KARL BARTH'S ANTHROPOLOGY
in Light of
MODERN THOUGHT

KARL BARTH'S ANTHROPOLOGY
in Light of
MODERN THOUGHT

Daniel J. Price

WILLIAM B. EERDMANS PUBLISHING COMPANY
GRAND RAPIDS, MICHIGAN / CAMBRIDGE, U.K.

© 2002 Wm. B. Eerdmans Publishing Co.

Wm. B. Eerdmans Publishing Co.
2140 Oak Inudstrial Drive N.E., Grand Rapids, Michigan 49505 /
P.O. Box 163, Cambridge CB3 9PU U.K.

Printed in the United States of America

07 06 05 04 03 02   7 6 5 4 3 2 1

Library of Congress Cataloging-in-Publication Data

Price, Daniel J.
Karl Barth's theology in light of modern thought /
Daniel J. Price.
p. cm.
Includes bibliographical references.
ISBN 978-0-8028-4726-3 (pbk.: alk. paper)
1. Man (Christian theology) — History of doctrines
— 20th century. 2. Barth, Karl, 1886-1968.
3. Christianity and the social sciences.   I. Title.
BT701.3.P75 2002
233′.092 — dc21

20021040273

www.eerdmans.com

Contents

CHAPTER 1

Introduction: Christian Anthropology
in a Modern Age

*Why do human beings learn so much, so soon, about technology, and
so little, so late, about loving one another?*

HENRI NOUWEN

The Dilemma of Modern Humanity

The psalmist, in one of the better-known statements of Scripture, asks:

> When I look at thy heavens, the work of thy fingers, the moon and the
> stars, which thou hast established; what is man that thou art mindful of
> him, and the son of man that thou dost care for him? (Psalm 8:4)[1]

This was written nearly three thousand years ago. While few of us would deny
that we have made progress in understanding the work of God's "fingers," the
material universe in which we have been placed, equally few would stand firm
in the assertion that we are nearer to finding an answer to the psalmist's question, "what is man?" than at the time it was written. The frantic accumulation
of scientific knowledge increasingly dominates the modern world in which
we live. Yet because of the heightened liabilities that this new technical knowledge entails, scientists, philosophers, and theologians of many persuasions

---

1. All Scriptural quotations are taken from the Revised Standard Version unless otherwise indicated.

1

are asking the human question — the question regarding the nature and destiny of human beings — with renewed urgency.

Albert Einstein was recently named "Person of the Century" by *Time* magazine.[2] Perhaps no one typifies the progress of science these past hundred years more than this shaggy-haired genius. Yet Einstein was more than an absent-minded physicist. He spoke eloquently and courageously against tyranny, and what he feared could become modern humanity's moral plight. He thus expressed his concern about the growing distance between science and human values:

> The scientific method can teach us nothing else beyond how facts are related to, and conditioned by, each other . . . knowledge of what *is* does not open the door directly to what *should be.* One can have the clearest and most complete knowledge of what *is,* and yet not be able to deduct from that what should be the *goal* of human aspirations. Objective knowledge provides us with powerful instruments for the achievements of certain ends, but the ultimate goal itself and the longing to reach it must come from another source.[3]

That Einstein would be alarmed about the separation between so-called scientific *facts* and human *values* indicates his understandable concern that they ought *not* to be separated. Einstein is only one among many modern thinkers to observe that the conditions of modern life have forced an urgent interest in the ancient question: "What is man?" Like the psalmist, we cannot afford to ask the question academically, for the hammer of modern technical achievement rings out in dangerous disproportion to moral progress. In the process of forging the conditions of our modern world, do we not have a pervasive sense that we may have lost some portion of our soul? The quest for modern humanity to find its soul is not merely a theoretical consideration, but one that gnaws at our modern reliance on material progress. It is also a quest upon which our very survival may depend.

On the cusp of the third millennium, questions about human nature and destiny pose a sense of urgency, part of which comes from the uncertainties unleashed by this staggering increase in scientific knowledge and its subsequent technological applications. We have grown materially rich, but many cry out that we are spiritually and relationally poor. In the Western world many seem undaunted — almost inebriated — by the rapid technical advances made possible by modern science. *Time* magazine's "Person of the

2. *Time,* vol. 154, no. 27, Dec. 31, 1999, pp. 62-95.
3. *Ideas and Opinions,* tr. S. Bargmann, ed. C. Seelig (New York: Crown, 1954) pp. 41-42.

Century," Albert Einstein, certainly represents modernity's pride at scientific accomplishment; our increased control of nature and its forces has been especially impressive in the past century. Yet even Einstein warned that if we fail to make commensurate progress in controlling ourselves, we do so at great peril.[4]

Is the plight of modern humanity uniquely desperate? Each age has had its wars, plagues, and surfeit of injustices. Even the modern pessimist must admit that those who live within developed countries today have witnessed an age when applied science has, for the most part, produced a wave of affluence heretofore unseen. In view of the many benefits accrued by modern science, hope that applied science will usher in a new age of human wealth and happiness is understandable. Yet modern discoveries have also produced many uncertainties. In the wake of the twentieth-century's ethnic cleansings, environmental destruction, cloning, use of chemical weapons, smart bombs, and a massive buildup of nuclear weapons, the frothy prospect of unhindered scientific development has crashed on the jetty of skepticism. The increased anxiety over technological misuse and abuse transcends ideology and national boundaries.[5] Alongside a higher standard of living have come technical weapons with ominously destructive capabilities. Alongside increasing amounts of leisure for the middle and upper classes have also come unforeseen strains and stresses on the nuclear family and shifting expectations for family roles. Alongside the wealth of developing nations, the poverty of the Third World stands out as a stark reminder that human equality remains an ideal that is far from being globally realized. The prospects for implementing the Enlightenment ideal of "liberty, equality, and fraternity" sometimes seem hopeful;[6] yet one could argue that scientific progress per se has so far yielded

---

4. Einstein expresses this dilemma by adapting a well-known phrase from Kant: "science without religion is lame, religion without science is blind" (*Ideas and Opinions,* p. 46). Einstein also published several lengthy books on the need for moral progress.

5. See Joan E. O'Donovan, "Man in the Image of God: The Disagreement Between Barth and Brunner Reconsidered," *Scottish Journal of Theology* (hereafter cited as *SJT*) 39 (1986) 433: "In the enthralling feats of biochemical technology the coming-into-being of individual human life is now the object of experimental making. Whether or not our mastery of the reproductive process will ever lay bare the mystery of human generation, it certainly throws open to an unprecedented degree the question of what human being is, and by what its uniqueness is constituted."

6. The Enlightenment theory of human progress, based on the advance of scientific knowledge, is characterized by the following expression from the Frenchman Antoine-Nicolas de Condorcet (1743-94), *Sketch for a Historical Picture of the Progress of the Human Mind,* tr. J. Barraclough (French original, 1795; London: Weidenfeld and Nicholson, 1955) p. 173: "Our hopes for the future condition of the human race can be subsumed under three important

just as much toward the inequitable distribution of wealth and the destruction of our planet as it has toward the alleviation of poverty and increase in wealth. Social scientists hardly need to inform us that yesterday's community *(Gemeinschaft)* is rapidly being transformed into today's impersonal society *(Gesellschaft)*. The local community that had formed the matrix for social and individual development for centuries past has been supplanted by diffuse and sprawling suburbs and crowded cities that contain increasing numbers of estranged individuals within the massive sea of humanity.[7]

The sense that we in the developed world have created a modern society with an increasing array of consumer choices is counterbalanced by the anxious suspicion that the cost of having consumer choices might be much higher than expected. The frenetic pursuit of attaining the "good life" may be eliminating some of the more important personal choices of life — at the least, the line between greed and the good life has blurred as we watch the senseless exploitation of our planet and its resources. The future seems both more promising and more foreboding than ever before; and therefore the question of who we are is being asked with a sense of urgency in nearly all of today's disciplines.[8]

---

heads: the abolition of inequality between nations, the progress of equality within each nation, and the true perfection of mankind." How quickly Condorcet disproved his own prophecy. He was imprisoned shortly after writing this and died almost immediately. I cite this because the lack of fulfillment of this Enlightenment prophecy should not be cynically interpreted, but seen in the light of the renewed cries for liberation from those within the church in the Third World. The cry of human liberation has been brought to the forefront of modern theology. Although it is not a particularly new cry, in many ways echoing the voices of the prophets in the Old Testament, it is not one that a contemporary Christian anthropology can ignore.

7. The sociological studies are filled with testaments to modern loneliness and alienation; e.g., Allan Bloom, in *The Closing of the American Mind* (New York: Simon & Schuster, 1987) pp. 117ff., says: "The aptest description I can find for the state of the students' souls is the psychology of separateness . . . people today must plan to be whole and self-sufficient, and cannot risk interdependence . . . we are social solitaries."

8. One example of those who see the anthropological question as primary is Ray Anderson: "Pondering the significance of Karl Barth's remark that 'theology has become anthropology since God became man,' I began to see theological anthropology at the heart of the theological course of study" (*On Being Human* [Grand Rapids: Eerdmans, 1982] p. vii). Others in theology with as wide-ranging opinions as Don Cupitt, *The Nature of Man* (London: Sheldon, 1979), see esp. the preface; and T. F. Torrance, *Theology in Reconstruction* (Grand Rapids: Eerdmans, 1966), indicate the urgent need for a deeper theological understanding of the human being. In an essay dedicated to Karl Barth, Torrance states, "At no point is theology more relevant today than in the issues it raises about our knowledge of man" (p. 99). See also David Cairns, *The Image of God in Man* (London: SCM, 1953) p. 9. Among philosophers, see John Macmurray, *The Self as Agent* (London: Faber and Faber, 1968), esp. pp. 29-38. In the psychological field, Harry Guntrip is one of the few who proposes that the task of theology is to help

All of this leads me to believe that Jürgen Moltmann's observation applies to the modern situation with special force: "technical progress for its own sake has become questionable."[9] Technical solutions alone have fallen short. Yet we would be naive to think that we could simply turn back the clock and deny the real progress that modern science has made. I therefore begin this study with the premise that any viable solution to the human dilemma of how to manage our accelerating technical accomplishments must respect both the empirical and the spiritual dimensions of human existence. An adequate anthropology must understand the significance of both science and morality: in the case of this study, a morality that flows from Christian faith. An adequate anthropology must allow science and theology to stand within their own respective spheres, at the same time being careful not to sunder one from the other. Scientific and dogmatic anthropologies should not be mutually exclusive. In other words, to borrow a phrase from Kant, if Christian anthropology without scientific anthropology is empty, then scientific anthropology without dogmatic Christian anthropology is blind.

Bringing the Resources of Christian Theology to Bear on Modern Thought

Reinhold Niebuhr has said, "There are resources in the Christian faith for an understanding of human nature which has been lost in modern culture."[10] In this study I propose that Karl Barth has brought many of these resources to light. I therefore explore Barth's theological understanding of the person, and conclude that his anthropology not only provides guidance for theological views of the human being, but serves surprisingly well as a springboard for theological anthropology to dialogue with the anthropologies of other sciences — particularly the human sciences. What is it within Barth's theology that lends itself to such a dialogue?

---

human beings find their own souls in order to keep us from the potentially disastrous consequences of the other sciences (*Personality Structure and Human Interaction* [London: Hogarth, 1961] p. 26). In Old Testament studies, Walter Eichrodt opens his book *Man in the Old Testament* with the comment: "The question how we are to understand human life is being asked among us to-day with a new intensity" (tr. K. and R. Gregor Smith, Studies in Biblical Theology 1/4 [London: SCM, 1951] p. 7).

9. *Man: Christian Anthropology in the Conflicts of the Present*, tr. J. Sturdy (London: SPCK, 1974) p. 23.

10. *The Nature and Destiny of Man: A Christian Interpretation*, 2 vols. (London: Nisbet, 1941) I, p. vii.

Barth's theology has cut a large swath across many dimensions of modern theology, including dogmatic theology, historical theology, Old and New Testament studies, and historical-critical method.[11] As the weight of Barth's theological anthropology has come to bear on a later generation of theologians and students, it may have an impact on other fields of human study in addition to dogmatic theology. One of the hindrances has been the sheer magnitude of Barth's own writings, especially the length of the *Church Dogmatics*. Barth's anthropology, which is contained in volume III/2 of the *Church Dogmatics,* has tended to be overlooked in favor of his earlier dialectical theology, expressed, for example, in his *Epistle to the Romans,* or in his supposedly angry dialogue with Emil Brunner in his now-famous rebuke of natural theology: *"Nein!"*[12] The bias toward interpreting Barth's later works in terms of his earlier dialectical theology continues even to the present,[13] with the result that Barth has sometimes been accused of being so theistically oriented that he neglects the human dimension.[14] However, careful reading of volume III/2 of the *Dogmatics,* and studies that have drawn on Barth's theology for social and political ethics, indicate that these criticisms were premature.[15] Emil Brunner is, ironically, one who has taken the time to peruse Barth's anthropology. He describes volume III/2 as "the culmination so far of the whole powerful work."[16]

I hope that the findings of this study will add to a growing body of literature that attests to the relevance of Barth's anthropology not only for theology, but also for any discipline that attributes importance to human interactions. I have therefore presented this study for the purpose of engaging those

11. See the excellent study by Christina Ann Baxter, "The Movement from Exegesis to Dogmatics in the Theology of Karl Barth, with Special Reference to Romans, Philippians and the *Church Dogmatics*" (Ph.D. thesis, University of Durham, 1981).

12. *Natural Theology: Comprising "Nature and Grace" by Professor Dr. Emil Brunner and the Reply "No!" by Dr. Karl Barth,* tr. P. Fraenkel (London: Geoffrey Bles, Centenary Press, 1946).

13. See Hans Urs Von Balthasar, *The Theology of Karl Barth,* tr. John Drury (New York: Holt, Rinehart, and Winston, 1971)

14. E.g., Robin Lovin, *Christian Faith and Public Choices: The Social Ethics of Barth, Brunner and Bonhoeffer* (Philadelphia: Fortress, 1984) p. 42. See also, R. E. Willis, *The Ethics of Karl Barth* (Leiden: Brill, 1971); and Reinhold Niebuhr, *Essays in Applied Christianity,* ed. D. B. Robertson (New York: Meridian, 1959) p. 184.

15. See George Hunsinger, *Karl Barth and Radical Politics* (Philadelphia: Westminster, 1963); and Stuart McLean, *Humanity in the Thought of Karl Barth* (Edinburgh: T & T Clark, 1981) pp. 6, 63. That Barth's theology could be almost entirely reduced to the political dimension (against Barth's own wishes) vis-à-vis socialist revolution in the thought of F. W. Marquardt, *Theologie und Sozialismus: Das Beispiel Karl Barths* (Munich: Chr. Kaiser, 1972) p. 127, would serve as evidence against those who accuse Barth of being politically irrelevant.

16. "The New Barth," *SJT* 4 (1951) 123. Brunner quotes from Prenter.

within the human sciences in an ongoing dialogue with Christian anthropology. My hope is that theologians might be willing to take a second look at Barth's doctrine of humanity, and acknowledge that he has traveled a long way from his second edition of the *Epistle to the Romans*. I also hope that, in light of this study, social and psychological scientists might find Barth's anthropology increasingly interesting, especially at the point where psychologists of a Christian persuasion seek both to integrate and differentiate Christian belief and scientific practice.

When it comes to delineating the respective roles of theology and natural sciences, Barth is particularly helpful because of his insistence that theology must stand its own ground, remaining faithful to its own particular object of inquiry, which is the self-disclosure of the triune God. At the same time, Barth also realized that theology could not be done in isolation from modern thought. Barth believed theology could best serve the other sciences by engaging in dialogue — a dialogue that respected, and sometimes *defended,* the establishment of clear boundaries between the disciplines.

Prior to Barth it was all too easy for nineteenth-century Protestant theology to adopt uncritically the thought forms of modern Western European culture. The accommodation of the gospel to the surrounding European culture obscured the real object of Christian belief by denying the power and transcendence of the almighty God who reveals himself. On the other hand, Protestant scholasticism, and even some contemporary evangelical theologians, have attempted to mount a reactionary retreat back to static[17] substan-

---

17. The term "static" is used in this study with special reference to the classical substantivalism, or essentialism, which began with Plato and Aristotle and continued into medieval thought largely through Augustine, Boethius, Aquinas, and others; its later representatives include Descartes. The world of Plato's forms is static in the sense that it is both isolated and immutable. Aristotle's thought is less static than Plato's, but, one could argue, only in matter of degree. Aristotle is more concerned than Plato with movements and actions of particular things, especially from potential to actual. Yet for Aristotle too the ultimate reality in which humanity participates is not so much through activity *(ergon),* but through the exercise of the mind *(nous),* which is not susceptible to change. See Stephen R. L. Clark, *Aristotle's Man* (Oxford: Clarendon, 1975); cf. Niebuhr, *Nature and Destiny of Man,* esp. chap. 1, §II. The term "static" contains an undeniably pejorative connotation; but it is also meant to be descriptive, mostly in terms of what it is not, as opposed to what it is, since the various ways in which it pertains to the thinkers mentioned above differ widely.

There have been many attempts to break out of the static categories; e.g., Alfred North Whitehead, in *Process and Reality* (Cambridge: Cambridge University Press, 1929), attempted to describe reality in metaphysical descriptions that incorporated the insights of both Darwin and Einstein. Whitehead's process philosophy might therefore be described as "dynamic," in contrast to the philosophies of Plato and Aristotle. However, I have a difficult time seeing process philosophy as a vast improvement over classical or neoclassical metaphysics when it comes to

tival categories of the Middle Ages, thereby rendering theology virtually irrelevant to modern conceptualizations of the person. I propose that if theology is to assume its proper task today, it must admit that there is no going back to the former substantival (or essentialist) categories.[18] This is not simply because the notion of the self as a thinking substance has gone out of fashion (especially after Hume and Kant), but also because these formulations have always exerted a foreign influence on biblical concepts of the person. The influence of Hellenic thought can be seen especially in the form of anthropological dualism that denigrated the body and elevated the importance of the soul. Subsequently, Hellenic modes of thought had great difficulty in adequately explaining the more unitary nature of soul and body that is found in biblical anthropology. Even more important for the church's mission in the world is the pernicious influence this Hellenic thought exerted on the church by tending to drive a wedge between the church and the world. Even more so is this alienation felt in a modern world driven by an earthy American movie industry and a global economy that frenetically provides consumers with every comfort imaginable and others unimagined until now. Anything that smells of Gnosticism is mostly repulsive to modern life — except for a few unsuspecting enclaves and cults loosely connected to Christian churches. But back to Barth.

In the theological anthropology of Barth, I propose that we find a way to understand ourselves that neither accommodates to the surrounding culture nor ignores the important insights of the human sciences. Barth seeks a way beyond the dualism found in so many traditional Christian anthropologies: he seeks to balance the importance of both the soul and the body, thereby providing a common ground between theology and human sciences to discuss the nature of the human being.

---

describing God, because Whitehead's dipolar God is ultimately abstract and impersonal. While I agree with Whitehead's attempts to produce a dynamic metaphysics that unseats God as the "Unmoved Mover," I believe that Barth's ontology of encounter, rooted in the trinitarian ontology of the Christological councils, does more justice to the Christian concept of God — and humanity. For a comparison between Barth and process theology, see Colin Gunton, *Becoming and Being: The Doctrine of God in Charles Hartshorne and Karl Barth* (Oxford: Oxford University Press, 1978).

18. For an attempt by a biblical scholar to reinstate substantival terms in biblical anthropology, see Robert Gundry, *Soma in Biblical Theology* (Cambridge: Cambridge University Press, 1976).

The Central Argument of This Thesis

In this book I propose that Barth's theological anthropology bears certain intriguing similarities to the anthropology of modern object relations psychology. The similarities between Barth's anthropology and modern object relations psychology should serve to correct some mistaken assumptions about Barth's supposedly hostile relation to the natural sciences. The similarities between Barth and object relations psychology serve as indicators that Barth's doctrine of humanity should not be interpreted as an attack on scientific anthropologies. At best, Barth is often seen as indifferent to the discoveries of modern human science. To the contrary, I argue that if he is rightly understood, Barth's theological reflections on human nature can provoke a thoughtful rapprochement between theology and the human sciences, stimulating a careful delineation of both the similarities and differences between the disciplines.

The most important parallel between Barth and object relations psychology is that both give due attention to the relational matrix of human personhood — both develop a "dynamic" view of the person. The meaning of the term "dynamic" will be spelled out during the course of this study, especially in chapters four–six. Following Barth, I give the term a highly technical meaning. Of course, it refers to motion, as opposed to an inert state, but much more than simple motion is meant. I use the term "dynamic" to refer to a very specialized kind of motion that applies to *interpersonal action*. Barth's dynamic anthropology stems from the convergence of several important strains of thought. First, Barth was influenced by existential philosophy with its suspicion of abstract modes of thought and its preference for action. Second, Barth's dynamic anthropology reflects certain elements of Calvin's anthropology that describe the human as a creature in immediate and momentary dependence on God.[19] But most of all, Barth's dynamic anthropology

---

19. See T. F. Torrance, *Calvin's Doctrine of Man* (London: Lutterworth, 1949), esp. pp. 29-30. Torrance points out that Calvin rejects Aristotelian categories, and instead describes the human being as constantly being "consumed and renewed" through relation to God. The "dynamic" interaction is therefore one of constant interpersonal relation to God. But Torrance perhaps underplays Calvin's occasional relapses into substantival categories (of a Platonic rather than Aristotelian type; I use the term "substantival" rather than "essential" because of the danger of using "essential" equivocally); see *Institutes of the Christian Religion*, ed. J. T. McNeill, tr. F. L. Battles, 2 vols. (Philadelphia: Westminster, 1960) I, xv, 2, where Calvin describes the souls as "immortal essences" awaiting to be delivered from the "prison houses of their bodies" (p. 182). There is an undeniable influence of modern existential thought here in Barth's definition of dynamic. In the *Dogmatics*, the English translation indicates that Barth is fond of the term "dynamic" to describe his own anthropology. E.g., denying that the human being is

issues from his interpretation of the *imago Dei* in light of his relational understanding of the Trinity.

The main thrust of this study is to uncover some new insights regarding the nature of the human being by comparing two very divergent disciplines: theology and psychology. But this study should also have implications for the interpretation of Barth's theology, particularly his perceived relation to the natural and human sciences. For example, if we look at the supposed disjunction between nature and grace in Barth's theology, we find that Barth has been accused of denying the rationality of theology because of his epistemology, which entails a "positivism of revelation."[20] Such a "positivism," say Barth's critics, created a distance between reason and revelation, and thus drove a wedge between the sciences and theology. By accusing Barth of revelatory positivism, Barth's critics were apparently referring to his insistence that the essential doctrines of orthodox Christianity must be upheld and believed as a whole or not at all. It is likely that the term refers to the equal but opposite tactic of the logical positivists, who insisted that all knowledge must be either logically consistent or empirically verifiable. This would apparently set Barth's revelatory positivism against the positivism of so-called modern scientific method, thus indicating the antipathy between Barth and science. Another way to interpret Barth's alleged positivism of revelation would be to suppose that Barth meant modern science could not in any way affect the truth claims of Christian dogmatics. This latter claim, that neither the methods nor the findings of natural science could negatively affect Christian dog-

---

"static" *(in sich selbst ruhendes)*, he affirms rather a person as one who is in encounter: "dynamic and active" *(ein sich selbst bewegendes, ein tätiges, ein handelndes)*. The German brings out the sense in which Barth marks the difference between dynamic and static. Human beings are "static" inasmuch as they "rest in themselves"; they are "dynamic" inasmuch as they "move, act, and interact." Cf. Karl Barth, *Church Dogmatics*, vol. III, part 2: *The Doctrine of Creation*, ed. T. F. Torrance and G. W. Bromiley, tr. H. Knight, et al. (Edinburgh: T & T Clark, 1960) p. 248 (hereafter *CD*, III/2), with *Die kirchliche Dogmatik*, vol. III: *Die Lehre von der Schöpfung* (part 2) (Zurich: Evangelischer Verlag, 1948) p. 297 (hereafter *KD*, III/2). See chapters four and six below for how Barth defines the difference between a dynamic history and a static state. In chapter five I show how object relations psychology also prefers an interpersonal "dynamic" description of the person over the more static mechanistic or organic models.

20. Viz., Wolfhart Pannenberg, *Theology and the Philosophy of Science*, tr. Francis McDonagh (Philadelphia: Westminster, 1976) pp. 32ff. Cf. Simon Fisher, *Revelatory Positivism? Barth's Earliest Theology and the Marburg School* (Oxford: Oxford University Press, 1988). It was Dietrich Bonhoeffer who first ascribed the term "revelatory positivism" *(Offenbarungspositivismus)* to Barth's theological method; see *Letters and Papers from Prison*, tr. Eberhard Bethge (New York: Macmillan, 1973) pp. 280-81, 286, 328-29. But Bonhoeffer was more irenic toward Barth than were many who expanded on his criticism. See Fisher, *Revelatory Positivism?* pp. 311-14.

matics, has some validity. However, does this lead to the conclusion that if one follows Barth, theology and science have been permanently severed with no point of contact between them?

In the midst of the dispute over Barth's supposed severance of theology from the empirical world, several things should not be overlooked. First, Barth, especially in his later writings, perceived certain interconnections and "parallels" between theology and science, grace and nature. For example, after establishing the ground of theology in Jesus Christ (i.e., in revelation), Barth goes back and looks at the view of the human being contained in Christian theology. He concludes that revelation does contain a type of human psychology. Therefore, Barth concedes that we should expect to find analogies,[21] some parallels, and common elements between the findings of those who study the human soul in psychological science and the psychology found in Christian revelation. The reservations that Barth holds regarding the compatibility between science and theology are based on his insistence that any analogies between nature and grace be taken from God himself: that they should be drawn out with respect to the interrelations within the triune God. This is expressed by Barth's well-known argument that theology should shift from predicating the relation between nature and grace from an analogy of being *(analogia entis)* to an analogy of relations *(analogia relationis)*. In proposing this change Barth is advocating more than a shift in terminology. He is advocating a major shift in paradigms with regard to both divine and human being. I propose that it is precisely this shift that makes a comparison between Barth and object relations psychology especially intriguing.

The point of this study is not to draw battle lines between those who respect Barth and others who reject him. Rather, it is to draw on a great theologian's basically orthodox reflections on Scripture and the triune God of the Christian faith and say: This material, drawn from the Scriptures and twenty centuries of Christian reflection on what it means to be human, can provide some food for modern thought — especially as we reflect on ourselves and our many modern dilemmas.

Barth's understanding of the triune God establishes both a material similarity with certain branches of modern human sciences, and at the same time a methodological means by which theology can maintain its integrity as a discipline by not capitulating to other sciences where it ought to hold fast. The former is important because it can provide theology a means for engaging in meaningful dialogue a modern culture largely under the spell of mod-

---

21. The analogies will, of course, be ones of relations, *analogia relationis*, and not of being, *analogia entis*. See Barth, *CD*, I/1, p. xiii; and discussion in chapter four below.

ern psychology; the latter is important because significant parts of the church and many of its seminaries have all but surrendered the preaching of the gospel to pop psychology.

The Common Ground between Barth and Object Relations Psychology

How might we explore what Barth and modern psychology have in common? T. F. Torrance has brought Barth's epistemology into dialogue with the physical sciences through exploring the analogies between Barth and the new physics, especially the discoveries of Albert Einstein. Torrance has maintained that Einstein's theories of relativity have opened the door for a friendlier atmosphere between physical science and theology, and he argues that Einstein's beliefs about the nature of the universe and his subsequent realist method of inquiry bear significant epistemic similarities to the theology of Barth.[22] Stuart McLean refers to this dialogue that Torrance has carried on with the "theoreticians and practitioners of the physical sciences," and urges that a similar discussion needs to take place in relating Barth's views to the social sciences.[23] I will attempt to make some headway in accepting this challenge.

In this study I propose that just as the realism which Barth brings to his overall theology invites some comparisons with modern physics, the realism which Barth employs in his anthropology also invites a comparison with the branch of object relations psychology developed by the British object relations theorists, especially the thought of W. Ronald D. Fairbairn (1889-1964).[24] I argue that significant parallels can be found between the concept of the person expressed in the trinitarian theology of Barth and object relations psychology, and that these parallels confirm the analogical relation between the revealed truths of Christian anthropology and scientific studies of human emotional development. In other words, the parallels between Barth and object relations psychology tend to confirm Barth's insistence that the analogy of *relations* is the best paradigm for exploring the relation between nature

---

22. *Transformation and Convergence in the Frame of Knowledge* (Grand Rapids: Eerdmans, 1984) pp. ix-x; see also idem, *Reality and Evangelical Theology* (Philadelphia: Westminster, 1982) pp. 14ff.; idem, *Space, Time and Resurrection* (Grand Rapids: Eerdmans, 1976) pp. 185-86.

23. *Humanity*, p. 7. McLean mentions the "social sciences" specifically, and I interpret this broadly to include the field of modern psychology.

24. Object relations is defined below, n. 52. For a more complete definition, see chapter five.

and grace, God and the world. The most discernible parallel is the relational definition of the human being that both Barth and object relations develop. Both disciplines emphasize the importance of explaining human existence only within the context of interpersonal relations. Both therefore understand the human being in dynamic terms.

Christian anthropology is concerned primarily with the human being's relation to God, and secondarily with the individual's relation to others. Nevertheless, while the relation to God is primary, one's relation to others is a necessary facet of relation to God. A major strength of Barth's anthropology is that he allows no cleavage between relation to God and relation to others. Regarding the relations between persons, both philosophy and psychology take an interest, as well as theology. Relation to others is, to borrow a phrase from John Macmurray, "the field of the personal." It is precisely on the "field of the personal" where we would expect to see some analogies between dogmatic anthropology and the discoveries of the psychologist. The field of the personal warrants our close attention because this is the area where theological anthropology has often said too little. Barth, on the other hand, is passionate in his protest against individualism. If Barth does nothing more than draw our attention to the inadvertent individualism of so many Christian theologies he will have served us well.

At the core of Barth's anthropology lies his persistent objection to the tendency in Christian theology to view the human being as an *isolated thinking individual*.[25] Battista Mondin puts Barth's emphasis on the determinative aspect of interpersonal relations positively. Regarding the interpretation of the image of God as male and female, he states that for Barth "God did not simply create man, but created him as a social being. Sociability is the most essential characteristic of human nature, since everything else is to be understood in the light of this fact."[26] In object relations a similar outlook is found: in normal human psychological development the individual is shaped by postnatal object relations. Object relations psychology, in its discovery that human psychology is shaped by our earliest social experiences, lends a flesh-

---

25. Boethius (c. 480–c. 524) described the human being as "an individual substance of a rational nature" *(Persona est naturae rationabilis individua substantia)*. Boethius's anthropology had an immense effect on medieval thought. Quoted in Clement Webb, *God and Personality* (London: Allen and Unwin; New York: Macmillan, 1918) p. 47. See also Anderson, *On Being Human*, p. 6; and Wolfhart Pannenberg, *Anthropology in Theological Perspective*, tr. Matthew J. O'Connell (Philadelphia: Westminster, 1985) p. 235, who cites the same quotation from *De duabus naturis*, *Patrologia latina* 64:1343C; cf. *CD*, I/1, p. 356.

26. Battista Mondin, *The Principle of Analogy in Protestant and Catholic Theology* (The Hague: Martinus Nijhoff, 1963) p. 165 n. 4.

and-bone illustration to the long-held Christian insistence that "if we love one another, God lives in us."[27]

In addition to certain material parallels, Barth's anthropology also points out some methodological similarities and differences between theological and scientific anthropologies. It is important to note the ways in which the respective disciplines of theology and psychology are defined by their object of study. Barth's anthropology is derived through careful reflection on Christian revelation in the context of its historical development and in light of modern thought. The subject matter of theological anthropology is not the human being per se, but the human being in light of the Word of God. Object relations, on the other hand, constructs its anthropological concepts through the constant revision of psychological theories in light of the scientific observation of individual emotional development. The element common to both anthropologies is the perception that the human being can be understood only in the context of relationship to an "other." It is being-in-relation to an other (or others) that shapes the individual into a human being. The dynamic of this relationship has been defined *theologically* by many different terms, such as: "being in communion," "I-Thou," "encounter," "being-constituting-relations," or "onto-relations."[28] All of these terms designate the importance of interpersonal relations for human beings to become homo sapiens in the fullest sense. These terms indicate that the person should not be seen merely as an isolated individual possessing certain attributes. Rather, the person is shaped by the relationship to an "other" at his or her ontological core. The particular nuances of meaning contained in these terms will be brought out in the course of this study, but the common element to all of them is the essential quality of being-in-relationship. Barth is fond of describing such a relationship as an interpersonal "history" *(Geschichte)*, which entails "being in encounter" *(Das Sein in der Begegnung)*.

In order to probe for the connections between theological anthropol-

---

27. 1 John 4:12.

28. With reference to the terms listed see, respectively, John Zizioulas, *Being as Communion* (London: Darton, Longman & Todd, 1985); Emil Brunner, *Man in Revolt*, tr. Olive Wyon, 3d ed. (London: Lutterworth, 1947); Martin Buber, *I and Thou*, tr. R. Gregor Smith (Edinburgh: T & T Clark, 1937), esp. pp. 3ff. The terms "being-constituting-relationships" and "onto-relations" were coined by T. F. Torrance; see *The Mediation of Christ* (Grand Rapids: Eerdmans, 1983) p. 57. Barth, like Brunner, borrows much of his terminology from Buber. Thus Barth uses the term "being in encounter" *(Sein in der Begegnung)* to describe the basic form of humanity. But Barth's interpretation of encounter bears a distinctively trinitarian interpretation, unlike Buber of course. See *CD*, III/2, pp. 222ff.

ogy and psychological studies of the person, we should presumably look for the connections between nature and grace. When it comes to sounding out the connections between nature and grace, traditional Christian anthropology has often seen the need for the presence of an ineffaceable rational faculty. But after Immanuel Kant's critical philosophy, the rational faculty was less acceptable as the basis of personhood in any speculative anthropology. For example, in the theology of Friedrich Schleiermacher, we see the attempt to circumvent the rational faculty by rooting anthropology in the "feeling of absolute dependence." One of the principal arguments of Barth's early theology was that liberal Protestant theology, following Schleiermacher, had become so imbued with subjective interpretations of religiosity that it was difficult to distinguish theology proper from the psychology of religion. Most theologians of Catholic persuasion, on the other hand, attempted to understand the connections between scientific and biblical psychology on the basis of "grace perfecting nature" *(gratia perficit naturam)*.[29] None of these pathways is open if we follow Barth. As I have shown, this is because of his rejection of the analogy of being *(analogia entis)* in preference for the analogy of relation *(analogia relationis)*. Barth's employment of the analogy of relation is one of the more important aspects of his theology that needs to be interpreted in the course of this study. It warrants mention from the start, however, that I believe Barth's usage of analogy provides one of the keys to understanding the relation between nature and grace. A proper understanding of Barth's usage of analogy is important because it has sometimes been assumed that Barth destroyed the possibility of analogical predication altogether. He did not. He did, however, seek to conform our analogical predications about God to the dynamic nature of God. Therefore, I argue that the analogical relationship between grace and nature has not been severed by Barth's insistence on the *analogia relationis*. Indeed, the analogy of relations is precisely what this study hopes to confirm. In comparing Barth to object relations psychology I hope to show that the analogy of relation is one means by which the distance *(diastasis)* between God and humanity is bridged in Barth's later thought.[30]

T. F. Torrance has also pointed out that, given Barth's theological prem-

29. E.g., W. W. Meissner, *Psychoanalysis and Religious Experience* (New Haven and London: Yale University Press, 1984) p. 9.

30. See H. Hartwell, *The Theology of Karl Barth* (London: Duckworth, 1964) p. 4, who mentions that the language of Kant, Plato, and Kierkegaard, the "mathematical point," "tangent," and "vacuum" used in *The Epistle to the Romans,* tr. E. C. Hoskyns, 6th ed. (New York: Oxford University Press, 1968), is language that Barth long since discarded by the time he wrote the *Dogmatics.*

ises, the similarities between natural science and theology are understandable based on the singularity of space and time as the place of divine revelation and also the place where human beings live their lives and study their sciences. The relation of revelation to Kant's understanding of the sensible forms of space and time in his first Critique inevitably comes up here. The question as to where Barth stands with regard to Kant's severance of the sensible forms of space and time from the realm of ethics and religion has an undeniable degree of importance in discussing Barth's relation to the human sciences. Barth's relation to Kant, therefore, has a large bearing on his relation to the other sciences. The perception that Barth is a Kantian has sometimes caused his critics to think that his dogmatics rest upon a type of revelation severed from the space-and-time sphere of natural science. Again, I hope to show that such interpretations are mistaken.

It is sometimes assumed that Barth's Christocentric emphasis has weakened his understanding of the relation between nature and grace. The Christian doctrine of creation has traditionally tended to serve as the theological bulwark against any dualism of nature and grace, theology and the other disciplines. But does Barth necessarily have a weak doctrine of creation? Or, to ask a related question, does a Christological understanding of creation necessarily weaken the link between theology and other disciplines? Barth's repeated objections to Gnosticism and Docetism indicate that both the incarnation and the resurrection took place within the realm of space and time: in other words, that God the Creator is also God the Redeemer.[31] Therefore, Christian anthropology must describe human beings as they exist in space and time.[32] Since space and time are also the place where natural scientific studies are undertaken, psychological science and theology must intersect, because in the incarnate Christ the divine and human intersect.[33] Some of the

31. See Barth, *CD*, I/2. Barth comments that we close the doors to Gnosticism with the formula: "Credo in Deum patrem, omnipotentem creatorem coeli et terrae, et in Jesum Christum, filium eius unicum, Dominum nostrum" (p. 655). On the incarnation see also I/2, pp. 132-71, and esp. 124-25. It seems clear that time and eternity share a unitary understanding in the incarnation, bearing an analogical relation not because of an analogy of being *(analogia entis)*, but because of divine grace. Cf. the preceding §14, "The Time of Revelation," esp. pp. 49ff.

32. See T. F. Torrance, *Space, Time and Incarnation* (Oxford and London: Oxford University Press, 1969).

33. Barth's theology can be understood from several specific vantage points, such as the freedom and sovereignty of the triune God, the primacy of revelation, etc. But the incarnation remains at the very heart of his and all trinitarian theologies, and there can be little doubt that Barth accepted the incarnation as an event in both space and time. See *CD*, I/2, pp. 132ff. The Word made flesh is "at once the mystery of revelation, which is the real object of

earliest church heresies such as Gnosticism and Docetism denied Christ a place in space and time. It has been the place of orthodoxy to deny those who would place Christ above or beyond our human world. In other words, there are grounds for stating the connections between theology and science, not merely because of the assumption that nature and grace are somehow connected, but, for those who follow Barth, because Christ and his creation are integrally related. It is not merely because of a general doctrine of creation, but also because of the unity of nature and grace in the incarnation that there can be no ultimate cleavage between exact science and theology. This relation is not always spelled out clearly by Barth. But it is a relation that is discernible for those who are willing to consider the paradigm shift that Barth advocates in his understanding of the relation between nature and grace based on his doctrine of the Trinity.

Let me state the relation between Barth's dogmatic anthropology and scientific anthropology in yet another way. If the analogy of relations holds true, then we should expect this analogy to be most evident precisely in the sphere of *relations* — especially human relationships. This, I argue, turns out to be the case. The analogy of relations is strikingly evident when we compare Barth to object relations psychology. The "I-Thou" relations that the theologians are fond of describing finds a counterpart in object relations psychology.

Nevertheless, there are some understandable reasons why relatively few comparisons of Barth and the human sciences have been carried out.[34] The trinitarian epistemology of Barth's dogmatics centers on the incarnation and resurrection; and while Barth did a good job of drawing out the implications for his view of time and history, it must be admitted that he did not fully draw out the implications of his Christology for the physical sciences, even less so

---

Christology, namely, the source and root of all the various problems and their solutions which are to engage us from now on" (p. 133). See also *CD*, III/2, pp. 519-26. See also Barth, *CD*, III/4, p. 24. Nevertheless, the implications of this were not fully drawn out in Barth, but remained to be drawn out by Barth's followers, especially T. F. Torrance; see *Space, Time and Incarnation*, pp. 65-66.

34. This is not to suggest that no studies comparing Barth and social sciences have been done. See, e.g., Walter Allan, "Sociology and Theology: A Study of Their Relationship with Reference to Berger, Luckmann and Barth" (Ph.D. dissertation, Drew University, 1969). This study is inadequate, however, since it fails to give attention to Barth's anthropology; in fact, it refers only to *CD*, I/2, and altogether ignores the other twelve volumes of the *Dogmatics*. The author draws the implausible conclusion that Barth failed to recognize that in addition to a transcendent source of knowledge, there are certain "socio-historical sources which exercise a profound influence upon theological thinking" (p. 154). Cf. Mondin, *Principle of Analogy*, pp. 147-51.

for the human sciences.[35] This, however, was not due to an inherently antiscientific bias that is sometimes attributed to Barth. It represents, I shall argue, an imbalance that Barth was in the process of correcting in his later volumes of the *Dogmatics*.[36]

Trinitarian Faith and Anthropology

I have mentioned that Barth's anthropology is trinitarian. Among other things, this means that he understands human nature based on the revealed humanity of Christ. Barth rejects universal ideas in favor of that which is particular and Christological. "Real man" is not derived by an abstract ideal of humanity, but from the historical Christ. He shuns general and a priori theoretical considerations of both God and humanity, arguing that when theology draws on universal ideas or principles in order to express its conceptions, it runs the risk of becoming an abstract system of thought that is cut off from its real foundation in Christ.[37] Therefore, Barth insists that theology should reason from the particular to the general, not vice versa. The reality of God is known from the Word of God revealed in the divinity of Christ, not from a priori concepts. The reality of the human being ("real man") is likewise known in the humanity of Christ.

35. See Roger Newell, "Participatory Knowledge: Theology as Art and Science in C. S. Lewis and T. F. Torrance" (Ph.D. thesis, University of Aberdeen, 1983) p. 479, who observes: "Torrance wishes to go beyond Barth in taking more seriously the relation between creation and redemption. For in Jesus Christ, the Word of God became a physical event in space-time and we must seek to understand it within the co-ordinate levels of created rationality. This means we must establish a closer and even intimate relation between natural and revealed theology, *but with a difference*." Newell continues to comment on Barth's rejection of the Thomist view on natural theology: "Barth was right on methodological grounds to attack a natural theology which functions as a prior, independent conceptual system, for no genuine science can permit itself to be controlled by an independent logical structure which claims to constitute an indispensable precondition or precomprehension." See also T. F. Torrance, *God and Rationality* (London: Oxford University Press, 1971) p. 141; idem, "Natural Theology in the Thought of Karl Barth," in *Transformation and Convergence*, pp. 285-301.

36. See Torrance, *Space, Time and Resurrection*, pp. ix-x.

37. See, e.g., *CD*, I/2, p. 862; and IV/1, pp. 3-7. In support of Barth is the insight of postmodern philosophy of science that the theoretical constructs which any science uses to investigate the world must bear some intrinsic relation to the world of time and space in which we live our ordinary lives. Thus most scientific theories that are held to be true have taken root from the intuitive grasp of reality that extrapolates on common sense. See, e.g., T. F. Torrance's essay "Ultimate Beliefs and the Scientific Revolution," in *Transformation and Convergence*, pp. 191-214, esp. p. 209.

I believe that Barth's delineation of Christ as "real man" is groundbreaking, and provides one of his more creative contributions to the church. As a preacher and sometimes pastoral counselor, I come from a tradition that has normally pointed to Jesus and said: "Now that we believe in Jesus, we can understand who God is." This is true. But the genius of Barth's theology of the human is that we can also point to Jesus to find out who *we* are. Few theologians have provided the pastor and Christian caregiver with a more useful tool for practicing the cure of souls. Barth's willingness to think of the whole human race in terms of the humanity of Jesus Christ has made a tremendous impact on Christian ethics; I would credit Barth with shaping the modern Western church's views on everything from Rogerian therapy to the demise of apartheid.[38]

As I have mentioned above, Barth's theology develops from his understanding of the personal dimensions and implications of God as triune. In spite of his decision to avoid using the term "person" to describe the immanent Trinity,[39] Barth's theology is interpersonal from start to finish.[40] As Mondin states regarding Barth's usage of theological language: "The problem is not whether God is a person; the problem is whether we are persons."[41] The dynamic ontology derived from Barth's understanding of the triune *God* is precisely the reason Barth's doctrine of *humanity* is especially dynamic — and to a large degree, I argue, contemporary.

---

38. Thomas Oden credits Barth's theology with making possible and acceptable Carl Rogers's therapeutic triad based on accurate empathy, congruence, and warmth (*Kerygma and Counseling* [Philadelphia: Westminster, 1966]; see esp. pp. 10, 109-45). Apartheid found little or no support from Barth's doctrine of election, unlike that of Calvin and the Calvinists.

39. *CD*, I/1, pp. 359-60. In describing the persons of the Trinity as "modes of being," Barth was reacting against the misuse of the term "person," *persona, prosōpon,* in modern theology. It is unfortunate that the German was translated "modes" of being, since it has an assonance with "modalism" — precisely the opposite of what Barth intended by the term. Had he lived another twenty years he might, in view of many contemporary developments in theology, have reversed his decision. Colin Gunton points out concerning Barth that because of "the connotations of the terms 'person' and 'personality' as they are now used he wishes to abandon the traditional designation of the three as 'persons.' . . . Remaining true to his intention of choosing the language to fit the facts, he finds that the term 'person' is more suitable as a description of the one God who exists in three modes of being than for each of the three modes taken individually. There is no doubt at all about his absolute insistence on the personal nature of God. Even when the expression 'mode of being' is employed, it is done with intent 'to express by this term, not absolutely, but relatively better and more simply and clearly the same thing as is meant by 'person'" (*Becoming and Being*, p. 141). See *CD*, I/1, pp. 355-56, 359. See also the editors' preface, p. viii; and *CD*, II/1, pp. 296-97.

40. *CD*, I/1, pp. 12ff. The truth is personal because it is revealed and known in the person of Christ.

41. *Principle of Analogy*, p. 157. Cf. *CD*, I/1, p. 157.

Of course, Barth is not the only theologian to take account of the shift in perceptions of modern thought. But he is one of the few theologians of the twentieth century to pay respect to the vast currents of intellectual change after the Enlightenment while at the same time preserving the substance of biblical trinitarian faith. Barth's methodological refusal to allow theology to have any grounds other than the trinitarian self-revelation of God in Christ keeps his theology from being overwhelmed by secular thought forms. It gives him a strong tie with the orthodoxy of the reformers and the church councils. In this sense, there is a bit of irony in the observation that Barth's theology can be described as both postmodern[42] and orthodox at the same time. The label "neo-orthodox" as attached to Barth's *Dogmatics* is perhaps understandable, but it does not stick.

If labels are ever helpful, Barth's theology should probably be labeled "orthodox," because it is founded on the trinitarian formulations of the early church councils.[43] Where Barth's theology achieves its aim, it derives from the revealed truths of Scripture and seeks to guide the faith of the church.

Finding a Way beyond Anthropological Dualism

One of the most important facets of a dynamic anthropology is its determination to move beyond the anthropological dualism that cleaves soul from body. Barth is not the only modern thinker to observe that Hellenic and medieval

---

42. In this study I occasionally use the terms "modern thought" and "postmodern thought." The former refers to a more general way of thinking that is mostly influenced by the Enlightenment. The latter refers to thought in the later twentieth century, which, particularly under the influence of the new physics, has challenged the Newtonian worldview. Philosophically, the origins of postmodern thought can be traced to the criticisms launched against logical positivism by Karl Popper, *The Logic of Scientific Discovery* (New York: Basic Books, 1959); Michael Polanyi, especially *Personal Knowledge,* corrected ed. (Chicago: University of Chicago Press, 1962); and Thomas Kuhn, *The Structure of Scientific Revolutions,* rev. ed. (Chicago: University of Chicago Press, 1971). Cf. Mary Stewart Van Leeuwen, *The Person in Psychology: A Contemporary Christian Appraisal* (Leicester: Intervarsity Press; Grand Rapids: Eerdmans, 1985) pp. 3-15. Personally, I prefer Polanyi's term, "post-critical," since it is more descriptive and less likely to be confused with the postmodern movement in contemporary philosophy foisted on us by Derrida, Foucault, Rorty, and others. "Post-critical" refers to the fact that Kant's critical philosophy no longer provides us with a thoroughly insightful way of understanding the methods of modern science, because Kant overlooked the need to integrate personal and objective knowledge. See *Personal Knowledge,* p. 354. Kant was deeply imbued with the worldview of Newtonian physics and, of course, knew nothing of the coming new physics with relativity, quantum mechanics, and the like.

43. See *CD,* I/1, pp. 370, 423ff.

philosophies still continue to have an adverse influence on our modern concepts of the person. For example, in *Angels, Apes and Men,* Stanley Jaki has pointed out that most modern anthropologies attempt to solve the dualistic problem in one of two directions. As indicated by his book title, Jaki believes that on one hand we exalt our rational capacity, thus making ourselves out to be "angels." On the other hand, we depose ourselves from our proper moral and spiritual position, making ourselves out to be purely biological creatures: "apes." These two forms of error, says Jaki, are represented, respectively, by Descartes and Rousseau: "Both were catalysts of the two main modern trends whose chief feature is to take only one half of human nature. Descartes seized on the mind and boosted man into an angel. Rousseau took the sentiments, but having no eyes for the head, he aimed at the heart and hit the target somewhat lower, where the beast loves to reside in man."[44] The unhappy result of choosing to side either with the rationalist anthropology of Descartes or the biological anthropology of Rousseau is summarized aptly by John Macmurray: "The Self must then be conceived either as a substance or as an organism, while in reality it is a person."[45] Yet this long-standing bifurcation between intellect and instinct did not die out with either Descartes or Rousseau. The problems contained in Descartes's "angelic" anthropology were handed on to, among others, Kant. Likewise, Rousseau's "apish" anthropology was recapitulated in an altogether different way in the thought of many modern anthropologies under the influence of Darwinism, including Freud.

In expositing both Barth's anthropology and that of object relations psychology, I will show how a dynamic anthropology can transcend the dualisms presented by both the angelic and the apish perspectives. Barth's reflections in volume III/2 of the *Dogmatics* demonstrate a concentrated effort to avoid both of these errors. He does not wish the human being to be reduced to a static point of thought. The goodness and dignity of our body and all that bodily existence entails are heartily affirmed by Barth. Neither does Barth fall into the equal but opposite error of assuming that we can reduce human life to animal instincts. Biological components alone are insufficient to explain the human being. As an alternative, Barth proposes that both the mind and the body must be integrated into a unitary human being who is an embodied soul and an ensouled body. Once again the traditional categories are shunned in favor of the dynamic categories; it is the dynamic relation of soul and body that constitutes the human being as a being created in God's image and sustained by the Spirit. The dynamic relations of self to others, and

---

44. (La Salle, Ill.: Sherwood Sugden, 1983) p. 41.
45. *Persons in Relation* (London: Faber and Faber, 1961) p. 15.

soul and body to one another, are discussed in chapters four and five, and especially in chapter six.

There is much made today about doing theology in context. Especially important is the theology of liberation coming out of Latin America and the long-needed reaction against oppressive expressions of Christian faith and practice. Many have turned away from European theology as a source of help for the church. In a very real sense, however, Barth addressed an ideological attack upon the church that is still in force. He was countering the Enlightenment insistence that "man is the measure of all things." In chapter two below we will see that Barth launches a protest against the "absolute man" of the Enlightenment. In denouncing the "absolute man," Barth rejects the primacy that the Enlightenment gave to human thought, and he therefore denies the validity of any anthropology that builds solely on the human capacity of abstractive reason. Whether the exaltation of reason be formulated on a rationalist and mechanistic model such as Kant's, or an organic-dialectical model such as Hegel's, Barth finds them both unhelpful and unbiblical. Humans are not disembodied intellects. We are not "angels."

On the materialistic end of the spectrum, we are faced in Freud's theory with the reduction of the human being to a complex configuration of instinctual impulses. It was not organic idealism, but organic biologism as interpreted by Darwin and Lamarcke that served as the working models for Freud's early psychoanalytic theories. Much of modern psychology, following Freud's lead, assumed that the human being is a very sophisticated and sometimes neurotic "ape," driven by a complex structuring of instinctual impulses. In spite of his amazing ability to uncover many of the unconscious processes that govern human behavior, Freud never fully freed himself from the assumption that human beings could be described in terms of instinctual impulses that can be curbed only by forceful conformity to societal demands.

With the development of object relations psychology, however, we see that instinctual theory is replaced by a personality theory that does justice to both the biological and the personal dimensions of human existence. In object relations psychology we see a unitary anthropology that overcomes the implicit dualism of Freud's psychology. Object relations, like Barth, avoids both the angelic and apish extremes in its study of the human being.

The Human Being in Scientific Psychology

On the psychological end of this investigation, I begin with one of the giants of modern thought and the founder of psychoanalysis, Sigmund Freud.

Freud set the field of psychology on an entirely new path from that of his predecessors. Like many turn-of-the-century researchers in the young field of scientific psychology, Freud's studies involved the application of the scientific method to the study of human behavior.

Freud had originally set out in his "Project" of early years (1895) to describe the psychology of the person in terms that would be acceptable to the positivist scientific reasoning of Helmholtz and Brücke. The models that Freud applied to his studies of the person were taken primarily from classical physics.[46] A close look at Freud's earliest theories reveals the remarkable extent to which the Newtonian physics has shaped the development of the modern human sciences. Where Kant applied the Newtonian paradigm to the a priori categories of the mind, Freud attempted to apply basically Newtonian categories to human biochemistry. True, Freud abandoned his attempt to reduce mental processes to neurology early in his career. Nevertheless, the paradigm of classical physics was never fully left behind.

Freud's early attempts to reduce psychological maladies to neurophysiology were interrupted by his discovery of the unconscious processes that, he argued, play such a critical role in shaping each person's psychology. Unlike his predecessors, Freud began to uncover the effects of certain interpersonal dynamics that were stored in the unconscious dimension of the mind. Freud could not long remain a strictly biophysical psychologist, because he began to realize that certain primitive or unconscious processes must be combined with interpersonal factors in order to shape the human psyche. Freud pushed beyond his original interest in neurology and became increasingly interested in the various manifestations of neurotic illness. As he took an increasing interest in human behavior, the inadequacy of his initial reductionistic presuppositions gradually unveiled itself. Freud partially rejected the reductionist model himself, even though he continually hoped for an organic solution for psychological illness. In this sense, Freud was a superb scientist, allowing the objective realities of human emotional development continually to cut back against the grain of his a priori assumptions about human nature. Nevertheless, Freud could not bring himself to accept fully the conclusions of even his own research. He never completely overcame his

---

46. See Guntrip, *Personality Structure;* he mentions that Freud's suspicion of both philosophy and theology caused him to accept uncritically the scientific *Weltanschauung* of his day, and thus he was especially influenced by the atomistic scientific theories of Helmholtz and Brücke, pp. 50, 120-21. See also Thomas Parisi, "Why Freud Failed," *American Psychologist* 42 (1987) 237-45. Finally, see Meissner, *Psychoanalysis and Religious Experience,* p. 3. More will be said on this in chapter five below.

emotional attachment to the scientific positivism of his day. In his definitive biographical work on Freud, Ernst Jones writes:

> In the realm of the visual, of definite neural activities that could be seen under the microscope, he had for many years felt entirely at home; he was as safe there as at the family hearth. To wander away from it and embark on the perilous seas of the world of emotions, where all was unknown and where what was invisible was of far greater consequence than what was visible, must have cost him dear . . . we may regard the feverish writing of the Project as a last desperate effort to cling to the safety of cerebral anatomy. If only the mind could be described in terms of neurones, their processes as synapses! How fond the thought must have been to him.[47]

Jones next quotes a letter written in 1898 by Freud:

> I have no inclination at all to keep the domain of the psychological floating, as it were, in the air, without any organic foundation. But I have no knowledge, neither theoretically nor therapeutically, beyond that conviction, so that I have to conduct myself as if I had only the psychological before me.[48]

It was the absence of an adequate theoretical framework for explaining the social dimensions of psychological phenomena that spurred some of Freud's successors to question Freud's overemphasis on instinctual impulses. In the United States, social psychology and the "cultural-pattern" school of psychology tended to counterbalance Freudian psychoanalysis, as did behaviorism in an altogether opposite way.[49] Yet both of these forms of scientific psychology largely overlooked the depth psychology begun by Freud, and carried on in different forms by Carl Jung (1875-1962), Alfred Adler (1870-1937), Otto Rank (1884-1939), and others.[50] In Britain, object relations psychology was given birth primarily through those connected to the Tavistock Clinic. The ideas of Melanie Klein (1882-1960), Donald Winnicott (1896-

---

47. Ernst Jones, *Sigmund Freud: Life and Work,* 3 vols. (London: Hogarth, 1954-57) I, pp. 420-21.

48. Ibid., p. 433.

49. Guntrip cites the influence of American culture-pattern psychologists such as Erich Fromm, Karen Horney, and Harry Stack Sullivan (*Personality Structure,* pp. 174ff.).

50. This is not to suggest that Jung, Adler, and Rank followed Freud without a good deal of variation from many of his original premises. From Freud's point of view, at least, each of these men became virtual apostates, having made some significant breaks with Freud's own psychoanalytical theories.

1971), and others might be seen as a synthesis of the depth psychology of Freud coupled with the cultural theory of American psychology.[51] Scottish psychoanalyst W. Ronald D. Fairbairn expanded on the ideas of Freud, Klein, and others. He reinterpreted many of the Freudian and Kleinian psychoanalytic ideas in the light of his work with schizoid patients, and also in light of some of the paradigms borrowed from the "new physics." Fairbairn's philosophical acumen therefore makes his psychological anthropology especially germane to this study.

Fairbairn proposed a dynamic view of the human being based on an inherent need to develop loving relations with a significant other (or "object"). With the gradual modification of the ideas of Freud by Fairbairn and others, object relations has grown into a respected subset of modern psychology.[52] I believe that object relations has gone a long way toward humanizing psychology without at the same time sacrificing its scientific integrity. Object relations theory is based on an accumulating amount of direct observation, especially of infants and children. It does not assume that the relationships between human beings can be exhaustively explained by biological functions or instinctual impulses. But neither does object relations ignore the biochemical factors and their influence on human behavior. Generally, object relations views the biological factors as necessary to human personhood, but not sufficient to explain human personhood in all its fullness and complexity. Object relations theory is based on the observation of the psychological development of the child from the earliest stages of infancy. In object relations the attachment of the child to the mother forms the primary matrix from which the self, in the context of an ever-widening circle of relations, is formed.

Once again, the dynamic relational view of the human being derives confirmation — this time from an empirical source. Object relations steers us away from thinking about the person in terms of the quantifiable biological functions of isolated individuals. Rather, it describes the person as a composite history of interpersonal relations. Precisely at this point I shall probe most deeply for analogies and parallels with Barth's view of the person. My pur-

---

51. See Guntrip, *Personality Structure*, pp. 50-51, 351.

52. Object relations psychology is sometimes loosely referred to as ego psychology, although Guntrip and others would prefer to make some distinctions between them. The choice of the term "object relations" seems unfortunate, since the "object" referred to is usually a person. The American term for "object relations" seems a bit more suited to what it describes: "interpersonal relations theory." But I shall stay with the British term since it is mostly British psychologists I cite, and it serves its purpose with suitable economy of expression. "Object" has a more technical ring to it, and since the external object can be internalized, it is perhaps best to stay with this technical-sounding term, in spite of its impersonal intonations.

pose in making such a comparison is primarily to see Barth's relation to the sciences properly understood. But such a comparison should also be of some practical value to pastors and leaders within the church. Providing a more adequate anthropology for the church can surely provide an important step toward improving the ancient art of the cure of souls in a modern world.

Reasons for Interdisciplinary Dialogue
between Theology and Psychology

Hans Küng has proposed: "Psychologists and theologians, 'doctors of souls' and pastors, have every reason today to enter into close cooperation. Fortunately both sides have made considerable progress in this respect."[53] There are several important reasons for bringing psychology into dialogue with Barth's anthropology. The first is practical.

As Küng points out, the church and psychology share a common ground in that both deal with persons directly, and both seek to provide some kind of practical relief, or "cure," for the human soul.[54] The proliferating usage of psychological tests by pastors and ecclesiastical bodies alike, the growing need for the minister to provide adequate counseling within the church attested by the proliferation of clinical pastoral education and practical theology, and the growth of small "support groups" within local churches, all attest to the convergence of these two disciplines on a practical level. Both the pastor and the psychologist adhere to a theoretical persuasion that effects a practical concern for human beings, and a practical concern that effects further theoretical reflection. In this sense they represent the respective "laboratories" that can test the validity of various anthropological theories.

As a pastor of a local congregation in northern California I constantly need to increase my awareness of self in order to minister to others. Conversely, I need to understand others in order to find myself and God. It is my hope and prayer that these theoretical reflections will have a practical benefit

53. *Freud and the Problem of God* (New Haven: Yale University Press, 1979) p. 100.

54. The etymologies of the terms for "pastoral care of souls" *(Seelsorge)* and "psychology" *(Seelenforschung)* suggest that the "soul" still remains the common ground between the two disciplines. There are of course many schools in modern psychology, and some of them would deny the existence of the soul, while others choose to ignore it. This need not concern us, unless they take up the philosophical task of attempting to disprove the soul's existence. See H. Misiak, *The Philosophical Roots of Scientific Psychology* (New York: Fordham University Press, 1961). See also J. T. McNeil, *A History of the Cure of Souls* (New York: Harper & Bros., 1951).

for myself and others who are seeking to shepherd the flock into the kingdom and treat their wounds with the healing balm of Gilead along the way.

What are we to think of this practical convergence between theology and psychology? In what ways might Barth provide us with some guidance? It will be helpful to keep in mind that, in spite of his extreme emphasis on revelation, Barth never strays far from the practical. I believe that Barth's realism, evidenced by his constant insistence that theology must be done within the context of the life and worship of the church,[55] lends particular viability to dialogue between Barth and modern psychology.[56] The anthropologies of both these disciplines are developed within the context of an enormous practical need. Both depend on the experience of pastors with parishioners, and of therapists with patients, to shape and inform their respective anthropologies. Barth developed his *Dogmatics* within the matrix of the church, and always kept the pastoral tasks well in mind, even when he was seeking answers for highly technical dogmatic questions.[57]

The second reason for comparing Barth and psychological views of the human being is to fill a theoretical void. To a large degree, Freud's explicit atheism cooled early efforts to explore in depth the interconnection between modern psychology and theology.[58] With the passing of time, the initial antipathies have gradually been set aside. Increasingly, psychology and theology have infiltrated each other's camps, and the trend is bound to continue. This integration, however, has been mostly pragmatic. For the most part, the relation between theology and modern psychology has developed as the popular understanding of psychology has gradually filtered into the church pulpits and pastoral counseling offices (especially in the United States).[59] Careful reflection on the proper integration of psychology and theology lags behind this pragmatic integration. Most ministers, and many theologians, know almost nothing about classical psychological theory, much less of object relations psychology. The minister's exposure is often limited to the popularized

---

55. "Dogmatics is a theological discipline. But theology is a function of the Church" (*CD*, I/1, p. 3). For Barth the church is, of course, defined by the Word of God.

56. See *CD*, I/1, pp. 3-11, 21, 47-87.

57. See, e.g., *CD*, III/4, p. xi. Cf. Eberhard Busch, *Karl Barth*, tr. John Bowden (London: SCM, 1976) pp. 219-20, who points out that even when he was writing the prolegomena to the *Dogmatics*, Barth was instructing young preachers.

58. See Meissner, *Psychoanalysis and Religious Experience*, p. 3.

59. For the one-sidedness of the flow from psychology to theology within the church, see Thomas Oden, *Agenda for Theology: Recovering Christian Roots* (San Francisco: Harper & Row, 1979) p. 164. Also see Paul Vitz, *Psychology as Religion* (Grand Rapids: Eerdmans, 1977) pp. 122, 124.

forms of humanistic psychology, with its tendency toward self-absorption.[60] Some fear and mutual suspicion still remain between those who practice psychology and those within the ranks of the church who do the pastoral counseling. This study is done with the hopeful prospect that a dialogue between the twentieth-century's leading theologian and the offspring of the twentieth-century's major psychologist might clear the way for a mutual and respectful exchange of ideas between these two disciplines. This is not to deny that many psychologists and theologians have begun to dialogue on a deeper theoretical level. It is only to point out that while some have done an admirable job of bridging the gaps between the two disciplines, few have attempted to integrate Barth's trinitarian theological insights and his ensuing definition of the human being as a "being in encounter" with the insights of any major psychoanalyst.[61] Much remains to be done in this area, and I am firmly convinced that systematic theologians should guard against relinquishing this dialogue to the supposedly quiet pastures of pastoral theology. I do not claim that this study in any way finishes the task of integrating good theology and psychology. I only hope that it might serve as a heuristic probe that can serve as a catalyst for some further dialogue.

Finally, I believe that three points are worth considering in light of the developing science of modern psychology — realities about the human being that theological studies of the person can ill afford to ignore.

First, Freud and his later followers discovered the powerful influence of unconscious and subconscious factors in human behavior. Can theologians continue to hold uncritically to the position that we are fully described by our rational faculty when the psychological evidence indicates that we are largely controlled by psychological factors which are mostly outside the realm of our conscious awareness? Psychoanalytic theory seems to me to present a stiff challenge to the common assumption in both philosophy and theology that the soul remains the seat of freedom while the body is trapped within the

60. See Vitz, *Psychology as Religion*, who castigates four contemporary psychological theorists: Erich Fromm, Carl Rogers, Abraham Maslow, and Rollo May, for their excessive emphasis on the self. See also Christopher Lasch, *The Culture of Narcissism: American Life in an Age of Diminishing Expectations* (New York: Norton, 1979); and Alan Torrance, "Self-Relation, Narcissism and the Gospel of Grace," *SJT* 40 (1987) 481-510.

61. A person who has made some initial attempt to bring Barth's insights into the psychological field is Thomas Oden, who draws comparisons between Barth's *analogia fidei* and Carl Rogers's client-centered therapy in *Kerygma and Counseling*. I greatly admire the effort by Frank Lake, *Clinical Theology* (London: Darton, Longman & Todd, 1966), to integrate trinitarian faith with depth psychology. I have one criticism: he built too exclusively on the thought of Otto Rank and thus overemphasized the dimension of birth trauma for psychological development.

fixed determinations of causation in space and time.[62] The unveiling of un-conscious motivations by modern psychology indicates that we are, for the most part, far less rational than we would like to admit.

Second, it could also be pointed out with regard to human rationality that psychological research has done a good deal of studying of the intelligence of other animals, and discovered that animal intelligence and creativity are much higher than had been previously thought. In light of these discoveries can theological anthropology insist that humans are distinguished from other animals by sole possession of a superior intellect (a *ratio*)? Can the *imago Dei* be reduced to reason, intelligence, and creativity, as so much of theology has previously proposed? Certainly there is something unique about the ways in which human beings reason and order their world, especially in our usage of language and speech. But once again, modern research has altered the conception of ourselves as rational creatures. Even if we cast aside all the research on animals, modern research tends to confirm that the development of human speech has a social component,[63] and it seems to me that theology will have an increasingly difficult time if it insists that the image of God in humanity is found in the human intellect alone, as an isolated faculty. In view of these discoveries, the human essence, and our means of understanding it as best we can, need to be reevaluated. Human rationality needs to be reinterpreted.

Finally, philosopher Paul Ricoeur rightly informs us that the choice of faith or unbelief does not rest with psychoanalysis. He does, however, believe that psychoanalysis can purge faith of some of its idolatries.[64] I believe that this is particularly true in the types of theology where the ground for theological reflection has been understood as the immediacy of religious experience. Into such experientially based theologies the insights of modern psychology can sometimes cut to the quick. For example, I will argue that the "feeling of absolute dependence," upon which the theology of Friedrich Schleiermacher

---

62. E.g., Kant sought to address the metaphysical problem of ethics with the assumption that human beings are noumenally free but empirically determined with regard to the same action (*Critique of Pure Reason,* tr. N. Kemp Smith [London: Macmillan, 1950] B xxviii-xxx, pp. 28-29; A 803, B 831, p. 634). Cf. Frederick Copleston, *A History of Philosophy,* vol. VI (Westminster, Md.: Newman Press, 1960) p. 336. See also Zizioulas, *Being,* pp. 35-49, who assumes that the biological nature of the person is determined, while the person as a "being in communion" has freedom.

63. See Rom Harré and Paul Secord, *The Explanation of Social Behavior* (Oxford: Blackwell, 1972) p. 6, and esp. pp. 84-100.

64. *Freud and Philosophy: An Essay on Interpretation,* tr. D. Savage (New Haven and London: Yale University Press, 1970) p. 230.

is based, is particularly susceptible to a psychological explanation.[65] I therefore pay close attention to the development of Schleiermacher's experientially based theology, carefully following Barth's critique of Schleiermacher, and near the end of the study (in chapter six) add a critique of my own in light of modern psychoanalytic theory.

After surveying Barth I will argue that human rationality is not to be discarded, but should be interpreted in light of our relations to God, self, and others. Subsequent to studying object relations psychology I will argue that pastors, church leaders, and theologians are simply naive to think that the insights of modern psychology can be overlooked or discarded. We need the insights and applications of modern psychotherapy, not in order to supplant theology with psychology, but in order to keep our journey into theological truth from becoming mired in our own psychological swamps.

65. This does not mean, of course, that an alternative psychological explanation to a theological belief invalidates the belief. Freud admits in his arguments against theism that he has not disproved the truth of theistic beliefs: he merely provides another explanation for their origin. Schleiermacher never intended to reduce his own theology to subjectivism. Nevertheless, the "feeling of absolute dependence," I propose, is particularly susceptible to explanations of a psychological type. See chapter six below.

CHAPTER 2

Enlightenment: Humankind at the Center

Who will show us any good? Let us say so, and let them hear: The
light of thy countenance is sealed upon us. For we ourselves are not
that light which enlighteneth every man that cometh into the world;
but we are enlightened by thee.

AUGUSTINE

My primary purpose in this chapter is to illumine Barth's theological anthropology by showing the kind of intellectual problems that the Enlightenment
presented for anyone who undertook a serious theological enterprise in the
early twentieth century. For Barth, theology framed in a war-torn and skeptical Europe could only be a very serious undertaking. I therefore show how
Barth develops his theology with a keen respect for the moral and intellectual
challenges of his time. Barth's theology was not spun in a vacuum; it is important to understand the milieu in which he wrote, including several key Enlightenment thinkers who shaped European intellectual life. All of this is
done with an eye to chapter four, where I develop the salient points of Barth's
anthropology.

In my original thesis the section on Kant was fairly extensive.[1] In this
book I have shortened this section in order to make it more readable. Few
things are more tedious than reading Kant's critical studies — especially dig-
ging through the turgid German volumes of his collected works. Study of

---

1. See Daniel J. Price, "Karl Barth's Anthropology in Light of Modern Thought" (Ph.D.
thesis, University of Aberdeen, 1991).

31

Kant is nevertheless warranted because Kant influenced European epistemology for almost two centuries. The more I studied Barth's life and work, the more I became convinced that in order to comprehend Barth's theology one must go back to Kant and trace the philosophical problems with which Kant wrestled so earnestly just over a century earlier. I am not the first to point out that Kant was tremendously influential in Continental theology during the earlier part of the twentieth century. This was especially true in the neo-Kantian school of theology at the University of Marburg. At roughly the same time when Barth was formulating his dogmatic theology, Kant's critical philosophy continued to present a formidable challenge to orthodox theology.[2]

The Enlightenment is also significant for this study in that it was during this period that the application of scientific methods to the study of human beings began to develop into the disciplines that would one day become the modern social sciences.[3] The historical perspective given in this chapter shows how both Kant and the incipient social sciences mistakenly applied Newtonian concepts to their respective fields and obscured the interpersonal dimension of being human.

Fortunately, our task of seeking the early influences on Barth's theology is made easier by the fact that Barth has written extensively on the major thinkers of the Enlightenment and interacts with them in many of his writings.

Barth's Critique of the "Absolute Man" of the Enlightenment

In his important work *Protestant Theology in the Nineteenth Century*,[4] Barth traces the development of the Enlightenment back through the Renaissance,

---

2. It must be admitted that Barth's anthropology draws on resources going back to a period well before the Enlightenment: to the Reformation, church councils, and the New Testament. While these resources serve as a foundation for many of Barth's *solutions*, the *problems* he dealt with stemmed primarily from Enlightenment idealism. It was also the Enlightenment that provided the impetus for the beginning of modern scientific psychology and the anthropological problems contained therein. This makes an understanding of the major thinkers of the Enlightenment important for this particular study.

3. Johann Friedrich Blumenbach (1752-1842) is considered the father of physical or cultural anthropology. But Immanuel Kant, as we shall see, made some contributions to physical anthropology himself in his *Anthropologie in pragmatischer Hinsicht*, in *Kants gesammelte Schriften*, 23 vols. (I-VIII, XIV-XVI, Berlin: Reimer, 1902-14; IX-XIII, XVII-XXIII, Berlin: de Gruyter, 1922-55) VII, pp. 117-333. Hereafter referred to as *GS*, with the volume indicated by Roman numeral.

4. Tr. B. Cozens, et al. (London: SCM, 1972; Valley Forge, Pa.: Judson, 1973). Eleven of the 29 chapters of *Die protestantische Theologie im 19. Jahrhundert* were first translated into English

and unravels what he considers to be an essential thread of Enlightenment thought:

> Eighteenth-century man began to become conscious of his power for science, and of his power through science. The development at the Renaissance, which had been hindered and reduced for almost one hundred and fifty years through the period of religious wars, now began to make immense strides. Once again man, led by a philosophy, which was only apparently disunited but was in essentials united, began to be conscious — and more forcibly than before — of a capacity for thinking which was responsible to no other authority than himself.[5]

Logic, observation, and mathematics began to displace the traditional authorities such as church and state during the Enlightenment.

Barth interprets the overall effect of the Enlightenment as the self-exaltation of "absolute man."[6] He traces the belief in "absolute man" to the heliocentric discovery of Copernicus. The Copernican revolution produced a paradoxical effect on the philosophy of the Enlightenment in that "the geocentric picture of the universe was replaced as a matter of course by the anthropocentric."[7] Copernicus theorized the heliocentric understanding of the solar system, and thus uncovered the fact that the human race was not at the center of the material universe. The result, Barth proposes, was that humans felt themselves to be displaced, having lost their centrality in the cosmos. Post-Copernican humanity were suddenly less sure of themselves than before. But rather than accepting this discovery as a humbling fact, humans created a compensating belief. The Enlightenment had already largely eroded the traditional Christian sense of faith in God. So a surrogate faith was invented: faith in humanity itself as the center of the universe, says Barth.[8] When Coper-

---

and titled *From Rousseau to Ritschl*, tr. Brian Cozens (London: SCM, 1959). Barth and others were not happy with the truncated version, and in 1972 the full document was published in English.

5. *Protestant Theology*, p. 39.

6. Ibid., pp. 40ff. Because the English term "man" is most often used to translate the German *Mensch*, I sometimes use "man" in order to avoid confusion while discussing Barth's thought. Where my own thoughts are expressed, I prefer to use the terms "person," "humankind," or "human being," rather than "man," because these carry a more concise meaning and less sexist connotations.

7. *Protestant Theology*, p. 38.

8. It is apparent that Barth is playing on the words of Kant, who referred to his critiques as "proceeding precisely on the lines of Copernicus' primary hypothesis." This is loosely interpreted to be Kant's "Copernican revolution." See Immanuel Kant, *Critique of Pure Reason*, tr. N. Kemp Smith, rev. ed. (London: Macmillan, 1950) B xvi-xvii, p. 22; cf. p. 25n. Hereafter cited as *CPR*, with "A" referring to the 1st edition (1781) and "B" referring to Kant's 2d edition (1787). See also Frederick Copleston, *A History of Philosophy*, 6 vols. (Garden City, N.Y.: Image, 1985) VI, p. 224.

nicus's cosmology undercut humankind's sense of self-importance, the emphasis turned from the cosmos to the human intellect. The human race was no longer at the cosmological center, but humans could maintain their sense of importance through the exercise of reason.[9] Barth argues that autonomous reason became the new center of human existence. The Enlightenment thinkers therefore developed an obsession with proving the superiority of the human intellect, which was viewed as the ground for freedom and autonomy over nature. Hence the exclusive anthropocentric interest that extends to contemporary theology and postmodern philosophy was spawned by the "Copernican revolution" in cosmology and the subsequent "Copernican revolution" in epistemology — the quest to make human achievement "absolute." Barth says that the Enlightenment "man" is "absolute" in that he shifts the focus of attention from God and the universe — to "himself, as the measure of both." Barth detects one of the evidences for this shift in the change from human rights and dignity based on the grace of God to rights based on self-evidence.[10]

Barth sees the Enlightenment as a "recrudescence of the Renaissance," a humanism that is the "autarchy of rational man in a rational world on the basis of the existence and dominion of a Deity guaranteeing this association and thus too man's complete autarchy."[11] This autarchy is especially evident in the

---

9. On a similar track, Reinhold Niebuhr states: "Men have been assailed periodically by qualms of conscience and fits of dizziness for pretending to occupy the centre of the universe. Every philosophy of life is touched with anthropocentric tendencies. Even theocentric religions believe that the Creator of the world is interested in saving man from his unique predicament. . . . This fact has not been lost on moderns, whose modesty before the cosmic immensity was modified considerably by pride in their discovery of this immensity. It was a modern, the poet Swinburne, who sang triumphantly:

> The sea of his knowledge is sure, the truth and his spirit are wed; . . .
> Glory to Man in the highest! for man is the master of things,

thereby proving that the advance of human knowledge about the world does not abate the pride of man" (*Nature and Destiny*, I, p. 3).

10. *Protestant Theology*, pp. 41-54. Barth is presumably contrasting the human-rights understanding of the reformers with the political individualism of the Enlightenment. He most likely has Calvin in mind for the former, and as an example of the latter cites Locke's *Treatise on Civil Government*. See *CD*, I/2, p. 562. See also W. Fred Graham, *The Constructive Revolutionary* (Richmond, Va.: John Knox, 1971) pp. 55-56; and Jean-Jacques Rousseau, *Of the Social Contract, or Principles of Political Right & Discourse on Political Economy*, tr. C. M. Sherover (New York: Harper & Row, 1984) p. 14, who states that the purpose of the social contract is "to find a form of association which defends and protects with the whole force of the community the person and goods of every associate, and by means of which each, uniting with all, *nevertheless obeys only himself*, and remains as free as before" (italics mine).

11. *Protestant Theology*, p. 76.

philosophy of Descartes.[12] Asserting that theology cannot think along Cartesian lines, Barth says: "The Modernist view from which we must demarcate ourselves here goes back to the Renaissance and especially to the Renaissance philosopher Descartes with his proof of God from human self-certainty."[13] Barth points out that the Enlightenment was the century of "Man, who discovers his own power and ability, the potentiality dormant in his humanity, that is, his human being as such, and looks upon it as the final, the real and absolute, . . . as something 'detached,' self-justifying, with its own authority and power, which he can therefore set in motion in all directions and without any restraint — this man is absolute man."[14] Subsequent to the scientific and technological advancement of the eighteenth century, the Enlightenment's "absolute man" considered himself "almost capable of anything."[15]

In spite of the scientific achievements of the eighteenth century, Barth proposes that they were not as significant as the political developments of that period, especially the casting off of the authority of the emperor and the Holy Roman Empire.[16]

In philosophical expression, the purest form of the Enlightenment, according to Barth, is found in the philosophy of Gottfried Wilhelm Leibniz (1646-1716), whose "self-sufficient monad" captures the essence of Enlightenment individualism.[17] Leibniz's theodicy was later politicized by Rousseau, who argued, "The natural state of man is the state in which no man has need of any other, neither for good nor for bad purposes, neither in friendship nor enmity."[18]

In Rousseau's thought the isolation of one from the others was in order to be "one with nature." With Leibniz the aloneness was enforced by his con-

---

12. Descartes served as a kind of bridge between the Renaissance and the Copernican hypothesis. Barth reacts negatively to Descartes's influence on subsequent thought because his epistemology ended in individualism; see David Livingstone Mueller, "Karl Barth's Critique of the Anthropological Starting Point in Theology" (Ph.D. dissertation, Duke University, 1958). Mueller states: "Barth sees the way prepared for religious individualism in the thought of the Renaissance, Descartes and Leibniz. Romanticism represents the highest expression of individualism. In theology it was Schleiermacher who gave classic expression to this approach" (p. 13n.).

13. *CD*, I/1, p. 195; cf. also p. 211.

14. *Protestant Theology*, p. 36. Cf. H. Hartwell, *The Theology of Karl Barth* (London: Duckworth, 1964) p. 4.

15. *Protestant Theology*, p. 41. See also *CD*, II/1, p. 293.

16. *Protestant Theology*, pp. 42-43.

17. Barth is referring to the fact that Leibniz's monads are self-sufficient substances, centers of psychic activity, which cannot be changed or altered by any other creature, for "the monads have no windows, through which anything can enter or depart" (*Monadology*, §7, quoted from *Leibnitz: Selections*, tr. P. P. Wiener [New York: Scribner, 1951] p. 533).

18. *Protestant Theology*, p. 181.

cept of the monad as indivisible self-contained thought. The former represents the human person as naturally good but tainted by civilization. The latter sees the human person as a self-contained substance, locked within its own world of thought. Both cases articulate a position that strains toward individualism. In both cases there is a reiteration of the admonition of Socrates to "know thyself" — quite apart from the need to know one's neighbor.

Granted, in his analysis of the rise of "absolute man" Barth is painting a picture of the Enlightenment in broad strokes. He readily admits the complexity of the picture, and the sense in which many components within the Enlightenment are not susceptible to a simple portrait. Yet he sees a forceful pattern emerging from the Enlightenment, one that tends to exalt the human status and isolate humans from one another and from God. The individualism contained in the rationalism of Leibniz and the romantic naturalism of Rousseau is important because both exert tremendous influence on modern views of the human person. The degree to which Barth rejects individualism in developing his own anthropology can hardly be exaggerated. It will be highlighted in the following chapters, especially chapter four.

With the Enlightenment approaching its zenith, Kant began to reflect on the theoretical problems presented to modern thought. In Kant's critical philosophy, the former metaphysical types of rationalism began to crumble. But with what did Kant replace the older dualistic anthropologies? I embark on this study of Kant to see if Barth's assessment that the Enlightenment person was "absolute" holds true of Kant. Furthermore, many have argued that Barth is "Kantian"; the best way to find out is to compare their respective ideas about God and humanity.

Kant's Idealist Anthropology

At the close of the nineteenth century, Friedrich Paulsen wrote, "Kant's philosophy is the door to the philosophy of our century, and the door to the Kantian philosophy is the *Critique of Pure Reason*."[19] When it comes to hu-

---

19. *Immanuel Kant: His Life and Doctrine*, tr. J. E. Creighton and A. Lefevre (London: John C. Nommo, 1902) p. xv. Cf. Benedict Ashley, *Theologies of the Body: Humanist and Christian* (Braintree, Mass.: Pope John Center, 1985) p. 635, who says that Kant is "rightly regarded as the most influential of modern philosophical systems." See also pp. 69-70. T. F. Torrance regards Kant as the "prophet of the 'modern' mind" (*Transformation and Convergence*, p. 7), and John Macmurray refers to Kant's thought as the most "adequate" of all modern philosophies (*Self as Agent*, p. 40). As an example of Kant's influence on Barth, every volume of the *Dogmatics* cites some aspect of Kant's philosophy at least several times (except the fragment IV/4).

man knowledge, Kant is unavoidably the central figure of the Enlightenment, and his Critiques have proved to be a major watershed for most modern philosophical and theological reflection thereafter.

In his first Critique, *Critique of Pure Reason*, Kant attempted a major synthesis between the rationalism of Descartes, Leibniz, and Wolff, and the empiricism of Locke, Berkeley, and Hume. Kant's first Critique resulted in the demise of "transcendent" metaphysics: that is, metaphysics as it had been traditionally understood right up until Hume and Kant. The challenge for most subsequent theologians was to do theology within the confines of Kant's critical philosophy — or find a way around it.

Kant's enlightened view of humanity is summed up in this quotation:

> The Enlightenment represents man's emergence from a self-inflicted state of minority. A minor is one who is incapable of making use of his understanding without guidance from someone else. This minority is self-inflicted whenever its cause lies not in lack of understanding, but in a lack of the determination and courage to make use of it without the guidance of another. *Sapere aude!* Have the courage to make use of your own understanding, is therefore the watchword of the Enlightenment.[20]

Kant's summons for humanity to "dare to reason" and thus break out of its status as a minor rests upon the exercise of autonomous human reason.[21] It is reason as an instrument of critical thought, which is Kant's most noticeable contribution to the age of Enlightenment.[22] Kant's enlightened emphasis on

20. Barth refers to a "little essay" written in 1784, but does not cite its place of publication or title (*Protestant Theology*, pp. 267-68). But see *GS*, VIII, pp. 36-41. ET, "What Is Enlightenment?" See *Critique of Practical Reason and Other Writings in Moral Philosophy*, tr. L. W. Beck (1949; repr. New York: Garland, 1976) pp. 286-92. Philosophical historian Peter Gay agrees with Barth's assessment of Kant; commenting on Kant's *Sapere aude*, Gay states, "Kant saw the Enlightenment as man's claim to be recognized as an adult, responsible being" (*The Enlightenment: An Interpretation*, 2 vols. [New York: Knopf, 1966] I, p. 3).

21. One of the foremost purposes of Kant's Critiques is to prove the autonomous as opposed to heteronomic nature of human reason, because he seeks to provide a metaphysics for human reason, and heteronomic reason defies freedom. It is primarily in the realm of the practical where human autonomy is possible; Kant affirms: "Natural necessity is, as we have seen, a heteronomy of efficient causes, for every effect is possible only according to the law that something else determines the efficient cause to its causality. What else, then, can the freedom of the will be but autonomy, i.e., the property of the will to be a law to itself?" (*Practical Reason and Other Writings*, p. 102).

22. *Protestant Theology*, p. 269. Barth claims that Kant's summary of the eighteenth century as an age "of true criticism" is even more to the point than the above quotation. We shall see, however, that they strain together: true criticism is seated in the faculty of human reason

the use of reason is "autonomous" inasmuch as it serves to challenge any subservience of reason to religion or revelation. In a sense Kant's critical philosophy severely curtailed the power of reason. Yet he did not bring reason into subservience to anything other than itself. Barth observes: "The critique of reason is reason arriving at an understanding of itself . . . the only kind of reason he considers worthy of his trust is the reason which has first of all come to be reasonable as regards itself."[23]

Kant's thought is important for this study for three reasons. First, because his influence on Barth and all of modern theology is almost immeasurable. The scope of modern theology and philosophy has been vastly curtailed by the Newtonian cosmology and subsequent Kantian philosophy. Modern thought may be attempting to push beyond Kant; but it is certainly not modern if it has tried to ignore or to go around him.

Second, Kant's philosophy contains a keen anthropological interest. Kant did not wish to ask his epistemological and ethical questions in a vacuum, but believed that they expressed answers to the question: What is man? In the *Critique of Pure Reason* Kant puts his philosophy within the following framework:

> All the interests of my reason, speculative as well as practical, combine in the three following questions:
>   1. What can I know?
>   2. What ought I to do?
>   3. What may I hope?[24]

But in his *Lectures on Logic* Kant espoused the view that philosophy should be put into an even wider context:

> The field of philosophy, in this sense, may be reduced to the following questions:
>   1. What can I know?
>   2. What ought I to do?
>   3. What may I hope?
>   4. What is man?
>
> The first question is answered by *Metaphysics*, the second by *Morals*, the third by *Religion*, and the fourth by *Anthropology*. In reality, however,

---

alone, and thus constitutes the way in which the human race is in fact "coming of age," according to the Enlightenment.

23. *Protestant Theology*, pp. 270-71.

24. A 805, B 833, p. 635.

all these might be reckoned under anthropology, since the first three questions refer to the last.[25]

Kant himself wrote and lectured extensively on the subject of philosophical anthropology, and some recent studies have brought to light the extent to which Kant's critical philosophy was undergirded by an anthropological interest.[26] We will see that Kant emphasized metaphysics as an a priori mode of knowing in the realms of physics, ethics, and aesthetics; and though he did not always mention his anthropological interest, his lectures indicate that in the back of his mind all the while was the question: What is man?[27]

My third reason for giving Kant a special amount of attention is that, as John Macmurray has pointed out, Kant's philosophy is the most "adequate" of modern philosophies because it is both critical and comprehensive.[28] Kant's philosophy truly served as the doorway for most of nineteenth- and much of twentieth-century philosophy, as he sought to find solutions to the problems created by science, morals, and aesthetics. He was particularly concerned to fit together the apparent necessity of the physical world under the influence of Newton's laws and the apparent freedom of morality. Kant believed that a genuine metaphysics would square with Newtonian physics as well as with the inner experience of moral freedom.[29] His *Critique of Pure Reason* deals with the former, the *Critique of Practical Reason* (and other writings related to practical reason that will be cited below) with the latter; and his third Critique seeks the foundation of aesthetics, *Critique of Judgment* (although the third Critique is also more than a mere critique of aesthetics). Taken together, the common thread that pulls the Critiques together is the question: What is man?

25. *GS*, IX, p. 25. Also cited in *Kant's Introduction to Logic*, tr. T. K. Abbott (London: Longmans, Green, 1885) p. 15. The translation is Abbott's.

26. E.g., Ernst Cassirer, *Rousseau-Kant-Goethe*, tr. J. Gutmann, P. O. Kristeller, and J. H. Randall Jr. (Princeton: Princeton University Press, 1945), esp. p. 5; also Frederick P. Van De Pitte, *Kant as Philosophical Anthropologist* (The Hague: Martinus Nijhoff, 1971), esp. chap. 2. See also Jaki, *Angels, Apes and Men*, pp. 27-34.

27. In favor of this assertion, I point out that Kant could write in 1765 (before he had written any of his Critiques): "If there is any science which man is really in need of, it is that which teaches him how to fulfill properly the position assigned to him in the creation and from which he can learn what he must be in order to be a man" (*GS*, XX, p. 45; tr. S. Jaki). Curiously, this passage is interpreted by Van De Pitte, "If there is any science which man really needs, it is the one *I teach*, of how to fulfill properly . . ." (*Kant as Philosophical Anthropologist*, p. 48). This is an inaccurate translation, but nevertheless captures the idea Kant had in mind as he wrote his philosophy.

28. *Self as Agent*, p. 39.

29. See *CPR*, B xvi-xvii, p. 22. See esp. A 803, B 831, p. 634.

Barth does not deal extensively with Kant's first Critique. He does, however, note its importance and then points out that Kant's essential anthropology is found in his practical writings.[30] I believe, however, that Paulsen is right to insist that the *Critique of Pure Reason* is the doorway to Kant's thought. Any serious student of modern theology needs to read and understand Kant's first and second Critiques.

A Synopsis of Kant's Critique of Pure Reason

In Kant's *Critique of Pure Reason*[31] he seeks to show how the objectivity of mathematical and scientific knowledge is possible.[32] He assumes that Newton has accurately explained the laws of universal motion and energy. Kant does not seek an a posteriori justification from experience for scientific knowledge, because he thinks this has already been provided by the successes of Newtonian science.[33] Rather, Kant seeks a metaphysical justification of mathematical and scientific knowledge.[34] This metaphysical justification, he

---

30. Barth affirms time and again that pure reason for Kant is ultimately practical (*Protestant Theology,* pp. 275ff.). Hence "Abstract man, the man who is held to be a creature of theoretical reason, is not the real man" (ibid., p. 276).

31. *Kritik der reinen Vernunft, GS,* III-IV.

32. Such a philosophical "justification" was thought to be necessary because of the problems raised by David Hume regarding the impossibility of demonstrating causality and necessity empirically. On the other hand, the rationalist school represented by Leibniz and Wolff found equal difficulty in demonstrating necessity from empirical observations, but treated the difference between the sensible and the intelligible as "merely logical." Since the truths of both mathematics and Newtonian physics seemed "necessary" to Kant, he found the lines of thought represented by both Hume and Leibniz-Wolff to be unacceptable. See, respectively, *CPR,* A 95-97, B 127-29, pp. 126-28; and A 44, B 61-62, pp. 83-84.

33. Kant was enormously influenced by Newton, and in many ways sought to transfer Newton's success into his own critical philosophy: "The true method of metaphysics is basically the same as that introduced by Newton into natural science and which had such useful consequences in that field" (*GS,* II, p. 286; trans. Van De Pitte).

34. Kant is commonly regarded as the philosopher who put metaphysical speculation out of reach for philosophy and theology thereafter. See, e.g., H. M. Kuitert, *The Reality of Faith,* tr. L. B. Smedes (Grand Rapids: Eerdmans, 1968), esp. pp. 11ff. Yet Kant calls the science of "metaphysics" the essence of his Critiques. See *CPR,* A xiii, xx, B xv. In a letter to Moses Mendelssohn, Kant expresses his disgust with metaphysics as it had been previously done, but then states: "I am thus far removed from regarding metaphysics itself, objectively considered, to be trivial or dispensable" (*GS,* X, p. 67). Both are true, because Kant distinguishes (though not very clearly) between "immanent" and "transcendent" metaphysics. See A 643, B 671, p. 532; and B xxiv-xxvii, pp. 26-28. The former is made possible by the "forms of sensibility" (space and time) and the twelve "categories." The latter, Kant says, is an illegitimate employment of the ideas of

thinks, can be provided only on an a priori basis. Since on an a priori under-standing of objects it seemed impossible to conform the mind to objects, Kant decided to see if it was more reasonable to conform objects to the mind. This method turned out to be his "Copernican revolution": the theory that objects conform to laws or a priori categories of the mind.[35] Kant was thus a rationalist, and in a qualified way an idealist — but of a different type; for he did not think that objects could be reduced to the human mind and its ideas. Rather, he accepted Hume's insistence that all knowledge begins *with* experi-ence. For Kant the mind is never wholly productive of its object. Objects are "given" through sensibility, which alone yields "intuitions,"[36] and all knowl-edge *(Erkenntnis)* is traceable to intuitions.[37]

Yet Kant did not assume, like the empiricists, that all knowledge arises *from* experience. Rather, any true knowledge results from the mind's synthesis of concepts and intuitions. As Norman Kemp Smith summarizes: "Our expe-rience may be a compound of that which we receive through impressions, and of that which pure reason supplies from itself."[38] We therefore approach nature not simply as the pupil, but also as the judge,[39] because the mind im-poses certain "categories of understanding" *(Verstandesbegriff)* on things that are given to consciousness. For Kant, then, there are always two components involved in judgments: the direct and sensual, and the conceptual or struc-tural. Kant proposes, "Without sensibility *(Sinnlichkeit)* no object would be given to us, and without understanding *(Verstand)* no object would be thought. Thoughts without content are empty; intuitions without concepts are blind."[40]

Kant frames his theoretical Critique by asking how synthetic a priori judgments are possible, first in mathematics, then physics.[41] Finally he asks if synthetic a priori statements are possible in metaphysics — to which he gives

---

reason (God, self, and world). See Norman Kemp Smith, *A Commentary to Kant's 'Critique of Pure Reason'* (repr.; London: Macmillan, 1979) p. liv.

35. *CPR,* B xvi-xvii, pp. 22-23; cf. p. 25 n. a. Kant meant it to be a "Copernican" revolu-tion in the sense that he thought the mind to be much more active than previous metaphysi-cians had thought. See Kemp Smith, *Commentary,* pp. 24-25. This creates the ironic situation that Kant saw the mind as "Ptolemaic" with regard to its central importance, but "Copernican" with regard to its modus operandi.

36. Kant is here talking about immediate sense perception or empirical intuition *(Anschauung).*

37. *CPR,* B 33, p. 65.

38. Cf. Kemp Smith, *Commentary,* p. 27.

39. *CPR,* B xiii, p. 20.

40. *CPR,* B 75, A 51, p. 93.

41. *CPR,* B 18-22, pp. 54-57.

a negative answer (with regard to speculative reason). An a priori judgment is that which is true independent of sense experience, and a synthetic judgment is one in which the predicate conceptualizes more than is contained in the subject. Analytic judgments are obviously a priori; but what about certain synthetic judgments? Could these too be a priori? Prior to Kant, an empiricist such as Hume would have said: "No! synthetic statements are necessarily derived from experience and are therefore a posteriori." Kant argues that this is not always the case; some synthetic judgments can be a priori.[42]

With regard to mathematics, Kant contends that mathematical judgments are both a priori and synthetic (Hobbes and others would argue that mathematical statements are a priori and analytic).[43] That is, mathematical statements are valid apart from sensible intuition, and yet they signify more than tautologies or mere analytic judgments. In the first Critique, Kant therefore delineates his "Copernican revolution" in epistemology by asking how synthetic a priori judgments are possible. Kant spends a major portion of his first Critique building his case that synthetic a priori judgments are possible in the realm of physics.

In the realm of the physical world, all sensible intuitions are mediated through space and time. Space and time are the "pure forms of all sensible intuition, and so are what make a priori synthetic propositions possible."[44] Since space and time are subjective forms, not an objective reality in the formerly understood sense, knowledge of objects is restricted to phenomenal reality, or "appearances."[45] Kant's treatment of space and time is highly complex, but for the most part he was greatly influenced by the Newtonian concept of absolute space and time; and although he adapted it to his own purposes, calling space and time the "forms of pure intuition," he nevertheless thought that such an a priori origin of the representation of space and time supported Newton's findings. Probably due to the fact that Galileo and Newton had insisted that essentialist categories be kept out of the realm of physics,[46] Kant reflected on

---

42. *CPR*, B 2-3, pp. 42-43. I use the terms "theoretical" and "speculative" interchangeably, referring to the type of reason employed in Kant's first Critique.

43. *CPR*, B 15-17, pp. 52-54.

44. *CPR*, A 39, B 56, p. 80.

45. An appearance *(Erscheinung)* is not merely an illusion *(Schein)*. See *CPR*, A 248, also B 69, p. 88.

46. See Enrico Cantore, *Scientific Man: The Humanistic Significance of Science* (New York: ISH, 1977) pp. 190ff. Cantore points out that the intrinsic intelligibility of nature is a discovery of postmodern physics, even though it is not essentialist. Kant's assumption that the absolute space and time of Newtonian physics were unquestionable led him to place such in the unreachable recesses of the mind (as "sensible forms"). The result was that they were not able to be

the Newtonian concept of absolute time and space, but then interpreted time and space as subjective forms of human understanding.[47] Because of the subjectivity of space and time, as well as the categories of understanding, Kant proposed that physical objects do not present themselves "as they are in themselves."[48] Here arises Kant's famous distinction between noumena (things in themselves) and phenomena (things as they appear).

The "Self" in the First Critique

From David Hume, Kant also inherited the problem of the identity of the self. The identity of the self had proved problematic for Hume's skeptical empiricism. Hume had concluded that there was no demonstration of identity from sense impressions, and concluded that the self was held together probably by memory.[49] Kant was not quite satisfied with this.

For Kant, there are two selves described in his Critiques — more accurately, two descriptions or perspectives of the same self. As we might expect, there are both a noumenal and a phenomenal self, that is, an intellectual and a sensible self.[50] The sensible self is locked in the empirical world and is therefore determined by the laws of causality.[51] Nevertheless, the sensible self can

---

modified by experience, and, T. F. Torrance observes, "this means that he built into the foundation of knowledge a disastrous ingredient of necessity or determinism" (*Transformation and Convergence*, p. 37). A similar criticism is voiced by Copleston, *History of Philosophy*, VI, p. 251. In addition, the more recent findings of cognitive research disallow such inflexible structures of the categories for understanding. The structures for human understanding have been discovered to change with certain developmental stages and are thus much more supple than Kant described them. With all of this in mind, L. W. Beck states: "No doubt the rigidity of the Kantian transcendental apparatus must be relaxed, alternative category systems must be conceded" ("What Have We Learned from Kant?" in Allen W. Wood, ed., *Self and Nature in Kant's Philosophy* [Ithaca, N.Y., and London: Cornell University Press, 1984] p. 20). We shall see in chapter five that Newtonian physics (rightly or wrongly interpreted) arises again in a strangely unsuspected corner, namely in Freud's psychological anthropology. Nevertheless, Kant cannot be faulted for adopting the scientific outlook of his day.

47. See A 518-32, B 546-60, pp. 455-64.

48. *CPR*, A 27, B 43, p. 71: "Space is nothing but the form of all appearances of outer sense. It is the subjective condition of sensibility under which alone outer intuition is possible for us." Cf. also A 39, B 56, p. 80. Kant's conception of time and space is immensely complex, and sometimes contradictory, especially if considered in the light of his entire works. Such technicalities lie outside the scope of this study, however. See Kemp Smith, *Commentary*, pp. 88-116.

49. See *A Treatise of Human Nature*, ed. L. A. Selby-Bigge (Oxford: Clarendon, 1896) I, iv, 6.

50. *CPR*, B xxviii, p. 28; cf. A 538-57, B 566-85, pp. 466-79.

51. *CPR*, A 544-45, B 572-73, pp. 470-71.

be known not as it is in itself but as an appearance.[52] The phenomenal self is thus the description of human persons as they appear in the sensible world, while the noumenal self is the person as a purely intelligible object — which can be approached only through practical reason.[53]

In the end, Kant's speculative self is painstakingly difficult to pin down. It seems to be predicated by the unity of the "I think." Yet the identity of the "I" as a unity is purely analytic, says Kant. The "I" of speculative reason is not predicable as simple substance, for such a predication would lie outside the field of the understanding.[54] Kant is unwilling to allow the self to make itself the object of its own knowledge because, as he points out, that would be incredibly circular.[55] It would also jeopardize everything Kant is trying to prove in pointing out that speculative reason is limited to knowledge that arises with sensible intuitions.

Kant has done us the service of pointing out how immensely difficult it is for the self to understand itself as a thinking subject. To a large extent he has debunked the myth of the self as a thinking substance. Yet what does he leave in its place? It seems that the speculative self is mostly a question mark.[56] This comes as little surprise if we remind ourselves that Kant was not (especially in his first Critique) seeking the empirical content of human knowing. Rather, he was seeking to explain the a priori conditions that make it possible to know. But more importantly, we see here the impasse that pure theoretical reason creates for a knowledge of the self. Even within the confines of the first Critique, the real identity of the self, Kant insists, can only be described practically — in terms of moral laws.[57] Kant has brought us to the

---

52. *CPR*, B 153-59, pp. 165-69.

53. *CPR*, A 547, B 575, p. 472.

54. *CPR*, B 408, p. 369. This points out the weakness of Descartes's insistence that the self can predicate its own self-subsistence and make itself the object of its own knowledge. See *Meditations on First Philosophy*, tr. Elizabeth S. Haldane and G. R. T. Ross, in *The Philosophical Works of Descartes*, 2 vols. (Cambridge: Cambridge University Press, 1931) I, pp. 149-50.

55. Hence Kant states in *CPR*, B 422, p. 377: "The subject of the categories cannot by thinking the categories acquire a concept of itself as an object of the categories. For in order to think them, its pure self-consciousness, which is what was to be explained, must itself be presupposed."

56. It warrants mentioning that the neo-Kantians at Marburg a century later found themselves dealing with similar problems regarding the identity of the self, and did not fare much better than Kant in seeking a theoretical resolution. See Fisher, *Revelatory Positivism?* chap. 1, "Marburg Neo-Kantianism." Both Kant and the neo-Kantians formulated many of the problems that Barth would deal with in his anthropology.

57. See *CPR*, B x, p. 18; B xxix, p. 28; B 432, p. 383; and esp. A 840-42, B 868-70, pp. 658-60.

boundary of speculative reason's limits in order to point us to a different form of reason that will illuminate that which remained darkly veiled to speculative reason:

> Rational psychology exists not as *doctrine,* furnishing an addition to our knowledge of the self, but only as *discipline.* It sets impassable limits to speculative reason in this field, and thus keeps us, on the one hand, from throwing ourselves into the arms of a soulless materialism, or, on the other hand, from losing ourselves in a spiritualism which must be quite unfounded so long as we remain in this present life. But though it furnishes no positive doctrine, it reminds us that we should regard this refusal of reason to give satisfying response to our inquisitive probings into what is beyond the limits of this present life as reason's hint to divert our self-knowledge from fruitless and extravagant speculation to fruitful practical employment.[58]

With the above statement in mind, we now turn to Kant's critique of morals, or pure practical reason, to trace further his concept of the self.[59]

Kant's Practical Critique and the "Self"

Like most philosophers, Kant was also concerned to discover the metaphysical foundations for ethical reasoning. Just as Hume had awakened him from his slumbers with regard to the problems posed by empiricism for philosophical speculation, Rousseau had awakened Kant to the necessity of human freedom.[60] With this in mind, Kant would attempt yet another synthesis. This time, it would not be a synthesis of two varying schools of philosophy, but an attempt to mediate the determinism of his own theoretical reason with the freedom demanded by morality. Rousseau propounded the necessity of political freedom, and Kant would seek to find its metaphysical foundation in much the same fashion as he had sought to explain the metaphysical justifica-

---

58. *CPR*, B 421, p. 377.

59. Kant's practical philosophy includes the *Foundations of the Metaphysics of Morals* (*Grundlegung zur Metaphysik der Sitten, GS,* IV), and also his *Critique of Practical Reason* (*Kritik der praktischen Vernunft, GS,* V).

60. See *GS,* XX, pp. 44, 58. Van De Pitte says: "What was for Rousseau a principle of the political order is thus developed by Kant into a moral and metaphysical doctrine which is essential to his Critical Philosophy. . . . Just as the natural freedom of man serves as the basis of Rousseau's political order, the object of that freedom, the moral law, forms the basis of Kant's practical philosophy" (*Kant as Philosophical Anthropologist,* pp. 54, 55).

tion of Newton's physics in his first Critique. It was impossible for Kant, therefore, to envisage his philosophy as a complete system of thought after writing his first Critique. Indeed, theoretical reason was able to say very little in a positive sense about the self, let alone God, freedom, and immortality. Given the Newtonian causality that Kant had assumed could provide a complete description of the physical world, the self of the phenomenal world was bound to be causally determined.[61] Yet given the influence of Rousseau and the political spirit of the Enlightenment with its emphasis on liberty, Kant sought to dig deep enough to uncover the roots of human freedom.[62]

Kant's Conception of the "Good Will"

Kant argued that just as there are a priori principles of our theoretical knowledge, which have their origin in the structure of understanding, so there are a priori principles of morality. Moral knowledge is reason in its practical application, that is, reason as applied to moral choices, not sensible intuition.[63] In the preface to his second Critique Kant reminds his readers that no form of anthropology is a sufficient source for moral knowledge in itself. Kant seeks a form of pure ethics, a metaphysics of morals. According to Kant, this metaphysics of morals, "applied to man, . . . borrows nothing from knowledge of him (anthropology) but gives him, as a rational being, *a priori* laws."[64]

In his oft-quoted opening words of *Foundations of the Metaphysics of Morals,* Kant says, "Nothing in the world — indeed nothing even beyond the world — can possibly be conceived which could be called good without qualification except a *good will.*"[65] The good will is the will that acts dutifully — in accordance with duty and "for the sake of" duty.[66] Kant thinks that all moral actions should be grounded in universal law. That is, all action should conform to a universally necessary imperative. "There is, therefore, only one cate-

---

61. *CPR,* A 546, B 574, p. 472.

62. See *CPR,* A 533-57, B 561-85, pp. 464-78.

63. See *CPR,* B x, p. 18.

64. *Foundations of the Metaphysics of Morals,* tr. L. B. Beck (Indianapolis: Bobbs-Merrill, 1969) p. 6. Kant thought the *Foundations* was a good framework, but an ultimately insufficient description of practical reason. See *Practical Reason and Other Writings,* pp. 122-23.

65. *Foundations,* p. 11.

66. Kant's extreme emphasis on duty has led him to be interpreted as founding a rather cheerless form of ethics; he nevertheless maintains that one should be cheerful about doing one's duty. Barth thinks this reveals a peculiar weakness in Kant's practical philosophy. See below, chapter four. Cf. Copleston, *History of Philosophy,* VI, p. 318.

gorical imperative. It is: Act only according to that maxim by which you can at the same time will that it should become a universal law."[67] Therefore, the true moral imperative is a *categorical* imperative.[68]

The Law and the Good Will

The finite will of the creature can only have respect *(Achtung)* for the moral law, in perceiving that it is both subject to natural conditions (usually described as feeling of pleasure, *Lust*), and yet commanded to conform to a moral law *(Sittengesetz)*. The feeling of respect does not necessarily engender morality, but makes the will aware of its own conditioned nature and of the absolute demand of the unconditional law. In the face of the law, the will is both humbled and ennobled.[69] Kant describes this respect for the law as a "moral feeling" *(Gefühl unter dem Namen des moralischen)*, but it is "produced solely by reason" (and therefore, in modern English, should probably not be labeled a "feeling"). Kant continues: "It does not serve for an estimation of actions or as a basis of the objective moral law itself but only as an incentive to make this law itself a maxim."[70]

Having followed Kant's argument thus far, we see that his anthropology rests on the limitations imposed by theoretical reason and the moral law imposed by practical reason. The real self, the noumenal self, is ultimately practical. For Kant, all respect for persons reduces to respect for the moral law.[71] The moral law is always over against the will as something holy (even though, strangely, the moral law is a product of human reason); therefore, in a very real sense, Kant cannot allow the law to be perfectly obeyed, for as soon as it would be perfectly fulfilled, it would no longer stand over against our natural (sensible) inclinations as a command. Hence the command of the law must always, to some degree at least, be against our natural inclinations:

> The command which makes this a rule cannot require that we have this disposition but only that we endeavor after it. To command that one do something gladly *(gerne)* is self-contradictory. For a law would not be

67. *Foundations*, p. 44.

68. One form of the categorical imperative is stated above. But other versions can be found; cf., e.g., *Foundations*, p. 63; and *Practical Reason and Other Writings*, p. 142.

69. *Practical Reason and Other Writings*, p. 185.

70. Ibid., p. 184. Cf. *GS*, V, pp. 76-77.

71. *Practical Reason and Other Writings*, p. 188n. For Barth, we shall see that all respect for law ultimately reduces to respect for persons.

needed if we already knew of ourselves what we ought to do and more-over were conscious of liking to do it . . . that law of all laws, like every moral prescription of the Gospel, thus presents the moral disposition in its complete perfection, and though as an ideal of holiness it is unattain-able by any creature, it is yet an archetype which we should strive to ap-proach and to imitate in an uninterrupted infinite progress.[72]

Kant makes several important points in this statement. First, he pro-poses that moral perfection is an impossibility. This follows from his empha-sis on law as a universal prescription that militates against our natural incli-nations as sensible creatures. Were creatures to attain holiness, the law would in some sense lose its "respectability," because it would no longer stand over and against our lower inclinations. Second, we see that Kant believes moral progress must be ongoing: not for this life only, but also into the next. The need for the infinite duration of moral progress is the premise for Kant's in-sistence on the immortality of the soul.[73] Finally, although obedience to the moral law can be accomplished spontaneously and freely, it cannot be done "cheerfully" *(gerne)!* This last point does not mean that Kant disallows for the possibility of happiness. Rather, it means that virtue is the supreme condition for all happiness. In the chapter entitled "Dialectic of Practical Reason," Kant agrees that happiness is part of the summum bonum, however: "the highest good means the whole, the perfect good, wherein virtue is always the supreme good *(oberste Gut),* being the condition having no condition superior to it, while happiness, though something always pleasant to him who possesses it, is not of itself absolutely good in every respect but always presupposes con-duct in accordance with the moral law as its condition."[74]

Kant concludes the second Critique by pointing out the advantages of the absence of an intellectual intuition that would lead to an understanding of God and immortality. He insists, instead, on his own demonstration of God and immortality through *practical* reason, arguing that if the theoretical knowledge of God could compel belief it would lead to a fearful form of moral conformity rather than a morality done from duty. The dignity of morals would thus vanish.[75]

In this brief synopsis of the first two Critiques we have come to see their logical continuity: the sense in which the first Critique is illumined by the

---

72. *Practical Reason and Other Writings,* p. 190. Barth will launch a pronounced rebuttal of Kant's cheerless ethic, as we shall see in chapter four below.

73. See *Practical Reason and Other Writings,* pp. 225ff.

74. Ibid., p. 215.

75. Ibid., p. 248.

second and the second rests upon the first. Given this survey of both theoretical and practical reason, we can more clearly understand the affirmation that Kant made in the beginning of his first Critique: "I have therefore found it necessary to deny *knowledge,* in order to make room for *faith.*"[76] If we studied Kant's writings on religion, we would see, however, that the faith Kant proposes is not a Christian faith. Rather, he proposes a faith based on reason and the sheer stoical necessity of obeying universal moral laws.

One cannot help but be more than a little amused at both the cheerlessness of Kant's sense of duty to obey the law, and (in spite of his concession that humans are normally inclined toward "radical evil") his naivete at supposing people would be universally willing to obey the categorical imperative.

Kant's A Priori Religion and Barth's Critique

In striking contrast to Kant, Barth views God and humanity in a realist and a posteriori way. Barth's theology and anthropology develop from the "given" of revelation;[77] his theology begins with the reality of God Incarnate. Barth's ethics develop from the reality of the humanity of God that is revealed in the historical person of Christ, and not Christ as an ideal to be emulated.

This indicates *in nuce* Barth's criticism of Kant's practical philosophy, and it is a difficult criticism to overlook. Here, at the practical level, is precisely where Kant's anthropology stands or falls. It begins to falter for two reasons. First, Kant has not shown the connection between the noumenal and the phenomenal self; nor is it apparent how they could be related. Second, his theory of human progress begs for some type of intervening grace in order to transform the corrupted will filled with radical evil into the good will; such a transformation is necessary for Kant's ethical philosophy to cohere.

Summary of Barth's Evaluation of Kant

In spite of Barth's objections to Kant's "negative ethic," Barth does not throw out Kant's Critiques altogether. From the first Critique Barth accepts the

---

76. *CPR,* B xxx, p. 29.

77. Barth's a posteriori method raises the question as to whether there are any "categories" of understanding that might be a priori with regard to human knowledge of God. This is one way to frame the famous debate with Brunner over nature and grace. I hope to clarify this issue and provide some insights on Barth's usage of the "point of contact" or a priori in chapter four, also in chapters five and six.

premise that unaided human speculation is in fact *in*capable of a right knowledge of God — thus throwing us into the position of needing revelation. From the second Critique, and the related writings on morals, Barth accepts the point that morality, including Christian ethics, does entail certain real obligations. And from Kant's writings in religion Barth adduces:

> It is only necessary to take quite seriously what Kant said half in mockery, in order to hear something very significant, even though we reserve in every respect our right to object to his formulations. Or is it not the case that the philosopher of pure reason has said something very significant to the theologian in telling him in all succinctness that *"The biblical theologian proves that God exists by means of the fact that he has spoken in the Bible?"*[78]

It is through the crack in the doorway of "revelation," one that Kant thought to have left open only narrowly, that Barth passes as he expands his own *Dogmatics* into one of the most wide-ranging theological statements in the history of the church.

Rejecting the Supremacy of Reason

One of Barth's chief complaints against the Enlightenment has been that it thrusts humanity too much upon the autonomous exercise of reason. Can this also be said of Kant's critical philosophy? As we have seen, Barth argues that Kant's "metaphysics" is ultimately a form of "anthropology and nothing but anthropology."[79] Barth is skeptical that we can deduce anything about God from mere anthropology, even practically considered.

It must be admitted, in Barth's favor, that Kant's "anthropological" emphasis provided a major impetus for the secularization of modern thought, even though this seems contrary to Kant's own intentions. Kant's distinction between appearance and reality has contributed to the modern split between fact and value, secular and sacred, science and religion.[80] This split between

---

78. *Protestant Theology,* pp. 311, 312.

79. See ibid., p. 303.

80. While Kant was himself a theist, or at least a deist, his challenge to classical metaphysics was later developed by Feuerbach, and ultimately passed on to Freud, where it was given a psychological interpretation that served to buttress one of the more aggressive atheistic positions in modern thought — ultimately pitting human reason in the form of science against religion. See the dialogue between Freud and the Lutheran minister, Oskar Pfister, who accused Freud, in *The Future of an Illusion,* of a naive optimism with regard to the future

fact[81] and value, science and religion, is evident from the very foundations of Kant's thought; for he was convinced that speculative reason could answer only the question originally posed in his *Lectures on Logic:* "What can I know?" while practical reason would have to be employed to answer the final three questions: "What ought I to do?" "What may I hope?" "What is man?"[82] It is not surprising then, in view of Kant's insistence that God exists as a necessary idea, about which very little can be known, or the moral legislator who serves to reinforce the categorical imperative, that he would conclude in the *Opus Postumum:* "God is not a being outside me, but merely a thought within me."[83]

Such a God, as the end product of human reason, is not acceptable for theology, Barth argues, for it reflects nothing more than an anthropological projection. Furthermore, Barth's allegiance to the Reformed tradition will not allow such a disparity between faith and knowledge as Kant thought to have demonstrated.[84]

---

of humankind in the hands of modern science: "Your substitute for religion is basically the idea of the eighteenth century Enlightenment in proud modern guise. I must confess that with all my pleasure in the advance of science and technique, I do not believe in the adequacy and sufficiency of that solution of the problem of life" (H. Meng and E. L. Freud, eds., *Psychoanalysis and Faith: The Letters of Sigmund Freud and Oskar Pfister* [New York: Basic, 1963] p. 115). Barth sees Kant as having begun a type of anthropological "reduction" (i.e., reducing metaphysics to a function of human reason) that led in succession through Schelling and Hegel to the anthropocentric reductionism of Feuerbach — from which, I must add, it is a very short step to the anthropology of Freud. See *CD*, I/1, pp. 193-94, 343. Ashley (*Theologies*, p. 635) also sees the humanism of Feuerbach "rooted in the critical philosophy of Immanuel Kant." On the connection between Feuerbach and Freud, see Meissner, *Psychoanalysis and Religious Experience*, p. 58.

81. A strange word to use, when Kant would have preferred to describe the same thing as "appearance."

82. *CPR* A 805-6, B 833-34, pp. 635ff.

83. *Kant's "Opus postumum,"* ed. A. Buchenau (Berlin: de Gruyter, 1938), I, p. 145.

84. See D. F. Ford, "Conclusion: Assessing Barth," in S. W. Sykes, ed., *Karl Barth: Studies in His Theological Method* (Oxford: Clarendon, 1979) p. 195: "Barth's theology is sometimes described as if it took the second of these ways [viz. privatized religion] and could not avoid being based on his personal decision of faith. This is to assume that he, with Kant and many others, thinks that no true knowledge of God is possible in faith and that therefore the individual's decision of faith goes beyond the facts. This is not Barth's position, for to him faith involves decision, but is primarily knowledge, a recognition of the facts, and is received because God is present and communicating." Cf. Calvin, *Institutes*, III, ii, 1-8. The knowledge that faith entails, for Barth, is plainly made possible by the incarnation. See *CD*, I/2, pp. 168, 877-78; II/1, pp. 12ff.

Reason and Individualism

Does Kant's critical philosophy also provide an example of the ways in which theoretical anthropologies strain toward individualism?[85] Apparently so. This is because the division of the human person into a sensible being on one side and an intelligible being on the other sets out the problem of human knowledge in a way that has not given any insight about how the theoretical and the practical can be joined together. The most that Kant can say is that they *must* be together somehow. This is problematic not only for our knowledge of God, immortality, freedom, and the self, but also for knowing other persons. As Macmurray has argued, the theoretical self, the self that has reason as its *differentia* from the lower animals, is bound to be egocentric.[86] If the ethical self is not conjoined with the theoretical self who exists in space and time, then what sense is there in acting ethically? For the only persons toward whom we could act ethically must dwell in our common world of space and time; yet Kant has distanced space and time from the arena of moral decisions.

Kant's concept of human autonomy was employed to preserve the practical reality of human freedom. In the end it seems that such an autonomous individual finds him- or herself *isolated*. For the moral law is not capable of providing a positive but only a negative ground for human relationships. Nothing prevents Kant's "kingdom of ends" from being a place where people politely avoid one another — or at best, tolerate one another on the basis of enlightened self-interest.[87] The kingdom of ends is the place where the categorical imperative is implemented, and Kant thought this would mean that all persons would be treated as ends in themselves: "Now, I say, man and, in general, every rational being exists as an end in himself and not merely as a means to be arbitrarily used by this or that will."[88] The world would certainly be a much better place if Kant's kingdom of ends were taken seriously, and

85. It must be admitted that Kant envisaged the destiny of the human race as an ethical commonwealth. However, such a social goal is based on "duty which is *sui generis,* not of men toward men, but of the human race toward itself" (*Religion Within the Limits of Reason Alone,* tr. T. M. Greene and J. R. Silber [New York: Harper & Row, 1960] p. 89). The motivation to attain such a unity is possible only with the employment of the concept of God. Hence, I would say, the criticism of individualism still holds.

86. See John Macmurray, *Persons in Relation* (London: Faber and Faber, 1961), esp. pp. 16ff. Macmurray builds, in my estimation, a very convincing case that the theoretical standpoint, adopted by both Descartes and Kant, is inherently egocentric. I mention more on this in chapters five and six.

87. *Foundations,* p. 52.

88. Ibid., p. 53.

even partially implemented. But is the prohibition not to treat others as mere means to my own selfish ends enough to encourage me to treat them lovingly? We have been warned what *not to do* toward others; have we been guided by Kant in knowing positively what it is we *need to do?* Modern and postmodern attitudes in the West that advocate for tolerance are remarkably Kantian and, I would argue, remarkably truncated versions of Christian charity. When Barth develops his anthropology he labors hard to explain not only how we ought *not* to treat other persons, but how we *should* treat them.

In summary, Kant's anthropology, for all its genius, reveals several shortcomings. First, it has failed to overcome the dualisms of classical anthropologies that divided soul and body into separate substances. Kant has mostly transferred such a dualism to the realm of the "noumenal" and "phenomenal." Second, some problems remain regarding how human destiny can appear so bright on the horizon of the future if, as Kant insists, every individual is filled with "radical evil." Barth is right to point out that Kant's corporate optimism and individual pessimism inevitably lead his philosophy to the need of some sort of intervening "grace." Finally, Kant's ethic is remarkably individualistic. It is always the solitary individual who stands alone at the bar of the almighty categorical imperative. One of the clearly stated points in Barth's anthropology, and a central point that I wish to highlight in this study, is that an exclusive emphasis on the rational faculty leads to an *individualist* anthropology. Barth is particularly critical of theoretical anthropologies that lead to individualism, and when he develops his own anthropology he is determined to cast out individualism. Unfortunately, Christian theology both before and after Kant has all too readily adopted the individualist model.[89] The myth of rugged individualism spawned and hatched in the United States bears a remarkably Kantian imprint.

Theological Options after Kant

Given the force of Kant's critical philosophy, Barth perceives three options for theology. First, to go along with Kant's Critiques just as they stand and view

89. E.g., W. T. Jones, *A History of Western Philosophy,* vol. I: *The Classical Mind,* 2d ed. (New York: Harcourt, Brace and World, 1969) p. 174, in a perfectly candid remark contrasting Plato to Christian anthropology, says: "Here again Plato is poles apart from the Christian tradition, which, in emphasizing the individual's effort to get into a right relationship with God, has tended to stress solitariness and to regard what sociologists call 'interpersonal relations' as a dangerous distraction."

Christianity in ethical categories, as did Albrecht Ritschl (1822-1889) and Barth's own teacher, Wilhelm Herrmann (1846-1922). Second, to accept the Kantian premise about the a priori condition of human reason but to seek yet another capacity, one found outside both the theoretical and the practical domains. Friedrich Schleiermacher attempted to circumvent Kant by emphasizing the a priori capacity of "feeling."[90] Following Schleiermacher, most of Protestant theology went down this path during the nineteenth century. Finally, Barth points out an option that questions not only the application of the Kantian conception of the problem, but the "conception itself, and therefore the autocracy and its competence to judge human reason in relation to the religious problem."[91] Barth proposes to take an option that he says was not considered during the nineteenth century:

> It might be possible to object that with the problem conceived as "religion within the limits of reason alone," only the one side of the problem, namely, religion as a human function, is seen, and not the other side, the significant point to which this function is related and whence it springs, the dealings, namely, for a God who is not identical with the quintessence of human reason, with the "God in ourselves." . . . This third possibility would, in a word, consist in theology resigning itself to stand on its own feet in relation to philosophy, in theology recognizing the point of departure for its method in revelation, just as decidedly as philosophy sees its point of departure in reason, and in theology conducting, therefore, a dialogue with philosophy, and not, wrapping itself up in the mantle of philosophy, a quasi-philosophical monologue.[92]

This third path that Barth proposes is the high road, and the one we will choose. But first we need to consider a couple of other Enlightenment thinkers.

---

90. Barth observes: "It is in pursuing these two lines of development that nineteenth-century theology is destined to be the direct continuation of the theology of the Enlightenment" (*Protestant Theology*, p. 306).

91. *Protestant Theology*, p. 307.

92. Ibid. The "dialogue" that Barth advocates between theology and philosophy confirms my sense that Barth would allow a "dialogue" to go on between his own theology and psychology, but would banish the idea that theology should take in psychological categories, or vice versa.

Barth's Trinitarian Theology
and Hegel's Dialectical Idealism

Hegel's influence on Barth was less significant than that of Kant. Neverthe-less, Hegel warrants our interest, for Barth insists that theology cannot afford to overlook either Kant or Hegel.[93] It was Hegel, along with the neo-Kantians, who influenced Barth to see the importance of history; and it was Hegel who would elevate the use of dialectic to its important status in modern thought.

The massive dialectical idealism of Hegel shaped Barth's theology in two specific ways. First, Hegel made an indelible impression on the logic of modern thought. According to Barth, Hegel's "boldest innovation" was that a concept does not simply exclude the concept that contradicts it, as most of Western logic previously held, but "includes it."[94] Hegel was influenced by Kant's critique of traditional metaphysics, but supplanted Kant's legal meta-phors with the metaphor of an organism. As an example of dialectic found in nature, Hegel writes:

> The bud disappears when the blossom breaks through, and we might say that the former is refuted by the latter; in the same way when the fruit comes, the blossom may be explained to be a false form of the plant's ex-istence, for the fruit appears as its true nature in place of the blossom. These stages are not merely differentiated; they supplant one another as being incompatible with one another. But the ceaseless activity of their own inherent nature makes them at the same time moments of an or-ganic unity, where they not merely do not contradict one another, but where one is as necessary as the other; and this equal necessity of all mo-ments constitutes alone and thereby the life of the whole.[95]

In exchanging the traditional logic of Western philosophy since Aris-totle for a dialectical form of logic, Hegel thought to break out of the tradi-tional limitations of reason and discuss God, truth, and history as real objects of human reason. Hegel was not, however, the innovator but the perfecter of the "dialectic." He advocated that thought proceeds by contradiction, and the

93. *Rousseau to Ritschl*, p. 280. Barth believes that Hegel's system of thought embodied the Enlightenment like no other, even though Hegel was not particularly well received in his own day. See *Protestant Theology*, pp. 386-87.

94. *Protestant Theology*, p. 401.

95. *The Phenomenology of Mind*, tr. J. B. Baillie (London: Allen and Unwin, 1949) p. 68. As another example of Hegel's affinity for organic metaphors see *Werke*, VI, p. 276, where he quotes Goethe's poem: "Natur hat weder Kern noch Schale, Alles ist sie mit einem Male."

reconciliation of contradiction: hence the method of thesis, antithesis, and synthesis. Hegel perfected the dialectic by expanding it into a system of universal truth, which contrary to Kant was unafraid to speak of God. Barth believes that the threefold rhythm of the dialectic was the "heart-beat of the Hegelian system."[96]

Barth's early theology has been characterized as "dialectical theology" and not unfairly so. In Barth's earlier theology the dialectic is evident in his emphasis on the "KRISIS" of faith caused by the *diastasis* between time and eternity, Christ and culture: the "No" and "Yes" of God that nevertheless find their synthesis in Jesus Christ.[97] Barth mostly abandoned the dialectical language by the time he began his *Dogmatics*. Nevertheless, some of his later thought still bears the imprint of the dialectic in the sense that Barth will at times take first one side of an argument, then another, and finally attempt to arrive at a conclusion, which could sometimes be called a "synthesis."[98] There is also an abundance of threefold movements within the *Dogmatics*.[99] The place where the residue of dialectical language is most detectable in the *Dogmatics* is in Barth's discussion of the nature of evil: he describes evil as the "antithesis"; but he balks when it comes to allowing a synthesis between evil and good.[100] Although Barth readily admits the importance of Hegel for modern theology, there is little evidence to compel the conclusion that Barth was overly influenced by Hegel. Nor do I accept that Barth's theology in toto can be summarized as "dialectical theology." (I will say more about this below when I discuss Kierkegaard's influence on Barth.) Barth's theological commitment to the Trinity is the more likely explanation for the triadic movements within the *Dogmatics* than either the conscious or unconscious influence of the Hegelian dialectic. Furthermore, Barth's careful reading of Søren Kierkegaard kept him from adopting Hegelian dialectic uncritically.

Timothy Bradshaw presents an interesting case: "Barth's doctrine of the

---

96. *Protestant Theology,* p. 401.

97. See Barth, *Epistle to the Romans,* pp. 10, 177-78, etc.; and below, chapter three.

98. See also *CD,* I/1, pp. 7-8, where Barth affirms the self-consistent path of theology, which nevertheless does not amount to an a priori acceptance of the law of noncontradiction (p. 9). None of this seems to compel the conclusion that Barth has not moved beyond dialectical theology, though he does utilize dialectic when he believes that it illumines the Trinity.

99. E.g., there is the threefold form of the Word: Revealed, Written, and Proclaimed, *CD,* I/1, p. 347, and God as Revealer, Revelation, and Revealedness, I/1, pp. 295ff. Not surprisingly, the doctrine of reconciliation takes three forms. See *CD,* IV/1, pp. 128-54. All of these are best explained by Barth's allegiance to God as Trinity. See, e.g., *CD,* I/1, §4, "The Word of God in Its Threefold Form." These and other threefold movements hint at a dialectic, although they do not, of course, imply a strict usage of dialectic.

100. See esp. Barth, *CD,* III/3, p. 302.

Trinity, the heart of his theology, is indebted to idealism specifically in that it reflects this seminal Hegelian principle, the logic of relation. This entails the free positing of the other, and the overcoming, without destroying, the distinction."[101] But Bradshaw admits that unlike Hegel, Barth never refers to God as "Mind." He also goes on to point out that any sense of idealism in Barth is clearly balanced by an existential actualism, which itself sometimes invokes the label "dialectical," but in a far different sense from Hegel's dialectic.

The end result of many discussions about Barth and Hegel indicates that the dialectical method is something that "later Barth"[102] used sparingly and consciously, and was always subject to the controlling idea of God in his revelation. The theology of the *Dogmatics* is not dialectical in a Hegelian sense; in fact, in the *Dogmatics* Barth's theology is not even dialectical in a Kierkegaardian sense. For even in Bradshaw's article showing that Barth wedded the Hegel-Marx-Bloch line with the Kierkegaard-Nietzsche-Heidegger line of thought, he mentions the Trinity as the means by which Barth achieved this "synthesis." Hence Barth's simple insistence that the Trinity shaped his later thought should be allowed to stand.

In the *Dogmatics* Barth is not attempting yet another synthesis of seemingly opposite philosophical systems (e.g., Kant's synthesis of rationalism and empiricism), but rather to be faithful to the true object of theology: God as triune and living Subject.[103] This is illustrated by an important statement:

> Here first and in final truth we have to do with a unity of identity and non-identity. Here God lives his divine life, which may be brought neither under the denominator of simplicity nor under that of multiplicity, but includes within itself both simplicity and multiplicity . . . here God Himself is really distinguished from Himself: God, and God again differently, and the same a third time. . . . Note that the divine being draws from this not only its inner perfection. But from it too draws the outer perfection

---

101. "Karl Barth on the Trinity: A Family Resemblance," *SJT* 39 (1986) 159.

102. When I refer to "later Barth," I mean Barth's theology after abandoning *Die christliche Dogmatik,* published in 1927, and beginning with *Die kirchliche Dogmatik* of 1932.

103. Barth's more conservative critics, such as Carl Henry, frequently accuse him of staying with dialectical theology, even in his later writings. See "Chaos in European Theology: The Deterioration of Barth's Defenses," *Christianity Today* 9 (1964) 15-19. But even those who think more highly of Barth sometimes cannot agree as to whether he has given up dialectical theology altogether. See McLean, *Humanity,* p. 13, who argues for the dialectical thought in the *Dogmatics,* with T. F. Torrance, *Karl Barth: An Introduction to His Early Theology* (London: SCM, 1962) pp. 106-7, 132, 141-42, 165, who argues that the dialectic had been left behind with the inception of the *Dogmatics.*

of its form, its thorough-going distinctiveness, as the unity of identity and non-identity. This is inevitable if God is triune.[104]

It is noteworthy that Barth ends the above statement with reference to the Trinity; he also follows up the above statement by emphasizing that we must not derive the *form* of God from a general necessity but from the necessity of its *content:* the triune being and life of God.[105]

Second, Barth thinks that Hegel is important for modern theology because of his emphasis on the historicity of the truth. Barth applauds Hegel's insight that truth might be history: an event. Barth proposes: "Of what use to theology was all knowledge of reported history, that of the Bible too, and of the Bible in particular, if at the same time it was incapable of recognizing real history, of recognizing the Living God?"[106] Partly due to Hegel's influence, Barth's understanding of both God and humanity is marked by careful attention to their "historicity."[107] In Barth's later thought, his understanding of history is not so much dialectical as dialogical and dogmatic — rooted in the eternal nature of God himself, and unfolded in the incarnation. Barth's dialectic is based not on the identity of human thought and divine reality, but on the distance that is overcome by God alone.

Hegel had alerted Barth to the importance of history as the stage upon which truth is played out as an active reality. But for Hegel history, and the dialectical movement that encompasses it, has a trinitarian foundation with a lower-case *t*. By contrast, Barth's trinitarian theology is undeniably particular, objective, rooted in the early church councils, and therefore refers to the triune God as personal: God is "Trinity" with a capital *T*.[108] While Barth applauds Hegel's inclusion of trinity in his system of thought, he nevertheless finds it "unsatisfactory . . . from the theological point of view."[109]

Barth concludes that Hegel, no less, and probably more, than any other Enlightenment philosopher, extols the virtue of human thought. Several

104. *CD,* II/1, p. 660.
105. *CD,* II/1, pp. 660-61.
106. *Protestant Theology,* p. 416.
107. Again, Bradshaw notes the marked difference between Barth and Hegel: "The 'historicity' or contingency in God is the ever new, dynamic *encounter* of freedom with form, and their *participation.* Barth's notion of 'historicity' has a definitely existentialist nuance" ("Karl Barth on the Trinity," p. 151).
108. See Hartwell, *Theology of Barth,* pp. 31-32, who points out that for Barth creation is history rooted in the eternal dynamics of the Trinity, thus history is *Heilsgeschichte;* see *CD,* III/1, pp. 65ff.
109. *Protestant Theology,* p. 414.

times Barth describes Hegel's system as the "apotheosis of thinking."[110] Barth goes on to reject Hegel's exclusive emphasis on truth as "the thinking which is conceived as the pinnacle and centre of humanity."[111] Barth does point out, however, that Christian theology can benefit from Hegel's dialectic because Christian doctrine itself contains apparent contradictions. This is an important insight with regard to Barth and his study of the person and work of Jesus. It illustrates that Barth was fully aware of higher-critical views of the Bible and Christ; rather than ignoring higher criticism, he sought ways to overcome its excesses.

When it comes to moral reasoning, there are certain limits to dialectical logic; Hegel's dialectic has its shortcomings with regard to the possibility of synthesizing such opposites as good and evil. Barth perceives this clearly: "Hegel in his paraphrase of the relation of man to God did not call a halt before the concept of sin. He included it in the unity and necessity of mind."[112] Whereas Kant stumbled on radical evil but honestly admitted it into his critical anthropology, Hegel saw no contradiction between good and evil that could not be dialectically synthesized. The dialectical synthesis of good and evil is a view that Barth rejects adamantly.

Barth begins his section on Hegel by saying that theology should give Hegel a "place of honor," and ends by saying that theology has "no occasion to throw stones at Hegel."[113] Overall Barth seems positive toward Hegel's dialectical idealism. Nevertheless, Barth rejects Hegel's notion of God. He takes issue with Hegel's idea of God as pure thought, and with it, rejects God as a dialectical method. This is because Hegel's dialectic limits God's sovereignty. For Barth, the final critique of Hegel is that his idea of God and humanity as objects of pure thought (and objects that can be somewhat confused at that) cannot encounter one another in a real relationship: "Hegel's living God — he saw God's aliveness well, and saw it better than many theologians — is actually the living man."[114] By identifying God with thought, Hegel ultimately limited divine freedom, and his God could not be the God of Christian theology. Once again, Barth rejects the theoretical conception of God and humanity because he believes that the idealist ontologies fail to do justice to the real distinction between God and human beings. The danger with such idealism is that the "God" whom it conceives is nothing more than a projection of human thought.

---

110. Ibid., pp. 398, 412.

111. Ibid., p. 417.

112. Ibid., p. 418. Barth cites Hegel, *Philosophy of Religion*, III, 110. "Hegel could even speak of the Devil in tones of unfeigned admiration" (p. 402).

113. *Protestant Theology*, p. 421.

114. Ibid., p. 419.

In sum, Barth follows not Hegel's idealist notion of history, but rather that of Kierkegaard and Martin Buber. Hegel argued for, and in some sense is the progenitor of, the organic arguments for God, humanity, and history. But most of all, Hegel represents the "absolute man" of the Enlightenment at his peak: Hegel places human thought at the summit, and therefore exalted the thinking faculty as did few others. Thus an all-important difference should be noted between Barth and Hegel in their respective concepts of history. For Hegel history is described primarily by categories that are organic: it is the self-movement of the mind unfolding from within itself like the petals of a flower. Barth, on the other hand, gives the concept of "history" an interpersonal interpretation based on the triune God.[115]

Summary of Barth and the Enlightenment

In Kant we studied a critical philosophy that rightly imposed limits on human reason, but nevertheless allowed reason to come in through the back door of practical thought. Kant's real "man" is circumscribed by moral considerations. He is defined by the will: the ultimate arbiter of practical reason. Hegel was on the other hand an uncritical rationalist. In Hegel's system, human thought is almost unlimited. Thus in these respective systems of thought, we see first a willing, then a thinking, human. In both cases we see the human being of the Enlightenment conceptualized as a rational being. Rationality thus becomes an end in itself. In light of Kant's influence on modern secularization, and Hegel's influence on Karl Marx, we do well to be wary of the exalted human intellect. Precisely here we see Barth's prophetic genius in rejecting such idealist anthropologies.

Barth voices two objections. First, idealism reduces any thought about God to humanity. If reason is the ultimate arbiter, then any thought about God that issues from such a system must be the product of human thought: nothing less, but nothing more. Second, the rationalist schema removes our humanity from the realm of space and time. The Enlightenment idealists espoused an "angelic" anthropology removed from the empirical world of human existence. Such anthropologies scarcely do justice to the earthy reality of human beings who exist as rational beings only because they are in relation to God and others.

---

115. Barth's concept of "history" will be spelled out in chapters four and six.

CHAPTER 3

Humankind at the Center
in Post-Enlightenment Theology

Barth's Critical Study of Schleiermacher's
Psychological Interpretation of the Christian Faith

In the theology of Schleiermacher we see the second major foil to Barth's own theology. Kant and the German idealists presented the first foil; Schleiermacher and the subsequent theologians of the nineteenth century represent the second. They are, of course, linked together, because Kant's critical philosophy shaped Schleiermacher's starting point decisively. Kant and Schleiermacher presented many of the problems that Barth would try to surmount in formulating his own theology and theological anthropology. A study of wider scope could, of course, mention Barth's rejection of some more contemporary Continental theologians such as Ritschl, Herrmann, and Harnack. But the theologies of the latter group mostly represent different variations on the theme begun by Schleiermacher.[1]

From the time of his writing the first edition of *The Epistle to the Romans,* until some of his very latest writings right before his death, Barth seldom failed to take issue with Schleiermacher.[2] In many respects Barth's theology represents a colossal effort to reverse the modern theological trend

1. See Dale N. Snyder, *Karl Barth's Struggle with Anthropocentric Theology* (The Hague: Wattez, 1966) p. 16: "Climbing this '*Gratweg,*' Barth had left Schleiermacher, Ritschl and Herrmann behind. While conscious of the difference in their respective theologies, he was even more conscious of the fact that they were all grounded in anthropology and not in the Word of God. They were anthropocentric."

2. See *Epistle to the Romans,* p. 202.

begun by Schleiermacher. Barth's theology is more than a reaction against Schleiermacher, of course; but one of Barth's major purposes in breaking with the Continental theology of the nineteenth century was to refute Schleiermacher's premise that the object of study for Christian theology is religious consciousness.[3]

In spite of Barth's differences with Schleiermacher, he frequently expressed admiration for Schleiermacher's willingness to take on the difficult intellectual problems of his day. Schleiermacher interpreted theology from the standpoint of human religious consciousness. In analyzing Barth's study of Schleiermacher, I advance an important point in terms of theological method: I side with Barth in his insistence that in the thought of Schleiermacher we see a confusion of the role of theology. It was Barth's contention that Schleiermacher reduced theology to a subset of the field of psychology.[4] This is important in itself for the purpose of gaining a historical perspective on Barth's theological development. And for purposes of this study, Barth's treatment of Schleiermacher is doubly important. If Schleiermacher had accurately described the limits of theological knowledge, then, I argue, theology would have lost its distinctive role as the science of the knowledge of God. If Schleiermacher's theology and so much of the subsequent theology of the nineteenth and twentieth centuries remain unchallenged, there can be nothing of an interdisciplinary dialogue between theology and the social sciences because a theology will have already become nothing more than a very specialized social science. Theology that derives from religious consciousness could be relegated to the branch of psychology known as psychology of religion.

A close look at the theologies of both Schleiermacher and Barth discloses that both sought to develop a theology of encounter. Both began with the broad-ranging premise that theology has at least something to do with the dialogue between God and humanity. The chief difference, however, is the extent to which Barth develops his theology of encounter upon a trinitarian premise. It remains in the chapters following to show why an anthropology that is trinitarian is better suited for a comparison with scientific psychology than Barth's critics claimed.

Barth acknowledges Schleiermacher as the church father of the nineteenth century,[5] and is not alone in ascribing to him a place of such impor-

---

3. Aside from Luther, Calvin, and Augustine, no other author is cited more often in the *Dogmatics* than Schleiermacher.

4. In this context, of course, the term "psychology" is meant in a general way, referring to philosophical psychology more than the modern discipline of scientific psychology.

5. *Protestant Theology*, pp. 425-26. Barth says C. Lülmann was "speaking the historical truth" when he coined the phrase in the essay "Schleiermacher, der Kirchenvater des 19. Jahr-

tance.[6] Nevertheless, Barth finds little that he agrees with in Schleiermacher's theology. In his lectures delivered in 1924 Barth said:

> I now know better than I did before that he was a great and gifted and pious man, that among all who came after him, whether they followed in his tracks or tried to kick against the pricks, there was and is none to hold a candle to him. Protestantism has not in fact had any greater theologian since the days of the reformers. But this theologian has led us all into this *dead end.*[7]

Barth follows with the assertion that if Schleiermacher represented the logical extension of the reformers' theology, "for me the right thing to do would be to become a Roman Catholic again."[8]

To some extent, Barth's criticisms of Schleiermacher followed on the heels of Brunner's scathing critique of Schleiermacher;[9] but, in deference to Schleiermacher, Barth thinks it important to remember the age in which the man lived. The problems that Schleiermacher inherited, wedged intellectually between the critical problems presented by Kant and Lessing, and the romanticism of Herder and Novalis, seemed almost insurmountable at the time.[10] Barth thinks that Schleiermacher did what he thought necessary to salvage Christian belief. However, the adequacy of Schleiermacher's mediation between Christian faith and culture is what Barth calls into question. At almost

---

hunderts" ("Schleiermacher, the Church Father of the 19th Century"). On the other hand, Barth thinks that Lülmann went a bit too far in proclaiming Schleiermacher "priest and prophet in one person and a king in the realm of the mind" (*Protestant Theology,* p. 426).

6. See, e.g., Otto Weber, *Foundations of Dogmatics,* vol. I, tr. D. Guder (Grand Rapids: Eerdmans, 1981) pp. 135-36: "Retrospectively, the dogmatics of the 19th century can be understood essentially as the direct, indirect, or negatively received influence of the theology of Friedrich Daniel Schleiermacher, one of the most powerful personalities in all of church history, in some ways comparable with Augustine." Even Emil Brunner, who was the first to break away from Schleiermacher, nevertheless concedes Schleiermacher's importance. See *Die Mystik und das Wort* (Tübingen: Mohr, 1924) p. 6. For a more recent work extolling Schleiermacher's importance, see B. A. Gerrish, *A Prince of the Church: Schleiermacher and the Beginnings of Modern Theology* (Philadelphia: Fortress, 1984) p. 20.

7. *The Theology of Schleiermacher: Lectures at Göttingen, Winter Semester of 1923-24,* ed. D. Ritschl, tr. G. W. Bromiley (Grand Rapids: Eerdmans, 1982) p. 259.

8. Ibid.

9. See Barth's review of Brunner's *Die Mystik und das Wort,* "Brunners Schleiermacherbuch," *Zwischen den Zeiten* 8 (1924) 49-64.

10. *Protestant Theology,* p. 427. Cf. Barth's respectful criticisms of Schleiermacher in one of his latest writings, "Concluding Unscientific Postscript on Schleiermacher," in *Schleiermacher,* pp. 266-67.

every turn Barth counters Schleiermacher's interpretation of the Christian faith, which, Barth argues, reduced the Christian faith to a culturally accommodating religion expressed in psychological categories.[11]

After the outbreak of World War I in 1914, and the manifesto of the ninety-three German intellectuals who identified themselves with the war policies of Kaiser Wilhelm II, Barth makes clear that he has rejected the culture-bound theology of Schleiermacher and begun a search for some other grounds for theology.[12] Barth sought to recover a theology that did not build on the psychology of religious experience,[13] but could be founded on a more objective foundation in God who self reveals through the Word. Barth concludes his 1924 lectures on Schleiermacher:

> If we reject the two suggestions above [that Schleiermacher has adequately encompassed the teaching of the reformers, and that his path had set Protestantism on a divinely ordained course], if we cannot find in Schleiermacher a legitimate heir or successor of the reformers, if we cannot see in the indubitable domination of his thinking the gracious guidance of God but the very opposite, a wrathful judgment on Protestantism which invites it to repentance and conversion instead of continuation, then the only possibility that remains — and I do not see how one can avoid this — is obviously that of a *theological revolution,* a basic No to the whole of Schleiermacher's doctrine of religion and Christianity, and an attempted reconstruction at the *very* point which we have constantly seen him hurry past with astonishing stubbornness, skill, and audacity. Schleiermacher undoubtedly did a good job. It is not enough to know that another job has to be done; what is needed is the ability to do it at least as well as he did his.[14]

Barth believes that Schleiermacher's thought develops along three important lines. First, Schleiermacher describes Christian faith as the root of the

---

11. See *Schleiermacher,* pp. 268ff. It was Franz Overbeck (1837-1905), the professor of church history at Basel during the 1880s, whose sarcastic comment that theology must be done "with audacity," provided the impetus for Barth to critically reexamine the culture-bound theology of neo-Protestantism after Schleiermacher. See "Unsettled Questions for Theology Today," in *Theology and Church,* tr. L. P. Smith (London and New York: Harper & Row, 1962) p. 72.

12. *Schleiermacher,* pp. ix and 263. See also Hartwell, *Theology of Karl Barth,* p. 8; Torrance, *Karl Barth,* pp. 6ff.; and Eberhard Jüngel, *Karl Barth: A Theological Legacy,* tr. Garrett E. Paul (Philadelphia: Westminster, 1986) pp. 59ff.

13. Once again, "psychology" in this section on Schleiermacher refers to the study of human consciousness, not modern scientific psychology.

14. *Schleiermacher,* pp. 259-60.

active life of the cultured Western European. Second, "feeling" provides the foundation for this active life. Third, Christian doctrine arises as the expression of feeling in specific instances of individuals within the history of the church.[15] In this section I will follow Barth's three-point outline of Schleiermacher (with some modifications), and trust that this will serve as a way to delineate Schleiermacher's thought, attempting to do justice both to Schleiermacher and to Barth's interpretation of him. Barth's critique of Schleicrmacher will itself be critically assessed at the end of this section. Because the second line of thought, the role of "feeling" in Schleiermacher's theology, holds most interest for this study, the largest proportion of attention will be given to understanding Schleiermacher's theological usage of "feeling."

Christian Faith and European Culture in Schleiermacher's Theology

Barth observes that Schleiermacher was a Christian and a thinking person, who "felt himself compelled to be a modern man with all his heart, with all his feelings and with all his strength."[16] By this Barth means that Schleiermacher's theology was cultural theology, a study of religion itself as the exaltation of nineteenth-century European life. Barth says of Schleiermacher:

> By birth and upbringing in its innermost sanctuary his theology is cultural theology: in religion itself which is the true object of his theology, it is the exaltation of life in the most comprehensive sense. . . . Civilization as the triumph of the spirit over nature is the most peculiar work of Christianity, just as the quality of being a Christian is for its own part the crown of a thoroughly civilized consciousness. The kingdom of God, according to Schleiermacher, is utterly and unequivocally identical with the advance of civilization.[17]

---

15. *Protestant Theology,* p. 448. This outline also approximates the manner in which Barth deals with Schleiermacher in his lectures and his more recently published book, *Theology of Schleiermacher.* See also *CD,* I/1, p. 37, where again Barth follows this basic outline in assessing the introduction to Schleiermacher's *Christian Faith:* "1. Anthropological possibility, 2. historico-psychological reality and 3. method do in fact constitute the schema which is actually followed in the introduction to Schleiermacher's *Der christlich Glaube* (§ 3-10, § 20-31)."

16. *Protestant Theology,* p. 434.

17. Ibid., pp. 434-35.

Schleiermacher's Christian life is the ethical life lived out in European culture *(Bildung)*. Although Schleiermacher ultimately describes the Christian faith as "the consciousness of being absolutely dependent,"[18] Barth points out that Schleiermacher did not merely seek to identify Christianity with the inner life of mysticism, but also attempted to show that religious consciousness provides the major impetus to "the movement of civilization." While Schleiermacher based his theology on the interior life of the religious individual, Barth emphasizes that Schleiermacher "prays because he wants to work; he is a mystic because without mysticism there could not be any civilization."[19] Schleiermacher felt obligated to work within the confines of Kant's critique of metaphysical speculation, and like Kant, saw the primary role of religion as the ethical improvement of the human race. But unlike Kant, Schleiermacher saw the philosophical function as one of persuading educated people that Christian religion was necessary and expressed the highest values of Western civilization.[20]

Barth delves into the form and content of Schleiermacher's writings, including his letters and sermons, leaving no stone unturned. Through it all, Barth is convinced that Schleiermacher's chief motivation was to be a defender of modern Western European civilization. It is only secondarily, Barth argues, that Schleiermacher is concerned with the inner psychology of religion, and tertiarily that Schleiermacher is concerned with Christian doctrine.[21] Barth proposes that Schleiermacher's theology was apologetic in both form and content, from his first writings until his last. His *Addresses on Religion*[22] were writ-

---

18. *The Christian Faith*, ed. H. R. Mackintosh and J. S. Stewart (Edinburgh: T & T Clark, 1928) §4, pp. 12ff.

19. *Protestant Theology*, p. 437. Barth equates mysticism with piety, but not with true spirituality, because mysticism lacks a real object while spirituality entails relation to God as its object. Cf. *Schleiermacher*, p. 224; and Barth, *The Humanity of God*, tr. J. N. Thomas and T. Weiser (repr. Atlanta: John Knox, 1978) p. 40. In *Die Mystik und das Wort*, Brunner argued that one must choose either between the Word of the reformers or the mysticism of Schleiermacher. Barth on the other hand does not think that Schleiermacher sought to identify Christianity with mysticism (although he lapsed into mysticism as an apologist) but rather with the "movement of civilization."

20. *Protestant Theology*, pp. 437-45. Cf. *CD*, I/1, pp. 192ff., where he describes Schleiermacher's attempt to define Christianity as "a human religious experience that can be established historically and psychologically." For differences between Barth and Schleiermacher on theological method, see also I/1, pp. 36-38.

21. *Protestant Theology*, p. 448. Barth frequently cites Schleiermacher's sermons and letters, e.g., to Friedrich Lücke, *On the Glaubenslehre: Two Letters to Dr. Lücke* (Chico, Calif.: Scholars Press, 1981). On whether Barth is correct in assigning this value to these sources, see below.

22. *Addresses on Religion* is the ET used in *Protestant Theology*, usually shortened to *Addresses*, translated from the German, *Über die Religion, Reden an die Gebildeten unter ihren*

ten to appeal to those who were especially influenced by the romantic movement. In summarizing Schleiermacher's argument in the *Addresses*, Barth proposes that the "unity of intuition" (which is later supplanted by the feeling of absolute dependence in *Christian Faith*) provides what is needed to complete one's cultural awareness.[23]

Statements like the following are interspersed throughout the *Addresses*, showing the extent to which Schleiermacher linked religious feelings with the advance of European culture:

> I have tried as best I could therefore, to show you what religion really is. Have you found anything in this description unworthy of our culture, indeed of the very highest culture of man? The more you are split apart and isolated within the world because of highly specialized culture or individuality, doesn't this make you long all the more for that sense of true relationship with the whole world which is possible only through your feeling? . . . Actually, I am only asking you to take seriously what is already of profoundest importance to you. Unfailingly, to be forced away from it will cause the finest aspects of your own cultured existence to be destroyed.[24]

An abundance of statements such as the above support Barth's insistence that Schleiermacher's theology is a theology of cultural affinity.

Even in his later work, *Christian Faith*, Schleiermacher makes his case for Christianity as a religion that necessarily encompasses both the aesthetic (primarily passive) and the teleological (necessarily active). Barth thinks it curious, if not contradictory, that Schleiermacher would advocate the active nature of the kingdom of God on earth, in spite of everything that points to the passive nature of Christian piety.[25] This serves as an indication to Barth

---

Verächtern, of which Schleiermacher prepared four editions (1799, 1806, 1821, and 1831). Barth follows the 1st edition in his lectures (see *Schleiermacher,* p. 244), hereafter referred to as *Reden.* Several English translations are available, including J. Oman, *Schleiermacher on Religion* (London: Kegan Paul, Trench, Trübner, 1893), using the 1st edition, hereafter referred to as Oman; and T. N. Tice, *On Religion* (Richmond, Va.: John Knox, 1969), using the 3d edition, hereafter referred to as *On Religion.*

23. *Protestant Theology,* p. 449. Concerning Schleiermacher's deference to culture, see *Reden,* pp. 33-34, 91, 158, 205, 220, 223.

24. *On Religion,* p. 145. See also pp. 27, 51, 54-55, 82-83, 143, 195, 272-73, 299-300 of *On Religion;* see also the author's note on the meaning of *Die Bildung zur Religion,* pp. 361-62 of *On Religion.* It is interesting and ironic to note how much Schleiermacher, the father of modern liberal theology, sounds remarkably like a contemporary Christian conservative.

25. *Protestant Theology,* p. 439; cf. Schleiermacher, *Christian Faith,* §9, pp. 39-44.

that Schleiermacher never veered from being an advocate of European culture, not even in *Christian Faith,* his *opus ingens.*

What caused Barth to resist so stubbornly the theology of Schleiermacher? After the signatures of 93 German intellectuals supported the war efforts of Kaiser Wilhelm II and Bethmann-Hollweg in 1914, Barth could no longer call Schleiermacher his theological father. This was not because Barth thought Schleiermacher himself would have supported the German war effort, but because Schleiermacher's culturally accommodating theology had so vastly influenced those who did sign the war declaration and later failed to resist.[26] The same issue surfaced again with the rise of German fascism before and during World War II. At the time of the Barmen Declaration Barth found himself asking to what degree theology should accommodate the surrounding culture. Writing during the time when he made a pronounced departure from the German Christians who supported Hitler, Barth once again perceived the pernicious effects of Schleiermacher:

> The period of the 16th-18th centuries was in its own way a great period, when European man resumed the powerful offensive which had been made by Graeco-Roman antiquity, beginning to discover himself as a man, his nature, his possibilities and capacities, humanity. The discovery of *"religion"* belonged, of course, to the same movement. It was in the very nature of things that theology should have its part in that discovery. . . . Ignorantly or stubbornly to ignore the anxieties and hopes of the immediate present is something which we do not expect or demand of theology for the sake of the Church. But it is quite a different thing openly to champion the predominant interest or even the demonism of an age, openly to identify oneself with that interest and to become the prisoner of that demonism. This is the very thing which theology must not do.[27]

It is clear that when Barth uses the term "religion," he is referring to the theology primarily of Schleiermacher and those under his influence.[28] Barth sees Schleiermacher's advocacy of culture as a damaging influence in regard to theology's inability to resist the trend toward both German nationalism and Hitler's fascism.

---

26. See *Schleiermacher,* pp. ix, 263-64.

27. *CD,* I/2, p. 293.

28. In Barth's well-known §17 of the *Dogmatics,* "The Revelation of God as the Abolition of Religion," he refers to Schleiermacher three times; see *CD,* II/1, pp. 290, 324, 350. See also *CD,* I/2, p. 290, where Barth asserts: "Neo-Protestantism means 'religionism.'" Cf. pp. 610-11, 692.

Barth interprets the theological Declaration of Barmen (1934) as a protest against natural theology and the political subversion of the church. Once again, the influence of Schleiermacher is perceptible in the inability of German theology to separate from its cultural surroundings: "What the 'German Christians' wanted and did was obviously along a line which had for long enough been acknowledged and trodden by the Church of the whole world: the line of the Enlightenment and Pietism, of Schleiermacher, Richard Rothe and Ritschl."[29] Barth believes the Barmen Declaration (which was largely written by him) is a protest, "without doubt directed against Schleiermacher and Ritschl. The protest was directed against the basic tendencies of the whole 18th and 19th centuries and therefore against the hallowed traditions of all other Churches as well."[30] In contrast to the nationalist and racist strains contained in the ideology of the "German Christians," the Confessing Church at Barmen declared "Jesus Christ is the one Word of God whom we have to trust and to obey."[31] Because of this, Barth believes that Barmen is already "one of the most notable events in modern Church history."[32]

Barth's protest against Schleiermacher's anthropological starting point for theology has some important ethical ramifications. Barth believed that any capitulation to a theology based on religious consciousness would strip theology of its capacity to give the church an objective basis on which to judge the surrounding culture. Conceding the humanistic interest that surfaced in Luther, Barth nevertheless observes:

> Even if we assume all this, however, the question always remains whether in face of the alleged anthropologising of the modern (or once modern) life-consciousness it is wise to follow in the steps of Schleiermacher and to orientate oneself to his life-consciousness even though under another sign. Theology has all too often tried to seek out and conquer the consciousness of an age on its own ground. We have protested already against theology allowing adversaries to dictate its action, since this can only mean conceding to them half or more than half of what should not be conceded, namely, the Church's lack of independence of life and thought over against the world and the primacy of the questions the world has to put to the Church over the questions the Church has to put to itself. Might it not be to-day that a theology which refuses even in method to make common cause with the aforesaid "humanising of life" will be more

29. *CD*, II/1, p. 174.
30. *CD*, II/1, p. 175.
31. Ibid.
32. *CD*, II/1, p. 176.

relevant — if this is the point — than one which admits at the very outset that it can speak only a second word, a word on the situation (the situation outside the Church).[33]

This quotation shows the extent to which Barth desires to keep theology from being overwhelmed by its surrounding culture. Theology must restrain itself to its primary concern, which is the God who reveals himself. This is the only means by which theology may stand its own ground, and perhaps speak a prophetic word to the world that has rebelled against its creator. We shall see that this will have many ramifications, not only for the relation between faith and culture, but also for the dialogue between theology and science.

In addition to the objection that Schleiermacher's anthropocentric theology fails to provide an objective ground for theology to transcend its cultural surroundings, Barth thinks that Schleiermacher's optimism regarding the evolution of science and human culture was simply naive. Schleiermacher, as a moralist much like Kant and an idealist like Hegel, "visualised the powerful onslaught and victory of spirit over nature and matter. . . . But the real picture which soon presented itself to all strata of the civilised nations except the dreaming philosophers, poets and unfortunately theologians, was very different."[34] Barth lists the "different" results, the sins and depersonalizing effects of Western industrialization that resulted in mass movements of humanity toward the cities, into the factories, forges, and mines. The end result of nineteenth-century industrialization Barth describes as "the figure of the human robot, who neither asks nor is asked about his soul and therefore cannot ask about that of others, who by an anonymous centre of power is made, moved, regulated, used and then discarded and replaced from an anonymous centre."[35]In view of the calloused treatment that many received at the hands of the industrial revolution, Barth asks whether the theoretical reduction of humanity to materialism matters near as much as the practical reduction, or even if it should be as great a concern.

Has Barth perhaps overemphasized the degree to which Schleiermacher wished to make Christian faith agreeable to modern European culture? We could object that although Schleiermacher was the sometimes champion of the Prussian state,[36] he deeply resented the intrusion of the state into the in-

33. *CD*, I/1, pp. 127-28.
34. *CD*, III/2, pp. 386-87.
35. *CD*, III/2, p. 387.
36. *Protestant Theology*, pp. 319f. See also Schleiermacher's nationalistic slurs against England and France: *On Religion*, pp. 48-49 and 63-64.

ternal affairs of the church.[37] Also, Schleiermacher's sermons contained a good deal of courageous preaching on social and political issues that did not necessarily flow with the trends of the time, for example, against social inequality.[38] The debate as to whether Schleiermacher saw the Christian faith evolving alongside Western European culture as if it were a natural effect (or at least the fullest expression) of culture, or whether he saw the need for Christian faith to shape the culture, could be carried on at length. Nevertheless, it would not be honest to accuse Barth of being either ignorant or unappreciative of Schleiermacher's homiletical courage, especially when it came to socially sensitive issues such as the redistribution of wealth.[39] Had Barth accused Schleiermacher of paving the way for a theology that would be a *positive* catalyst for the atrocities committed in Germany during the two world wars, this would be more than a little slanderous. In Barth's arguments against the culturally accommodating theology of Schleiermacher, however, he is careful to say that Schleiermacher's theology was not a positive preparation for German nationalism, but only a "negative preparation for this phenomenon."[40] That Barth was supported in his stand against Hitler by only a handful of pastors and theologians in 1934 and thereafter would seem to be ample witness to this "negative preparation."

Barth is right to point out that Schleiermacher's primary purpose in his theological writings was apologetic in the sense that Schleiermacher undeniably aimed his speeches on the Christian religion at the cultured people of his day.[41] The point does not warrant lengthy discussion within this study, since it does not refer directly to Schleiermacher's view of humanity. It does, however, indicate the direction in which Schleiermacher's doctrine of humanity is headed. For Schleiermacher theology begins with a discussion of the inward human capacity to engender religion to the benefit of the culture. For Barth, theology begins with a form of address, from God to humanity, which therefore challenges the foundations for any understanding of God other than the revelation of God himself, and ultimately challenges the culture to which the Word of God is addressed. The distance between "religion" as a cultural phenomenon and "revelation" as the foundation for Christian dogmatics defines one of the major differences between Schleiermacher and Barth. Barth concludes that the real tragedy of modern Protestant theology "was that theology lost its object, revelation in all its uniqueness. And losing that, it lost the seed

37. See *On Religion,* pp. 262ff., 265.
38. Cited in Barth, *Schleiermacher,* p. 38.
39. See *Protestant Theology,* pp. 438-39.
40. *CD,* III/4, p. 307.
41. E.g., *On Religion,* pp. 51, 54, 68-69, 82-83, 110.

of faith with which it could remove mountains, even the mountain of modern humanistic culture. That it really lost revelation is shown by the very fact that it could exchange it, and with it its own birthright, for the concept 'religion.'"[42]

Standing on the cusp of a new millennium, we may find it difficult to measure the exact amount of progress the human race has made. Any ten persons asked about the subject are likely to render ten very divergent opinions. Regardless, it is my position that the utopian predictions of the romantic era, including those of Schleiermacher, did not come to pass and still can be viewed as mostly a dim wish.

The Role of "Feeling" in Schleiermacher's Theology

Here again Barth has left no stone of Schleiermacher's writings unturned. Barth engages in a detailed study of Schleiermacher's letters and sermons in addition to his major works.[43] Yet, for all the emphasis he places on the importance of Schleiermacher's sermons and letters,[44] Barth admits that in the introduction to *Christian Faith*[45] (§§1-31), we have the essence of Schleiermacher's theology,[46] and in §§3-6 we enter the "holy of holies of Schleiermacher's theology."[47] We thus turn to this major work of Schleiermacher with a view to understanding the role of feelings.

Schleiermacher's *opus ingens* begins with a discussion of piety. Barth points out that this is not a fundamental change from any of Schleiermacher's

---

42. *CD*, I/2, p. 294.

43. Robert R. Williams, *Schleiermacher the Theologian* (Philadelphia: Fortress, 1978) p. xi, accuses Barth of "sloppy, fragmentary, and piecemeal" treatment of Schleiermacher. He even accuses Barth of creating a caricature of Schleiermacher's theology, although he later concedes that Barth is "one of the few theologians who actually read Schleiermacher" (p. 17, n. 12) He would perhaps have been more honest to admit that Barth's treatment of Schleiermacher is thorough but happens to disagree with his own interpretation.

44. See *Schleiermacher*, pp. 47 (on the importance of sermons) and 185 (on the importance of the *Sendschreiben*).

45. *Der Christlich Glaube, nach den Grundsätzen der evangelischen Kirche im Zusammenhang dargestellt*, originally published in 1821, 2d ed. 1830. ET, *The Christian Faith according to the principles of the Evangelical Church systematically set forth*, usually shortened to *The Christian Faith*, sometimes translated and shortened to *The Doctrine of Faith*, e.g., as in *Protestant Theology*. The volume used in this study (unless otherwise specified) is *The Christian Faith*, ed. and tr. H. R. Mackintosh and J. S. Stewart, from 2d German ed. (Edinburgh: T & T Clark, 1928).

46. *Schleiermacher*, p. 193.

47. Ibid., p. 212.

previous works, but rather represents a continuity.[48] Piety is therefore the beginning, end, and center of all Schleiermacher's works; it is in human piety, says Barth, that Schleiermacher finds the "peace which passeth all understanding."[49] Like Barth, Schleiermacher begins his most important work with the attempt to describe the theology of the church.[50] But unlike Barth, who describes the theology of the church from the reality of the Word of God,[51] Schleiermacher points from the church to the piety of the believer. For Schleiermacher, "The piety which forms the basis of all ecclesiastical communions is, considered purely in itself, neither a Knowing nor a Doing, but a modification of Feeling, or of immediate self-consciousness."[52] By "feeling" Schleiermacher refers to something like a spontaneous emotion, and by "self-consciousness" he means a self-awareness of a particular inner state, such as "self-approval and self-reproach."[53] Schleiermacher derives his dogmatic starting point from human psychology, particularly religious self-consciousness. This is evident when he discusses the relation between knowing, doing, and feeling:

> Now, if the relation of the three elements above-mentioned were anywhere set forth in a universally recognized way, we could simply appeal to that. But, as things are, we must in this place say what is necessary on the subject; though this is to be regarded as simply borrowed from Psychology, and it should be well noted that the truth of the matter (namely, that piety is feeling) remains entirely independent of the correctness of the following discussion. Life, then, is to be conceived as an alternation between an abiding-in-self *(Insichbleiben)* and a passing-beyond-self *(Aussichheraustreten)* on the part of the subject.[54]

Schleiermacher draws a clear distinction between knowing, feeling, and doing. Knowing and feeling constitute abiding-in-self, while doing proper is the passing-beyond-self. Feeling stands in antithesis to knowing and doing.[55]

---

48. Cf. J. Arundel Chapman, *An Introduction to Schleiermacher* (London: Epworth, 1932) p. 17: "*The Christian Faith* is to a large extent an elaboration — a very massive elaboration — and a more balanced statement of the chief ideas which are unfolded in the earlier work [*Addresses*]."

49. *Protestant Theology*, p. 454. Barth cites Schleiermacher's *Sermons*, III, p. 167. Cf. *Schleiermacher*, pp. 10ff. Barth's description is taken from Phil. 4:7.

50. Cf. *CD*, I/1, pp. 3-11, 80.

51. See *CD*, I/1, pp. 126-27.

52. *Christian Faith*, §3, p. 5. Cf. Barth, *Schleiermacher*, pp. 212-14.

53. *Christian Faith*, §3.2, p. 7.

54. *Christian Faith*, §3.3, pp. 7-8. Cf. Barth, *Schleiermacher*, p. 214.

55. *Christian Faith*, §3.3, p. 8.

This does not mean that piety is excluded from knowing and doing; rather, "feeling" is polemically separated because it constitutes the seat of both knowing and doing. Since piety and knowledge cannot be equated, Schleiermacher argues that piety is prior. *Piety* is thus the object of knowledge in dogmatics.[56] Neither knowing nor doing constitutes the essence of piety, but both are constituted by it. This leads Schleiermacher to conclude that "Christian doctrines are accounts of the Christian religious affections set forth in speech."[57] Having found what he believes to be the proper foundation for dogmatics, Schleiermacher sets out to describe the common element of religious self-consciousness. This he finds in the "feeling of absolute dependence" *(das Gefühl schlechthiniger Abhängigkeit).*[58] Absolute dependence can be qualitatively distinguished from all other feelings of dependence, which are relative. Both animals and infants can sense dependence in a relative sense, but the religious consciousness can be explained only as the feeling of absolute dependence, which Schleiermacher describes as mutually exclusive of the lower animal level of self-consciousness.[59]

In order to evaluate Schleiermacher's feeling of absolute dependence, we must take a careful look at Barth's analysis of §§3-5 of *Christian Faith*. A prima facie reading of passages such as found in §4 suggests that Schleiermacher does *not* wish the feeling of absolute dependence to become an end in itself, apart from God. Indeed, he says, the feeling of being absolutely dependent is the same thing as "being in relation with God."[60] The feeling of absolute dependence is supposed to lead to a real sense of dependence on God himself; any lesser form of dependence is not the feeling of *absolute* dependence.[61] Again, Schleiermacher appears to point theology beyond mere human states of consciousness when he says: "All propositions which the system of Christian doctrine has to establish can be regarded either as descriptions of human states, *or as conceptions of divine attributes* and modes of action, or as utterances regarding the constitution of the world; and all three forms have always subsisted alongside of each other."[62] Schleiermacher intends to bridge the gap between God and the human being, between object and subject, with the feeling of absolute dependence. Schleiermacher is

---

56. Ibid., §3.4, p. 10. Cf. Barth, *Schleiermacher*, pp. 213-14.

57. *Christian Faith*, §15, p. 76. Schleiermacher's doctrine of God is of course tied directly to the feeling of absolute dependence. See *Christian Faith*, §50, p. 194.

58. See §4, p. 12n.

59. *Christian Faith*, §5.2, pp. 20ff.

60. Ibid., §4, p. 12.

61. Ibid., §8.2, pp. 118, 132.

62. Ibid., §30, p. 125. Italics mine.

attempting a theology of encounter. But has the feeling of absolute dependence succeeded in bridging this gap between God and humankind? Is there a real encounter? Or has Schleiermacher, as Oman says in the introduction of his translation of the *Addresses*, "solved the difficulty by saying that one part of the mind can take the other for the object"?[63] We shall see below that Barth is especially concerned to find out if Schleiermacher's conception of piety can really reach out to God himself and provide an adequate description of the divine attributes.

Taking up the thread of his thought, in §4 Schleiermacher says that all true feeling is a determined self-consciousness, determined by *"something other."* In Schleiermacher's own words: "in every self-consciousness there are two elements, . . . a self-caused element *(ein Sichselbstsetzen)* and a non-self-caused element *(selbstnichtsogesetzthaben)*; . . . a Being and a having-by-some-means-come-to-be *(ein Sein und ein Irgendwiegewordensein)*."[64] No one can deny this, said Schleiermacher: no one who unconditionally accepts the ability to "answer this question of the priority of receptivity or activity by means of self-observation."[65] Schleiermacher argues that absolute freedom and absolute dependence do not arise in response to anything of the world. Schleiermacher thinks it self-evident that the feeling of absolute dependence does not derive from anything earthly, because things of worldly origin usually create a sense of *relative* freedom and *relative* dependence. Hence, in positing a feeling of *absolute* dependence, Schleiermacher thinks to have found the ground of all religious consciousness.

Barth poses two important questions regarding the feeling of absolute dependence. First, does it necessarily follow from the *relative* nature of freedom, from the perception that freedom has its limits, that dependence is therefore *absolute?* Schleiermacher's absolute dependence constitutes the boundary of the continuum of freedom and dependence as its *prius* because it transcends both. Barth concludes that Schleiermacher naively "equates what is psychologically first with the absolute. He introduces the absolute here, and in so doing he can posit the feeling of absolute dependence where he ought only to have put a question mark."[66] Second, given the purely passive, receptive nature of feeling stated in §3.3, and its lack of object in §3.2,

---

63. Oman, p. xliii.

64. *Christian Faith*, §4.1, p. 13. Barth summarizes this important section in Schleiermacher: "Determined by something other we feel dependent. Determined by ourselves, which also occurs, we feel *free*, and we ourselves are then active in relation to the other" *(Schleiermacher*, p. 214).

65. *Christian Faith*, §4.2, translation Barth's, *Schleiermacher*, p. 214.

how does feeling assert itself as something absolute? How can this absolute dependence, grounded in pure receptivity, spring into action, as Schleiermacher claims it is vital for religion to do? How absolute dependence and relative dependence square with one another is not fully understandable, says Barth. Barth concludes, regarding the contradictory nature of the feeling of absolute dependence, "at the climax of this train of thought, logically considered, an impasse is reached from which there is no exit."[67] In chapter six, after I have surveyed certain aspects of Freudian and post-Freudian psychoanalytic theory, I will take a closer look at Barth's criticism that Schleiermacher has substituted psychology for the "absolute." In other words, Schleiermacher has blurred the real distinction between human psychology and the groundwork for Christian theology, which, according to Barth, should be revelation.

One must admit that Schleiermacher's feeling of absolute dependence is not a static thing. An analysis of §5.3 reveals the way the feeling of absolute dependence develops. It grows as the lowest or animal grade of consciousness gradually disappears, and it forms a kind of "symbiosis" with the middle, sensory grade of self-consciousness. Barth describes this growth of piety as comparable to a plant growing: "I intentionally say the plant rather than the child, for if we did not already know, would we really think that the process described in §5,3 concerns living people in their relation to the living God?"[68] For a further analysis of the way the feeling of absolute dependence develops, or fails to develop, we shall have to discuss Schleiermacher's view of sin and redemption.

Thus far, through an analysis of Barth's critiques we have seen that the feeling of absolute dependence has not really bridged the gap between subject and object, the human being and God. It has only described the human being as a creature with a natural capacity to develop God-consciousness, which evolves gradually, while God himself is so far removed as to be insusceptible to our counterinfluence.[69] It might provide an acceptable account of the psychology of religious experience, but falls short of describing the object of theology — who is God. In agreement with Barth, I find the feeling of absolute dependence contradictory and unacceptable as the starting point for Christian theology.

66. *Schleiermacher,* p. 216.
67. Ibid.
68. Ibid., p. 219.
69. Cf. *On Religion,* p. 293, for the organic evolutionary character of human religion.

Schleiermacher's Doctrine of Sin and Redemption

For Schleiermacher the connection between feeling *(Gefühl)* and redemption *(Erlösung)* is so integral that redemption nearly represents an unfolding of feeling. While redemption is explained by the quantitative growth of the feeling of absolute dependence, the negation of the growth explains human sin; with this understooding, Schleiermacher claims that sin and grace are antithetical to one another.[70] Schleiermacher explains that redemption "denotes what is common to all Christians even in different ways, representing a transition from a bad state, presented as bondage, to a better one."[71] Redemption is an evolution of God-consciousness, from the depths of the human soul in which God has been only partially forgotten,[72] but of which people can be reminded.

Here the parallels between Schleiermacher and Plato are difficult to overlook — especially Schleiermacher's view that the sensory self-consciousness hampers God-consciousness and creates a forgetfulness toward God.[73] Sin is therefore a dormant God-consciousness, depicted by the quantitative absence of the feeling of absolute dependence. Redemption is a process in which God-consciousness progresses from a worse state to a better one. This leads to the inevitable conclusion that Schleiermacher's doctrine of redemption is essentially commensurate with his anthropology because redemption does not represent anything coming *to* humanity from a transcendent source; rather, it is represented by the reversal of human "God-forgetfulness." Schleiermacher asserts:

> Then the evil condition can only consist in an obstruction or arrest of the vitality of the higher self-consciousness, so that there comes to be little or no union of it with the various determinations of the sensible self-

70. See esp. *Christian Faith*, §62.1, p. 250.

71. Ibid., §11.2, p. 54. Barth also cites §§62.1; 62.2-3; 64.2.

72. *Christian Faith*, §11.2, p. 54. Cf. Barth, *Schleiermacher*, pp. 195-96.

73. See Richard B. Brandt, *The Philosophy of Schleiermacher* (New York: Harper and Bros., 1941) p. 146. See Plato's idea of "recollection" *(anamnēsis)* in the earlier Dialogues of *Laws*, tr. A. E. Taylor (London: 1934). Also R. S. Bluck, ed., *Plato's Meno* (Cambridge: Cambridge University Press, 1964), who points out that *anamnēsis* is the foundation for understanding the *ousia* of a thing, and therefore the foundation of a priori knowledge (pp. 44-50, 53-54). But also Schleiermacher's idea of redemption bears a certain resemblance to the upward ascent of the soul. See "The Myth of the Cave," *Republic*, tr. F. M. Cornford (Oxford and New York, 1945) pp. 514ff.; cited in Jones, *Classical Mind*, pp. 135ff. Among secondary sources that refer to Plato's influence on Schleiermacher, see Williams, *Schleiermacher the Theologian*, pp. 13ff.; Tice, "Introduction," in *On Religion*, p. 25.

consciousness, and thus little or no religious life. We may give to this condition, in its most extreme form, the name of *God-lessness,* or better, *God-forgetfulness.*[74]

Schleiermacher described the image of God in humanity as the feeling of God-consciousness, and rejected the views that it could refer either to the lower faculty of the soul (*appetitus sensitivus,* which is actually the middle faculty),[75] or the capacity to govern the external world.[76] Sin is described as a pervasive lapse of God-consciousness or, more specifically, "the bondage of the feeling of absolute dependence."[77]

Barth is perturbed by Schleiermacher's anthropocentric description of sin, and constantly takes issue with it in different sections of the *Dogmatics.* For example, Barth describes Schleiermacher's view of sin in §§67-68 of *Christian Faith* as "a derangement of human nature but no more."[78] For Schleiermacher sin seems more akin to a mental derangement than an infraction committed against a transcendent and holy God. Schleiermacher's organic description of sin and redemption is remarkably modern, and almost postmodern in the sense that it is subjective. His views have more than a few adherents in modern theological and philosophical circles.[79]

Barth points out that while Schleiermacher upholds the redemption of Christ, he does not entail a real pardon *by* Christ on our behalf. For example, Schleiermacher could say, "To attribute mercy to God is more appropriate in language of preaching and poetry than to that of dogmatic theology."[80] Regarding Schleiermacher's doctrine of redemption, Barth concludes: "He was unable to exhibit the peculiar reality of sin, for he was unable to exhibit the reality of grace."[81] Once again, Barth expresses his dissatisfaction with a system of thought that fails to give adequate consideration to the reformed doctrine of grace.

---

74. *Christian Faith,* §11.2, p. 54.

75. Ibid., §61, p. 253 n. 1.

76. *Christian Faith,* §61, pp. 252-53.

77. Ibid., §63.2, p. 263.

78. *CD,* III/3, p. 320.

79. For example, Pierre Teilhard de Chardin, *The Phenomenon of Man,* tr. B. Wall (London: Collins, 1959).

80. *Christian Faith,* p. 353.

81. *CD,* III/3, p. 324. Barth qualifies his criticism of Schleiermacher by admitting that Schleiermacher did believe that sin was real, in so far as it could be described within the religious consciousness. The fault with this description of sin, however, is that Schleiermacher predicated the objective reality of sin based on the subjective reality of sin.

Barth's objection to Schleiermacher's theology as a whole rests on Schleiermacher's exclusive interpretation of Christian faith in terms of religious consciousness — a consciousness that fails to refer ultimately to God in himself. In spite of Schleiermacher's claims to the contrary, his "feeling of absolute dependence" fails to reach its real object: the God of Christian faith. Concerning Schleiermacher's doctrine of sin, Barth concludes:

> There is no recollection of the Jesus Christ in whom God covenants with man and therefore genuinely confronts him, negating, judging and condemning sin and thus opposing it as an objective reality. Just as Schleiermacher denies that real encounter and real history are involved in the relationship between God and man, or God and creation, so he refuses to admit that in the relationship between God and sin.[82]

I conclude, along with Barth, that Schleiermacher's doctrine of sin and redemption does not describe the struggle between the sinful self and a righteous God. For Schleiermacher, sin and redemption could be more precisely characterized as an intramural struggle within the confines of human consciousness than an encounter between God and humanity.[83]

Summary of Barth's Rejection of Schleiermacher's Theology

Historical Setting and Theological Differences

I have attempted to highlight the major differences between Barth and Schleiermacher. Their chief differences are unquestionably theological ones, stemming from real differences in their perspectives about both God and humanity. Nevertheless, the respective eras in which these two men lived and worked must be given some consideration. Would Schleiermacher have maintained his undaunted optimism about the inevitability of human prog-

---

82. *CD*, III/3, p. 328.
83. See *CD*, I/2, pp. 813-14. Cf. James B. Torrance, "Interpretation and Understanding in Schleiermacher's Theology: Some Critical Questions," *SJT* 21 (1968) 273: "No doubt the events of the Gospel are the occasion for the rise within the Christian of the specifically religious feeling of redemption, but can they in any way constitute, within the framework of Schleiermacher's epistemology, the objective content of faith, as they do in traditional Christianity? No doubt Jesus is the perfect embodiment of religious self-consciousness and the feeling of absolute dependence, and the One through whom redemptive energies are released within the world, but how far can he be, for Schleiermacher, the One in whom God *gives Himself* to men to be the object of faith and worship?"

ress, and the overcoming of nature by human religious effort, had he lived closer to the twentieth century and further from the eighteenth century?[84] Had he witnessed two world wars, the Holocaust, and countless other assaults to human decency and dignity in the twentieth century, would Schleiermacher have been able to follow the Enlightened optimists who proposed that the technological development of modern weapons might lead to the more humane type of warfare, with less killing than battles fought with ancient weapons?[85] Would he still be inclined to identify the kingdom of God with the advance of civilization?

These are only speculative questions, but it seems that the answer, to some of them at least, must be a resounding, "Of course not!" Schleiermacher was shaped by the surrounding idealism and romanticism of early-nineteenth-century Europe. And this is precisely Barth's case against him. Barth proposes that Schleiermacher was so shaped by his cultural mileu that he compromised the integrity of theology as the study of the triune God of grace. As we have seen, Barth's real objections to liberal theology in general, and Schleiermacher in particular as liberalism's forefather, center upon substantial theological differences — differences that would hold true in any age. This does not mean that Barth managed to transcend the historical setting of his own *Sitz im Leben,* as if he could do theology in a historical vacuum. It does point out Barth's objection from the beginning of our study: that he takes issue with the notion that Schleiermacher's theology was the only option for modern theology and one providentially given. Barth objects to Schleiermacher, and the whole trend of modern theology, because he thinks the lessons of the twentieth century should not be ignored.[86]

Early in his theological career, Barth had made his parting of ways with Schleiermacher clear:

> Those who accept the thoughts I have brought forward as germane to the essential facts thereby acknowledge themselves descendants of an ancestral line which runs back through *Kierkegaard,* to *Luther* and *Calvin* and

84. *On Religion,* pp. 201-3, and especially his insistence that the revival of religion and national destiny of Germany are almost identical, pp. 341ff. Cf. Barth, *Protestant Theology,* pp. 435, 438; and *CD,* III/2, pp. 386-87.

85. See Barth, *CD,* III/4, p. 453.

86. Thus Barth says that idealism led to self-consciousness in DeWette and Schleiermacher, and thus to the basis of piety, and therewith the noetic principle of Christian dogmatics. However, modern ontology, "better instructed theoretically by Kierkegaard and practically by world war and revolution, interprets human existence not merely secondarily, but from the very outset as history, and materially not so much as capacity, but rather as 'being projected into nothingness' (M. Heidegger)" (*CD,* I/1, p. 37).

so to *Paul* and *Jeremiah*. . . . And to leave nothing unsaid, I might explicitly point out that this ancestral line — which I commend to you — does *not include Schleiermacher*. With all due respect to the genius shown in his work, I can *not* consider Schleiermacher a good teacher in the realm of theology because, so far as I can see, he is disastrously dim-sighted in regard to the fact that man as man is not only in *need* but beyond all hope of saving himself; that the whole of so-called religion, and not least the Christian religion *shares* in this need; and that one can *not* speak of God simply by speaking of man in a loud voice.[87]

Much later, Barth spoke of Schleiermacher in less strident terms, even saying that he would like to think that he *might* have misunderstood Schleiermacher.[88] He nevertheless maintained that Schleiermacher had set theology on the wrong track by allowing theology to rest on the subjective expression of human religious consciousness as the essential buttress to European culture. Barth did not take issue with the fact of human dependence on God; this he steadfastly maintains in his own dogmatic theology. Rather, he rejected Schleiermacher, on the basis of Kierkegaard's insight that the form of human dependence is a sickness unto *death*.[89] It is a sickness that indicates a human crisis for which there is no earthly solution. While Schleiermacher extolled the subjective dimensions of dependence as the essence of religious consciousness and the content of Christianity, Barth on the other hand exclaims along with Kierkegaard that the fact of dependence indicates only the impossible predicament of the human race apart from relation to an eternal God, and the impossibility of initiating that relationship from the human side. Thus Barth concludes: "it must not be overlooked that after praising everything worthy of praise in my writings in Schleiermacher, I still had ringing in my ears the venerable 'Apostles'' and Nicene Creeds. Theologically speaking, I could not revert to Schleiermacher."[90]

What Is the Proper Role of Religious Consciousness in Christian Theology?

Barth has shown that Schleiermacher consistently reduced the Christian faith

---

87. *The Word of God and the Word of Man*, tr. Douglas Horton (London: Hodder and Stoughton, 1928) p. 195.

88. *Schleiermacher*, pp. 274-79.

89. *The Word of God and the Word of Man*, p. 150. Cf. *CD*, I/1, p. 37.

90. *Schleiermacher*, p. 267.

to human psychology in the broadest sense. Barth's most forceful critique of Schleiermacher is that Schleiermacher reduced theology to the study of religious consciousness. Theology has therefore lost sight of its true object, and its viability as a discipline has been compromised. If the subject matter of theology must be contained by the "feeling of absolute dependence," then what is to prevent theology from becoming nothing more than a subset of human psychology? The question is one that Barth entertained quite seriously, and it explains why he saw a direct theoretical link between Schleiermacher and Feuerbach. If predications about God can be made only from the standpoint of human consciousness, what might happen to those predications if we discover that the feeling of absolute dependence is largely reducible to early childhood patterns of socialization? Would talk about God then be reducible to mere human projections and wishes, as both Feuerbach and Freud argued?

What shall we make of Schleiermacher's "feeling of absolute dependence"? It has an undeniable appeal to it; but the question remains as to what kind of reality it does in fact refer. In chapter six below I contend that the feeling of absolute dependence can be accounted for on other grounds than that of religious consciousness. If ever there was a theological maxim that is open to psychological explication, it would have to be Schleiermacher's "feeling of absolute dependence." Schleiermacher affirmed that the feeling of absolute dependence was derived from psychology in the general theological sense, and did not seem to be bothered by such an admission. Pushing even beyond Barth's criticism of Schleiermacher, however, we are compelled to ask: Has Schleiermacher described the ground of religious experience, or has he unwittingly uncovered a most powerful description of early childhood dependence, one that might be accounted for by insights found in modern scientific psychology?[91] In chapter six I argue for the latter, and I believe that such an argument highlights the importance of Barth's critique of Schleiermacher.

Summary of Barth's Critique of "Absolute Man"

In light of Barth's discussion and criticisms of Scheiermacher and Kant we have reached an important conclusion, one that shall establish a premise for

---

91. *Christian Faith*, §4.3, p. 15. This is not to say that Schleiermacher intended to reduce theology to psychology. As Paul Ricoeur suggests, however, psychology might be able to "purge theology of idolatries" by pointing out that the feeling of absolute dependence is dangerously susceptible to psychological explication. I take this up in chapter six.

the relation between theology and the other disciplines. Barth has established a proper boundary between theology and other fields of study: theology is the science of the revealed Word of God and it should not be confused with the other disciplines such as philosophy, speculative psychology, or the human sciences. In comparing the revealed anthropology of the Bible with the speculative anthropologies of the Enlightenment and post-Enlightenment theology, what kinds of objections does Barth raise against the latter?

Barth's critique of the "absolute man" of the Enlightenment stands on a twofold objection. First, the "absolute man" of the Enlightenment was overly self-confident of his intellectual capacities. This proved to be no less true for Kant, who trimmed the rational capacities with his Critiques, than for Hegel, who elevated reason to a historical system of truth. Second, the "absolute man" of the Enlightenment was far too isolated. The human *ratio* is by definition a function that occurs in isolation from others. This self-sufficient and isolated definition of the human being has been traced from the Enlightenment thought of Rousseau, Hegel, and Kant.

One must admit that Schleiermacher's theology cannot be classed with Enlightenment rationalism. His theology was, rather, a romantic reaction against rationalism. Nevertheless, we have seen that his theology based on "intuitions" is no less anthropocentric than a philosophy based on reason. Even in his attempt to incorporate the social dimensions of religious consciousness,[92] Schleiermacher's theology described the relational component as a mere coincidental development of individual religious consciousness. Schleiermacher therefore failed to transcend the influence of the Enlightenment, which Barth argues placed humankind at the center of all respective discussions about God and the world.[93] After rejecting the so-called providential guidance of Schleiermacher, Barth needed to find a better route for modern theology. He began to probe for a "wholly other" foundation for theology. The startling destruction wreaked upon Europe during World War I, combined with Barth's extended studies of the epistle to the Romans, served to start a theological revolt against the prevailing theology of Schleiermacher and the nineteenth century.[94]

Hemmed in as he was by so many social and theoretical impasses, Barth's break with modern theological liberalism seemed to be an event waiting to happen. But Barth could not make such a break on his own. In addition to his reacquaintance with the "strange new world of the Bible" — especially

---

92. See *Christian Faith*, §6, pp. 26-31.
93. Cf. Oman, pp. 89, 91.
94. See Eberhard Busch, *Karl Barth*, tr. John Bowden (London: SCM, 1976) pp. 68ff.

Paul's epistle to the Romans,[95] Barth needed the intellectual support of a number of different thinkers from various times and places. The skeptical criticism of Franz Overbeck (1837-1905), the social radicalism of Leonhard Ragaz (1868-1945), the eschatological radicalism of the Blumhardts,[96] and perhaps most of all, the existential thought of Søren Kierkegaard, all converged to provoke Barth to cry out against the subservience of Christian theology to the prevailing optimism and individualism of nineteenth-century European thought and life.

The Influence of Søren Kierkegaard on Barth's Anthropology

In this section I discuss Kierkegaard primarily to attain a better understanding of Barth's early anthropology (c. 1920s), to clarify the relation between theology and philosophy, and to show the extent to which Barth used Kierkegaard as a lever to pry theology away from the consciousness theology of Schleiermacher. I give special attention to the way Barth acknowledges Kierkegaard's insights in his *Epistle to the Romans*. The extent to which Kierkegaard continued to influence Barth's later thought, including his *Dogmatics,* is highly disputed in contemporary theological circles, and I do not attempt to settle that dispute here. I believe that even in Barth's latest works, Kierkegaard's influence is perceptible, although it has been transmuted and adapted to Barth's own creative purposes.

The "Existing" Individual in Kierkegaard

As a so-called existential philosopher,[97] Kierkegaard is concerned with the existence of an individual person. Kierkegaard is deliberate, and usually highly polemical, in sounding the alarm against almost every form of speculative thought that deals with universals or abstractions while overlooking the existence of the particular individual. Where rationalists such as Spinoza and Hegel seek to find the unity of the reasoning subject and the universal truth to which reason could appeal, Kierkegaard seeks to explain what distin-

---

95. Ibid., pp. 97-98.

96. Ibid., esp. pp. 37, 76ff., 83ff., 115-16. Cf. Jüngel, *Karl Barth,* pp. 54-70; and Torrance, *Karl Barth,* pp. 36-47.

97. See H. R. Mackintosh, *Types of Modern Theology* (1937; repr. London: Nisbet, 1962) pp. 218-20.

guishes them. He wishes to point out how great is the distance between the thinking subject and the eternal truth, especially the distance between the individual and God. Kierkegaard attempts to shatter the myth that God is immanent to the faculty of unaided human reason:

> The fundamental misfortune of Christendom is really Christianity, the fact that the doctrine of the God-Man (the Christian understanding of which, be it noted, is secured by the paradox and the possibility of offense) is taken in vain, the qualitative distinction between God and man is pantheistically abolished — first speculatively with an air of superiority, then vulgarly in the streets and alleys.[98]

Kierkegaard attacks immanence because he believes that the virtual pantheism of Hegel and other philosophers who attempted to build "systems" blurs the distinction between God and humanity. In attempting to bridge the gap between the thinker and the universal truths of reason, the rationalists, according to Kierkegaard, overlook the simple fact of the existing individual.[99]

Nevertheless, Kierkegaard's "God" is not locked away in some unreachable transcendence. It is important to note that Kierkegaard does not deny that God and humanity have in fact been brought together. He merely denies that God and humanity could be brought together apart from an act of God himself — apart from the incarnation of the "God-Man."[100] Rationalist systems circumvent the incarnation because they deny that God himself has accomplished anything that unaided human reason has not already been able to accomplish. In raising this objection, Kierkegaard believed he was pushing theology back to the reformers' cry of *sola gratia*. If God is immanent in everything that exists, and thus to be apprehended by the use of either reason (or some other human faculty or power, such as the will or the feelings, etc.), then there would be little need for God to reveal himself. The God who can be known immediately through human effort could easily be confused with human consciousness. Such a God might not be the God of the Christian faith. Furthermore, the person who thinks he knows God directly may find his or her own existence in a state of confusion. As Kenneth Hamilton observes: "Kierkegaard explains that every theory of immanence, as it strives for consistency, is driven toward pantheism, and in the process the individual invari-

---

98. *Fear and Trembling and the Sickness unto Death*, tr. Walter Lowrie (Princeton: Princeton University Press, 1954) p. 248.

99. See *Kierkegaard's Concluding Unscientific Postscript*, tr. David F. Swenson and Walter Lowrie (London: Oxford University Press, 1941) p. 203.

100. Cf. *Sickness unto Death*, p. 248; and Barth, *CD*, I/1, pp. 242-43.

ably becomes swallowed up in the general idea of humanity."[101] Kierkegaard is convinced that the immediacy of relation between God and the self runs contrary to the Christian teaching on the transcendence of God:

> All paganism consists in this, that God is related to man directly, as the obviously extraordinary to the astonished observer. But the spiritual relationship to God in the truth, i.e. in inwardness, is conditioned by a prior irruption of inwardness, which corresponds to the divine elusiveness that God has absolutely nothing obvious about Him, that God is so far from being obvious that He is invisible.[102]

The Hegelian dialectic sought to relate all things through the intellect, to overcome all antitheses through pure thought. Kierkegaard, on the other hand, points out that such a relation should arouse our suspicion, because it relates to everything in general and nothing in particular: "This pure thought, hovering in mystic suspension between heaven and earth and emancipated from every relation to an existing individual, explains everything in its own terms but fails to explain itself."[103] We shall see that Barth is well advised by Kierkegaard, especially in his *Epistle to the Romans,* and therefore takes care to avoid the pitfalls of rationalist philosophical systems. But just as importantly, Barth's concept of being — both of God and of the individual — is shaped by Kierkegaard in some crucial ways. More will be said about this below.

As I have mentioned above, Barth's early theology was often characterized as "dialectical" theology. But rather than a dialectic of Hegelian synthesis, we might say Barth employs the dialectic of Kierkegaardian differentiation: Kierkegaard sought to appreciate the significance of divine revelation by pointing out the naturally occurring distance between God and humanity apart from the incarnation.[104] Unlike Hegel's dialectic, Kierkegaard's was a dialectic of intellectual humility.[105] It was humble because it was suspicious of any wholly consistent system of thought. It was humble because any possible synthesis between God and humanity, between time and eternity, came from divine initiative and not from human thought. Barth's affinity for Kierkegaard (among others) led him to conclude that Christian theology had been held captive for too long by the consciousness theology of Schleiermacher and the

---

101. "Schleiermacher and Relational Theology," *Journal of Religion* 44 (1964) 32.

102. *Postscript,* p. 219.

103. Ibid., p. 278.

104. Cf. Mackintosh, *Types of Modern Theology,* p. 227.

105. See the section on Hegel in chapter two above, and also Torrance, *Karl Barth,* p. 83.

idealism of Kant and the neo-Kantians. Kierkegaard's dialectic shattered — or at least attempted to shatter — the forms of immanence between God and humanity that overlooked the incarnation. Barth therefore stood on the shoulders of Kierkegaard in challenging the ideas of immanence apart from incarnation.

In place of a theology based on immanence Barth chose a theology of "encounter."[106] In the place of intellectual systems, Barth chose to focus on particular existence and actions. Both rationalistic and romantic systems fell under the sweeping "No" of Barth's dialectical theology. The resounding "No" of the *Epistle to the Romans* is Kierkegaardian to the extent that it denies the human possibility of knowing God apart from the incarnation.[107] To some degree, then, it would seem that Barth's suspicion of natural theology derived from his reading of Kierkegaard. The intellectual apprehension of God apart from incarnation and revelation was, according to both Kierkegaard and Barth, contrary to *sola gratia*.

Kierkegaard was fond of stating: "truth is subjectivity."[108] The most important kind of truth, according to Kierkegaard, can be attained only through taking account of the person as an existing subject.[109] No one is able to think universal thoughts apart from their prior individual existence. "Truth is subjectivity" therefore expresses a supreme skepticism toward philosophical systems, especially those which tend to blur the separation between subject and object, between thinking and being. For Kierkegaard, "The systematic Idea is the identity of subject and object, the unity of thought and being. Existence, on the other hand, is their separation."[110] He does not deny that philosophical systems are capable of some degree of understanding about God; he does deny, however, that systems are compatible with the Christian means of knowing God. Philosophical systems may have some application to the God-relationship within the self; but this has little to do with Christianity, argues Kierkegaard. In Christianity, the God-relation is always "something outside the individual, the individual does not find edifi-

---

106. See Busch, *Karl Barth*, p. 144: "The adjective 'dialectical' describes a way of thinking arising from man's conversation with the sovereign God who encounters him."

107. See Kierkegaard's *Philosophical Fragments*, tr. David F. Swenson (London: Oxford University Press; New York: American-Scandinavian Foundation, 1936) pp. 24-28. Barth's early dialectic harks back not only to Kierkegaard, but also to "Paul and the Reformers" (esp. Luther). Most of all it refers to the incarnation itself. See Barth, *The Word of God and the Word of Man*, pp. 206ff.

108. *Postscript*, pp. 33, 112, 141, esp. 169-224.

109. Ibid., pp. 101-5.

110. Ibid., p. 112.

cation by finding the God-relationship within himself, but relates himself to something outside himself to find edification."[111] In describing truth as "subjectivity" Kierkegaard is not denying the objective truth of Christian faith; rather, he is protesting against the possibility that a Christian in pursuit of the truth could indulge in "thinking dispassionately about God and eternity." The claims of Christ demand a decision; they do not allow the option of bland assent to objective doctrines or glib conformity to institutional norms. The incarnation confronts the individual with a historical fact that commands an individual response. Kierkegaard does not deny the objectivity of the incarnation as a historical fact; he merely points out the importance of the personal response of faith.

Here we have an insight that would prove to influence Barth greatly. For both Kierkegaard and Barth, truth is not exhausted in the right relation between propositions and historical realities abstractly conceived, but it must ultimately relate to an existing individual. In other words, Kierkegaard's insistence that truth is subjectivity emphasizes that truth is ultimately personal. Truth does not "hang in the air"; it resides in an existing subject.[112] It follows from this that God, for Kierkegaard, is not given in the will, intellect, or religious consciousness, but as an Other — that is, as an object who is living Subject.[113] God, therefore, is not immanent to any human faculty, but always present as the One who stands over and against us.[114] God is "Wholly Other." If there is any means for relation with the "Wholly Other" God, it is in the moment of "encounter" — an encounter that is a human response made possible by divine initiative. The encounter between the human subject and the transcendent God is one of the major themes that runs throughout Barth's theology.

Kierkegaard's insistence on the differentiation between God and humanity, time and eternity, gave Barth the lever with which to pry theology away from Schleiermacher and the theoretical systems of the Enlightenment. In the place of the consciousness theology of Schleiermacher, Barth develops

111. Ibid., p. 498. See pp. 493-98 on the differences between "religiousness A" and "religiousness B." The former is religion that is immanent to human reason or experience, the latter belongs to faith. For Barth, the former is worship of "No God," and the latter, worship of the "Wholly Other" or "Unknown" God of whom Paul speaks.

112. *Postscript,* pp. 112-13.

113. Ibid., pp. 178-79. This is not to deny the role of the intellect, will, feelings, etc., but merely to point out that they are meaningful only within the context of existing individuals. This is a point that Barth seizes on for most of his theological career; it will be spelled out more clearly below in chapter six.

114. *Postscript,* p. 239.

a theology of encounter based on the distinct existence of both God and humanity; the distance between God and human persons is transcended only in the mediating existence of the God-man.[115] In place of the Enlightenment understanding of human rationality, Barth will interpret human rationality (as it functions in relation to the Christian faith) in terms of the capacity to form relations to God and others.[116]

It should be almost self-evident at this point that the Kierkegaardian dialectic is vastly different from the dialectic of most of his immediate predecessors. Whether it be Hegel, Kant, or Schleiermacher, their mode of dialectic was linked to a system of thought. For Kierkegaard, the dialectic is taken back to its Socratic meaning in the sense that the truth is usually pursued in the context of a dialogue between individual persons. It is a dialectic that highlights the existing individual.

The Diastasis between God and Humanity
in Barth's Epistle to the Romans

Kierkegaard's overall influence on Barth has been well documented, but sometimes misunderstood.[117] Barth makes no secret of his appreciation for Kierkegaard during the period when he broke with modern liberalism. In the frequently cited passage from the preface to the second German edition of the

---

115. See Torrance, *Karl Barth*, p. 83: "It is obvious how much this dialectical thinking of the early Barth owes to Kierkegaard: to his conceptions of 'indirect communication', 'the paradox', and 'fragments' which Kierkegaard found forced upon him through his efforts to take in deadly earnest the fact that, as he put it, the absolute fact had become a historical fact. It all hinges upon the concrete historical reality of God in Jesus Christ."

116. See chapter six below.

117. See, e.g., W. W. Wells, "The Influence of Kierkegaard on the Theology of Karl Barth" (Ph.D. dissertation, Syracuse University, 1970) pp. 262-65, who presents the dubious argument that Barth had been either unwilling to acknowledge, or unable to see, the continuing influence of Kierkegaard well into the period of his writing of the *Dogmatics*. In his chapter on Barth's doctrine of revelation, Wells mistakenly assumes (pp. 215ff., citing Henri Bouillard, *Karl Barth: Parole de Dieu et existence humaine*, 3 vols. [Paris: Aubier, 1957] II, p. 186) that Barth's rejection of the *analogia entis* of Thomistic theology is an equivalent expression for the infinite qualitative distinction between God and humanity. Wells makes no positive assessment of Barth's trinitarian theology, or the *analogia fidei* or *analogia relationis;* hence it is no surprise that such an oversight leads him to conclude that for Barth, "knowledge of God seems to be beyond man's reach" (p. 264). For a more plausible interpretation of Barth's *analogia relationis,* see Colin Gunton, *Becoming and Being: The Doctrine of God in Charles Hartshorne and Karl Barth* (Oxford: Oxford University Press, 1978) pp. 140-48; also H. Hartwell, *The Theology of Karl Barth* (London: Duckworth, 1964) pp. 9-10. Cf. also below, chapters four and six.

Epistle to the Romans (1921), Barth states that if he has any system, it is taken from Kierkegaard's insistence on the "'infinite qualitative distinction' *(den 'unendlichen qualitativen Unterschied')* between time and eternity."[118] Such a distinction establishes the difference between God who is in heaven and each human individual who is on the earth: it expresses the fundamental distinction between God and humanity.[119] Barth follows Kierkegaard in denying that knowledge of God is available through the immediacy of human experience. The gospel is available only to those who respond to the divine initiative with faith: "Only for those who believe is it the *power of God unto salvation*. It can be neither directly communicated nor directly apprehended. Christ hath been appointed to be the Son of God — *according to the Spirit* (i.4). 'Now, Spirit is the denial of direct immediacy. If Christ be very God, He must be unknown, for to be known directly is the characteristic mark of an idol' (Kierkegaard)."[120]

Several things need to be said about Barth's adoption of the "infinite qualitative distinction between time and eternity." First, as with Kierkegaard, the mystery that surrounds God and the distance *(diastasis)* between time and eternity do not mean that they are distinguished in such opposition that they can never be reconciled or brought into relation.[121] For Barth, as with Kierkegaard, the distance between God and humanity is bridged through God's love, which cannot resist "annihilating the unlikeness that exists between them."[122] The *diastasis* is indicative of the fact that God calls the world into question. In the *Epistle to the Romans,* this means that the "Gospel is not a truth among other truths. Rather, it sets a question-mark against all truths.

---

118. *Epistle to the Romans,* p. 10. This is taken almost verbatim from Kierkegaard: see *Sickness unto Death,* p. 257; cf. *On Authority and Revelation,* tr. Walter Lowrie (Princeton: Princeton University Press, 1955) p. 112; and *Postscript,* pp. 195, 369. But, more importantly, the "infinite qualitative difference" between God and humans indicates a prominent Kierkegaardian theme. It sometimes indicates a distance created by human sinfulness: e.g., *Sickness unto Death,* esp. pp. 162-68, 249-57; *Philosophical Fragments,* pp. 10ff., 37; *Postscript,* p. 240; but at other times seems more Hellenic, as if eternity and time were sheer metaphysical opposites. See *Postscript,* pp. 295, 439-40; *Sickness unto Death,* pp. 162-68.

119. Cf. Barth, *The Word of God and the Word of Man,* pp. 190-91.

120. *Epistle to the Romans,* p. 38. For further references to Barth's emphasis on the distance between God and humanity, see also pp. 28, 29, 41, 45, 50, 52-53, 97-98, 100-101, 278-79; indeed, this is a theme that jumps from almost every page of Barth's work. That the Spirit is needed to bridge the distance between God and humanity also serves to indicate the distance that exists between the self and other human beings. Hence, the need for the Spirit to bring together the community of faith. See 1 Cor. 12:13.

121. See *CD,* III/4, pp. xii-xiii.

122. *Philosophical Fragments,* p. 19.

The Gospel is not the hinge but the door. The man who apprehends its meaning is removed from all strife, because he is engaged in a strife with the whole, even with existence itself."[123] There is a questioning by God that causes a "KRISIS" for the creature, with a subsequent "dissolution" *(Aufhebung)* of the type of direct knowing that had been advocated by Schleiermacher, Hegel, and others.[124] To know is to know a difference — to know a distinction. But even with the dissolution, the infinite distance between God and humanity does not remain intractable. There is a commensurate sense in which the gospel, after dissolving, provides for the "establishment" *(Begründung)* of the world.[125] This is an example of Barth's early dialectic in which all human aspirations — including religious aspirations — are dissolved by the wrath of God and established by the grace of the incarnation. Even in this early stage of theological development, Barth gives an indication of the direction he intends his later theology to go: the intersection between the unknown God and the known world is made apparent in Jesus Christ.[126] Since God is beyond our comprehension, it is only in the revelation of God in Christ that the distance between God and humanity can be overcome;[127] any attempts to reach God apart from revelation represent the vain experiences of a this-worldly "religion."[128]

Kierkegaard emphasizes repeatedly that the gospel calls into question the status quo of human culture; this has a twofold impact on Barth's theology. First, it helps Barth to distinguish the gospel from human culture. Christian faith and European culture are not to be confused: "The kingdom of men is, without exception, never the Kingdom of God."[129] In his dialectical period Barth accentuates the *diastasis*, the distance between God and humanity. An important aspect of the *diastasis* is that the gospel creates a necessary offense.[130] The deity of Christ demands a type of obedience that disallows indifference; it demands a passionate commitment to God in the face of uncertainty.[131] Later, in the *Dogmatics*, Barth attempts to find the manner in which

---

123. *Epistle to the Romans*, p. 35.

124. Ibid., p. 91.

125. Ibid., pp. 92ff.; cf. W. Lowe, "Barth as a Critic of Dualism: Re-Reading the *Römerbrief*," *SJT* 41, 377-95, esp. 384-85.

126. *Epistle to the Romans*, pp. 29-30.

127. Ibid., p. 279.

128. See ibid., pp. 49-54, 91ff., 159, 192-93, 299-300. The tension between religion and revelation is sustained in Barth's *Dogmatics*. See CD, I/2, §17.

129. *Epistle to the Romans*, p. 56.

130. Cf. ibid., pp. 42-54, 276ff., with *Philosophical Fragments*, pp. 39-43.

131. See *Sickness unto Death*, pp. 260-62.

God establishes continuity between himself and creation through incarnation. But at this earlier stage, Barth is compelled to understand the incarnation in the Kierkegaardian terms of the mystery of God and the distance between God and humanity. Barth believes it is necessary to emphasize the transcendence of God and the distance between God and human understanding in order to free Christian theology from its captivity to the realm of religious feelings and its subsequent absorption into European culture. In the *Epistle to the Romans,* Barth reiterates Paul's affirmation that Jesus Christ himself presents a stumbling block. The gospel is *not,* therefore, the highest embodiment of European culture. Contrary to the culture-bound consciousness theology spawned by Schleiermacher, Barth states:

> In Jesus the communication of God begins with a rebuff, with the exposure of a vast chasm, with the clear revelation of a great stumbling block. "Remove from the Christian Religion, as Christendom has done, its ability to shock, and Christianity, by becoming a direct communication, is altogether destroyed. It then becomes a tiny superficial thing, capable neither of inflicting deep wounds nor of healing them; by discovering an unreal and merely human compassion it forgets the qualitative distinction between man and God" (Kierkegaard).[132]

Second, Kierkegaard's critique of idealism began to shape Barth's philosophical framework for doing theology. After reading Kierkegaard, Barth could no longer allow the abstract, and more or less static, philosophical categories of being to provide a suitable framework for understanding the being of God or humanity. To be is to act. To be is to exist in relation to an other, and such relation requires a clear differentiation between the self, as subject, and the object that is known. Real human existence takes place through encounter: human existence is not static being, but entails the dynamic of *becoming.*[133] The human capacity for abstract thought cannot adequately explain human life. Human life is better explained by the spheres of relations that surround each person. The primary relation is, of course, one of relationship to God. God is known only as he is encountered as a living reality: a "Wholly Other" who makes himself known through his Son. The God of Christian faith is known not through his immanence, availed to the experi-

---

132. *Epistle to the Romans,* pp. 98-99.
133. This is Jüngel's observation of Barth's later doctrine of God in *CD,* I/1. See *Gottes Sein ist im Werden (The Doctrine of The Trinity: God's Being Is in Becoming* [Grand Rapids: Eerdmans, 1976] pp. viii, 61-108)

ence of the mystic or the reason of the intellectual, but primarily through the encounter of the sinner with divine grace.[134]

I have attempted to show some of the ways in which Kierkegaard's philosophy influenced Barth's sharp theological distinction between God and humanity, eternity and time, thus establishing a *diastasis* that broke with the types of immanentism characteristic of much nineteenth-century theology. This has some important implications for theological anthropology, for it sets the human person as an individual over against the eternal God. In distinguishing between the existing individual and the sovereign existence of God, Kierkegaard established the foundations for a theology of encounter that differentiates God from humanity. Barth was quick to see that the apparent cleavage between God and humanity throws humanity into a crisis (KRISIS) of real dependence. It reveals that the very thing human beings need is the very thing they lack. Relation to God is the sine qua non of human existence, but it is the thing that we are unable to establish on our own. Relation to God is not, however, a capacity of the human religious affections, but rather is established by God himself through the incarnation.

Kierkegaard's Concept of the Person and Mind-Body Dualism

Having surveyed several anthropologies that were developed on the European continent during and after the Enlightenment, we have seen how each placed emphasis on one of the faculties: Kant ultimately emphasized the will, Hegel the intellect, and Schleiermacher the feelings. Kierkegaard, however, did not focus on one or another faculty, but on the importance of the existing and acting individual and the choices facing the individual. Such an emphasis tends toward a type of holism that would take root in Barth's later anthropology.

Kierkegaard's iconoclasm extended beyond the God-humanity relationship to his intrapersonal anthropology. He was interested not only in the self's relation to God, but also in the self's relation to itself. He rejected the traditional dualism that posited the person as a synthesis of body and soul (or mind), and replaced it with a more dynamic anthropology that emphasized the ability of the self to act as an agent. The spirit, which is the true self according to Kierkegaard, is an essentially free element that unites the body and soul into a dynamic acting agent. The self may choose to act within the framework of various spheres of existence. The self is in relation

---

134. *Epistle to the Romans*, pp. 59, 64, 68.

both to itself and to the Power that constitutes it.[135] The options available to the self in forming relations to God, self, and others are significantly more open than the traditional notion that each person could feed either the higher or lower appetites. The self can act selfishly, following its own desire for aesthetic satisfaction. Or it can act ethically, religiously, or even at the highest level, sacrificially. This break with the dualism of body and soul provided one of the seminal influences on Barth's dynamic anthropology. When Barth develops his doctrine of the human person, he proposes that a substantival dualism between body and soul cannot do justice to biblical anthropology.

In the end, Barth makes some significant modifications of Kierkegaard's anthropology. Barth's departure from the camp of Kierkegaard stems primarily from his discomfort with Kierkegaard's individualism: Kierkegaard described the relations of the self to itself and God, but mostly neglected to give sufficient treatment to the relations with one's neighbor.[136]

The Rejection of Existential Philosophy as a Foundation for Theology

The beginning of the *Kirchliche Dogmatik* in 1931 followed the "false start" of the *Christliche Dogmatik* (1927). With the *Church Dogmatics* Barth attempted to reject Kierkegaardian existentialism, along with any philosophical a prioris, as a starting point for dogmatic theology. There are several reasons for Barth's perception of the need to scrap existentialism. First, Barth proposed that theology must begin with its own premises and not with those of philosophy; otherwise it could never be sure that it would be a truly distinct

---

135. See, e.g., *The Concept of Dread,* tr. Walter Lowrie (1944; repr. Princeton: Princeton University Press, 1973) p. 123.

136. The common elements of thought contained in Barth's and Kierkegaard's anthropologies could be explained by their mutual allegiance to biblical anthropology, coupled with their attempts to surmount the problems presented by Hellenic and Enlightenment mind-body dualism. Some have written plausible but not overly convincing arguments that Barth continued to be influenced by Kierkegaard well into the period of the writing of the *Dogmatics.* E.g., in addition to the Ph.D. thesis by W. W. Wells (n. 117 above), who discredits Barth for his unconfessed association with Kierkegaard, see also Alastair McKinnon, "Barth's Relation to Kierkegaard: Some Further Light," *Canadian Journal of Theology* 13 (1967) 31-41, who discredits Barth for not giving Kierkegaard more credit in the shaping of Barth's own later dogmatic theology. However, it is mostly academic to attempt to trace the influences that might, or might not, have come to bear on Barth's later thought, without giving the thoughts themselves primary attention.

discipline from philosophy.[137] In his attempts to describe the paradoxical nature of the God of Abraham, Kierkegaard wrapped God up in a mystery, a paradox that obscured God almost as much as it revealed him. But second, and more important for the purposes of this study, Kierkegaard's existentialism lent itself all too readily to individualism. He failed to emphasize sufficiently that relation to an "other" is the key to self-relation. Tracing his need to accept Kierkegaard's insights with an increasing amount of discrimination, Barth says:

> What about the individual in whose existence nearly everything seems to be centred for Kierkegaard? Where in his teaching are the people of God, the congregation, the Church; where are her diaconal and missionary charge, her political and social charge? What does it mean that, in interpreting the command "Thou shalt love thy neighbour as thyself," Kierkegaard could agree with St Augustine and Scholasticism against Luther and Calvin that there must be a love of self that takes precedence over love of others? How strange that we, who were just coming from an intense preoccupation with the relation of Christianity to the social question, did not immediately become suspicious at the point of Kierkegaard's pronounced holy *individualism*.[138]

When Barth sat down to write his doctrine of humanity, one of his most pronounced goals was to purge Christian theology of its not-so-holy individualism.

In spite of his many positive contributions to the issues facing modern theology, Kierkegaard's anthropology espoused a type of individualism that allowed the person to exist in cheerless isolation. Kierkegaard's heavy emphasis on the individual indicates that perhaps he had not separated from the acculturating influences of the Enlightenment and Schleiermacher as much as he had supposed. "Truth as subjectivity" may save the individual from

137. See *CD*, I/1, pp. 20-21; III/4, pp. xii-xiii.

138. *Fragments Grave and Gay*, tr. E. Mosbacher (London and Glasgow: Collins, 1971) p. 99. Italics mine. As to whether Barth is completely right regarding Kierkegaard's individualism is another question. It would seem that Kierkegaard's critiques of the aesthetic sphere of existence and preference for the ethical and religious spheres suggest a social dimension to human existence, e.g., in his emphasis on commitments to relationships such as marriage, etc. Nevertheless, Kierkegaard's own psychological problems promoted a kind of aggressive individualism within his writings that proved to be both a blessing and a curse. H. R. Mackintosh suggests a similar criticism: "Kierkegaard's thinking starts from the real self, in presence of the real God, as though the man stood out before the Most High alone in empty space" (*Types of Modern Theology*, p. 234). See also Mackintosh, pp. 251, 257-58; and Barth, *CD*, III/2, p. 113.

drowning in a vast sea of intellectual abstractions; but it surrendered the capacity to understand the individual on a deeper personal level due to its inadvertent self-absorption. "Truth as subjectivity" may engender a rightful amount of respect for the individual person, but in Kierkegaard's thought it obscured the social coefficient of knowing and being, which is the cornerstone of both biblical anthropology and modern object relations psychology. Apart from interpersonal relations, no individual can have meaningful existence. This is a theme that Barth returns to again and again as he develops his own anthropology. But where does Barth derive his understanding of the social dimension of human personhood? Could it be that his leftward-leaning politics of his earlier days played itself out in his later writings?

It is neither from socialism nor Darwinism that Barth would attempt to develop a more dynamic and socially based anthropology. It is, rather, from revelation itself, specifically the revelation of the triune God. Barth develops a dynamic anthropology predicated on the *analogia relationis*, the analogical relation between God and humanity based on the relation within God himself as Father, Son, and Spirit. In formulating such an anthropology Barth hopes to show how biblical anthropology avoids both the individualism of the theoretical and psychological anthropologies, and the reductionism of the materialist anthropologies.[139] In the next chapter I turn to Barth's doctrine of humanity and show how he interprets many of the anthropological problems in light of the person of God revealed in Jesus Christ.

139. It is unfortunate that I cannot take up Kierkegaard's specifically psychological philosophy, especially in a cross-disciplinary study such as this one. The existential psychologists such as Rollo May and Victor Frankl are certainly deeply indebted to Kierkegaard's "personal" psychology; but tracing Kierkegaard's influence on modern psychology would entail an altogether separate study.

CHAPTER 4

The Core of Barth's Theological Anthropology

The man whom we can with justice call "modern" is solitary.

CARL JUNG

Having traced some of the theoretical problems that Barth inherited from the theological climate of the nineteenth century, we now take a closer look at Barth's later doctrine of humanity. The salient feature of Barth's mature anthropology is that it is dynamic. Barth's anthropology is not dynamic merely in the sense that it indicates raw motion as opposed to a static state — but also in the sense that "dynamic" refers to interpersonal relations. In order to fully understand the relational character of Barth's anthropology, a shift in perspective from the former categories of Christian anthropology is required. The relational implications of Barth's anthropology are highlighted by his adoption of the Latin phrase: *Si quis dixerit hominem esse solitarium, anathema sit.*[1] This statement comes in the middle of Barth's volume on theological anthropology and it holds both ends together. This Latin phrase indicates the social character of Barth's anthropology: to be human is to participate in a shared experience. Therefore, no accurate understanding of the human being can be derived if we look at a person in isolation from God and others. This phrase is the negative affirmation of Barth's positive insistence that "real man" can only be understood as a being in encounter: a being in covenant relation with God and fellow humans. To find the human essence, Barth insists we must view the person in relation to God, others, self, and time. It is, there-

---

1. *CD*, III/2, p. 319. "If anyone will have said that man is solitary, let him be anathema."

fore, the overlapping spheres of relationships that constellate to form a human being. If modern men and women are alienated and solitary it is to their detriment as creatures made in the image of God. Separation is a sign of human brokenness. The purely solitary person is a human being in crisis. Those who attempt to climb up the path of life without a partner tread on the brink of an abyss. Like a mountain climber whose strength wanes while climbing solo, the person who is truly alone stands on a precipice with little hope of reaching the summit.[2] The need for an anthropology that is couched in terms of the shared experience of human community is integral to Barth's discussion of the human being as a creature made in God's image and likeness.

The communal aspect of our human beinghood occupies Barth's attention for the first half of his impressive volume on Christian anthropology.[3] What provided the stimulus for Barth's interest in this relational anthropology? Two possible sources come to mind. Barth cultivated a deep suspicion of Western individualism, perhaps due to his earlier interest in Christian socialism. The influences of Christoph Blumhardt, Hermann Kutter, Leonhard Ragaz, and others, who thought that socialism was about to deliver us from the excesses of the industrial revolution and bring about a better world, quickly come to mind.[4] But in Barth's later thought it is far more likely that his anthropology grew out of his reading of the Bible, especially the Gospel of John, and most especially the important chapter 17.[5]

Let us turn now to Barth's *Dogmatics*, volume III/2, in order to spell out his doctrine of the person. I begin with Barth's section on method, highlighting Barth's comparison of the respective methods of science and dogmatics. Near the end of this chapter I point out how Barth endorses a type of joyfulness that he thought was lacking in Kant's practical reason. Finally, I uncover the surprising fact that Barth does *not* consider the image of God in humankind to have been eradicated by human sin. The thread that pulls this chapter together, however, is one that runs throughout the *Dogmatics*: Barth's understanding of the Trinity. From his understanding of the triune God Barth develops his Christological and relational doctrine of the human being. It is precisely this "dynamic-relational" emphasis that I will later compare to object relations psychology in order to indicate a number of significant parallels between them.

---

2. See Eccl. 4:9-12.

3. *CD*, III/2.

4. See Busch, *Karl Barth*, pp. 76ff.

5. *CD*, III/2, pp. 220-21.

The Human Being as God's Creature

As a creation of God, the human being can be considered only in the context of his or her relation to God, and subsequently to other persons. Barth's understanding of the Word of God makes explicit that in God's self-revelation through Jesus Christ the human being is the redeemed creature of God. Barth's method of deriving the truth about human nature is, of course, Christological. In order to unify creation and redemption, however, he initially turns his attention to the doctrine of creation, and finds implied in the meaning of the term "creation" *(ktisis, creatura)* both that God is the Creator and the human being is his creature.[6] Barth points out that the human being as a creature of God is in need of constant relation to the Creator. Barth comments on the creation saga in Genesis 2:

> Like the beast, man is formed of dust, animated by God and destined to return to dust and non-existence. But in contrast to the beast, he is animated by God directly and personally. Of all creatures he is chosen and called by Him immediately. And he stands or falls by reason of the fact that God does not abrogate this relationship to him but maintains and continues it.[7]

Following the theology of reformers such as Calvin, Barth does not see the human being composed of inherent qualities, gifts, or attributes, but rather as a being who possesses the image of God by virtue of relation to God.[8] The human essence cannot therefore be the possession of any individual, but comes only as a gift through relation to the Creator.[9] While Barth holds some reservations regarding the *creatio continua* of Calvin, he nevertheless maintains the strength of the idea that God is immediately and personally related to humanity, through his emphasis on the doctrines of providence and divine election.[10] The idea of human beings as beings in dynamic

---

6. *CD*, III/2, p. 3.

7. *CD*, III/4, p. 238.

8. Cf. T. F. Torrance, *Calvin's Doctrine of Man* (London: Lutterworth, 1949) pp. 29, 56, 74-75. See also Pannenberg, *Anthropology,* pp. 49-50.

9. See CD, III/1, p. 200: "Was der Mensch nicht besitzt, das kann er wie nicht vererben, so auch nicht verlieren [What man does not possess he can neither bequeath nor forfeit]." The *imago Dei* is thus not capable of being forfeited because it is not possessed by humans — apart from Christ, that is.

10. Cf. *CD*, III/3, pp. 6, 68ff.; and *CD*, I/2, pp. 688-89. Cf. *Institutes*, I, XV, 2; XVI, 1-2; *Commentary on Genesis*, 2:2; 2:9; *Commentary on Acts*, 17:28. Calvin is prone to use essentialist Platonic language in his anthropology. Yet he "baptizes" his language in the biblical doctrines of *creatio continua* and *creatio ex nihilo*. Cf. Torrance, *Calvin's Doctrine of Man,* pp. 61ff.

relation to God is one that Calvin began and Barth amplifies; Barth, unlike Calvin, anchors his anthropology in the bedrock of Christology.

Because Barth takes both creation and redemption seriously, several implications arise for his doctrine of the human being. First, the question of method: How are we to understand the human being in light of revelation? Anthropology for Barth will be tied to the revealed doctrines of creation and incarnation. Second, Barth will not attempt to formulate an anthropology based on the individual's possession of one or more of the human faculties. Neither the intellect nor the will nor the emotions can serve as an adequate tool for understanding the human being. This does not mean Barth eliminates the importance of these faculties. Rather, he interprets them dynamically, that is, in terms of their development from relations to God, self, and others.

Is There a Biblical Cosmology?

Quite typical of many Europeans who work in the German-speaking world, Barth starts with methodological considerations. How shall we understand humanity? By what means can dogmatics discover real humanity? And what should be the relation of theological anthropology to the methods employed in both natural science and philosophy?

Human beings are creatures placed in the cosmos by God. However, Barth insists that theology is not obligated to accept any particular cosmology (*Kosmologie*) or worldview (*Weltanschauung*).[11] Barth proposes that the "Word of God does not contain any cosmology of heaven and earth themselves."[12] The rejection of any particular cosmology as representative of the biblical picture stems from Barth's belief that cosmologies are only incidental to the primary message of the Word of God, which is the relation of God in his Word to humanity. The Word of God conveys its essential message through adopting many different cosmologies — but no particular cosmology can be singled out as *the* biblical cosmology. Barth is fond of saying that cosmologies are found only in the "sterile corners where the Word of God is not found."[13] Regarding dogmatics he says: "To the extent that it is faith in God's Word, and is even partially true to itself, it cannot become faith in current worldviews but can only resist them."[14] Barth proposes: "we lose nothing and gain everything

---

11. *CD*, III/2, p. 6. Barth uses "cosmology" and "world-view" with no discernible change in meaning.

12. Ibid.

13. *CD*, III/2, p. 11.

14. Ibid.

if we resolutely refuse to make the doctrine of the creature a doctrine of the universe, a cosmology."[15]

It is likely that Barth denies that the Bible advocates a specific cosmology in order to take up the challenge presented by Bultmann, who proposed that the modern worldview, which is heavily influenced by the insights of modern science, had undermined confidence in the biblical-mythological cosmology to such an extent that the latter must be rejected, or at least radically reinterpreted. In his denial that any particular cosmology serves as *the* biblical worldview, Barth is taking a stand against Kant and the "Marburg Kantians" in their various interpretations of deistic cosmology. When interpreting the Bible, Barth believes it is important to reject any a priori assumptions about a mechanistic universe that may preclude miracles such as the resurrection.[16]

Nevertheless, the general cosmological distinction between heaven and earth serves an important function. The cosmologies that are employed in the Word of God provide limits for theology; they establish the cosmological border, or boundary *(kosmologische Grenze)*, for theology, as well as for other disciplines. Barth asserts:

> The Word of God has a cosmological border. It illuminates the world. It makes it known — heaven and earth — as the sphere in which God's glory dwells and in which He concerns Himself with man. . . . It points to heaven as the sum of the created reality which is invisible and unknown and inaccessible to man . . . and it points to earth as the sum of the created reality which is visible and known to man and under his control. . . . The twofold reference is unmistakeable. Heaven corresponds to the being and action of God. Earth corresponds to the being and action of man. The conjunction of heaven and earth corresponds to the covenant in which the divine and human being and action meet.[17]

While the Word of God contains no independent cosmology, it does establish a cosmological border. Hence the Word of God is helpful in defining both the similarities and differences between theological science and "exact science" *(exakten Wissenschaften)*.[18] After Barth discusses the simi-

---

15. *CD,* III/2, p. 19.

16. See esp. III/2, p. 447.

17. *CD,* III/2, pp. 11-12.

18. *Exakten Wissenschaften* is sometimes translated as "inductive science," other times as "exact science." I thus use these terms interchangeably. It is difficult to know precisely which sciences Barth includes in his usage of the term "exact science." It seems that he probably means physics, biology, and chemistry. However, this contains implications for the relation of theology to the human sciences that should not be overlooked.

larities between theology and exact science he also points out their differences.

The Similarities between Natural Science and Dogmatics

Theology and natural science have three methods in common. (1) Natural science is "exact" in "that it confines itself to the study of phenomena but does not lose itself in the construction of world systems."[19] Neither dogmatic theology nor the exact sciences should function with an a priori assumption about a specific worldview. To the contrary, both are done with respect to the given reality of their particular objects of study. So they have a common method: the investigation of a particular object of study. Barth's method throughout the *Dogmatics* is one in which he moves from "the particular to the general." In this sense Barth's method, like that of exact science, is a posteriori. Neither science nor theology should, according to Barth, attempt to deduce their truths from universal a priori axioms. They deal instead with a particular object of study: science with various aspects of the natural world, dogmatics with the revelation, especially as it comes through the particular person and work of Christ. Hartwell comments on Barth's method and its movement from the particular to the general:

> The Word of God is not an abstract general idea conceived by the human mind but a particular fact, namely the particular fact of God's actual revelation of Himself and of His will for man in and through the concrete person and work of Jesus Christ, who is Himself the incarnate Word of God, the Lord . . . who became a servant and the servant (the royal man) who became Lord.[20]

We might wonder, however, at Barth's insistence on the methodological similarities between theology and natural science by observing that agreement regarding theology's particular object is not all that easy to achieve. What is the real object of theology? Is it the Bible? revelation? religious experience? How is this particular object of theological study to be found? If anything seems to be an a priori concept in a universal or general way, it would seem to be the concept of God; this was certainly the case with Kant and Hegel, as we have seen, and even Schleiermacher to some degree. In Barth's thought, however, the particular object of theology is found in the incarna-

---

19. *CD*, III/2, pp. 12-13; see also pp. 23, 199.
20. *Theology of Karl Barth*, p. 23.

tion: in God-become-flesh. It is also found in the particular acts of God in the history of Israel that serve as the prior condition for Israel's admiration of the power and majesty of God. Barth's theology is not based on universal or idealistic conceptions of God; it is based on the history of God with Israel, culminating in the incarnation. In discussing the omnipotence of God in the context of his saving acts toward Israel, Barth observes: "It is not the general which comes first, but the particular. The general does not exist without this particular and cannot therefore be prior to the particular. . . . It is from this particular that we come to this general."[21]

Barth's emphasis on the particular events of revelation as the particular subject matter for theology has not really solved the problem or forged a consensus among theologians. But we should remember that neither do philosophers of science always agree on questions regarding the true subject matter and exact procedures of the so-called hard sciences. The best course seems to be to follow Barth's line of reasoning and evaluate the success of his program as it unfolds.

(2) Barth points out that another similarity between exact science and theological science can be found in their anthropocentric mode of inquiry. Theology must be "anthropocentric." In this context Barth uses the term "anthropocentric" positively. He is referring to the fact that an understanding of humankind composes one of two foci of the ellipse of revelation: the Word of God focuses on both God *and human beings*. Barth affirms, "Who and what man is is no less specifically and emphatically declared by the Word of God than who and what God is."[22] Exact science is anthropocentric because it investigates the cosmos "from the standpoint of human observation and inference" as "the cosmos of man." By "anthropocentric" *(anthropozentrischer)* Barth means that both theology and exact science are the result of a specialized and particular activity of human beings. They are activities in which human subjects engage.[23] Theology is anthropocentric because it is a study of

21. *CD*, II/1, p. 602. In support of his contention that the particular precedes the general, Barth cites Calvin's *Commentary on Luke*, where Calvin warns against the danger of considering God's power, *extra verbum, si quid visum est* (*Corpus Reformatorum*, XLV, pp. 32-33).

22. *CD*, III/2, p. 13.

23. The "anthropocentric" nature of exact science has been pointed out by increasing numbers of philosophers of science in recent times. See especially Michael Polanyi's concept of "personal knowledge," of which the primary purpose is to show that the study of nature cannot be disjoined from the human subject; see his *Personal Knowledge: Towards a Post-Critical Philosophy*, corrected ed. (Chicago: University of Chicago Press, 1962) pp. vii-viii, 19-32, 49-55, 63-65, 132-202, 255-56, etc.; *The Study of Man* (London: Routledge & Kegan Paul, 1959) pp. 12-13, 27, 72. Polanyi's thought is discussed in T. F. Torrance, ed., *Belief in Science and in Christian Life* (Edinburgh: Handsel, 1980), esp. pp. 10ff.; and also Torrance, *Reality and Scientific Theology* (Edinburgh: Scottish Academic Press, 1985), esp. chap. 4, "The Social Coefficient of Knowl-

the Word of God, which also illumines human self-understanding.[24] In the Word of God the knowledge of humankind in relation to God is revealed inasmuch as the Creator becomes the creature — not just any creature, but the human being, Jesus of Nazareth.[25] Christian dogmatics therefore contains the truth about humanity just as much as the truth about God.

In affirming the anthropocentric nature of both natural science and theology, Barth does not mean that humanity is the "measure of all things." Quite the opposite: science is anthropocentric in that it consists of the human activity of drawing inferences about particular objects of study, "of which it clearly recognizes the limits *(Grenzen)*." The limits that exact science must recognize are those which prohibit it from making any statements that go beyond the boundaries of the cosmos. Exact science is therefore anthropocentric without being "theanthropocentric." The latter term refers to the fact that only theology can understand the human being as the creature in relation to God. The revealed content of theology is God-and-humanity, in that order: God revealed in his Word as a human, thus humanity disclosed in its full reality. It is only by God that God is known; it also is only by God that real *humanity* can be known. The discussion of God himself is the task taken up by theology, and not other sciences (although Barth does admit elsewhere that other sciences *could* take up the dogmatic task in correcting the church's talk about God).[26]

Barth's insistence on the anthropocentric character of science does not suggest that it is a subjective enterprise without a specific body of objective knowledge. To the contrary, science is objective when it acknowledges that it is a human enterprise, in pursuit of knowledge about objective things in the cosmos. While exact science studies a particular object, neither the object in itself nor the method of investigation provides a full explanation of the exact scientific enterprise. Exact science describes the cosmos, says Barth, and it "describes the cosmos only as the cosmos *of man*."

Contemporary scientific studies of both the cosmos itself and quantum physics indicate that the human observer is integral, invariably exerting an influence on that which is observed.[27] Here T. F. Torrance notes the similarity be-

---

edge." See also Enrico Cantore, *Scientific Man: The Humanistic Significance of Science* (New York: ISH, 1977).

24. "In thy light do we see light," Ps. 36:9. Cf. *CD*, II/1, pp. 110ff.

25. See *CD*, III/2, pp. 13, 18-19. We see here that Barth is less skeptical of the anthropological dimension of Christian revelation than at his earlier stages of development, such as *Epistle to the Romans*.

26. See *CD*, I/1, pp. 6-7. Other sciences, however, seldom do take up the dogmatic task of helping the church reflect accurately on its talk about God (p. 6).

27. Both the theory of general relativity and quantum mechanics, as well as the more re-

tween Barth's theological method and the observationalist structure of modern science.[28] If both theology and exact science are anthropocentric as Barth claims, then it should not be surprising that they both would have respective dogmatic starting points; in other words, both would adhere to personal beliefs that are axiomatic and that could only be explained, but never proved. Stuart McLean comments on Barth's dogmatic method: "The critical question is not dogma, but the spirit and awareness with which the inquiry proceeds. Recognition of one's presupposition, awareness of the limitations of human constructs, and openness to impinging 'newness' — all three — characterise the scientific spirit, whether in social, physical, or theological thought."[29] There is therefore a methodological similarity between dogmatics and exact science, inasmuch as both function optimally when they acknowledge their respective premises, allowing those premises to be adjusted in order to describe the object of study with increasing degrees of accuracy. It might surprise the reader to see that the twentieth-century's greatest theologian, and a dogmatic theologian at that, advocates an "opennness to impinging 'newness.'"

(3) Barth proposes that exact science, like theology, should recognize two distinct spheres. Exact science does not label the two spheres "heaven" and "earth" as does theology, but it nevertheless respects the distinction between heaven and earth, reckoning with the sphere that is "within the range of human observation and thought, to which it turns and which it investigates and describes."[30] When exact science presses against the boundaries of the physical sphere, it should respect the border and not attempt to trespass into the domain proper to theology.[31] Barth is not saying that scientists al-

---

cent ideas such as the so-called anthropic principle, are indicators of the personal dimensions of scientific knowledge. In other words, they indicate each in a different way that the human observer affects that which is observed, and in some way plays an interactive role. This could apply to what Barth interprets as "anthropocentric." See Sir John Eccles, *The Human Mystery* (Berlin and Heidelberg: Springer, 1979) pp. 30-31, 96ff., 236-37. See also Stanley Jaki, *Cosmos and Creator* (Edinburgh: Scottish Academic Press, 1980) pp. 41ff. With regard to quantum mechanics, I am thinking about the way in which the observer affects the specification of the position and velocity of the electron. Cf. Polanyi, *Personal Knowledge*, p. 393, who argues that it is the measuring instrument, not the observer, that affects the result. Whichever the case may be, my point is that there is no such thing as objective science apart from a human subject who does science.

28. See *Karl Barth*, pp. 179-80.

29. *Humanity in the Thought of Karl Barth* (Edinburgh: T & T Clark, 1981) p. 7. McLean's first sentence is a bit obscure but seems to indicate that dogma and science are not exclusive.

30. *CD*, III/2, p. 13.

31. This does not mean that exact scientists are compelled to admit the existence of the so-called heavenly sphere. Nevertheless, are cosmological scientists and astronomers pushing against the boundaries of science when they describe the beginning of the universe? E.g., Eccles

ways acknowledge the reality to which the theologian appeals; he means, rather, that the scientist must acknowledge certain limitations that exist to the mode of inquiry peculiar to science, and that the sphere of religious inquiry lies outside the domain of scientific studies.[32]

I, for one, wish that Barth had said more about the relation between exact science and dogmatics; he nevertheless exhibits a keen perception of the basic issues. Barth shows a good deal of acumen in his insistence on the anthropocentric character of exact science. He made this observation at a time when scientific positivism was only beginning to loosen its grip on the philosophy of science, a positivism that had all but eliminated the personal element from its interpretation of scientific method.[33] Barth was convinced that the framing of scientific hypotheses should not be expanded into a worldview. Rather, scientific hypotheses represent a temporary means of measuring the present limitations of knowledge as they allow the scientist to engage in dialogue with a particular object of study. Exact science must therefore lay aside worldviews so that the particular phenomena can be studied and the bounds of knowledge expanded. Barth believes that theologians have too easily fallen prey to anxiety over their need to give allegiance to the supposed scientific worldview, when it remains doubtful that there is any such thing as "*the* view of exact science."[34] The methodological rejection of any cosmology as *the* particular biblical or scientific worldview marks a dividing line between Barth and the "Marburg Kantians" such as Bultmann, who have placed themselves in an "anthropological strait-jacket" because they have accepted at the outset of their theology a worldview "shaped for good or ill by modern science."[35]

Finally, Barth also observes that scientific inquiries might prove especially enlightening if they begin with or "presuppose a knowledge of real man."[36] In

---

points out that scientists may be pressing against the borders of scientific knowledge when they piece together evidence that surmises that the universe likely had a beginning with a sudden "Big Bang" some 10-12 billion years ago, beyond which they do not have the tools available to investigate (*Human Mystery,* Introduction).

32. The acknowledgment of a limit beyond which exact science cannot inquire has also found acceptance by certain theoretical physicists, such as Clerk Maxwell. See Torrance, *Transformation and Convergence,* p. 224.

33. See Arthur Peacocke, *Intimations of Reality* (Notre Dame, Ind.: University of Notre Dame Press, 1984) pp. 16-23.

34. *CD,* III/2, p. 12.

35. *CD,* III/2, pp. 446-47. The latter part of the quotation is taken from Bultmann, but Barth says this line of cosmological reasoning can also be traced back through Ritschl, Herrmann, and Schleiermacher.

36. *CD,* III/2, p. 202.

other words, Barth speaks favorably with regard to the prospect that Christian theology might provide a viable theoretical foundation for various scientific considerations of human beings. Here Barth endorses the prospects for an integration and dialogue between theological anthropology and the findings of other sciences.[37]

We have seen that three points of agreement between exact science and dogmatic theology are the absence of worldview, the anthropocentric nature of investigation, and the recognition of fundamentally different spheres. Given these points of agreement, what makes them distinct from one another? Barth reminds us that in addition to similarities, there are also some important differences between the methods of exact science and dogmatics.[38]

The Differences between Natural Science and Dogmatics

According to Barth, the primary difference between exact science and dogmatics is defined by the different objects that the respective disciplines study: exact science studies particular things — including living things — in the cosmos, whereas theology studies the triune God in his self-revelation. Therefore, theology has an obviously different task from that of natural science.

In his first volume of the *Dogmatics*, Barth proposes that theology can learn little from other sciences with regard to its own method.[39] This is no longer the attitude that we find in the third and fourth volumes of the *Dogmatics*. Barth's later writings contain a more positive outlook regarding the similarities. Barth remarks that exact science, as long as it keeps to its given task, "cannot be the enemy of the Christian confession."[40] It is important to remember that Barth is drawing this comparison between dogmatics and exact science at the beginning of his volume on anthropology; therefore, any possible rapprochement between theology and science applies to the human

---

37. Ibid.; see also pp. 430ff.

38. This also raises the very important question regarding the dogmatic nature of theological inquiry. If Christian dogmatics claims to be a science, mustn't it also be willing to subject its premises to some criterion for verification and falsification? In other words, there must be some criteria by which its premises could be proven either true or false, if it wishes to stake a claim to truth.

39. See *CD*, I/1, pp. 8-10. Nevertheless, he concedes in the same volume that theology can be classified along with the other sciences, avoiding both its own self-exaltation and the exclusive right of other sciences to wield the credibility of such a term (p. 11).

40. *CD*, III/2, p. 24.

sciences, as well as the so-called hard sciences. In the context of this discussion Barth allows that the study of human phenomena might prove to be misleading, but it could just as well be "relevant, interesting, important and legitimate. . . . And it may well be that its results will be significant and even instructive for us."[41] Barth allows for the possibility that scientific studies of humanity can be helpful for theology, as long as they describe human behavior as "symptoms of the human phenomena" and avoid encroaching on the domain of theology by asserting that their findings are "axiomatic, dogmatic and speculative."[42] Theology is prepared to welcome the general knowledge of humankind presented by natural science — provided that natural science describes human beings in their relation to the natural order, not in relation to God or ultimate reality.

This means that scientific anthropology must keep its hypotheses tentative. If exact science is to remain exact, it must refrain from "consolidating its hypotheses as axioms and therefore treating them as revealed dogmas."[43] Exact science is concerned with appearances, and with specific and partial human phenomena. Theological science must make a claim to truth. Exact science strives to achieve a consensus of opinion in its study of the human phenomena, and communicates its results to a community of scientists who have given themselves to that task, adding to the knowledge as the research grows. Barth argues:

> Scientific anthropology gives us precise information and relevant data which can be of service in the wider investigation of the nature of man, and can help to build up a technique for dealing with these questions. Since it is itself a human activity, it presupposes that man is, and what he is, and on this basis shows him as to how he is, in what limits and under what conditions he can exist as the being he is. It is not concerned with his reality, let alone with its philosophical foundation and explanation. But it reveals the plenitude of his possibilities.[44]

It is only dogmatic anthropology that can speak of "real man," which means human beings in relation to God, and "perceptible in the light of God's Word."[45] This does not mean that theological anthropology speaks infallibly about the nature of the human being, only that it must speak of man

41. *CD*, III/2, p. 79.
42. *CD*, III/2, p. 25.
43. *CD*, III/2, p. 23.
44. *CD*, III/2, p. 24.
45. *CD*, III/2, p. 25.

"within and as a whole." Barth concludes: "As theological anthropology concerns itself with this reality *(Wirklichkeit)*, it is fully aware of its own shortcomings, but it raises the claim to truth *(Wahrheitsanspruch)*. Scientific anthropology cannot do this."[46]

It is somewhat unfortunate that the language Barth employs can give the impression that he considers dogmatic theology to have an exclusive claim to truth that might appear to impugn the truth claims of the natural sciences. To propose that dogmatics alone can speak about the human "reality" while scientific anthropology describes human "possibilities" makes it sound as if scientific studies of the person yield only superficial knowledge.

To some degree this discussion harks back to Kant's distinction between the noumenal and phenomenal types of knowing. It would seem that Barth accepts Kant's general distinction between the phenomenal "appearances" and the noumenal "thing-in-itself," arguing that science is limited to the former, while the theologian is capable of speaking of the latter. In some respects then, Barth adopts this fundamental Kantian paradigm. The scientist, physiologist, or psychologist looks at the human phenomenon *(Phänomen Mensch)*, while the theologian looks at his or her inner reality *(wirklichen Menschen)*.[47] However, Barth has made at least two important modifications of Kant. First, Barth does not relegate the discussion of "truth" or claims of ultimate reality to the realm of practical reason as did Kant. The reality claims of the dogmatic theologian are predicated on the human being seen in relation to God, in light of the Word of God, not in light of practical reason.[48] Second, although Barth has argued that scientific anthropology cannot make a claim to "truth," he is not arguing that the scientist cannot stake out a claim to truth. We should not conclude prematurely that the truth claims of the theologian necessarily drive a wedge between science and theology. Barth is simply saying that the task which is peculiar to theology is the task of reflecting on the human subject *in light of the revealed Word of God.* Dogmatics is given the task of explaining how the Word reveals the truth, or inner reality, concerning the human being.

It is odd that Barth would mention the similarities in method between dogmatics and exact science, and then proceed to put them on seemingly different levels of knowledge, such that the hypotheses of science must remain

---

46. Ibid.

47. *CD,* III/2, p. 26; *KD,* III/2, p. 28.

48. In this sense, Barth fell under the influence of Kant through his mentor, Wilhelm Herrmann; but at the same time, he also inherited Herrmann's insistence that theology did not need to be cowed by philosophy and could make claims to truth that neither philosophy nor natural science could make. See Busch, *Karl Barth,* pp. 44ff.

tentative while the truth claims of dogmatics are virtually incontrovertible. This raises an important question concerning Barth's theological method and its relation to natural science. If Barth's methodological comparison between natural science and dogmatics holds true, it must be that there is some manner by which dogmatic statements can be either verified or falsified. Dogmatics, Barth argues, is defined by its real object; therefore, like natural science, it must have some objective referent to which it must bring its own statements into conformity. Barth admits this condition when he mentions that in order for theology to speak *sub ratione Dei,* it must acknowledge that it cannot survey or control its real object, which is the Word of God. Therefore, dogmatics should not be occupied with any a priori decisions; rather dogmatics should be "ready to receive those decisions with which the object will urgently confront human thinking and speaking. It is ready for new insights which no former story of knowledge can really confront on equal terms or finally withstand. Essentially dogmatic method consists in this openness to receive new truth, and only in this."[49] Once again, for a dogmatician Barth's theology and especially his methodology are dramatically open.

We must press the question further and ask whether Barth would seriously entertain the possibility that every dogmatic presupposition, including the Word as the revelation of God, or the Trinity, would be open to new truth that might overturn its reliability. Barth admits that the Trinity is the best expression of the reality of God, and therefore the presupposition of all doctrinal statements about God: "It describes the fact that God confronts us as Creator, Mediator and Redeemer, that as such He speaks and deals with us, that He is God and Lord in this threefold way. This being of God in His work and activity is not a dogma, or a basic view, or a controllable principle which can be used as such for the construction of a system."[50] The Trinity is not to be expanded into a dogmatic system of belief, but refers to the reality of God in his act and being. Therefore, the question as to whether the Trinity could be superseded, for example, by the Jungian concept of God as quaternity, is one that Barth could not seriously entertain any more than the biologist would entertain the notion that living things could cease to be an object of study for natural science. It would defy the rationality of the study of God to speculate how God might be studied if he were utterly unlike the way he reveals himself.[51] This would be to engage in fruitless speculation. It is true,

---

49. *CD,* I/2, p. 867.

50. *CD,* I/2, p. 879.

51. See Barth, *Anselm: Fides Quaerens Intellectum,* tr. I. W. Robertson (London: SCM, 1960) p. 52: "The 'rational' knowledge of the object of faith is derived from the object of faith

Barth insists, that dogmatics is always open to change; it is "open-textured,"[52] and open to reformulation in the light of further insight into its real object: God the living Subject. Nevertheless, if dogmatics loses sight of its object, who is a living Subject, it will lose not only its scientific ground but its real existence as a discipline.[53] If we ask how one may know that the triune God is the real starting point for dogmatics, Barth would simply say that it is one of the "givens" of Christian dogmatics. The self-revelation of the triune God is axiomatic. Dogmatics should not, however, erect any systems, but always be ready to yield to the "Word of God which presupposes itself and proves itself by the power of its content."[54]

It may seem odd to the nontheologian that someone like Barth would construct his theology on belief in the triune God, as if it provided the bedrock of unshakeable certainty. Belief in the trinitarian God of traditional Christianity might seem idiosyncratic, if not obscurantist in light of modern thought — and even in light of many modern theologies. It will seem less odd, however, if we allow ourselves to see that the exact sciences proceed with a number of implicit "fundamental beliefs" that can neither be refuted nor proved, but that nonetheless function as the foundation for the scientific enterprise itself.[55] Once again, many beliefs are better proven by their capacity to support a wider body of beliefs than by their inherent capacity to provide certainty. We shall see later in this chapter how Barth describes the human reality in terms of his understanding of the Trinity.

A Comparison of Barth and Pannenberg's Anthropological Method

In order to better understand Barth's anthropological method, it will prove illuminating to contrast Barth with the noteworthy study by Wolfhart Pannenberg, *Anthropology in Theological Perspective.*[56]

Pannenberg proposes to do "fundamental-theological" anthropology, by which he means that his anthropology does not argue from dogmatic pre-

---

and not *vice versa*. That means to say that the object of faith and its knowledge are ultimately derived from Truth, that is, from God and from his will." Cf. Stephen Sykes, "Barth on the Centre of Theology," in Sykes, ed., *Karl Barth: Studies of His Theological Method* (Oxford: Clarendon, 1979) pp. 36-37.

52. See Gunton, *Becoming and Being*, p. 124.

53. See Barth, *Anselm*, pp. 46-49.

54. *CD*, I/2, p. 868.

55. See Polanyi, *Personal Knowledge*, pp. 269ff., 299-300.

56. See above, n. 8.

suppositions. "Rather," Pannenberg proposes, "it turns its attention directly to the phenomena of human existence as investigated in human biology, psychology, cultural anthropology, or sociology and examines the findings of these disciplines with an eye to implications that may be relevant to religion and theology."[57] Pannenberg proposes that it is possible to set out from a more or less "neutral" (in the sense of being nondogmatic) standpoint to evaluate the anthropological data, in order to see if there is within the human phenomena, as observed by these respective disciplines, something of relevance to religion and theology. Pannenberg makes an admirable attempt to trace basic themes, such as "exocentricity" or "openness to the world" through the various disciplines: beginning with the biological, then progressing to the sociological, and finally the historical phenomena of personhood. All the while Pannenberg builds his case for the critical usage of the term "spirit," apart from any dogmatic understanding of the relation between human "spirit" and divine "Spirit."

Pannenberg's study contains an impressive amount of material that should further the dialogue between theology and the various social sciences. Yet his method could hardly be more opposite from that of Barth. Pannenberg assumes that one must abandon dogmatic presuppositions in order to evaluate directly the phenomena of human interactions on their own terms. Given such a starting point, he thinks that he can build his case for the critical understanding of the human "spirit," thus forging common ground between theology and other sciences. The crucial point on which Pannenberg's whole argument hinges is this: Can he really find the neutral ground between theology and human sciences to evaluate the potential for finding common themes? How does one observe the "phenomena of human existence" apart from at least some commitment to a theoretical framework? As we have seen from Barth's argument above, no science can be exempt from certain implicit and explicit beliefs, and it would therefore seem that the best form of science is the open declaration of its premises. This is true of both dogmatics and science. Therefore, the prospect that one could look at the human disciplines directly and discover the "spirit," without first assuming something about the identity of the "spirit" that one is looking for, seems unlikely. And if we are looking for the "spirit" in very general terms, how can we know that the "spirit" has anything at all in common with the Christian understanding of the *imago Dei* and sin? We would certainly expect to find interconnections (Barth uses the term "parallel[s]," *Parallele*) between the phenomena of the human being and the dogmatic truths revealed about humans

---

57. *Anthropology,* p. 21.

by the Word. But can there be such a thing as neutral ground, some *tertium comparitionis,* from which we can directly observe such connections? A critical question to put to Pannenberg is whether his adjective "fundamental-theological" is nothing more than a dogmatic starting point. If not, then we might ask in what sense he is not, after all, doing a very sophisticated form of natural theology, even though the arena of study has been shifted from the cosmological proofs of classical theism to the anthropological proofs of his extensive studies.

A similar isssue was at stake in Barth's objection to Schleiermacher's method, in which Barth accused Schleiermacher of supplanting the classical proofs with an anthropological proof.[58] The methodological questions all reduce to a single question: Can the observation of any finite phenomena lead to the necessity of the infinite? This seems on one hand to be what Pannenberg attempts to do. He wishes to "demonstrate the universal validity of religion by doing fundamental-theological anthropology," by investigating the "religious and therefore theologically relevant implications of anthropological data" to see if they lead to "the concepts of image of God and sin."[59] This type of theological inquiry is what Barth calls doing theology "from below to above." That is, it reasons from the historical probabilities in an attempt to establish some degree of credibility for revealed truths.[60]

In spite of my Barthian bias, and hence the criticisms of Pannenberg, I admit Pannenberg has made a very important contribution to contemporary theological views of humanity. He has reopened the apparently undying question regarding to what extent the revealed truths about the person are pertinent to the actual discoveries of the social sciences. Barth has shown that there is a formal, methodological similarity between dogmatics and exact science, including the psychological sciences. If I have a criticism of Barth's method, it would be that he left too much unsaid regarding the material relation between theological anthropology and other anthropologies. Barth assumes at the outset that there is hostility between dogmatics and philosophi-

---

58. See *Christian Faith,* §33, pp. 133-34, and compare Barth, *Schleiermacher,* p. 210; and *CD,* III/1, pp. 8-9.

59. *Anthropology,* p. 21.

60. Barth's correspondence with Pannenberg in response to reading Pannenberg's earlier work, *Jesus, God and Man,* tr. Lewis L. Wilkins and Duane A. Priebe (Philadelphia: Westminster, 1968), accentuates their basic difference in method, and Barth's disappointment with Pannenberg's "path from below to above" (*Karl Barth: Letters 1961-1968,* ed. J. Fangmeier and H. Stoevesandt, tr. and ed. G. W. Bromiley [Grand Rapids: Eerdmans, 1981] pp. 177-79). In the earlier work to which Barth refers, Pannenberg attempted to rest revelation in the historical probability for the resurrection of Jesus.

cal or "speculative" anthropology, whereas there is less hostility between theology and science.[61] However, the distinction between scientific and speculative anthropologies is not always easily drawn. Many anthropologies straddle the line between speculative and scientific, developing their theories from the simple empirical data concerning various aspects of human existence, and then venturing a theory that might most comprehensively explain the data.[62] Would these anthropologies be understood as a "speculative" anthropology, to which Barth is so adamantly opposed? Or would this simply be a temporary hypothesis, which would have to be constantly adjusted according to the experimental facts of exact science?

Barth is aware that many theories of the human being begin with, or at least bear a certain similarity to, the hypotheses of natural science. As long as they remain hypotheses, Barth sees no reason to oppose them. However, they often have been expanded from tentative hypotheses, which attempt to account for the current stage of knowledge about the phenomena, to universal axioms, which are no longer susceptible to revision. When such theories "go beyond the hypotheses of exact science," Barth sees them as speculative worldviews that stand halfway between philosophy and myth.[63] This is anthropology in which "man is confident that he can be both the teacher and the pupil of truth."[64] As such it must be in opposition to dogmatic anthropology.

Barth does not, however, spell out in detail how we might distinguish between a scientific premise, framed as a tentative hypothesis in order to serve a heuristic scientific function, and a hypothesis that is purely philosophical. The distinction between the former and the latter is not an easy one to make, but it is a very important one, because Barth rejects the compatibility between dogmatics and philosophical anthropology, while allowing for large areas of agreement between dogmatics and the scientific findings about humanity.[65]

61. *CD*, III/2, pp. 21-23.

62. The relation between phenomenology and phenomenological psychology might serve as an example of a philosophical anthropology that eventually finds some of its insights incorporated into certain dimensions of scientific psychology.

63. *CD*, III/2, p. 22.

64. Ibid.

65. This raises the whole question regarding what Barth thought of the relation between theology and philosophy. A full treatment of this topic would create far too lengthy a diversion. But one can generally say that Barth assents to the employment of certain philosophical concepts and terms by theology, with the important condition that theology must bend the terms of philosophy to meet the needs of its own particular subject. Philosophy, if it is to serve the church, must be brought into conscious subjection to the Word of God. Philosophy poses a

Barth, then, has defined the distinction between theological anthropology and other anthropologies that are based on speculation. As helpful as his method may be in defining boundaries, his definition is primarily a negative one. We might wish that he had spelled out more fully the possibilities for a positive connection between the content of theological anthropology and that of exact science. Along the same lines, T. F. Torrance observes concerning Barth and natural theology: "if we are to take as seriously as Barth claims to do the unitary interaction of God with our world in creation and Incarnation, there must surely be a closer connection between the conceptualities of theological science and those of natural science than we find in Barth's thought."[66] In an age when the social and behavioral sciences have made a good deal of progress toward becoming "exact" sciences,[67] Pannenberg is right to raise the question regarding the common elements between theological anthropology and the findings of other anthropological inquiries. If such connections cannot be uncovered, then we would begin to question whether there is any correlation between nature and grace, between the God of creation and the God of redemption. Barth clearly does not wish to divorce the two, but rather views nature as embraced and redeemed by grace. Nature is thus known by grace, just as the law is illumined by the gospel. This represents the unitary way of knowing that Torrance is fond of ascribing to Barth's theological method.

It would seem that Pannenberg's method lacks the simplicity of Barth's dogmatics, while Barth's method runs the risk of becoming irrelevant to other disciplines. I argue, however, that this criticism of Barth is not necessarily the case. A dogmatic theology is capable of formulating a doctrine of humanity that is sufficiently open-ended to engage in a meaningful dialogue with scientific anthropologies. Indeed, I propose that it is precisely the dogmatic character of Barth's anthropology that allows him to develop a truly novel understanding of the person based on the triune God. The human be-

---

danger, according to Barth, when it slips into theological reflection unconsciously, or tries to claim direct knowledge of God apart from revelation. See Giovanni Miegge, "A Roman Catholic Interpretation of Karl Barth," *SJT* 7 (1954), pp. 59-72, esp. p. 64. Also, *CD*, I/2, pp. 728ff.; II/1, pp. 84, 187-88; and I/1, pp. 125-32, 165.

66. *Transformation and Convergence*, p. 297.

67. See Larry Hedges, "How Hard Is Science, How Soft Is Science?" *American Psychologist* 42 (1987) 443-45. In this article the author argues that based on meta-analytical statistical studies, the empirical cumulativeness for both the physical sciences and so-called soft sciences indicates similar degrees of consistency for both. This is presumably one of the meanings that Barth attaches to "exact science" — disciplines that are susceptible to an increasing degree of statistical consistency; if so, then modern psychology appears to be closing the gap in its relation to other sciences.

ing fashioned after the image and likeness of God reflects God's trinitarian-relational character, and therefore needs to exist as a creature who is "in relation" to God and others. It is the relational character of the human being that bears certain analogies to modern object relations psychology. This point remains to be substantiated in the remainder of this study.

A Summary of Barth's Anthropological Method

Barth's dogmatic method for studying the human being is helpful at three points. First, he argues forcefully that theological anthropology must begin with dogmatics, not with an a priori philosophy, cosmology, or speculative worldview. Theological anthropology differentiates itself from other forms of anthropology by beginning with God in his revelation and moving to an understanding of the human being contained in that same revelation. It thus opposes theoretical views of the human being, not because dogmatic views of humanity claim to be infallible, but because dogmatics must stake a claim to truth in its study of humanity that is not found on any other level of study. A speculative theory that omits the Word of God overlooks the truth about our human personhood, even though it might contain some specific truths about human beings.[68] This points out that Barth takes the unique truth claims of revelation quite seriously.

Second, theological anthropology respects the boundaries between itself and the natural sciences. These boundaries are determined by the respective object with which each is concerned. Exact sciences deal with particular objects of study and their accompanying phenomena. Theology deals with God as its object: the triune God who reveals himself as living subject. In spite of the different objects of study, however, theology and exact science contain certain methodological similarities with one another, and they may engage in dialogue provided each respects the boundaries of its own field.

Third, the knowledge of "real man" can derive only from the Word of God, because only the Word of God reveals the reality of human sin and corruption. The reality behind the sinfulness of human beings tends to reinforce

---

68. E.g., Barth acknowledges that there are general elements of truth in the respective disciplines that study the human being. E.g., natural science describes humanity in his creaturely setting, idealism points out his distinctiveness from the chemico-biological processes, existentialism sees the human being in his or her openness to a transcendent Other, and theism perceives the human being as theonomously rather than autonomously determined (*CD*, III/2, pp. 200-202). These are all positive contributions to the study of humanity, but need further illumination from revelation.

the fact that grace is needed in order for human sin, and the real human being apart from sin, to be revealed. Speculative human self-understanding is therefore unable to understand "real man" because of both the ontic and noetic effects of sin.[69] Due to the extent of human sin and brokenness, Barth argues that the "real man" can be known only as the human reality is revealed by God.[70] Human sinfulness points to the pressing need for a revealed source of our true humanity. This will be found, of course, in the one true man, Jesus Christ.[71]

The Human Being as a Being in Encounter with God

The Imago Dei *as Relationship to the Word of God*

On the basis of Barth's earlier dialectical theology, and also his debate with Brunner, many theologians have concluded that Barth believed the image of God had been thoroughly effaced by sin. If nothing else, I intend to show in the remainder of this chapter that this is a mistaken interpretation of Barth's anthropology. Barth does not believe that the image of God has been destroyed by human sin; he believes rather that the image of God has been misinterpreted. Barth proposes a major paradigm shift in theological anthropology: one from seeing the human being as an individual defined by innate faculties to seeing the person as a dynamic-interpersonal agent whose faculties arise only as they exist in relations to others.

In Barth's debate with Brunner over the point of contact, Barth interpreted the *imago Dei* as being in relationship to God. Barth denied that humans possess an inherent a priori potential to form the relationship.[72] Therefore, it is the Word of God that sets the human being apart because the Word establishes the relationship:[73] "As God speaks His Word he not only estab-

---

69. On the role of sin in dogmatic anthropology see *CD*, III/2, pp. 26-48.

70. See *CD*, III/2, pp. 197-98, 319, 347, 402-3, 555.

71. More will be said about the ways in which Christian anthropology can provide guidance for the human sciences in their struggle to determine what criteria may determine human "normality." See chapter six below.

72. See Brunner and Barth, *Natural Theology.* For some good synopses of the Barth-Brunner debate over natural theology and the "point of contact," see Stanley G. Lott, "The Significance of Man in the Theology of Karl Barth" (Ph.D. dissertation, New Orleans Baptist Theological Seminary, 1968) pp. 81-111; also Dale N. Snyder, *Karl Barth's Struggle with Anthropocentric Theology* (The Hague: Wattez, 1966) pp. 19-24, 138-39.

73. See *CD*, I/1, p. 244.

lishes the fact but reveals the truth of His relationship to this, the human creature . . . this is the distinction which makes him the object of theological anthropology."[74] Theology in general is given the task of presenting the relationship between God and humanity "in light of the biblical witness to its history as a whole," whereas theological *anthropology* in particular "confines its enquiry to the human creatureliness presupposed in this relationship and made known by it, i.e., by its revelation and biblical attestation." Christian anthropology therefore "asks what kind of a being it is which stands in this relationship with God. Its attention is wholly concentrated on the relationship."[75]

According to Barth, there is no point in trying to go around the divine-human relationship to find some faculty that is prior to it, because this would mean that we must attempt to find a faculty that is present regardless of one's relation, or absence of relation, to God. Barth admits that there must be a point of contact between God and humanity, otherwise there could be no such thing as revelation. Nevertheless, this does not mean that the so-called point of contact is found within the human faculties; Barth concludes that the point of contact is something provided in the revelation itself.[76] This sets the stage for Barth's discussion of the image of God in humanity *(imago Dei).*

Barth brings the subject of the *imago Dei* to a point when he interprets it in terms of the humanity of Christ. Barth states that the simplest thesis of theological anthropology is "that every man as such is the fellow-man of Jesus."[77] Therefore, the *imago Dei,* and the point of contact between God and humanity, which other theologians hold to be inherent in human nature, is seen by Barth to reside in an ontological relationship with the one who is both the Son of Man and the Son of God.[78] The *imago Dei* is sharpened to its finest point when Barth equates the image of God with the humanity of Christ himself: "The humanity of Jesus is not merely the repetition and reflection of His divinity, or of God's controlling will; it is the repetition and reflection of God Himself, no more and no less. It is the image of God, the *imago Dei.*"[79] The image of God interpreted in terms of the humanity of Christ is no static thing, but a reflection of a dynamic relationship of the triune God. The *imago Dei* is divine love as it is reflected in the human creature.[80]

74. *CD,* III/2, p. 19.
75. Ibid.
76. See *CD,* I/1, p. 29.
77. *CD,* III/2, p. 134.
78. Ibid.
79. *CD,* III/2, p. 219.
80. See *CD,* III/2, pp. 218-19. This will be further developed below in this chapter in the section "Encounter and Trinity."

These methodological considerations have important ramifications for this study, because they bring to light the ways in which theology and social sciences can best engage in fruitful dialogue. When I compare Barth's anthropology with the findings of modern object relations psychology, I am not arguing that the findings of the latter can provide the basis for us to discuss the image of God and human sin, or any other theological dogma. I shall argue, rather, that on the basis of the more dynamic anthropology of Barth, we should expect to find analogies between the anthropology which is revealed and that which is derived through careful study of the human being. In other words, we should expect to find that relations are essential to one's humanity both on the theological and on the scientific level. This, I shall argue, is precisely what we find when we compare Barth and object relations psychology.

Relationship as "History"

In order to further clarify what I mean when I describe Barth's anthropology as "dynamic," I present a study of Barth's usage of the term "history."

Barth distinguishes his anthropology by carefully defining what he means by "history." Barth gives the important term "history" *(Geschichte)* a technical meaning peculiar to his own theology. A history involves encounter: a relationship of one with an other. A history should therefore be distinguished from a self-contained movement or action. Barth contrasts a history with a "state." A state cannot be a history, even if the state in question might move or change, because a state is self-contained. What makes the state a state, as opposed to a history, is that it lacks the crucial dimension of interpersonal encounter. Barth explains:

> In contrast to the concept of history *(Geschichte)* is that of a state *(Zustands)*. There are states that are very much in movement, developing through many changes and varied modes of behaviour. The conception of a stiff and motionless uniformity need not be linked with that of a state. But the idea of a state does involve the idea of something completely insulated within the state in question, the idea of a limitation of its possibilities and therefore of its possible changes and modes of behaviour. It is never capable of more than these particular movements. Even the concept of the most mobile state is not therefore equivalent to that of history.[81]

81. *CD*, III/2, pp. 157-58. In chapter six below I show that there are a number of significant parallels between Barth's concept of encounter as a "history" and object relations psychology as it describes the history of the individual's psychological development.

119

In order to clarify his technical usage of the term "history," Barth explains that a plant can have no history, as such. It may grow, move, take in nourishment, and eventually die. But a plant has no history because it always functions within the fixed circles of change that are characteristic of its own state of existence. On the other hand, a history is introduced when something happens to a being at the deepest level that induces it to act outside the usual circles of its fixed biological behavior. Therefore, a history does not describe what happens when an entity makes changes intrinsic to its own nature, but only when some other being impinges on an individual, eliciting a free response. Barth reasons: "The history of a being begins, continues and is completed when something other than itself and transcending its own nature encounters it, approaches it and determines its being in the nature proper to it, so that it is compelled and enabled to transcend itself in response and in relation to this new factor."[82]

A "history" therefore occurs when someone breaks outside the circle of one's usual behavior; but since this is impossible for any being on its own, a being can transcend its own movement only as it is encountered by an other, engaging in a reciprocal relationship in which there is mutual change at the deepest level of being. Any such historical being, therefore, does not simply *have* a history, but *is* a history, and the particular qualities and attributes of its nature constitute only the manner of its historical being. Where then do we find such a history? Clearly, a history such as Barth defines it cannot apply to events that occur between mere physical objects. Inanimate objects are capable of effecting external changes only on one another, such as changes in direction and velocity due to forces like chemical, gravitational, or atomic reactions, and so forth. Physical events, regardless of how much motion may be involved, do not encompass a "history" as Barth defines it. History for Barth is not just action; it necessarily includes interaction, and the interaction must be between free and living subjects.

We have shown that an organic movement of plant life and the like fail to deserve the designation of a "history" in the theological sense; for Barth this exclusion would also apply to animal life. What about normal human intercourse? Are mundane human interactions describable as a history? Buber and other existential philosophers would argue that most people's interactions are a history. Barth disagrees. Normal human encounters rarely break through the closed circle of human subjectivity. Barth expands his concept of a history to encompass the whole field of interpersonal encounter between God and humanity; he concludes that we find authentic

82. *CD*, III/2, p. 158.

"history" only in the man Jesus. Only there do we find a dynamic movement of the Creator to the creature, and a response from the creature to the Creator. In other words, apart from the man Jesus, we would find only a human race that is locked up within its own selfish and more or less determined existence: the human race would be in an unchangeable state. We would have no hope of changing at the deepest level of our being. On the other hand, Jesus' existence cannot be described by any state, because his life is not one of simply being self-moved or self-directed. The history of the man Jesus is God revealed to humanity as a man. As such, the life of Christ is primal history *(Urgeschichte)*; other human beings are in relation to God only as they are in relation to him, because in him they encounter both creature and Creator, both elected man and electing God.[83] To say that Jesus enables human history is to say that Jesus enables the encounter between God and humanity.

Perhaps we can now glimpse the degree to which Barth's anthropology differs from that of Pannenberg and Schleiermacher (both of the latter under the perceptible influence of Hegel). Barth's careful description of the history of an individual draws an important line of demarcation between himself and others who hold to an organic anthropology.[84] The organic view holds that the unfolding of an inherent characteristic within human beings best describes human nature and destiny. Generally, organic models of the person have an advantage over mechanistic ones in that they tend to recognize the importance of the systems to which individuals have a functional relation. But Barth moves even further toward a truly dynamic interpretation of the person: in his "historical" understanding of the human being Barth differentiates a still higher level of being, contending that neither an insulated self-movement nor an organic relation to a larger whole can disclose the character of a being who is truly human. Unless one holds to an extreme form of pantheism, it would seem Barth is on safe ground to assert that a plant has no history. Barth expands this concept of a history to universal proportions when he insists that apart from the incarnation, apart from the union of God and humanity in Christ, the human race would be in much the same condition as the plant; apart from Christ, the human being is consigned to fulfill the particular qualities that are inherent within its own self-contained nature. A plant has the capacity for living according to its design, but even under the best of circumstances it cannot become any-

---

83. *CD,* III/2, pp. 160-61; cf. II/2, pp. 94ff.

84. I use the term "organic" in its broadest sense here and not just in the limited sense of applying to the processes of biology described from an evolutionary perspective.

thing other than what it is determined to become; it has no capacity for response. Humans are unique in the respect that we can respond to God's issue of grace. As we peek inside the meaning of Barth's usage of the word "history," we begin to get a glimpse of why he is considered the theologian of freedom.[85]

According to Barth each person's history is tied up with primal history in the being of the man Jesus. In his existence as both God and man we see the possibility of encounter between God and humanity. His primal history enables all other humans to have, more accurately to "become," a history. Apart from this history, human affairs, while changing on the surface, remain essentially a steady state.

It is interesting to note the extent to which Barth develops his anthropology along similar lines to Kant in his first two Critiques. Like Kant, Barth agrees that to allow the mere phenomena to determine the "real" nature of human beings would be unthinkable. Christian anthropology is not founded on the study of human phenomena in order to determine what human nature is. This is not to deny that human beings are creatures within the phenomenal world. Human beings are objects in the real physical world as surely as we are subjects. Yet human beings are more than objects; we are thinking and acting subjects. Barth thinks that Kant was going in the right direction to prefer the practical over the theoretical definition of the person.[86] Barth argues that the naturalist anthropologies that hold uncritically to Darwinian or other materialist dogma always end up pointing beyond themselves. Naturalism points beyond itself because in the very act of studying ourselves as human beings "scientifically," we cannot avoid the insight that we are simultaneously thinking, willing, and acting beings who have attained a degree of self-transcendence.[87] We can see ourselves as objects for study, as animals with certain characteristics who stand alongside the other creatures of the animal kingdom. However, Barth raises the following objection to naturalism with an almost casual confidence: "We are constantly aware of ourselves as other than what is perceptible to our senses . . . this different approach which has to be considered can be only that of our practical reason, of ethics."[88] This much of the Kantian philosophy is allowed to stand: to build an anthropology on the phenomena alone would be to construct an anthropology on the basis of appearances and not the human reality. In addition to being physical creatures,

85. See Clifford E. Green, *Karl Barth: Theologian of Freedom* (San Francisco: Harper-Collins, 1989).

86. See *CD*, III/2, pp. 92-94.

87. See *CD*, III/2, p. 92.

88. *CD*, III/2, p. 91.

humans are thinking, willing, and valuing creatures; thus far, Kant was right.[89]

Yet, in Barth's view, the Kantians did not go far enough: "It is certainly good to have advanced from the narrowness of naturalism to the breadth of the ethical approach. But it is not so good that we may think that we have attained to real man, to his uniqueness in creation."[90] Barth does not accept the Kantian position that the pathway to the real person can be found where the universal truths of practical reason call us to act according to duty. Barth's "real man" is not found where the categorical imperative beckons. The "real man" is found rather in the very specific person of Jesus Christ, who is fully human but not merely human.[91] Theologians who followed Kant did not traverse far enough; they may have advanced from the theoretical to the practical, but they have not yet reached the domain of Christian anthropology. Christian anthropology cannot be grounded in the abstract or universal call of the law, but on the personal call of the man Jesus. It is only as human beings are in relation to Christ that the human image can be restored from its tarnished condition to its original luster.[92] There is, of course, a human phenomenon. There is also an ethical urgency to the gospel: a command that issues from the person and work of Christ. But neither provides a sufficient understanding of what it means to be truly human; neither the human phenomenon nor the command of a precept that issues from human reason can penetrate to the "real man." The "real man" is brought into being only by the transcendent call of God — a call that seeks to engage the whole person in a life-shaping encounter with God in Christ. This is what Barth means by a "history."

Has Barth merely created some clever technical terms here in attempting to incline things favorably toward his own view? Has he redefined the term "history" so as to distort its original meaning beyond recognition? Is he being creative or merely equivocating when he uses the term "history" to describe the divine-human encounter as it is effected through Christ? Or has he revealed something profound about human ontology? I hope to show that the

---

89. It was, of course, most of Western philosophy from Plato and Aristotle onward, and not just Kant, that argued that in addition to being physical beings we are rational and moral beings. Cf. Emil Brunner, *Man in Revolt*, tr. O. Wyon (London: Lutterworth, 1947), esp. pp. 43ff.

90. *CD*, III/2, p. 94.

91. Barth is careful to maintain the uniqueness of Christ even while he develops his anthropology Christologically. Cf. *CD*, III/2, p. 49.

92. Barth lists six criteria by which a true anthropology may be determined. True anthropology has to do with God and human beings, with God's action toward them, with the glory of God in their existence, with God's lordship over them, with their action in relation to God, and with the service of God that humans must accept in this relation. See *CD*, III/2, p. 95.

last is the case. But for now we have established that he has offered the reader a real alternative to the organic concept of humanity, which has been so prevalent in historical sciences after Hegel, and biological science after Darwin. Barth plainly rejects the possibility that human nature could be described by a *state* of development that is defined by its own self-contained existence.[93] The real nature of human beings is not discoverable by analyzing any human phenomena, or even by examining the ethical dimension of human actions. Our real humanity surfaces only where one is able to hear the higher calling of God in the humanity of Christ. Our real humanity is visible only when our brokenness and rebellion are exposed by the obedient humanity of Christ.

"Real Man" and Sinful Humanity

Barth has brought to our attention the problem that occurs when we attempt to understand the human being by means of self-assessment. We see ourselves, but how do we know when we perceive our *real* self? We can study various human phenomena and sift through the data, but how do we know what is normative? Can the social scientist find that which is normative by casting the research net in ever-wider circles, seeking some golden mean through statistical analyses of vast numbers of people? It may be helpful to know "averages," but in the case of human beings, "average" cannot always be equated with "normal."

Barth argues that the problem of self-understanding surfaces with the fact that "real man" has fallen into brokenness and sin. Sin has distorted the human character to such an extent that we humans cannot clearly perceive ourselves. Sin veils "real man" from himself. Sin bars us from finding ourselves by looking within. Sin therefore presents a major problem for our knowledge of ourselves. Yet how can we even know that such a problem exists? For sin even blinds us to the reality of our sin.[94]

A solution comes only when we grasp that the grace of God cancels human sin. At this point Barth manages to agree with at least one thought of Schleiermacher: it is only in the light of grace that sin can be illumined.[95] The

93. This does not mean that Barth rejects the biological concept of evolution. It does seem, however, that his thought bears more semblance to those in the evolutionary debate who emphasize the environment as an essential component of the process of development, as opposed to those who think that the genetic coding of the particular organism itself is the source of evolutionary development.

94. See *CD,* III/2, p. 33. Cf. Emil Brunner, *Revelation and Reason,* tr. O. Wyon (Philadelphia: Westminster, 1956) p. 383.

95. *CD,* III/2, pp. 35ff.

darkness of human sin is brought to light by divine grace; grace is needed in order to reveal the even greater truth that "the true nature behind our corrupted nature, is not concealed but revealed in the person of Jesus, and in His nature we recognise our own, and that of every man."[96] In the man Jesus, human nature is not concealed, "but revealed in its original and basic form."[97] Barth's "real sinner" is therefore determined by the humanity of Jesus. In a pithy statement Barth sets forth his anthropological starting point:

> The ontological determination of humanity is grounded in the fact that one man among all others is the man Jesus. So long as we select any other starting point for our study, we shall reach only the phenomena of the human. We are condemned to abstractions so long as our attention is riveted as it were on other men, or rather on man in general, as if we could learn about real man from a study of man in general, and in abstraction from the fact that the one man among all others is the man Jesus. In this case we miss the one Archimedean point given us beyond humanity, and therefore the one possibility of discovering the ontological determination of man. Theological anthropology has no choice in this matter. It is not yet or no longer theological anthropology if it tries to pose and answer the question of the true being of man from any other angle.[98]

Jesus has been and is "true man," and this unalterably affects our humanity.[99] He is our neighbor and we cannot break free from him. Since every human being is the "fellow-man" of Jesus, Christology is at the core of Christian anthropology. The ability to penetrate the veil of human brokenness and sin is granted only as we see a human being in relation to Christ. Barth declares: "Basically and comprehensively, therefore, to be a man is to be with God. Godlessness is not, therefore, a possibility, but an ontological impossibility for man."[100] By this Barth does not mean that godless people do not exist; sin surely exists and exerts a powerful influence over human affairs. Barth means that sin is a mode of being "contrary to our humanity."[101]

---

96. *CD*, III/2, p. 43.
97. *CD*, III/2, p. 52.
98. *CD*, III/2, p. 132.
99. *CD*, III/2, p. 133.
100. *CD*, III/2, p. 135.
101. *CD*, III/2, p. 136. There is a sense, of course, in which Barth's anthropology, based on Christ, sets him up as an "ideal" of humanity. Nevertheless, we should not overlook the importance of Barth's insistence that this "ideal man" is also "real man" and one who had historical existence in a specific time and space, and whose history continues to influence human history (both in the common sense, and in the sense in which Barth reinterprets "history") through the presence of his Spirit.

As usual, Barth does not want to draw on generalizations in his formulations about humanity. Our real humanity is not related to God in a general and unspecified relationship. Neither does our real humanity come to us by way of our ancestral endowment from Adam.[102] It is rather the concrete and specific relation between God and humanity through Christ that is the foundation of Christian anthropology. "Real man" is with God because he is with Jesus. Barth does not allow this "being-with-God" to rest on human initiative, but on God's initiative. By becoming a human, God expresses his solidarity with all creatures and all of creation; but God especially identifies with fallen humanity because he has come into the human sphere himself. This means that God initiates the relation between himself and humanity, a relation that is often expressed by the reformers in the doctrine of election.[103]

Before discussing Barth's doctrine of election, I should mention that Barth's emphasis on the need to be "with God" in order to be truly human bears certain analogies to some aspects of object relations psychology. Certain branches of object relations that root their theories in the research of ethologists such as Konrad Lorenz have discovered that individual human existence is invariably shaped by the need to be "with another." For example, Bowlby's studies propose that the need to be is necessarily linked with the need to be in close proximity with an other — normally the infant's mother. The proximity to a primary or original object has psychological significance because it builds the foundation for later social behavior.[104] The analogy should not be stretched too far, because Barth is careful to mention that dogmatic theology is most concerned to find whatever is unique to the human being, as opposed to the things that we hold in common with the other animals.[105] Nevertheless, attachment behavior of both humans and animals points out a basic truth: to "be" and to "be with" are inseparable.

---

102. See *Christ and Adam: Man and Humanity in Romans 5*, tr. T. A. Smail (Edinburgh; London: Oliver and Boyd, 1963) p. 43: "Much in true human nature is unrelated to 'religion,' but nothing in true human nature is unrelated to the Christian faith. That means that we can understand true human nature only in the light of the Christian gospel that we believe. For Christ stands above and is first, and Adam stands below and is second. So it is Christ that reveals the true nature of man. Man's nature in Adam is not, as is usually assumed, his true and original nature; it is only truly human at all in so far as it reflects and corresponds to essential human nature as it is found in Christ."

103. See *CD*, II/2, pp. 3-506, for Barth's treatment of the doctrine of election.

104. See, e.g., John Bowlby, *Attachment* (New York: Basic Books, 1969), esp. pp. 177-209.

105. *CD*, III/2, pp. 80-81.

"Real Man" with God: The Doctrine of Election

As we might expect, Barth expands the traditional doctrine of election by interpreting it in terms of Christology.[106] Barth seems less concerned with the election of individuals than with this simple affirmation: Jesus is the man elected by God. A human being does not elect him- or herself, but is elected by God. Therefore, predestination "is the basis of the fact that the Creator and creature, God and man, are united at this point and the kingdom of God comes."[107] This happens in the coming of Christ, who reveals the will of God to his creatures. What is God's will? Barth continues: "that all men and all creatures should be delivered from evil, i.e., from that which God the Creator has rejected, and preserved from its threat and power."[108]

We might say that Barth holds to the reality of human sin by keeping it in dynamic and necessary tension with "real man."[109] That is, Barth acknowledges the reality of evil and the fallenness of humanity; on the other hand he does not want to define the ontology of human beings merely by the generally observable phenomena of human actions. An adequate understanding of human sinfulness is not something that we can achieve merely by reading the morning paper, however bad the news may be. Sin is, rather, a revealed truth.

Until revealed, sin has a blinding effect. It locks us into an inability to see ourselves for who we truly are. We thus need help from an external source, from an Other, an Object (who in this case is living Subject), to reveal the extent of our brokenness. As human creatures we cannot rescue ourselves from our ontological impossibility. But the Creator can, and has decided to, rescue us from nonbeing. This decision is made in the election of the one man, Jesus; in him God's decision to deliver us from evil is effected. Barth reminds us time and again that our real humanity lies in our "being with God":

> We spoke of the man whose being is a being with God. Yet it is only as we fill out this concept with that of the divine election of grace that we reach solid ground. For man cannot now appeal to his defencelessness, to the natural weakness of all being in face of the overwhelming power of nonbeing. He cannot bewail and justify himself as a sinner on the ground that he is inevitably delivered up to the forces of evil.[110]

---

106. Cf. *CD*, II/2, p. 145. Jesus Christ is both electing God and elected man.

107. *CD*, III/2, p. 143.

108. Ibid.

109. Of course, this is not a sort of Hegelian dialectic that synthesizes evil as if it were a mere stepping stone for historical process.

110. *CD*, III/2, p. 146.

Why, according to Barth, is the human race now without excuse? Because we have been elected with this man, Jesus. As the fellow elect of Jesus, humankind is destined to be the victor over nonbeing.[111] It is incumbent upon us, therefore, to conform to our restored humanity in Christ.

Our humanity consists of our being summoned to a dialogue, in our "listening to the Word of God."[112] The man Jesus is the sum of the divine address, the Word of God to the cosmos. Jesus not only *speaks* the Word of God, he *is* the Word. Human beings are thus "those who are summoned by this Word."[113] Is there anything prior to this Word? Barth answers: "The question of anything preceding our being apart from the divine summons can arise only if we try to explain ourselves by ourselves instead of by our concrete confrontation with God."[114] Barth continues: "Perhaps the fundamental mistake in all erroneous thinking of man about himself is that he tries to equate himself with God and therefore to proceed on the assumption that he can regard himself as the presupposition of his own being. The presupposition of man is God in His Word."[115] In denying that the "real man" could exist outside election in Christ, Barth concludes: "He is a man as he is summoned, and his endowment merely follows as part of the summons. . . . God in His Word is the basis of this too, and on the foundation thus laid his being as man is a being summoned."[116]

From this brief treatment of Barth's understanding of the doctrine of election, we see that the human distinctive lies not in the fact that we want to be with God — in spite of our great need to do so — but first in the fact that God wants to be with us. Scripture is full of metaphors that capture the importance of this primary relationship of God seeking out his people. As a Re-

---

111. This does not necessarily imply universalism, the *apokatastaseōs pantōn* (Acts 3:21), as some have accused Barth of teaching. Rather it shows how Barth will develop his teaching on human freedom. The human being is not a creature who falls into the category of either elect or nonelect, as if God had made some predetermined choice based on the limited application of the covenant of grace. Rather, God has elected the entire human race in the election of Jesus. Just as the need for help is universal, the offer of help in Jesus Christ is one of universal election. Election, thus understood, entails real freedom and the necessity of a real choice on the human side to respond to God's election in Christ. This goes a long ways toward improving the determinism inherent in so much Calvinism. See, e.g., F. Klooster, *The Significance of Barth's Theology* (Grand Rapids: Baker, 1961) pp. 41ff. Cf. Barth, *CD*, II/2, pp. 149ff.; *CD*, IV/3, pp. 473-78.

112. *CD*, III/2, p. 147.

113. *CD*, III/2, p. 150.

114. *CD*, III/2, p. 151.

115. Ibid.

116. *CD*, III/2, p. 152.

117. See Isa. 8:8-10; Matt. 1:23: *meth' hēmōn ho theos*. Cf. *CD*, IV/1, pp. 3-21.

formed theologian, Barth imbues his reader with this truth about election: the human capacity to reach out to God is not nearly as important as God's capacity to reach out to us.[117]

Human Destiny as the Covenant Partner of God

We have seen how Barth has argued that "real man" *(der wirkliche Mensch)* is a person in relationship to God. Next, Barth develops the content of that relationship by describing "real man" as the one who lives with God as his covenant partner: "God has created human beings for Himself, and so 'real man' is for God and not the reverse. He is the covenant-partner of God. He is determined by God for life with God."[118] But why is the partnership between humanity and God so frequently obscured? And what are the real effects of sin on this relationship?

Barth ponders the truth of the matter that so many people stubbornly deny their partnership with God. He admits: "Real man can deny and obscure his reality."[119] This fact, however, cannot be explained; it can only be described as the paradoxical, yet very powerful, reality of sin. Barth calls the power of evil the "dreadful possibility," "impossible possibility," or at other times the "ontological impossibility."[120] Human evil then is the unfathomable denial of relation to God; and whoever denies relation to God denies their real humanity. Nevertheless, the reality of God's choice to override human sin and establish a covenant with the human race means that God determines something about the human race that remains constant.

Election and Christology

In Barth's view, the free sovereignty of God and his right to elect the human race overcome the paradox of human evil. Like Calvin, Barth leans heavily on the doctrine of God's electing activity, an election that begins in the divine self-disclosure and results in the downward motion of grace. But unlike Calvin, Barth does not agree with a "double election": one for the elect in Christ,

118. *CD*, III/2, p. 203.

119. *CD*, III/2, p. 205.

120. Ibid.; see also Barth, *CD*, IV/3, pp. 178ff., where Barth admits that evil is best described as an irrational paradox, and these terms are but meager attempts to describe the paradox.

121. See *CD*, II/2, pp. 104-5.

the other for the reprobate. If there is any double election, it is that Jesus is both elect man and electing God.[121] This leads Barth to ask: What is the constant, the thing that corresponds between the human being as determined by God and his own phenomenal humanity? The "correspondence" *(Entsprechung)* must be found Christologically. In one of his more important anthropological affirmations, Barth says: "If the divinity of the man Jesus is to be described comprehensively in the statement that He is man for God, His humanity can and must be described no less succinctly in the proposition that He is man for man, for other men, His fellows."[122]

The Human Being as a Being in Encounter with Others

Jesus the Man for Others

In the humanity of Jesus, in his being as a man for others, Barth finds the basis of human encounter. Jesus was not first for himself, or for a cause or ideal; Jesus was first and foremost a man for others. Barth says, "What interests Him and does so exclusively, is man, other men as such, who need Him and are referred to Him for help and deliverance."[123] In the life of Jesus we see the living embodiment of a man who is for others. Jesus is thus not able to be seen in isolation, apart from others. He is, rather, one who encounters his brothers and sisters. He lives "to them and with them and for them. He is sent and ordained by God to be their Deliverer. Nothing else? No, really nothing else."[124] Jesus is ontologically related to the human race. By this Barth of course means that Jesus was fully human. But the humanity of Jesus could be no other than a man for others. He could not be indifferent and still be Jesus. His relation to others is not accidental, but essential, because it flows from the eternal love of the Son for the Father.[125] Jesus is not able to look on human suffering and sin with stoical indifference; the afflictions of others affect him in his innermost being.[126] Jesus helps others not from without, or even beside, but from within, taking their place, and creating something new from nothing. Jesus' being is both from and to his fellow humans:

121. *CD*, III/2, p. 208.

122. *CD*, III/2, p. 208.

123. Ibid.

124. *CD*, II/2, p. 209. Barth cites Luke 2:11; Dan. 7; Phil. 2:6-7; 2 Cor. 8:9; Heb. 12:2; 2:14, 17-18; 4:15, as evidence that Jesus is a deliverer for humans.

125. *CD*, III/2, p. 210.

126. See Barth's word study on *splangnizesthai* in *CD*, III/2, p. 211.

127. *CD*, III/2, p. 216. An interesting objection to Barth's emphasis on the dynamic and

If we see Him alone, we do not see Him at all. If we see Him, we see with and around Him in ever-widening circles His disciples, the people, His enemies and the countless millions who have not yet heard His name. We see Him as theirs, determined by them and for them, belonging to each and every one of them. It is thus that He is Master, Messiah, King and Lord. "Selfless" is hardly the word to describe this humanity. Jesus is not "selfless." For in this way He is supremely Himself. The theme of the New Testament witness is a kind of incomparable picture of human life and character. What emerges in it is a supreme I wholly determined by and to the Thou. With this twofold definition Jesus is human.[127]

Therefore, Jesus in his divinity is from and for God, and Jesus in his humanity is from and to his fellow "man" *(der Mensch)*.[128] These are not at odds with one another but closely correspond. There is similarity between the divine and human in Jesus; hence the I of Jesus is determined by the Thou of God the Father, but also the Thou of his fellow humans. Jesus' being for God and being for his "fellow man" are treated by Barth in light of the Chalcedonian formula regarding the two natures of Christ.[129]

---

interpersonal character of human personhood is that he overlooked the need for an individual to remain distinct from the group — as well as to be connected to it. On the level of everyday life, Barth was strongly individual, but in his theology might he tend to overemphasize human interconnectedness at the expense of individuality, especially in light of Jesus' frequent withdrawal from the masses? See Matt. 8:18; Mark 1:35-45. This objection is worth considering; and yet it could be argued, especially from the passages in the Gospel of Mark that refer to the supposed "messianic secret," that when Jesus withdrew from the masses he was actually seeking a deeper communion with, and guidance from, the Father. He was not necessarily seeking isolation for its own sake. But, conceptually, neither should the individual be pitted against the group, as though they were exclusive. A genuine encounter is primarily defined by its capacity to enhance individual identity while at the same moment leading to communion, one with the other.

128. Rather than the term "man" *(der Mensch)*, Barth sometimes uses the more inclusive term "cosmos" *(der Kosmos)* to refer to humanity and its historical setting. Jesus does not redeem humanity, understood abstractly, but humanity in the cosmos. See *CD*, III/2, p. 216.

129. Both the positive formulation of the Christological councils *(vere Deus, vere homo)* and the negative adverbs describing the hypostatic union of the two natures of Christ *(asynchytōs, atreptōs, adiairetōs, achōristōs)* have been employed by Barth to illumine the understanding of "real man." The Chalcedonian formula especially serves as a limit and guideline for Barth's Christological anthropology. Barth's affirmation that "man" is "soul of his body — wholly and simultaneously both, in ineffaceable difference, inseparable unity, and indestructible order," has *mutatis mutandis* an unmistakable Chalcedonian ring to it. Of course, the two natures within the one person of Christ are unique in their hypostatic union, but the relation between soul and body within the human being bears a certain analogous relation to the hypostatic union of the two natures of Christ. See *CD*, III/2, pp. 325, 437; also *CD*, I/2, p. 499,

Jesus is from and to God, and from and to his fellow man; these cannot be separated. Hence love for God and love for neighbor are not "separate but conjoined." But neither does Barth think that love of God and love of neighbor should be confused, as if God were merely some immanent presence in every neighbor. The twofold law of love in Mark 12:29-34 prohibits the separation of the love of God and the love of neighbor, but they are not identical. Barth points out that in Matthew 22:38-39 the command to love God is the first and great commandment, and the love of neighbor is the second. They are thus not to be confused, but neither are they to be separated. Barth insists, "the command to love the neighbour is not merely an appended, subordinate and derivative command. If it is the second, it is also described as like unto the first in Mt. 22:39. A true exposition can only speak of a genuinely twofold, i.e., a distinct but connected sphere and sense of the one love required of man."[130]

The Heart of Trinitarian Anthropology:
Analogia relationis

Here we come to the core of Barth's anthropology. Barth's development of yet another technical term, *analogia relationis,* may one day prove to be his most lasting contribution to modern theology. We must, however, undergo a major paradigm shift with regard to classical conceptions of being in order to appreciate the significance of the analogy of relations.

Just as there is correspondence between the humanity and deity of Christ, there is also correspondence between human love and divine love described by the term that has become one of Barth's key theological concepts, *analogia relationis.* The *analogia relationis* is Barth's alternative to the Thomistic *analogia entis,* which undergirds so much of Catholic theology, and it is related closely to the terms that Barth uses in the earlier volumes of the *Dogmatics: analogia fidei,* taken from the reformers via the Greek text of Romans 12:6, and *analogia gratiae.*

There is a good deal of dispute in contemporary theological circles regarding whether Barth accurately understood Aquinas's usage of the term

---

where in similar fashion Barth describes the divine humanity of the Scriptures as analogous, but not in exact relation, to the divine humanity of Christ. Finally, see *CD,* IV/1, pp. 127ff. Cf. Calvin, *Institutes* II, xiv, 1-2. I say more about the relation of soul and body below, and especially in chapter six.

130. *CD,* III/2, pp. 216-17.

analogia entis.[131] It is beyond the scope of this study to settle this intricate dispute.[132] Since the human ability to predicate meaningfully about the relation between the "real man" of dogmatic anthropology and "scientific man" of modern psychology depends on a correct usage of analogy, however, some comments need to be made. The employment of analogy might provide a key for rightly understanding the relation between theological anthropology and the human sciences.

A consensus is forming that Barth misinterpreted, to some degree at least, Aquinas's usage of *analogia entis.* Yet, even supposing this to be the case, does this necessarily abrogate the importance of Barth's preference for the term *analogia relationis?* I think not. In questioning the *analogia entis,* Barth is attempting to preserve both the "indirectness" and the openness of revelation, to keep God from being the immanent possibility of human reason or religious affections. With the *analogia relationis,* Barth is attempting to preserve the transcendent freedom of God, and the importance of revelation for right knowledge of God. He is attempting to uphold *sola gratia,* to avoid Catholic synergism (with regard to salvation that places a strong emphasis on human works) on the one hand, and liberal immanentism on the other.[133]

But *analogia relationis* also serves a positive function: it represents an attempt to formulate a more dynamic ontology than that represented by *analogia entis.* The term *relationis* refers to a type of being that incorporates the action of a personal agent: a being that is becoming. The *analogia relationis* represents a theological attempt to express the fact that God loves the human race with trinitarian love.[134] Barth points out that John 17 reveals the filial relationship between Father and Son as the foundation for the relationship between the human race and God. Commenting on this chapter in John, Barth observes:

> He who is already glorified by the Father in His relationship to Him is again glorified in them, in His relationship to men. Thus the divine original creates for itself a copy in the creaturely world. The Father and the Son are reflected in the man Jesus. There could be no plainer reference to

131. See Battista Mondin, *The Principle of Analogy in Protestant and Catholic Theology* (The Hague: Martinus Nijhoff, 1963), esp. pp. 147ff.

132. See *CD,* I/1, pp. 41-42. Barth perhaps leaned too heavily on the interpretations of the Polish Catholic scholar Erich Przywara in order to understand the *analogia entis.* Barth is not attempting to drive a wedge between grace and nature; cf. I/1, pp. 134, 172-73.

133. See *CD,* I/2, pp. 144-45.

134. *CD,* III/2, p. 220.

the *analogia relationis* and therefore the *imago Dei* in the most central, i.e., the Christological sense of the term.[135]

In rejecting the *analogia entis* and offering instead the *analogia relationis,* Barth has pushed beyond substantival predication, with regard to both God and human beings. Concerning Barth's shift in terminology, Colin Gunton concludes that it is thus "impossible to conceive God in the old substantial categories."[136]

The epistemological questions raised by Barth's rejection of the *analogia entis* are significant.[137] It is therefore important to pause to consider the significance of the *analogia relationis* before going further.

Gunton comments that few theologians have fully appreciated the radical shift in ontology that Barth advocates, except for Eberhard Jüngel. According to Jüngel, Barth's understanding of revelation has made possible a radically different conception of God's independent reality *(Selbständigkeit),* in which God is seen as an *essentially* relational being, in which the being of God *for us* is not something foreign to God's essence but is grounded in his very character. God is thus a "being in becoming": Father, Son, and Holy Spirit.[138]

A question might be raised here concerning the relation between being and action: Does being follow action *(Esse sequitur operari),* or action follow being *(Operari sequitur esse)?* Any adequate ontology must entail both. Perhaps because he is reacting so strongly against Aristotelian substantivalism, Barth emphasizes the former based on the action of God in history.[139] The latter position Barth accuses of being a metaphysical abstraction.[140] Likewise, for Barth, human existence consists in willing and acting. Barth argues that

135. *CD,* III/2, p. 221.

136. *Becoming and Being,* p. 143. Cf. Plato *Phaedo* 78d.

137. It is not surprising, therefore, that in view of this momentous shift that Barth advocates, a theologian who agreed with Barth as much as Brunner would still quarrel with Barth at this particular point regarding the "point of contact." As to whether Barth correctly understood the Thomistic usage of *analogia entis,* a good deal of controversy has arisen. Even if Barth has misunderstood the *analogia entis,* as von Balthasar and others argue, it does not negate the need to move beyond it. See Hans Urs von Balthasar, *The Theology of Karl Barth,* tr. John Drury (New York: Holt, Rinehart, and Winston, 1971) p. 245.

138. Jüngel, *Gottes Sein ist im Werden (The Doctrine of the Trinity: God's Being Is in Becoming* [Grand Rapids: Eerdmans, 1976] pp. 63-64).

139. R. W. Jenson comments that for Barth, God is "the eminently historical being" (*Alpha and Omega: A Study in the Theology of Karl Barth* [New York: Nelson, 1963] p. 76). As we shall see, the same thing will be the case with Barth's anthropology.

140. *CD,* II/1, pp. 83-84.

the human being "exists in that he acts."[141] "Real man" is "active, engaged in movement." Human freedom cannot be explained by the mere *potential* to act, but is constituted only in the acting itself:[142]

> We recall the point that it is not merely a question of man's static but of his active responsibility before God. If his being in this responsibility has the character of freedom, then freedom too means the actualisation of this responsibility — the event of his knowledge of God, his obedience to Him and his asking after Him. The word "freedom" might easily be misunderstood in this connexion, since as an abstract noun it can suggest a passive condition. But it must not be taken in this way. Man is, as he knows God; he is as he decides for God; he is as he asks after God and moves to His judgment.[143]

One thing becomes apparent in our study of Barth's usage of analogy: he does not deny the usefulness of analogy. He merely denies an analogy of "being" that assumes an ontic connection between God and humanity that may serve as a noetic bridge for us to reach out to God apart from his prior reaching out to us.[144]

Objections have been raised by theologians of various persuasions who believe that Barth (and others of the Reformed tradition who emphasize "relation") has overemphasized the importance of *relations* and failed to focus enough on the importance of *being*. It is as if the metaphor of a bridge applied here, with Barth overemphasizing the bridge to the exclusion of the river banks at both ends. Let us suppose that the bridge represents the relation between two things that find themselves linked together. In any relation there must be at least two separate entities or things, in order for the relation to occur. For example, while the bridge spans the distance between two bod-

---

141. *CD*, I/2, p. 793.

142. Nevertheless, if there is to be free action, there must be a *capacity* for acting. According to Arnold Come, the "covenant capacity" is seen as the seat of freedom in Barth's anthropology (*An Introduction to Barth's Dogmatics for Preachers* [Philadelphia: Westminster, 1963] p. 153). Cf. *CD*, III/2, pp. 399-400. But we must be careful not to turn the capacity into a faculty.

143. *CD*, III/2, p. 195.

144. For *analogia fidei* see *CD*, I/1, pp. 12, 243; I/2, p. 471; II/1, pp. 82-83; II/2, pp. 530-31; for *analogia relationis* see III/2, pp. 220-21, 323-24. Torrance, in *Karl Barth*, pp. 142-56, refers to yet another term that Barth employs: *analogia gratiae*. The *analogia gratiae* is probably best understood as that which serves as the foundation for the *analogia fidei*; both terms have roughly the same meaning and refer to the more fundamental principle of *sola fides*. It is important to note that the analogies of relations and being are both analogies that apply to modes of being, whereas the analogies of grace and faith refer to modes of predication. See also Jüngel, *Karl Barth*, p. 43.

ies of land, it could not stand were it not for the preexisting reality of the two land masses that support its towers. Has Barth focused on the relation itself to such an extent that he describes the bridge apart from the terra firma at both ends?[145] Would he have done better to discuss the particular entities themselves before describing the nature of the relations that hold between them?

Once again, the bridge metaphor points out that the shift in perspective, which Barth is asking his reader to make, has not been made. While the reality of the land masses at either end of a bridge cannot be denied, the bridge metaphor is too crude to explain the complexity of real relations, especially interpersonal relations. It is a mistake to assume that being and "being-in-relation" can be separated, that entities first exist, then connect via a third entity. For the relation itself determines to a great extent the nature of the entities themselves. In other words, it is pointless to ask whether entities precede relations or relations precede entities. There cannot be one without the other. They exist simultaneously, much in the way that subatomic particles exist apart from human observation, yet when observed bear the impact of observation.

However, it would distort Barth's own teaching on this matter if we allow the issue of being and becoming to be dealt with abstractly. Barth did not develop his ontology or anthropology theoretically, but in accordance with the revealed nature of God. Barth's reflections on the nature of being and becoming derive from his understanding of the Trinity. God's being *is* in his becoming; to isolate God's eternal being from his temporal becoming in revelation and incarnation would destroy the only proper framework for understanding the triune God. As T. F. Torrance puts it, the relevance of Barth's theology is found primarily in his doctrine of God, in which "he brought together the Patristic emphasis upon the Being of God in his Acts and the Reformation emphasis upon the Acts of God in his Being, thus combining as never before the ontic and dynamic aspects of knowledge of God."[146]

Has Barth hemmed himself in by saying that the order of God's being dictates the order of human knowing? In insisting on both the ontic and noetic priority of divine freedom in grace, has Barth lapsed into fideism? Has he sundered theology from its rational ground, and therefore alienated it from knowing of the natural order? If the answer to any of these questions is affirmative, then this would obviously throw into serious question the possibility of finding a connection between Barth's dogmatic anthropology and scientific anthropology.[147]

145. See Berkouwer, *Man: The Image of God,* tr. D. W. Jellema (Grand Rapids: Eerdmans, 1962) pp. 35, 259.

146. Torrance, *Transformation and Convergence,* p. viii.

147. For an extensive bibliography of those who criticize Barth's usage of analogy of relation, see Gunton, *Becoming and Being,* pp. 171-72 n. 17.

The implications of Barth's insights will become clearer as we pursue the relation between being and acting. The human being has his or her being as he or she is in relation to God and others. The need to be in relation presupposes the need to act; to act is implicitly a relational category because one acts toward another. In Barth's thought we cannot comprehend act apart from being, nor being apart from act. This applies both to God and to the human creature. According to Barth, nature is an expression of God's grace, and is therefore ordered according to his sovereign will, both obscuring and revealing his character. Therefore the *analogia relationis* is one way of affirming that at the core of both nature and grace is the person of God who reveals himself in Christ. The *analogia relationis* establishes the relation between nature and grace based on the premise that God's sovereign personal reality is the ground of all reality: it grounds being in personal action, rather than grounding act in the prior condition of being, which has been the case with most of Western philosophy since Plato. This insight allows us to peel Barth's anthropology down to its core.[148] Reality is ultimately personal because it is created and sustained by the triune God, who reveals himself as personal.

In spite of Barth's occasional failure to distinguish clearly between the ontic and noetic dimensions of the *analogia relationis,* it seems safe to conclude that being and knowing do closely correspond. This is why Barth objects to the *analogia entis;* if analogies can be predicated about God based on the notion of like causes producing like effects, then God could be known apart from revelation. This, at least, is Barth's interpretation of Aquinas's employment of analogy. The rejection of *analogia entis* is another way to say that Barth is opposed to natural theology, or to any form of theology that would circumvent grace. But, in addition to a negative reason, Barth finds a positive ground for developing the analogy of relations in the nature of divine love as found in the Trinity and expressed through the love of the Father for the Son, and analogously, in the Son's love for humanity *ad extra,* both in his historical existence in the flesh and after the resurrection in the embracing love of the Spirit.[149]

If we accept the analogy of relations as the truth that nature bears the constant imprint of grace, then we should expect this to have some noetic implications. Should we be surprised, then, at the insight of modern object relations psychology that in the developmental stages of human psychology, personal knowledge, that is, a primary interpersonal relation, precedes knowl-

---

148. Understood in the dynamic sense, of course.

149. Von Balthasar, *Theology of Karl Barth,* p. 247. Even a Catholic theologian like von Balthasar could accept the *analogia relationis* in so far as it means: "The whole order of reason is theologically imbedded in the order of grace."

edge of the natural world and lays the very foundation for subsequent cognition? The social structure of human emotional and intellectual development that is affirmed by object relations psychology and interpreted by Macmurray and others would tend to confirm Barth's insistence on the *analogia relationis*. In other words, to *be* is to be in relation. To be rational, it is therefore necessary to share in a social experience with other rational creatures. Any anthropology that overlooks the fact that human emotional and cognitive development grow out of a shared experience would be inadequate. More will be said about this in the following chapters.

"Being in Encounter": The Identity of "I and Thou"

As we have seen, in Barth's theological anthropology, "what man is, is decided by the primary text, i.e., by the humanity of the man Jesus."[150] Because Jesus is a man for others, the human being who is abstractly considered — apart from coexistence with his or her fellow humans — is not fully human. This means that for authentic humanity, relationship to others is *actual,* not potential or optional. It is in the relationships that the human being is essentially formed. We might say that for Barth the real self is formed only as it finds itself in others.

Barth believes that the negation of the human being as fellow humanity is the individual who exists as "I am."[151] Individualism will lead us astray because it considers humanity *in abstracto,* and the abstraction leads us to entertain fictional views of humanity.[152] The "I am" is a fictional self because it

---

150. *CD,* III/2, p. 226. This indicates a marked shift from Barth's early position, in his *Epistle to the Romans,* which separated the Godness of God, as "Wholly Other," from the humanity of human beings in radical discontinuity. Barth admits that his anthropology in this section of the *Dogmatics* is predicated on the assumption that "Jesus' being for others, implies some likeness with ourselves." But even this likeness does not deny the uniqueness of Jesus. Hence the uniqueness of God is preserved, alongside his likeness to us in the man Jesus. See *CD,* III/2, pp. 222ff.; cf. IV/1, p. 186.

151. See *CD,* III/2, pp. 229-30. This is the term Barth uses to indicate the inherent arrogance of the self that seeks constant self-expansion and ultimately isolates itself from any other.

152. By "abstract" *(abstrakte)* here, Barth apparently opposes an idealized concept of humanity that is the standard by which we gauge ourselves. But more importantly he emphasizes that the person considered abstractly is always a person in isolation from others ("abstrakte, d.h. eine von der Mitexistenz seines Mitmenschen abstrahierte Existenz zugeschrieben wird"), whereas Jesus was a historical individual, whose humanity was always with and for others (*KD,* III/2, p. 270; *CD,* III/2, p. 226). In some sense we see here the influence of Kierkegaard, with his resistance to abstractions. But Barth shifts from Kierkegaard's emphasis on individual existence to the communal existence of humanity, based on the historical life of Jesus.

is a self without relations. It is a self that is only for itself, and not for or toward others. "I am" is not merely a self that *happens* to be alone, but "I am" describes the self that *chooses* to be alone, to remain within the closed radius of a "self-imposed autism." Even in the forming of external relations, the "I am" only projects him- or herself upon others. Interpersonal relations are therefore viewed as incidental.

The *I AM* of God is different from the "I am" of the human subject precisely because Yahweh is not alone; God's being is in constant communion. Such is not the case with human beings. We do not have communion within ourselves. Even though we can have some sense of relation to self, we know this relation only in the context of our relations to others. The individual who claims to be self-sufficient is arrogant and therefore attempting to mock God.[153] Barth illustrates this in a very moving section that exposes Nietzsche's pathetic individualism as the prime example of that which opposes fellow humanity *(Mitmenschlichkeit)*.[154]

"I Am as Thou Art"

The problem of self-conscious individual identity is expressed by Barth with the question: What is meant by "I"? In speaking of "I" the individual makes not only a distinction, but also a connection. "I" does not make sense in isolation, but only in relation to "Thou." Here Barth adopts the technical term "encounter," which was developed by Martin Buber. Barth, however, makes some important modifications of Buber's I and Thou.[155]

---

153. And God will not be mocked. Barth does not offer a proof text; but see Gal. 6:7, which follows after 6:2: "Bear one another's burdens and so fulfill the law of Christ."

154. See *CD*, III/2, pp. 231-42. Barth concludes that Nietzsche was the "most consistent champion and prophet of humanity without the fellow-man" (p. 242).

155. The language of I and Thou is sometimes referred to as "dialogical personalism." In his analysis of dialogical personalism, Pannenberg thinks that Barth is the evangelical theologian closest in thinking to Buber, especially in vol. III/2 of the *Dogmatics*. Pannenberg rightly points out that Barth does not interpret the human I as constituted by the Thou, but makes the combination of I and Thou in its totality point to God, that is, to the trinitarian coexistence of Father and Son. For Barth, the *ad intra* relation serves as the prototype of the human and, remarks Pannenberg, "as far as the provenance of the dialogical understanding of the person in the history of ideas is concerned, he may well be correct" (*Anthropology*, p. 183 n. 73). But Pannenberg criticizes Barth for his concept of the interhuman I and Thou, which he says was adopted uncritically from Buber. And Pannenberg thinks that Buber's position fails to break outside traditional philosophical subjectivism when it posits the "Thou" on the basis of the subjective awareness of "I" (ibid.). Pannenberg is apparently criticizing Barth

In the logic of interpersonal encounter, human dialogue must take place between an I and a Thou. What does Barth mean by "I"? "I" does not make sense in isolation, but only in relation to "Thou": "The declaration 'I' in what I say is the declaration of my expectation that the other being to which I declare myself in this way will respond and treat and describe and distinguish me as something like himself. . . . Thus the word 'Thou,' although it is a very different word, is immanent to 'I.'"[156] For Barth the "I" is relationally understood in the sense that the "I" always stands over and against the "Thou." "I" is in relation to "Thou," and I cannot say "I" without simultaneously implying "Thou." The self-sufficient I is an illusion because, as Barth points out, even the concept or thought of an I implies relation to another: to a Thou, who necessarily stands over against myself as an I. The I and Thou are related because the I stands over and against the Thou — and only in distinction to the Thou does the I have an identity. In developing this interpersonal ontology, Barth takes issue with the isolated *cogito* of Descartes:

> A pure, absolute and self-sufficient I is an illusion, for as an I, even as I think and express this I, I am not alone or self-sufficient, but am distinguished from and connected with a Thou in which I find a being like my own, so that there is no place for an interpretation of the "I am" which means isolation and necessarily consists in a description of the sovereign self-positing of an empty subject by eruptions of its pure, absolute and self-sufficient abyss.[157]

Therefore, the I is not absolute but is defined by both distinction from and connection with the Thou. The necessary relation between I and Thou is one

---

for allowing the *interpersonal* I and Thou to lapse into the subjectivism of personal consciousness of the I. Hence, like Buber, Barth's "Thou" is simply a case of "the idealist philosophy of the autonomous subject . . . transposed into a thinking centered on a heteronomous subject" (p. 184) and has no objective grounds. That is, the Thou is only a logical extension of my own self-consciousness. But it is difficult to understand the weight of the criticism, because the problem of the likeness between I and Thou is not interpreted by Barth in an a priori theoretical framework. Rather, it is rooted in a particular history, in Christology, and ultimately in the Trinity, as Pannenberg acknowledges. Pannenberg seems to overlook that for Barth the Trinity cannot be considered separately from humanity; rather, it provides the ontological foundation for real humanity through the incarnation. This also tends to negate Pannenberg's criticism that dialogical personalism in general tends to consider I-Thou relations in isolation from I-It relations. On the basis of the incarnation, Barth did not see these two as necessarily exclusive.

156. *CD*, III/2, p. 245.
157. *CD*, III/2, pp. 245-46.

of the chief descriptions of a dynamic anthropology. It is "dynamic" because it always entails the active relation of one person to another.

Just as the I cannot be understood without distinguishing from the Thou, neither can the I see the Thou without concluding that the Thou is like "I am." Barth puts it this way: "As I am, the other is like me."[158] There must be an acknowledgment that the other, the Thou, with whom I am in encounter, is like I am: hence, thou art like I am. Apart from this, there can be no I and Thou. Buber would say that there can be only "I and It" where the other is not seen as "I am."

Thus far it seems as if Barth's understanding of I and Thou is predicated on the understanding that the other is like myself. If so, the identity of the other, the Thou, can be reduced to a logical extension, and the other's actual existence would continue to be problematic, because there is no way to prove that the other is not a heteronomic other. In other words, what warrant would there be for saying "I am as Thou art" and vice versa? Here the philosophical problem of other minds could rear its ugly head. However, the problem of the likeness between I and Thou is not interpreted by Barth in a theoretical framework. It is rooted in a particular history, and ultimately rooted in Christology. Barth makes this clear when he asks, What is the content of the encounter? It is: "I am as Thou art." But Barth is cautious at this point in his argument not to allow the encounter to become the tail that wags the dog, as if the I am is constituted solely by the human, Thou art. The I does not lose his or her own identity in the Thou. In the statement "I am as Thou art," the "as" is *not* meant to be constitutive of the I am. "I am" does not formally disappear with "Thou art." Rather, the continuity between "I am" and "Thou art" derives from their being created by the same God.[159]

Once again we see how Barth's articulation of the human is active and dynamic. The form of humanity is not based on *esse*, but on *existere*. As we have seen, for Barth, "to say man is to say history *(Geschichte)*." In emphasizing the historicity of the encounter, Barth is pointing to the encounter not as a theoretical possibility or ideal to which humanity must measure up. Rather, he is pointing to the fact that the basic form of humanity is best described as event, as actions that take place between particular human beings. When in-

---

158. *CD*, III/2, p. 246.

159. *CD*, III/2, p. 248. The accusation that Barth's theology in general is based on "heteronomic thinking" is an old one, put forth by Paul Tillich, *The Protestant Era*, tr. and ed. James Luther Adams (London: Nisbet, 1951) pp. 52, 61-62, 95. But both Pannenberg and Tillich fail to appreciate fully that it is the Otherness of the triune God that is, in Barth's view, the only way to solve the problem of the identity between self and Other. See Hartwell, *Theology of Karl Barth*, p. 181.

dividual humans posit themselves as an "I am," they create a history.[160] Therefore human encounter is not a predicate of history in the abstract; rather, the "little histories" of the human encounter are the predicate of "I am as Thou art." As human beings encounter one another they create a history, not in a primary sense — only God is the Creator of history in the primary sense *(Heilsgeschichte)* — but in a secondary sense, what Barth calls a "little history" *(kleine Geschichte)*.[161] This is another way for Barth to stress the primacy of action in his understanding of human ontology. He is not placing the accent on an abstract or isolated view of human individuals. In light of the humanity of Jesus, human beings are agents who are divinely determined to act in a certain way; we are to act toward one another as Christ has acted toward us. This dynamic quality of the encounter is illustrated in Barth's statement: "Similarly, the statement 'Thou art' denotes a history. Therefore in our formula: 'I am as Thou art,' we do not describe the relationship between the two static complexes of being, but between two which are dynamic, which move out from themselves, which exist, and which meet or encounter each other in their existence. The 'I am' and the 'Thou art' encounter each other as two histories."[162]

We now begin to see more clearly what Barth means when he refers to a dynamic anthropology. It is "dynamic" in the sense that it refers to a necessary relation between persons.

If we refer back to Kant, we can see that Barth does not try to reconstruct an anthropology based on metaphysical speculation. He has to some degree constructed his anthropology on the plane of the "practical"; yet it is not a practical anthropology that suffers from the restrictions that Kant applied to his own philosophical anthropology. It is rather a practical anthropology that has been expanded by the "given" quality of the revealed truth of the God-man, Jesus Christ. It is grounded in the historical existence of the man, Jesus. As such, it could be labeled "existential" because it is grounded in

---

160. Otto Weber sheds light on Barth's view of history: "Revelation is never a predicate of history; on the contrary, history is a predicate of revelation" (*Karl Barth's Church Dogmatics*, tr. Arthur C. Cochrane [Philadelphia: Westminster, 1953] p. 58).

161. See *CD*, III/1, pp. 65ff.; IV/3, pp. 685ff. The seminal idea for this "encounter," which comprises a little history, can be found in *CD*, I/2, pp. 41-42, where Barth agrees (in part) with Feuerbach that the ego cannot be self-existent, but must stumble upon another, an object *(Gegen-Stand)*, with in order to emerge from the sea of non-ego. Barth cautions, however, that we are perfectly capable of "dodging a Thou." Hence the real need is to be in encounter with God — which is impossible unless God accommodates himself to us as a human being. This is where Barth brings in the objective possibility of revelation: "The Word of God a man, a man the Word of God" (I/2, p. 40).

162. *CD*, III/2, p. 248.

the particular existence of Jesus of Nazareth. Barth's theological anthropology is not a philosophical anthropology; but that does not mean it is nonphilosophical. Barth's "real man" is not derived from speculative philosophy; but this does not mean he conceives of the person as "nonthinking."[163] Rather, he borrows certain terms and categories from various philosophical thinkers in order to illustrate the richness of biblical anthropology.

As we have seen, Barth did not conceive his dynamic description of the basic form of humanity on his own. From Calvin came the basic idea of the individual person's immediate creaturely dependence on God. From Kierkegaard he derived the concept of the human being as a being who exists in particular, and therefore a being who is compelled to act. In Buber, Barth found the language of encounter. Barth's understanding of "history" as an interpersonal encounter bears marked similarities with both Buber and Friedrich Gogarten.[164]

Yet Barth made some important innovations in developing his theology of "encounter." From his reflections on the triune God, Barth developed the theology of intratrinitarian encounter as the foundation of the *imago Dei*. It is this development that marks Barth's most profound contribution to theological anthropology. We next examine the particular content of Barth's trinitarian thought in order to appreciate fully his trinitarian anthropology.

Encounter and the Trinity

Barth unfolds his understanding of the human I and Thou from the intratrinitarian I and Thou between Father and Son. In Barth the I and Thou relation between humans is not considered theoretically but Christologically. His description of the continuity between I and Thou is not gained by extrapolating from the self-consciousness of "I," nor from empirical observations

---

163. See 2 Cor. 10:5. *CD*, I/1, pp. 84-85, 138, 203-5.

164. See Martin Buber's *I and Thou*, tr. R. Gregor Smith (Edinburgh: T & T Clark, 1937), where Smith comments in the introduction regarding Buber's influence on Gogarten's *Ich glaube an den dreieinigen Gott*: "The controlling affirmation of [Gogarten's] thesis is the reality of our consciousness of other selves; history for him is constituted where two persons meet. Applying this thought to the modern theory of history as a process within an unbroken causal system, where facts are to be demonstrated in the light of controlling 'eternal' values or 'interpretations' of reality, he demonstrates convincingly the inadequacy of its abstract presuppositions about reality. The concrete reality, for him as for Buber, is the situation where responsible persons confront one another in living mutual relation" (p. x). Smith's statement could apply equally to Barth. Nevertheless, one should take note of Barth's later departure from Gogarten, especially from Gogarten's sociopolitical interpretation of I and Thou.

based on statistical averages. Rather, the "I am" is always rooted in the humanity of Jesus.[165] The Thou is understood as "like I am," because both human beings have Christ for their brother. "I am as Thou art" is thus more than an idealistic formula for Barth. It represents a reflection of the divine love: a love between Father and Son in the Spirit. Hence: "He is the original I and source of every I and Thou, of the I which is eternally from and to the Thou and therefore supremely I. And it is this relationship in the inner divine being which is repeated and reflected in God's eternal covenant with man as revealed and operative in time in the humanity of Jesus."[166]

It should be observed that the relational anthropology that is based on the dynamic love of the Trinity creates a certain "response-ability" for the human subject. With a relational anthropology comes a responsibility to enter into relationship. In other words, the trinitarian ground for Barth's anthropology creates an immediate ethical obligation to my neighbor as the Thou, who is "like I am." Remember, the Thou is "like I am" because we both have our humanity in the humanity of Jesus. Jesus' being for others implies some likeness with ourselves. In view of the analogy of relations, it is incumbent on us to bring our actions into correspondence to the love that Jesus showed us. We are destined not only to be covenant partners with God, but also to reflect the divine love in our relations one to another. We see that for Barth, the *fact* of human existence rooted in history creates an *ought*, a moral obligation that has been created by the ontological reality of humanity revealed in Christ. Being and action, fact and value are thus integrally connected when it comes to dogmatic anthropology based on the analogy of relations.[167] In sum: to be is to act, and to act rightly is to act in correspondence with the act of God toward us in the humanity of Jesus.

This unity of fact and value can be achieved in dogmatics, because, once again, Barth roots his anthropology in his understanding of the Trinity. God the Creator creates a relationship with humanity that is not alien to himself as Creator. His relation to humanity *ad extra* is rather a reflection of his essential relationship *ad intra* as Father, Son, and Holy Spirit. Regarding the relationship God initiates with the human race through his covenant, Barth says:

> Entering into this relationship, He makes a copy of Himself. Even in His inner divine being there is relationship. To be sure, God is One in Him-

---

165. *CD*, III/2, p. 244.

166. *CD*, III/2, pp. 218-19. Cf. III/2, pp. 323-24.

167. This is in contrast to the opening statement of Einstein, who inadvertently adopts the position of so many modern philosophers under the influence of Kant: that knowledge of what *is* cannot lead us to knowledge of what *should be*. See above, p. 2.

self. But He is not alone. There is in Him a co-existence, co-inherence and reciprocity. God in Himself is not just simple, but in the simplicity of His essence He is threefold — the Father, the Son and the Holy Ghost. . . . He is in Himself the One who loves eternally, the One who is eternally loved, and eternal love; and in this triunity He is the original and source of every I and Thou, of the I which is eternally from and to the Thou and therefore supremely I. And it is this relationship in the inner divine being which is repeated and reflected in God's eternal covenant with man as revealed and operative in time in the humanity of Jesus.[168]

Because the relational nature of God is reflected in the humanity of Jesus,[169] and therefore is the determination or destiny of every human being, it follows that the person who corresponds to and reflects the being of God *(analogia relationis)* bears the stamp of God's own dynamic character. Each human being then is destined to be in relation, to be I and Thou. I implies Thou, and Thou refers back to I. I and Thou are not coincidental or incidental but "essentially proper to the concept of man."[170] Hence I encounter the other only as the other also encounters me. I am limited and imposed on by this encounter, says Barth. "I am" also posits the condition of the other: the Thou; I stand as Thou to the other. Barth argues that unless the "I am" is in encounter, then it is an empty "I am." The encounter is not secondary or an auxiliary function of the individual; the encounter is at the very root of the individual's being. In other words, the fact of God's love and the reality that human beings are created in his image determine the obligation for human love. We now are in a position to see the logic of Barth's argument unfold as he develops his anthropology from his theology. Real humanity can be dynamically understood, because God's own being is dynamically revealed as an encounter, a primal history, proceeeding from *ad intra* to *ad extra,* and finally creating the basic form of humanity that is a "little history."[171]

168. *CD,* III/2, p. 218.

169. Barth cites John 17:5-21. He concludes that here "the divine original creates for itself a copy in the creaturely world" (III/2, p. 221).

170. *CD,* III/2, p. 248.

171. McLean is one of the few commentators on Barth's anthropology to bring this out: "Barth sees the I-Thou-ness of our humanity not only as a reflection of the inner Godhead, but also as a reflection of the I-Thou form of real man (God-man). . . . Thus humanity (man-man) reflects and points to man's destiny which is to realize that we are covenant-partners of God (man-God)" *(Humanity,* p. 37).

The Fourfold Basic Form of Humanity

What form does being in encounter take? What would it look like to correspond to the divine love and so live our lives in likeness to God's dynamic love? When he describes the basic form of humanity, Barth begins to touch on ethics. The reader might wish that I omit this section, since the primary argument contained in this study deals with anthropological theory. However, several important points in this section ought not to be overlooked. First, it shows the universal scope of Barth's anthropology. It comes as little surprise that this form of humanity is one that is not limited to those inside the walls of the church. Second, and this will be a great surprise for many of Barth's readers, this section shows the culmination of one of the few Christian anthropologies that appeals to human dignity and joyfulness rather than human depravity. Finally, Barth's practical interpretation of "being in encounter" as mutual seeing, hearing and listening, and rendering assistance, bears a strong similarity to many of the more humanistic forms of psychotherapeutic intervention. The practical and pastoral implications of this section should not be overlooked.

In asking what are the categories *(Kategorien)* for being human, Barth urges caution. The categories of eating, drinking, sleeping, working, propagating the species, and so on are not the special interest of theological anthropology because they have no "categorial" *(kategoriale)* significance in the description of humanity. These are merely the field on which our humanity gets played out. Hence these common human activities can be either human *(menschlich)* or inhuman *(unmenschlich)*. But the real form of humanity takes the form of encounter; it actualizes the "I am as Thou art."[172] Barth describes four categories that being in encounter entails. He describes them in ascending order of importance.

First, being in encounter is a "being in which one man looks the other in the eye."[173] Seeing eye to eye is seeing our fellow human being, and this seeing eye to eye makes us human. To see the other, to look them in the eye, is not only to see them but also to be seen by them. Barth reminds us of the obvious but shameful truth that we can look *at* other human beings, yet fail to see them as human. Our sight can be dimmed by viewing them as something other than human; we thus "see past them," to use a common phrase. We see them as an "It," rather than a "Thou." Seeing eye to eye is more than looking at someone; it includes an openness both to see the other as human and to allow the other

---

172. *CD*, III/2, p. 249. Cf. Anderson, *On Being Human*, pp. 20-21.
173. *CD*, III/2, p. 250.

to see my own humanity. Barth describes this seeing eye to eye as a "two-sided openness."[174] Such openness is the first element of humanity. Where openness is lacking, real humanity does not occur. But "conversely, where openness obtains, humanity begins to occur."[175]

Second, being in encounter takes place where there are mutual speech and hearing. Even more important than seeing and being seen is the event of speech: hearing and being heard. Barth insists that both persons must express and receive, then receive and express. Speech and hearing are so important because they cross over the "frontier of visibility." That which is purely seen needs to be interpreted with the "human use of the mouth and ears. Humanity as encounter must become the event of speech."[176] But speech can at times be deceptive; it may not be particularly human if in speaking the words there is no genuine self-expression, but merely a guise for something deeper and better known, which is withheld from the Thou for no good reason. With penetrating insight, Barth reminds the reader that words can sometimes be used as a mask to prevent the I from encountering the Thou; when this takes place authentic humanity is obviously absent. Barth asks: "How can I take the Thou seriously as a Thou if I express myself to him but do not really intend to express myself at all? How can I then be in true encounter with him?"[177] What matters here is "the humanity of my hearing, and this is conditioned negatively by the fact that at least I do not hear this other with suspicion, and positively by the fact that I presuppose that he is trying to come to my help with his self-expression and self-declaration."[178]

If we critically analyze Barth's argument on the basic form of humanity thus far, we might raise the objection that human beings sometimes do not speak a word of kindness, or listen attentively. If and when this is the case, am I nevertheless obligated to "make myself known"? Barth answers with a clear

---

174. *CD*, III/2, p. 251.

175. Ibid. Barth mentions that we are more likely to share openly when in the depths than in the heights, and are therefore usually more human when we go through such difficult experiences together. It is surprising, especially in view of Barth's Christological foundation, that Barth says very little about suffering as a category of our human experience.

176. *CD*, III/2, p. 253. Here Barth emphasizes the importance of the auditive sense in clearing up much of the ambiguity and equivocation contained in sight without speech. In human interaction, words often clear up the equivocal acquaintance of sight. Barth will continue, of course, to point out the even greater importance of "rendering assistance," i.e., action on behalf of others. On the primacy of the auditive and tactile over the visual sense, see Macmurray, *Self as Agent*, esp. pp. 106-11. Barth's insight here has found a remarkable amount of confirmation in the field of interpersonal communications and childhood development.

177. *CD*, III/2, p. 254.

178. *CD*, III/2, p. 255.

yes. The word of address is necessary even if it looks to be unsuccessful: "Address is coming to another with one's being, and knocking and asking to be admitted. . . . In certain cases this may be a thankless task."[179] Barth responds that the individual should not withhold one's speech and listening from a Thou, simply because the results seem to be uncertain: "I cannot withhold it, because he encounters me as a man, and I should not take him seriously as a man if I did not seriously try to find the way from me to him. No matter what the results, I cannot refrain from knocking."[180]

This speaking and listening is not human if it stems only from my own need to speak and listen. It is human when it is done without regard to the results, and without the presumption that even the modest demands of the other can be met by me. So the first question is not what we can achieve for the other, but, Barth proposes, "The first question is what is to become of us if we do not listen to him, if we refuse to allow this penetration into our sphere either as a whole or in part."[181]

What is it that compels me to listen, to share and speak in openness toward the Other when there are precarious uncertainties in such an enterprise? Is there some kind of rational moral principle in operation here? a categorical imperative, which might be comparable to Kant's analysis of practical reason? If the obligation to mutual speech and hearing is based on an abstract universal duty, then Barth has not gone beyond Kant, and his accusations that the categorical imperative is cheerless would lose force. However, a categorical imperative does not seem to be Barth's intention here. In Barth's insistence that we must give to the other a "human" hearing, regardless of what kind of assistance we think we may be capable of rendering, he is basing the need to listen on his definition of the basic form of humanity. It is humanity in the image of God; it is humanity that is vicarious in the identification with the need of the other because such a vicarious humanity was lived out by Christ on our behalf.[182] Hence to fail to listen seriously is to fail to respect not only the other's humanity,

179. *CD*, III/2, p. 256.
180. *CD*, III/2, p. 257.
181. *CD*, III/2, p. 258.
182. Cf. James B. Torrance, "The Vicarious Humanity and Priesthood of Christ in the Theology of John Calvin," in *Calvinus Ecclesiae Doctor*, ed. W. H. Neuser (Kampen: Kok, 1978) p. 70. Torrance affirms the Reformed origin of Barth's emphasis here: "So we pray to Christ as God, and at the same time in our prayers He prays for us and with us to the Father. There is thus a duality-in-unity in the confession that 'Jesus Lord.' As Calvin argued, He is Lord and Head as Creator and He is Lord and Head as the leader of our humanity." Torrance cites Calvin's *Commentary on Hebrews* (2:12); *Sermons on Acts* (1:9-11); and *Institutes* III, xi, 8, 12, among others. Cf. also *Institutes* IV, xvi, 18.

but also my own. And even though God alone can help with that problem, I am compelled by my own humanity to listen to their problem and identify it as my own. The fellow humanity of Christ is the basis for mutual speech and hearing.

For Barth human listening is not self-*less*. It is rather the grounds on which the self corresponds to its humanity. In listening, the self is concerned both with his or her own humanity and with the humanity of the other. This must be reciprocal. There must be a realization that I need to listen to the other in order to be human, and the other needs to encounter me. Reciprocity is essential to human speech and listening. Barth reminds us that, just as "we can look past people, we can also talk past them and hear past them. . . . Two monologues do not constitute a dialogue."[183] By this Barth apparently means that we can pretend to hear and not truly be listening; we might even be very skilled at certain listening techniques, but if we fail to appreciate the other's humanity in the encounter, then we have failed to be human. Thus we "hear" past them, hearing their sounds and even their words, but not listening to their true humanity. Barth awakens the reader to this subtle truth: "as hearers, we can find only what we seek . . . a dialogue begins only when the hearers are concerned about themselves, about the removal of their own difficulty in respect of the other, so that the words of the other are received and welcomed as helping this embarrassment. Without this presupposition, hearing is merely a common endurance of a commonly produced sound of words."[184]

It is important to note the extent to which mutual speaking and listening are interpreted within a dynamic framework. The faculty psychology of the rationalistic theologians would emphasize the rationality that speech requires; the emphasis lies on the faculty that gives rise to the speaking itself. But a relational interpretation puts the speech in the context of a relationship. Speaking requires listening, just as listening requires speaking. The therapeutic value of modern psychoanalysis and counseling could hardly be given a better rationale than Barth provides here. When we speak and listen one to another on the interpersonal level, we are conforming to our true humanity; we have rediscovered one of the fundamental forms of what it means to be a person. Mutual speaking and listening shape our personhood at a very deep level from the earliest stages of childhood. The importance of listening for emotional health is explained by Frank Lake:

If present loneliness can induce neurotic anxiety, then its opposite, namely genuine company, can combat neurotic anxiety. Just as recent so-

---

183. *CD*, III/2, p. 259.
184. Ibid.

cial isolation can arouse a reverberation of the separation-anxieties of infancy through into consciousness, so the return of good relationships, in which the lonely person is cared for, will replace the resonance of early anxiety-provoking situations by the resonance of such other good experiences of infancy as are available on the reverberating circuits of memory. The anxious person is then "re-mind-ed" that his infant loneliness was often met by mother love coming down to meet him, to look and to listen, with patient attention, gentle talk and welcoming eyes. In this way, the mere provision of an attentive listener can put to flight an army of irrational fears.[185]

Lake has been one of the few psychotherapists to combine a Christological perspective with an object relations theory of personality. Like Barth, he sees listening not only as a therapeutic skill but as a necessity, both ontologically and theologically.[186] Lake's weighty tome provides a rich resource for the pastor, counselor, and theologian alike.[187]

At this point Barth admits, with characteristic realism, that the kind of speaking and listening he is talking about seldom occur. On the contrary, "Most of our words, spoken or heard, are an inhuman and barbaric affair because we will not speak or listen to one another. We speak them without wanting to seek or help. And we listen to them without letting ourselves be found or helped."[188] This "barbaric affair" takes place not only in private conversations but also in pulpits, lectures, books, and articles. Much of what we speak, write, hear, and read is propaganda, and this could make us cynical and suspicious about the efficacy of words and human speech altogether. However, Barth offers the rejoinder that a cynical retreat will not solve the problem, for "it is not the words that are really empty. It is men themselves when they speak and hear empty words."[189] While suspicion and disillusionment about human speech and listening may be justified, Barth concludes that we must not "in any circumstances allow them house-room."[190]

It is not precisely clear where Barth discovers the "mutual speech and hearing" dimension of our humanity. Presumably, he develops it Chris-

---

185. *Clinical Theology* (London: Darton, Longman & Todd, 1966) p. 10.

186. Ibid., esp. p. 11.

187. Again, see *Clinical Theology,* chap. 1, "Listening, Dialogue, Witness and Counseling," pp. 1-100. There are abridged versions of *Clinical Theology* available as well, but they are less weighty and less interesting.

188. *CD,* III/2, p. 260.

189. Ibid.

190. Ibid.

tologically, because for Barth, the vicarious humanity of Christ means that Christ's life of servanthood, including his speaking and listening to those around him, provides a paradigm for personhood. Perhaps Barth was influenced by the insights of Dietrich Bonhoeffer: "Christians, especially ministers, so often think they must always contribute something when they are in the company of others, that this is the one service they have to render. They forget that listening can be a greater service than speaking."[191]

Third, being in encounter consists also in "the fact that we render mutual assistance."[192] This third step is higher than the previous two, which should not surprise us, given the emphasis Barth places on the importance of action. Since God's being is an act, likewise being human must culminate in acting. Yet the way from the lower levels to the higher is not easy; Barth alleges that it may sometimes be the case that the initial perception that one will be called on to render assistance precludes the openness of speaking and hearing between one person and another. Rendering assistance is where the basic form of humanity takes shape — where the proverbial "rubber meets the road":

> We see that it is this higher [level] which claims us. We must see and be seen, speak and listen because to be human we must be prepared to be there for the other, to be at his disposal. We thus hesitate. We are afraid. This is too much to ask. And because this is too much, everything that leads to it is too much: sincere seeing and letting oneself be seen; sincere speech between man and man. There is indeed a necessary connexion at this point. If I and Thou really see each other and speak with one another and listen to one another, inevitably they mutually summon each other to action.[193]

Yet Barth warns that an action in and of itself is not necessarily human. Some actions can be inhuman. Even altruism can be inhuman if it does not take place within an encounter. How can altruism be inhuman? Again, Barth emphasizes the need for reciprocity in rendering assistance. Barth reasons that an altruist may render assistance, thinking the person needing help stands in unilateral need of help; that they, as a helper, do not need the helpee. Such is not the case, says Barth. Truly human assistance is based on the truth that I need the other just as much as I am apparently needed by them. In order for action to be truly human, it must be arrived at with "the

---

191. *Life Together*, tr. J. W. Doberstein (New York: Harper & Row, 1954) pp. 97-99.
192. *CD*, III/2, p. 260.
193. *CD*, III/2, pp. 260-61.

twofold correspondence that the other has summoned me and I him; that he really needs me and I him; that I act as one who is called but who also calls."[194]

Again, Barth carefully guards the identity of the individual within the event of the encounter. The differentiation between I and Thou is not abrogated. I can act in rendering assistance to Thou, but can *not* act on his or her behalf. Only God can act on behalf of the other. This is Jesus' prerogative, and in this Barth insists that Jesus is incomparable in his vicarious humanity. We cannot serve as another person's savior. In correspondence to Jesus in his humanity, however, we humans must render and receive assistance. Our rendering and receiving assistance is mutual, unlike that of Jesus the Son of God.[195] To be human, then, is to cry out for help. Not to cry out for help is to attempt to emulate God, and to therefore fall into the abyss. Barth declares in one of his more metaphorical assertions: "My humanity depends upon the fact that I am always aware, and my action is determined by the awareness, that I need the assistance of other as a fish needs water."[196] Again, Barth explains that rendering assistance must work reciprocally:

> I also know that what he expects of me — namely, a little support — does not exceed my powers, that this little assistance is not in any sense a divine but a very human work which may rightly be expected, that I am able to render it, and under an obligation to do so. I cannot evade my fellow who asks for it. I must stand by him and help him. I become inhuman if I resist this awareness or try to escape the limited but definite service I can render.[197]

On the other end of the encounter, Barth also says that I need to *give* assistance to the Thou as a fish needs water. Barth does not derive the need to give and receive assistance from an ethical ideal or abstract general principle. Rather, it is the real man, Jesus, who paints for us a picture of rendering assis-

194. *CD*, III/2, p. 261. It is not precisely clear whether Barth means that (1) the I, as the one rendering assistance, should keep in mind my potential need for assistance in the future, or (2) even in the very act of helping the other, the I actually needs their assistance. In view of his aversion to potentiality, it is probably the latter meaning. This seems to be confirmed by following Barth's argument below.

195. It might be pointed out that Jesus did cry out for help from the cross, and often received help of all kinds. See Mark 15:34; Luke 23:26. In mentioning that Jesus did not need assistance, Barth is referring to Jesus' deity, not his humanity. See *CD*, III/2, p. 262.

196. *CD*, III/2, p. 263.

197. Ibid.

tance. Barth contrasts his portrait of "real man" with Nietzsche's Zarathustra, who serves as an example of ideal humanity.[198]

Finally, Barth mentions a condition that must be present in all the forms of humanity thus far described: "being in encounter consists in the fact that all the occurrences which we have so far described as the basic form of humanity stands under the sign that it is done on both sides with gladness."[199] "Gladly" *(gerne)* is the category of the encounter that humanizes the above three categories. Barth insists that this attitude of "gladly" is all-important. Without it, all of the preceding may be simply "an inhuman description of the human." The "gladly" springs forth from the great secret of humanity, that he or she is God's covenant partner.

Being in encounter means meeting gladly and in freedom as "companions, associates, comrades, fellows and helpmates."[200] Barth develops this view from his understanding of human freedom. Just as God's freedom expresses itself in his love, so human encounter is truly human only when it is a free reciprocal relationship. Therefore, "Humanity lives and moves and has its being in this freedom to be oneself with the other, and oneself to be with the other."[201]

At this point it is important to recall that freedom for Barth can never be depicted by a neutral stance poised between two (or more) alternatives. Freedom is an action and a reality. Therefore, Barth argues that it is a loss of freedom to choose *not* to be in relation to one's fellow human gladly. The choice of nonfreedom is a "fatal possibility." On the other hand, freedom involves choosing fellow human beings *gladly.* Freedom consists in conforming to our human reality — the reality of our need to be in encounter with others. In this sense Barth denies that sin is endemic to human nature: "It is not by nature, but by its denial and misuse, that man is as alien and opposed to the grace of God as we see him to be in fact."[202] This clarifies an important anthropological distinction that Barth now spells out explicitly: the basic form of humanity, viewed against the background of the man Jesus, is "good and not evil." Barth concludes: "We do not associate ourselves, therefore, with the common theological practice of depreciating human nature as much as possible in order to oppose to it the more effectively what may be made of man by divine grace."[203]

198. *CD,* III/2, p. 264.
199. *CD,* III/2, p. 265.
200. *CD,* III/2, p. 271.
201. *CD,* III/2, p. 272.
202. *CD,* III/2, p. 274.
203. Ibid. Cf. *CD,* IV/1, p. 379. For a likely illustration of what Barth has in mind with regard to those who depreciate human nature, see Calvin's *Sermons on Job.* Whether Barth is right in assessing Calvin this way is outside the scope of this discussion.

When Barth says that human nature is good, he means that the goodness and dignity of every human being is Christologically rooted. All that has been predicated about the form of humanity has been spoken in the light of revelation, specifically the revelation of the humanity of the man Jesus. The correspondence between the basic form of humanity and the humanity of the man Jesus stands, even if it is corrupted and disguised by sin. Therefore, human evil in the form of resistance to God's grace is not natural, but a denial and misuse of human nature. This helps to explain the origin of the "gladly" that Barth insists must be present in all the other forms of being in encounter. The "gladly" stems, so to speak, from the "point of contact" between God and humanity.[204] As we have seen, this is not a point of contact that humans possess apart from the grace of God in his revelation. Rather, this point of contact is the secret of humanity, hidden before the ages by the grace of God. The secret of humanity (and hence dignity) is found in its kinship with the humanity of Jesus.[205]

Barth makes what will be a surprising assertion to many of his readers. He lets it be known that in delineating the basic form of humanity, he is not talking about Christian, *agapē* love. Rather, he is talking about the human being as a human being, not necessarily filled with the Holy Spirit, but simply fulfilling his or her human nature. Thus the basic form of humanity that

204. As we have seen in the discussion earlier in this chapter, Barth never denies the reality of the point of contact between God and humanity. He only disputes a point of contact that might be incorrectly understood as an autonomous human endowment. See *CD*, I/1, p. 29.

205. See *CD*, III/4, "The Honour of Man," p. 564: "How high is the honour of man even as the creature of God and object of His world sovereignty is revealed in the inconceivable fact that God Himself becomes man in Jesus Christ — man in all the limitation in which every other man is also man. Can we ever overemphasise the significance of this for the unlost and unlosable distinction which belongs to every man in his limitation, whatever his attitude to it? What are all human declamations about the intrinsic dignity of man compared with the foundation which it is given here according to the witness of the Bible? . . . how can this honour be overlooked, forgotten or denied in face of this foundation? How can 'dignity' be denied to even the most miserable of men when the glory of God Himself was the honour of this man nailed in supreme wretchedness to the cross? Furthermore, how high the honour of man is in its proper form, as his honour on the basis of his calling is revealed in the second inconceivable fact that in Jesus Christ, even in the limitation in which every other man is also man, the man called by God and placed in his service exists after the manner of God . . . no word is strong enough to bring out the bearing of this on the honour of every man called by God. There are familiar Christian declamations concerning the honour of this calling but what are they compared with the foundation which it is given according to the New Testament in the resurrection of Jesus from the dead, in His exaltation to *kyriótēs*? . . . man becomes and is free when he takes to heart the honour paid him by God in his limitation."

Barth ascribes to human nature is not limited to the Christian community.[206] What further surprises us here is that Barth's description of the basic form of humanity is not a description of *agapē*, but of *erōs*. Barth discloses this when he mentions that he admires the freedom and gladness contained in the Greek concept of *erōs*. It is surprising because *erōs* is usually presumed to have its origin outside revelation, and apart from *agapē*. To hear Barth speak so highly of a kind of love that seemingly comes not from revelation, but from human inspiration or intellection, is not what one would expect from a theologian who had become so well known for his previous assertions to the effect that grace destroys nature rather than perfecting it. Here we must pay close attention to Barth's argument.

The "gladly" of *erōs* may be, and often is, outside the sphere of the church and of special revelation of Christ. However, this "gladly" is not outside the sphere of grace. It is important to see that Barth casts the net of grace widely when he discusses the humanity of Christ. The humanity of Christ is not limited by any prior judicial or penal theories of atonement. It is rather a vicarious humanity that is universal if anything at all. In opposition to those who would think to enhance the grace of God by demeaning humanity, and thus emptying *erōs* of any significance, Barth says, "But in light of grace itself, of the connexion between the humanity of Jesus and humanity generally, this representation cannot be sustained. Man cannot be depicted as a blotted or empty page."[207]

So we see that even within this sphere of natural human knowledge, there is a form of knowledge that is informed by grace. Barth urges the church not to overlook the common humanity of those outside when it makes its appeal for them to come inside. When an effort is made to shame the non-Christian, or blacken their humanity, the appeal will fail to be taken seriously. The non-Christian "will not be convicted of his sin if he is uncharitably — and falsely — addressed concerning his humanity."[208] Their unwillingness to be maligned is understandable in light of the fact that every human being is a recipient of some degree of grace because they dwell "in the sphere in which Jesus too was man." They can therefore possess the "gladly," the "freedom of the heart open to the fellow-man."[209] Barth concludes that it is *erōs* which contains within it the "gladly," and thus an element of freedom that describes true humanity: "The Greeks with their *erōs* — and it was no inconsiderable but a very

---

206. *CD*, III/2, p. 276. Barth cites Luke 16:8, which says the children of the world may be wiser, and thus more human, than the children of the light.

207. *CD*, III/2, p. 278.

208. *CD*, III/2, p. 279.

209. *CD*, III/2, p. 278.

real achievement — grasped the fact that the being of man is free, radically open, willing, spontaneous, joyful, cheerful and gregarious."[210]

Here we might pause to ask if Barth has softened his stance against natural theology. A prima facie glance might lead one to think so. But this is not necessarily the case. In spite of all the positive statements about *erōs*, Barth derives his anthropology not from Hellenism, but from the revealed humanity of Christ. Yet given the anthropology that he has developed through the source of revelation, and the common humanity in Christ, Barth sees a "legitimate relationship between Christianity and Hellenism." The positive side of the relationship between *erōs* and *agapē* (and Barth *has* emphasized that there is a negative side to the relationship) confirms that Christian love is an awakening of humanity to find its true fulfillment in Christ. Humanity may be distorted and perverted, but Barth affirms that it has not been forfeited.[211]

Commenting on 1 Corinthians 13, Barth says that love *(agapē)* redeems *erōs* — not *erōs* in the abstract, but *erōs* as it expresses itself in the joy of that person's humanity. The connection between *agapē* and *erōs* points out a possible point of contact between the Christian and the world; or it may become a sore spot if the Christian overlooks the solidarity between *agapē* and *erōs*:

> The *agapē* of the Christians would perhaps not be all that it professes to be if the Greek man with his *erōs* could not see that even in the Christian he has to do with a man and therefore with a being with which he can at least feel and proclaim solidarity in respect of that root of his *erōs*. If this were not the case, the love of the supposed Christian would surely be a very loveless love.[212]

Barth summarizes his section on *agapē* and *erōs*:

> This downward connexion of love by way of humanity to the *eros* of the Greeks was obviously present in New Testament times for all the differentiation of the spheres, and it is hard to see why the connexion cannot and should not be seen, respected and used in our own day as well. What we have here is a relationship between the Church and the world without which the Church cannot discharge its function in the world because without it it would not be the Church, the Church of Christian love.[213]

---

210. *CD*, III/2, p. 283.

211. See *CD*, III/2, p. 284. Barth cites Phil. 4:8, and the dominating *aretē*, of the epistle to the Philippians, to enforce his point that *erōs* and *agapē* maintain something in common.

212. *CD*, III/2, p. 285.

213. Ibid.

It is obvious here that Barth, in his delineation of the basic form of humanity, is describing more than does the natural scientist. The interpersonal indicatives of revelation have inspired a set of imperatives about human conduct. In his methodical unfolding of the trinitarian foundation of grace, Barth goes beyond the boundaries of exact science and beyond the phenomena of human existence to describe the humanity of Jesus. Barth therefore prescribes what our real humanity must become. If our destiny is in Christ, then the basic form of humanity revealed in Christ is who we *ought* to become.[214] The gap between who we are and who we ought to become creates an imperative. We become human as we see eye to eye, speak and hear, and render assistance gladly. Unlike the anthropologies of natural science, Christian anthropology is both a descriptive and a prescriptive anthropology: there is an unmistakable "oughtness" about it. Such an anthropology does not simply describe the phenomena, the facts about human existence, but rather judges the phenomena by the reality of what human beings are as cohumans with Christ.[215] Barth is thus practical, in the Kantian sense, without depending on an abstract ideal or disembodied law that stands over against us. In Christ, Barth sees a real connection between the theoretical and the practical. Christ calls out for the fulfillment of our humanity by standing within the stream of history as one who can be seen with the eyes and touched with the hands,[216] and also as one who demands our allegiance and obedience every bit as much as does the categorical imperative.

The boldness with which Barth affirms the "gladly" of real humanity points out one of his chief differences with Calvin and the Calvinists. Barth emphasizes the "gladly" to such a degree, in part, because he wants his anthropology to break out of the sober mold forged by Calvin's doctrine of double election and reinforced in his doctrine of total depravity.[217] It is also likely that Barth desires to proclaim his departure from the melancholy individualism of most existentialist philosophers, including Kierkegaard.

But even more than Calvin or the existentialists, it is likely that Barth

---

214. E.g., Christ is the "head" *(kephalos)* in whom all Christians are urged to "grow up" *(auxēsōmen)*, Eph. 4:15; cf. Rom. 8:29.

215. It is interesting that Barth, atypically, does not provide much scriptural evidence for his fourfold basic form of humanity, though that does not mean that we find the scriptural evidence to be lacking. On seeing eye to eye, see Luke 6:20; 24:16; John 6:5; Acts 3:4; Rev. 1:14; 2:18; 7:17; 19:12; 21:4. On mutual speaking and listening, see Matt. 11:15; 13:9, 43; Luke 11:28; 14:35; 15:1; 19:48. On rendering assistance, see Matt. 8:7; 12:15; Luke 9:11; 4:40-41. On gladness, see 1 John 1:4; 2 John 12; 3 John 4; Jude 24.

216. 1 John 1:1.

217. See *CD*, IV/1, pp. 365-66.

has Kant in mind when he emphasizes the "gladly." Barth attempts to show how dogmatic anthropology contains more joy than Kant's so-called categorical imperative. Like Kant, Barth realizes that there must be some form of duty woven into the fabric of Christian ethics.[218] But, unlike Kant, Barth does not see the basic form of humanity as an onerous duty under the cheerless weight of the categorical imperative. Rather, the basic form of humanity is a conformity to the real human determination (or destiny) that is revealed in the humanity of Jesus. Our real humanity has been graciously revealed in Christ — in the real humanity of Christ, and not Christ as an ideal of humanity. Therefore it is a destiny to which we are called by grace, hence comes the joy, the "gladly" that characterizes the real form of humanity.[219] Barth advocates an ethic that flows out of the riches of grace, not one that precedes grace. It is an ethic that flows out of the basic form *(Grundform)* of our humanity, which, even though it has been despised and dishonored, cannot be completely shattered. We see, therefore, how Barth attempts to overcome the impasse Kant reached with regard to radical evil: while the mystery of how the uncorrupted will became corrupt has not been solved, the mystery of how the corrupt will can become good is now revealed in the man Jesus. And Barth insists that we can meet the grace that affirms our real humanity, *gladly.*[220]

"Being in Encounter" and Sexual Polarity

Having established that the human being is "fellow-human" in the encounter of I and Thou, Barth does not wish to leave the basic form of humanity up in the air, so to speak. He thus grounds the encounter in the basic differentiation between male and female. Barth has shown that even if theory and practice sometimes contradict it, fellow humanity is a constant that cannot be com-

218. See *CD*, II/2, pp. 650-51. Barth admits that the "ought" is something that Kant correctly perceived, but goes on to show that "the essence of the idea of obligation is not that I demand something from myself but that, with all that I can demand of myself, I am myself demanded" (p. 651). Thus even Kant's categorical imperative demands to be grounded in something higher than the self-legislation of reason. This requirement is met by Christian ethics in its Christological foundations. Christology is also the means by which Barth thinks we can meet the demand to treat people as ends in themselves and not merely means to an end, as Kant's kingdom of ends rightly demanded but sometimes failed to achieve.

219. The ethical implications of the "gladly" are worked out by Barth in *CD*, III/4, pp. 374ff.

220. Barth describes the "joyful" character of Christian ethics in a very moving passage in *CD*, IV/3 (2), pp. 661-62. From §71, "The Liberation of the Christian."

pletely obscured. Fellow humanity is most specifically illustrated by sexual polarity. Barth proposes:

> May it not be that this particular place is attended, at least in the so-called civilised nations, by so much interest and curiosity, but also so much reticence and anxiety, so much phantasy, poetry, morality and immorality, and so much empty talk and sighing and sniggering on the part of the inexperienced, because there are so few who realise they they have to do here with the centre of the human, the basic form of primal humanity? . . . There is no being of man above the being of male and female.[221]

Barth is clear that he does not wish to discuss the psychology of the sexes, the specific outworking of the sexual differentiation that may refer to either cultural stereotypes or psychological archetypes. What interests him here is the encounter between male and female itself, in which each may have the same thing: "the other."[222] In describing male and female as our most basic form, Barth is not implying that there can be no relationships between male and male, or female and female. He means that all relationships are subsumed under the original relationship of male and female. Even in the relations of male to male and female to female, male and female is the basic structural distinction; by this Barth means that we cannot exist other than as a male or a female. But he also is pointing to a less obvious fact that in the differentiation of male and female we find a clue to the meaning of our existence: we are made to be in relation to "the other." Barth reasons that eventually "even human being which is temporarily isolated will definitely bear and in some way reveal the character of this one particular distinction and connexion."[223]

---

221. *CD*, III/2, p. 289. See also *CD*, III/4, pp. 117ff.

222. *CD*, III/2, p. 289.

223. *CD*, III/2, p. 287. The ready objection that Barth does not do justice to either the reality or the ontology of homosexuality, or even celibacy, is one that must be taken seriously. The phenomena of homosexuality or celibacy might at first seem to be a denial of Barth's insistence that fellow humanity means male and female in differentiation and encounter. But the life of a celibate, a hermit, or a homosexual would contradict fellow humanity as male and female only, if a closer look at the apparent absence of male and female encounter failed to reveal some sign of its essential importance, even in its absence. More needs to be said about this, but it cannot be dealt with at length here. See *CD*, III/1, pp. 186ff., 288ff.; III/4, p. 166. See also Anderson, *On Being Human*, pp. 107ff., 127-28.

Sexual Polarity and the Covenants

The relationship between male and female is rooted in the covenant of God with Israel. Thus marriage is a reflection of God's covenant with his people — first with Israel, and later with the church. Barth cites the J creation saga (esp. Gen. 2:18-25) and its theological unity with the P saga (esp. Gen. 1:26-27) as evidence for the rejection of human beings in isolation.[224] Therefore, "this basic distinction, the differentiation and connexion of I and Thou, must be explained as coincident with that of male and female. All other relationships are involved in this as the original relationship."[225] Furthermore, the poetry of the love songs, says Barth, is possible only in the context of Yahweh as the faithful protector of his covenant with Israel. The covenant of marriage thus rests on the covenant of Yahweh with Israel. Ephesians 5:21-33 provides Barth with the exegetical grounds for saying that the marriage covenant reflects the divine covenant. Christ's relationship to the church serves as the prototype for humanity as male and female. Barth concludes that against the background of Ephesians 5 and the New Testament as a whole:

> the basic thesis of theological anthropology, that human being is a being in encounter, loses every shred of similarity with a mere hypothetical assertion. It acquires an axiomatic and dogmatic quality. In the Christian Church we have no option but to interpret humanity as fellow-humanity. And *si quis dixerit hominem esse solitarium, anathema sit.* We can now regard this as secured and demonstrated. And the future history of humanity may well depend to some extent upon whether the Christian Church can agree to recognise this as secured and demonstrated, and thereafter assert that anathema with a stringency for which it has so far lacked both the perception and the resolution.[226]

One might object that Barth has packed too much into the category of "male and female." In what sense does every human encounter indicate the male and female differentiation? Barth has perhaps made a sweeping generalization in subsuming every type of relation under that of male and female.

---

224. *CD*, III/2, p. 291. Cf. III/1, pp. 288-89. For Barth's impact on Old Testament scholars with regard to his exegesis of Genesis 1 and 2, see Johann Jakob Stamm, "Die Imago-Lehre von Karl Barth und die alttestamentliche Wissenschaft," in *Der Mensch als Bild Gott*, ed. Leo Sheffczyck (Darmstadt: Wissenschaftliche Buchgesellschaft, 1969) pp. 49-68. Cf. Berkouwer, *Man: The Image of God*, p. 74.

225. *CD*, III/2, pp. 292-93.

226. *CD*, III/2, pp. 318-19.

For example, the relation between parents and children, an individual to a nation or institution, or friends of the same sex cannot be immediately explained in terms of male and female relations; and it is perhaps insulting to state that any relation other than that of male and female is only a "preliminary accompaniment for this true encounter."[227] Barth concedes that there are diverse forms of human relationships; yet he insists that whatever form relationships might take, they all point to the male-female relation as their "subterranean motive." Here Barth is close to Freud in some respects, inasmuch as both of them argue that sexuality is the motivating force behind almost every human interaction — whether or not it appears that way on the surface. While there are certain similarities, there are also important differences between Barth's interpretation of sexuality and Freud's. A closer comparison will come in the following chapters.

If the reader stumbles over Barth's heavy emphasis on sexual polarity, his chief point should not be lost: human beings are created more for companionship than solitude.[228] This insight nails down a theological linchpin for all who labor as pastors, Christian counselors, and mental health professionals. In spite of the much needed contemporary emphasis on personal meditation, contemplation, and spiritual development, we must still remember that our spirituality cannot be successfully developed in isolation.

The Human Being as Soul and Body

I discuss the relation of soul and body briefly here, and expand on it in chapter six.

Barth continues to explore the Christological implications for what it means to be human. He turns his attention to the relationship between soul and body with the following statement, which is laced with Chalcedonian language: the human being is "soul and body totally and simultaneously, in indissoluble differentiation, inseparable unity and indestructible order."[229]

This terminology may sound a bit strained at first glance, but its occasionally awkward bulkiness yields to its thoughtful balance. Barth is fighting a battle on two fronts, and must achieve a balanced clarity in order to win his case; he is opposing both the reductionist anthropologies of positivist science of his day, and the stubborn dualism of soul and body that has so weightily

---

227. *CD*, III/2, p. 293.
228. See *CD*, III/2, pp. 291ff.; III/1, pp. 288-89.
229. *CD*, III/2, p. 437. See also p. 325.

influenced Christian anthropology from the time of the Gnostics right up until and including the twentieth century. The former anthropology reduced the human being to a body without a soul, the soul being either denied or conceded as a mere epiphenomenon of the higher bodily events. The latter denied the necessity of the body to human existence, nearly reducing the human being to a discussion of the soul, wherein the human body "was almost always emphatically disregarded."[230] Barth is convinced that neither position satisfies the requirements of biblical anthropology.

Barth's purpose in this section is to prove that the human being is a unity; soul and body are not, therefore, intrinsically opposed substances. This proof is undertaken, once again, in a theological sense. It is taken from Christology, and is not beholden to anthropologies in any other science, even if one might find "parallel or divergent presentations in other disciplines."[231] The relation between body and soul will nevertheless have many similarities with the problem of the relations between mind and body with which the philosopher and psychologist must deal. Since my purpose in delineating Barth's anthropology is to point out the significant parallels with object relations psychology, I will draw out a fuller sketch of the relation between soul and body in pages 249-57.[232]

Summary of Barth's Anthropology

In summarizing Barth's anthropology, it should be apparent that while Christology is necessary for Barth's anthropology, it is not sufficient. Barth's anthropology is not built on the life of Jesus apart from his trinitarian relationship to the Father in the Spirit. A careful reading of this important volume of the *Dogmatics* reveals that Barth's anthropology is interpreted foremost in terms of the triune God. It can hardly be stated more clearly than Barth has already put it himself, that just as God is a being in relation with himself as Father and Son in the Spirit, so the human essence is reflected in the being of the man Jesus, a man who lived his life in encounter with God and others. This is the divine determination for human beings that overcomes human sin and restores the image of God. Jesus' solidarity with the human race, his essential humanity, reveals the human essence. Human essence, therefore, is re-

230. *CD*, III/2, p. 325.
231. *CD*, III/2, p. 327.
232. Barth also discusses the human being in relation to time. This is an illuminating discussion that might also prove very interesting in interdisciplinary dialogue with other sciences. However, it falls outside the specific scope of this study.

lational. It is being in encounter. It is the existing human being, acting within the field of relations one to another. It is seeing, hearing, helping, and enjoying the companionship of others. It is encounter as opposites: I and Thou, male and female. Being in encounter is a "history" because it is here, and only here, in the life of Jesus that we encounter one who is truly human, and yet truly "Other" than we are — one who is capable of breaking through our sinful and inward bent and establishing a life-giving relation that restores our vital humanity. There is therefore no human being who is isolated, static, or purely individual. Isolation from God and others is the essence of brokenness and sin. Thus understood, Barth's concept of the person is "dynamic."

Barth develops his dynamic anthropology on four levels of relations: the human being is constituted by simultaneous relations to God, others, self, and time. Relation to God is primary; it is the first and foremost relation that the theologian must describe. It is a relation that other disciplines will for the most part disregard (perhaps rightly so). The relation of the self to God defines the field of theological anthropology. No other field will have the relation to God as its primary concern. But the relation to God does not end there: it necessarily entails relations to self and others. Barth has affirmed forcefully that we are by nature creatures who need relationships with others. Here, in the being-constituting relations of the self with others, we should expect that any science which studies human behavior might provide some parallels to what Barth is saying. It is here, in the social field, what Macmurray calls "the field of the personal," that we would expect to find parallels between theological anthropology and scientific psychology. This, I argue, is precisely what we find when we compare Barth to modern object relations psychology. We discover that human psychology can be greatly illuminated by examining the field of relations that surround the individual from the earliest moments of infancy and into early childhood. The similarities and differences between Barth and modern object relations psychology are the subject matter of chapters five and six.

The important thing to recall once again from Barth's anthropology is that the human being is not a solitary being. This point needs to be constantly reemphasized in the Western world — especially the United States — where alienation, isolation, and rugged individualism have held us hostage for a long while. The Western church, too, is particularly susceptible to the isolating forces of modernism and postmodernism unless it pays attention here.

Barth's friend and faithful critic, Emil Brunner, aptly summarized his review of volume III/2: "Whatever may be said about this volume, there is one thing no one can leave unsaid: It is of all Barth's works his most human."[233] It

233. "The New Barth," *SJT* 4 (1951) 135.

is precisely this human element that should enable the church to reach beyond its bounds to see the vast sea of human need and respond on behalf of Christ. It is also this human element that could enable theology to reach beyond its bounds and engage in mutual dialogue with other disciplines that also seek through their discoveries the ennoblement and service of the human race.

CHAPTER 5

The Human Being in Object Relations Psychology: Empirical Evidence for a Relational Psychology

For close to a century now, many psychologists have seemed to suppose that the methods of natural science are totally specifiable and specified. . . . The stipulation that psychology be adequate to science outweighed the commitment that it be adequate to man.

SIGMUND KOCH

This chapter involves a discussion of the person from the standpoint of object relations psychology. In order to understand object relations,[1] one must have some familiarity with its seminal beginnings in Freud's psychoanalytic theory. I thus begin with Freud, and show how object relations developed both negatively, as a rejection of his instinctual theory, and positively, from the object relational elements that were present in many of his works. In order to narrow the scope of discussion, I have chosen the object relations theory of W. Ronald D. Fairbairn to represent the object relations school.[2] This chapter therefore begins with Freud, moves on to the object relations theory of Fairbairn, and concludes by drawing out the implications of object relations psychology for a modern concept of personhood. In the conclusion of this chapter, I indicate why I believe object relations contains a high degree of significance for theology. The purpose of this discussion is not to outline mod-

1. Hereafter when I use the term "object relations," I am referring to a specific branch of modern psychology. For a further definition of object relations psychology see below.
2. I give my reasons for choosing Fairbairn below.

ern object relations psychology per se, but to assess its salient points for the purpose of comparing the respective anthropologies of Barth and object relations in chapter six.

I have shown in chapter four on Barth that the human being cannot be considered in isolation from God and others. The "real" person is rather a whole person, in dynamic encounter with God and others: an "I" who exists in encounter with a "Thou." Barth arrived at his dynamic anthropology Christologically, from drawing on the resources of Christian revelation. When we survey the theoretical development of psychoanalytic theory, we find a similar theme on an altogether different level of discussion.

Obviously, the method of inquiry in modern psychology is markedly different from the method used by Barth in his attempts to explain a dogmatic Christian anthropology.[3] Nevertheless, Christian anthropology is not "dogmatic" because it supersedes the truth-claims of other disciplines; as we have seen in chapter one, dogmatic anthropology that takes seriously the Christian doctrine of the Trinity should be grounded in the same space-time reality as the other sciences. There must therefore be certain parallels between theological anthropology and the human sciences; Barth sometimes refers to the points of agreement between theology and psychology as "material parallelism" *(sachliche Berührung).*[4] These "parallels" are most intriguing because their respective modes of investigation are so different that we would hardly suspect theoretical collusion. A full comparison of the similarities will be made in chapter six below, but let me state briefly what I think are the major points of similarity.

In tracing the theory of the self from the genesis of Freud's psychoanalytic insights to object relations, we will see that in object relations theory a fundamental shift of the understanding of the nature of the person takes place. In Fairbairn's thought the self, or "ego,"[5] cannot exist alone. The ego

3. It is usually acknowledged that object relations derived its seminal beginning with some of the essays of Freud. Who can deny that no one would be less likely to accept the premises of Christology than Freud? There is thus a certain irony in comparing the findings of these two thinkers. Nevertheless, most of Freud's successors parted sharply with his contention that religion is an illicit illusion, mostly explained away in terms of a psychological need for the protection of an idealized father figure.

4. See *CD*, III/4, p. 138. The English term "parallel" is a rather poor word to convey what Barth is getting at here, since it almost sounds as if Barth is advocating some type of parallelism in order to explain the connection between nature and grace. Such is not the case. Barth is rather describing similarities between actual points of fact in theology and the human sciences. The translation "parallel" is used here because on the following page (and elsewhere) Barth uses the more common German word for "parallel," *Parallele,* to describe this relation.

5. "Ego" is a fluid term, depending largely on the theorist who is using it, but usually referring to the integrating agency of the psychological self.

grows through the stage of "*infantile* dependence" to "*mature* dependence" as the individual forms personal relations to an "other" — technically referred to as "object." The psychological development of the person in object relations is essentially social: a whole person, body and mind (psyche), shaped by relations to other persons. The ego, or self, in object relations theory is motivated not by detached instincts, but by the need to form a relationship to an external object. Whereas Freud posited the individual as inherently instinctual and pleasure seeking, in object relations the individual is inherently social: in Fairbairn's terms, "object-seeking." Fairbairn's object relations theory shows how the organic categories of modern evolution fall short of providing a comprehensive explanation of the observable human phenomena. In other words, there is a point at which the organic anthropologies reach an impasse in their capacity to explain human love and human society. Interpersonal love is more than a complex layering of crude impulses.

Object relations has become a branch of modern scientific psychology that is broadly defined. Object relations is sometimes equated with, other times contrasted to, ego psychology. It has nevertheless become a discernible field of study within the psychoanalytic tradition.[6] Object relations is one among a number of psychoanalytic theories that attempts to describe the enormous complexity of the formation of the human personality. The term "object" generally refers to another person; hence the term might seem ill chosen in light of what it describes. However, the "object" may also refer to a more complex internalized psychological representation of the person — or part of the person — to which the child or infant relates; hence the technical employment of the term is sometimes both necessary and useful.

Although most object relations theorists have moved well beyond Freud, they are divided in their opinions about the importance of instinctual theory. As studies continue, and data revise psychoanalytic theory, Fairbairn's insights are becoming increasingly dated as well. In my view, however, Fairbairn has done a good job of pointing out the inherent shortcomings of instinctual theory. Fairbairn built his personality theories largely on the depth psychology of Freud, but departed sharply from Freud's biological reductionism.[7] I have chosen to focus on Fairbairn because I believe that

6. Thus Peter Buckley, ed., *Essential Papers on Object Relations* (New York and London: New York University Press, 1986) p. xi, observes that the diversity within object relations theories is so great that it is better described as a continuum than a uniform theoretical persuasion. Cf. Sue Walrond-Skinner, *A Dictionary of Psychotherapy* (London and New York: Routledge & Kegan Paul, 1986) s.v. "Object Relations."

7. The chief advocate and interpreter of Fairbairn's object relations theory is Harry Guntrip. I refer extensively to his works on the development of psychoanalytic theory. Some

he was able to take the important insights of Freud and push beyond Freud's conceptual framework at certain critical junctures. In this sense, his departure from Freud represents a significant landmark in our understanding of persons. Furthermore, Fairbairn's ability to interpret the basic notions of psychoanalytic theory in light of the insights of the new physics indicates that he was one of the few social scientists to attempt to break free from the influence of logical positivism. Such a positivist stance was largely instigated by Comte and reigned from the nineteenth century until well past the midpoint of the twentieth century. Positivism often forced the application of classical Newtonian concepts to fields of inquiry outside physics with disastrous consequences. For example, Freud's ideas were perceptibly influenced by the Newtonian worldview and the discoveries of many of the laws of thermodynamics. He began his work with the implicit assumption that the discoveries of contemporary physics and chemistry could provide instructive paradigms for the study of human mental processes. In my view, he went wrong from the start. Nevertheless, Freud's perspectives are engaging for anyone interested in modern concepts of the person. This is partly because his observations were so keen and his theoretical applications so original. It is also because Freud's works aspired to discuss all aspects of human life from his own psychoanalytic perspective, including theories of human civilization, philosophy of science, and religion.

In tracing back the beginnings of object relations to Freud's psychoanalytic theories, one finds that Freud's implicit anthropologies defy easy categorization. For the most part, Freud's model of the person evolved through three stages, each succeeding the former as it proved insufficient to explain the complexities of the psyche. Freud developed first a mechanical, then an instinctual, and finally he *began* to construct a truly interpersonal, or psychodynamic, theory of the person. While these three stages unfold generally during the course of Freud's writings and research, they did not develop in a strict chronological order. Within the same essay Freud would frequently employ concepts that were both biologically reductionist and interpersonally dynamic. I outline Freud, then, primarily to provide a context for understanding object relations theory. But secondarily I wish to show that in many instances psychology had become overly enamored with the success of the supposedly more precise physical and biological sciences, and thus short-

---

have criticized Guntrip's interpretation of Fairbairn; but I find the criticisms due mostly to the perspective of the authors who wish to take issue with Guntrip's interpretation that Fairbairn made a clean departure from Freud's psychology based on instincts. See Otto Kernberg, *Internal World and External Reality* (New York and London: Aronson, 1980) pp. 58-59.

circuited its attempts to become a science of the psyche.[8] In this chapter I hope to convince the reader that a true science of the human soul should not attempt to force the concept of the person into mechanical or organic categories, because the languages appropriate to both mechanisms and organisms cannot fully comprehend the reality of human beings.

My second purpose in outlining the three stages of Freud's anthropology is to give an example that corroborates Barth's insistence that the materialist anthropologies — both ancient and modern — have proved inadequate to describe the human soul. Even by the requirements of modern psychoanalytic theory alone, the human being cannot be contained solely within the categories of physics, chemistry, or biology. Freud struggled first with mechanistic, then organic, and finally with a more dynamic-interpersonal model of the person in order to explain human psychology. His attempt to find an adequate explanation for the human mind seems a fitting illustration of the fact that the truth about us as humans must be viewed as hierarchical, or "stratified," with any scientific interpretation of human "nature" always dependent on both a lower, physical explanation of who we are, and a higher metascientific understanding that can be provided only by a philosopher, theologian, or any honest soul who is willing to incorporate meaning, values, and purpose into the discussion. It is precisely this need to take into account the higher level of interpersonal dynamics that occurs in object relations. Object relations thus converges with more recent scientific paradigms in bursting the bonds of the materialist and reductionist assumptions that were originally adopted by Freud and most social scientists of the nineteenth and early twentieth centuries.[9] Freud's ways of explaining the human mind were undeniably brilliant; yet psychology was bound to build on his insights and push beyond them. Object relations is one field of psychology that did.

It is worth noting that both Barth and object relations psychology advocated major paradigm shifts in the way we construct our self-concept. Each cries out against a prevailing view by making some piercing criticisms of anthropologies that are either dualistic or materialistic. Yet it was the genius of both Barth and Fairbairn that they could point the way beyond the

---

8. See, e.g., Arnold Modell, "Primitive Object Relationships and the Predisposition to Schizophrenia," in Buckley, *Essential Papers,* pp. 329-49, who argues that the imprecision of psychoanalysis should not induce it to prematurely employ the methods of the physical sciences. This would emulate the sciences that mistakenly applied Newtonian methods to fields of study outside classical physics. See esp. pp. 329-31.

9. For a basic definition of truth as "hierarchical," see Torrance, *Reality and Scientific Theology,* esp. chap. 5, "The Stratification of Truth."

former models and paradigms. It is difficult to pinpoint the weaknesses of the prevailing views, but much more difficult still to provide an alternative view that will stand up even under the weight of one's own criticisms. Barth did not merely reject the idealist anthropologies of ages gone by — he provided a positive alternative through a different approach. Fairbairn likewise put his finger on some of the weaknesses of Freud's anthropology. He then proceeded to provide a fresh alternative to the anthropology based on an evolutionary understanding of the instincts, by advocating an object relations approach.[10]

In many of the recent psychological theories it is encouraging to see that certain reductionist assumptions and post-Kantian dualisms have been called into serious question. It is likely that some recent developments within psychology have opened up the possibilities for an increased dialogue between "religion" and modern psychological science. Some of these insights are based on some psychologists' willingness to embrace the so-called postmodern or post-critical understanding of reality.[11] While this new stage of potential openness between psychology and religion is highly encouraging, it also warrants some caution. In any rapprochement there is the risk that one discipline will take the other hostage even in the midst of a seemingly warm embrace. In my view, interdisciplinary dialogue will not prove fruitful if it obscures the particular object of study with which the respective subjects deal. In simplest terms, theology should deal with God as its object of study. Exact sciences deal with physical objects and the replicable patterns of relations that pertain to those objects. Psychology must deal with the soul. If the fragmented view of reality advocated by many postmodern philosophers continues to advance, then we should expect to find cross-disciplinary studies of the person both increasing and decreasing: increasing in the sense that almost "anything goes," and decreasing in the sense that finding common intellectual ground will become increasingly difficult.

A psychology that takes the existence of the soul seriously does not mean, of course, that the biological components of human life can be ne-

---

10. The difference of course is that Fairbairn's criticisms of Freud are still just that: the voice of a minor prophet building on and dissenting against a major one. With Barth, his theology can no longer be viewed merely as a reaction against scholastic, Roman, or liberal theology, but as a major achievement in and of itself.

11. See, e.g., R. W. Sperry, "Psychology's Mentalist Paradigm and the Religion/Science Tension," *American Psychologist* 43 (1988) 607-13. Nevertheless, the new eagerness of behavioral science to embrace a wider worldview must itself be critically assessed by philosophers and theologians who might see the expansion of open-ended scientific worldviews as encroachment on the domain of theology and philosophy.

glected. Both Freud and object relations make a sound case for the importance of the biological realities of life. They demonstrate that the biological dimension plays an important role in the constitution of the human being. Modern theologians should listen to their findings. Modern psychology's serious consideration of the biological components of human life provides a much-needed corrective to many anthropologies of the classical and medieval periods that denied our physical side. Furthermore, a due consideration to the physical and biological realities of life fits well with Hebraic-biblical anthropology in which the unitary structure of the material and spiritual is specifically assumed. The latter view, I believe, has been followed more closely by Barth than most theologians of Western Christendom.

While the many parallels between Barth's anthropology and the anthropology of object relations are both intriguing and significant, I nevertheless respect the boundaries between theology and psychology. These are separate disciplines with very distinct objects of study. Psychology's theoretical task is to match its language to the nature of the human mental events, or psyche, through continued research and clinical observation. On the other hand, theology's task is to discuss the human being in relation to God. Psychology would overstep its own boundaries by seeking to discuss the person in relation to God. In the first four chapters I spent a good deal of time attempting to put Barth's theological anthropology into its proper context. In this chapter I attempt to do the same for object relations psychology. This is because I am committed to the view that both disciplines must first be understood on their own ground before they can be compared. Another way of saying it is this: the relationship between the similar terminology in Barth and object relations is analogical, but not univocal. The language and technical terms of both respective disciplines depend on an appropriate semantic context in order to obtain a viable comparison with the ideas of another discipline.

In spite of the differences, we should expect to find significant parallels between theological anthropology and psychology. From their respective frames of reference they are, after all, attempting to study the same object: the human subject. As noted in my first chapter, any radical disagreement between theological anthropology and scientific anthropologies, between nature and grace, would pose a threat to the unity of truth. In spite of the supposed influence of postmodern philosophy, most persons today still assume that where science and religion disagree, "someone got it wrong." I still operate from the premise that all truth is cut from the same fabric. Hence a theology detached from space and time would fall into an unacceptable dualism that separates faith from history, fact from value, and mind from matter.[12] One of my motivations for developing an extended comparison between Barth and object relations psychology is to point out that Barth's anthropology is in fact embedded in the space-time plane of the real world. In other words, Barth's trinitarian anthropology cannot be rightly understood if we insist on viewing it as a self-enclosed circle that hangs on revealed truths suspended by the clouds. Barth's doctrine of the person, contrary to the opinions of many of his critics, is capable of carrying on a meaningful and sustained dialogue with the scientific studies of the person.

Another concern in this chapter is to illustrate how biological reductionism fails to provide a good basis for a concept of the person. In my study of Freud, I hope to show how neither instinctual attraction nor repulsion can fully explain human love.[13] The realities of human interactions cannot be adequately explained apart from love itself. Only love can comprehend the various dimensions of human existence — including love's absence. These and other findings of object relations psychology, I will argue, are strongly analogous to what Barth has discovered on the theological level.

Freud's Developing View of the Human Being: From Psychophysiology to Psychology

Many psychologists would agree with Guntrip's observation that Sigmund Freud has become to psychoanalytic theory what Isaac Newton is to classical

---

12. Thus Meissner argues that the religious perspective embraces the entire spectrum of reality, and if the ego functions related to the supernatural as well as the natural world are granted, there must be some arena where psychoanalysis touches on theology and depends on theology, "since it makes explicit what revelation tells us about the character of the supernatural" (*Psychoanalysis and Religious Experience* [New Haven and London: Yale University Press, 1984] p. 210). Meissner develops his views on a *gratia perficit naturam* model. Meissner's point still holds, even though I argue that Barth's trinitarian and incarnational model is even more adaptable for such a dialogue with psychology.

13. The basic themes of biological reductionism have been carried into the present-day anthropologies by a host of modern social scientists, including those in the recently blossomed field of sociobiology. Many of these are quick to claim Freud as their progenitor: e.g., Edward O. Wilson, *Sociobiology: The New Synthesis* (Cambridge: Harvard University Press, 1975); idem, *On Human Nature* (Cambridge: Harvard University Press, 1978). He extends population biology and evolutionary theory to human social development in order to explain even unique human behaviors such as altruism. See also Frank J. Sulloway, *Freud: Biologist of the Mind* (London: Burnett, 1979), esp. p. 500.

physics.[14] Both were pioneers in their respective fields. But, as Guntrip observes: "it is not the function of the pioneer to say the last word but to say the first word."[15] It was Freud who first observed the psychological importance of the childhood relationships to the parents, and it was Freud who developed the terminology that began the field of psychoanalysis. Freud's observations on the importance of childhood for adult life, and the terminology, including the term "sexual object," were expanded by object relations psychology into a theory of human personality that delineates the importance of interpersonal relations especially during the time of infancy and early childhood. As I survey the development of Freud's assumptions about the person, I attempt to show how the "interpersonal" elements within his own later discoveries outstripped his earlier premises.

It was in the latter half of the nineteenth century that scientific psychology made a marked break with philosophical and theological psychology.[16] The commonly acknowledged founder of scientific psychology is Wilhelm Wundt (1832-1920). In his Leipzig laboratory, Wundt was allegedly the first to study the human mind according to causal laws. His research was coupled with a theory of psychophysical parallelism that avoided any theoretical explanation of how the mind and body interact. It was not long, however, before Wundt's structural dualism gave way to a more monistic theory of the human being.[17] Such monism was often based on a positivist understanding of the world, and leaned toward a more empirical psychology. In contrast to the parallelism of Wundt, the perceptual studies of Hermann von Helmholtz (1821-1894) and Ernst Brücke (1819-1892) were wedded to a neo-Kantian philosophy that was based on strongly anti-vitalist, and ultimately positivist, premises. While Freud was attending the medical university at Vienna, both Helmholtz and Brücke were tremendously influential in his early training and intellectual development. Freud became one of Brücke's outstanding students. Upon completing his studies the young

14. See *Personality Structure and Human Interactions* (London: Hogarth, 1961). Guntrip writes (p. 43): "In sober truth all the fundamental new ideas *did* come from Freud himself."

15. *Psychoanalytic Theory, Therapy, and the Self* (New York: Basic Books, 1973) p. 3.

16. An excellent survey of the history of modern psychology can be found in H. Misiak and Virginia Sexton, *History of Psychology* (New York and London: Grune & Stratton, 1966). Less specific, but more pertinent to Christian theology, is the survey in Mary Stewart Van Leeuwen, *The Person in Psychology* (Leicester: Intervarsity Press; Grand Rapids: Eerdmans, 1985) chaps. 1–5.

17. By "monist" I am referring to the monist anthropologies as they were promulgated by William James (1842-1910) and later by Bertrand Russell, wherein they theorized that subjective feelings were stimulated by bodily changes caused by some kind of "excitation." It has little to do with the monist metaphysics of idealists such as Hegel and Spinoza.

Freud was expected to land a post in physiological research. No posts were open at the time, so financial necessity compelled him to become a medical doctor rather than a research physiologist.[18] It is important to note that Helmholtz, usually acknowledged as the school's leader, had provided the mathematical background for the formulation of the law of the conservation of energy. The concept of energy equilibrium greatly influences Freud's psychological theories.[19]

Many who have studied Freud have found that three successive models of the human being emerge from his thought: (1) the neurological model of "The Project for a Scientific Psychology" (1895), (2) the apparently more psychological model of "The Interpretation of Dreams" (c. 1900-1920), as superseded by (3) the endopsychic structural scheme of the id, ego, and superego found in such works as "Beyond the Pleasure Principle," "Group Psychology and the Analysis of the Ego," and "The Ego and the Id" (1920s-30s).[20] Freud based the first model on physical and biochemical types of changes, employing the language of neurology and the conceptual framework of thermodynamics that at the time was under the influence of Helmholtz's energy conservation theory.[21] The second probed the depths of the unconscious, and basically employed organic-evolutionary models of the person to explain the origins of hysteria and other psychological symptoms through sexual repression.[22] The third took account of human relations in forming the psychology of the individual person. The last stage reveals a relational and psycho-

18. See Sulloway, *Freud,* pp. 14ff.

19. According to Sulloway, *Freud,* p. 66, Freud was not the first to introduce the mechanistic thrust of Helmholtz into psychoanalytic theories. Rather, the neo-Kantian psychophysicist Theodore Fechner first introduced the idea of the law of conservation of energy into psychology. For Freud's mention of the influence of Fechner on his own thought, see *The Standard Edition of the Complete Psychological Works of Sigmund Freud,* ed. J. Strachey, tr. J. Strachey, et al., 24 vols. (London: Hogarth, 1953-74) XX, p. 59. Hereafter referred to as *S.E.* with volume indicated by Roman numeral.

20. E.g., K. M. Colby, *Energy and Structure in Psychoanalysis* (New York: Ronald, 1965). This is also the basic outline followed by Sulloway, *Freud,* although Sulloway's intent is to minimize the importance of Freud's third stage and root Freud's thinking in biology. See also Guntrip, *Personality Structure,* pp. 17, 55-118, 159. It must be admitted, however, that any single synopsis of the writings of so complex and vast a thinker as Freud is always susceptible to oversimplification.

21. Meissner, *Psychoanalysis,* pp. 6-7, observes that the laws of thermodynamics in particular provided Freud with his scientific paradigm, e.g., exchange of energy, inertia, the thresholds of stimulation and response, inertia and constancy.

22. Although the former thermodynamic model that adhered to energy homeostasis was never completely absent.

dynamic dimension to Freud's thought that was especially evident in his writings about the superego and the Oedipus complex.[23]

Guntrip and others have observed that Freud could not push ahead and fully develop his dynamic model for fear of leaving behind the positivistic presuppositions that he thought could not be questioned. Freud's concern to integrate the biophysical and psychological dimensions of the human being was understandable, especially in view of the unacceptable tenet of structural psychology that isolated the mind from the body in the form of parallelism.[24] In Freud's view, the biophysical explorations of early psychology seemed to provide its only possible foundation for becoming a science. He therefore held to his instinctual theory, even when he was pushing well beyond it in his later essays that stressed the importance of ego and relations to external "objects."[25] Fairbairn explains that in Freud's later thought, "a developing psychology of the ego came to be superimposed upon an already established psychology of impulse." We shall see that Fairbairn thought such a structure unwieldy in explaining the psychological facts, a situation that he hoped to remedy in his own theory.[26]

Attempts at a Physiological Anthropology: "The Project for a Scientific Psychology"

The purpose of the Project at the time it was written appears to have been to supplant vitalist categories of understanding human behavior with a framework for understanding human actions from brain physiology.[27] In 1895 Freud was convinced that mental processes were hidden, or represented, in some form in the brain. In the Project Freud equated mental

23. See Guntrip, *Psychoanalytic Theory,* pp. 29-30.

24. For Barth's discussion and rejection of the parallelism advocated by Wundt, Fechner, Paulsen, et al., see *CD,* III/2, pp. 428-29.

25. On the importance of the ego, see "The Ego and the Id," *S.E.,* XIX ([1923] 1961); and regarding objects as important in psychological development, see esp. "Civilization and Its Discontents," *S.E.,* XXI ([1929] 1961), esp. p. 95.

26. *Psychoanalytic Studies of the Personality* (London: Tavistock, 1952) p. 59. See also p. 83.

27. The "Project" was published only posthumously in 1950. Its original title in German was *Aus den Anfängen der Psychoanalyse* ("From the beginnings of psychoanalysis"). It was retrieved from Freud's letters to Wilhelm Fliess. Freud's final attitude toward the Project is hotly debated in psychological circles even up to the present. See n. 40 below. It nonetheless remains a highly important work, for it reveals the ideas that undergird so much of Freud's later theories.

events with neurological events. Freud's expressed intention in the Project was to "furnish a psychology that shall be a natural science: that is, to represent psychical processes as quantitatively determinate states of specifiable material particles, thus making those processes perspicuous and free from contradiction."[28]

Freud's Project assumed a passive and mechanistic view of the human being, an assumption that was largely shaped by the neurological research that he had undertaken with Brücke.[29] Freud's vocabulary in the Project is dominated by terms such as "contact barriers," and the flow of energy through "permeable" and "impermeable neurones." [30] To the unsuspecting reader of the Project it would seem to be nothing more than a description of the neurological mechanisms of memory and perception. Meissner observes: "The view of man adopted by Freud in his early attempts to conceptualize a model of human behavior was essentially this mechanistic one. . . . The principles on which the Project is constructed are both neuronal and thermodynamic."[31] Ernest Jones also describes the scientific knowledge available in the fledgling field of brain physiology during the time in which Freud undertook the Project as essentially employing the language of "physics — with terms like energy, tension, force, etc. — in another sphere."[32]

Writing just five years before the turn of the century, Freud believed that the energy level in the nervous system could be interpreted in roughly the same terms as the contemporary thermodynamic models. Thus a constant state of physiological tension or excitation was assumed, and a stimulus of input would result in an immediate discharge along the path of least resistance in order to return to the constant level of excitation. Sources of the excitation were the presumably "endogenous stimuli"[33] related to the major needs of the body for food, respiration, and sexual release.

---

28. "Project for a Scientific Psychology," S.E., I ([1950] 1978) p. 295.

29. Thus Freud could say, concerning the continuing influence of Brücke, "In a certain sense I nevertheless remained faithful to the line of work upon which I had originally started. The subject which Brücke had proposed for my investigations had been the spinal cord of one of the lowest of the fishes (Ammocoetes Petromyzon); and I now passed on to the human central nervous system" ("An Autobiographical Study," S.E., XX [(1925) 1959] p. 10).

30. The term "synapse" had not yet been invented; this is what Freud meant by "contact barrier."

31. Psychoanalysis, p. 191. Cf. The Origins of Psycho-analysis, Letters to Wilhelm Fliess, Drafts and Notes: 1887-1902, which includes "Project for a Scientific Psychology" (New York: Basic Books, 1954) pp. 295-397.

32. Sigmund Freud: Life and Work, 3 vols. (London: Hogarth, 1953-57) I, p. 416.

33. These "endogenous stimuli" (hunger, respiration, and sexuality) were later replaced by a term that indicates their biological counterpart: "instinct." See S.E., I ([1950] 1966) p. 297 n. 1.

It now becomes clearer how the laws of physics and chemistry — especially as they came to be interpreted by Helmholtz — provided the framework for Freud's Project.[34] Yet the Project was not simply a matter of transferring the laws of thermodynamics to neurophysiology. For in describing the neurological processes of perception and memory, Freud was clearly attempting to explain human *consciousness*. His amazingly complex description of the neurological processes was not meant to apply to mere physiological processes, but rather to describe such specifically human phenomena as the "experience of satisfaction" and "the exigencies of life."[35] It was precisely this attempt to describe the psychical in terms of the neuronal that led students of Freud to label the Project as "neurophysiological reductionism."[36]

In order to apply the concepts of classical physics and chemistry to the mind, Freud was forced to adopt a concept of the human mind and mental processes that was essentially static — in this instance, "homeostatic." The homeostatic assumption can be seen in Freud's insistence on the human mind as a closed system that always seeks equilibrium, designed to maintain a constant level of energy and thus resist excitation.[37] Again, Meissner observes: "In Freud's early, relatively closed view of the mental apparatus, it seems clear that the basic principles of inertia and constancy were calculated specifically to maintain such homeostatic balance."[38]

34. Meissner comments on Freud's early theory (esp. the Project): "reality consisted of nothing but material masses in motion, and that the basis of the perceptual processes lay in the physical excitation of neural elements by external physical stimuli" (*Psychoanalysis,* p. 192). Cf. Guntrip, *Personality Structure,* pp. 119ff. Cf. also C. Barrett, ed., *Wittgenstein — Lectures and Conversations* (Oxford: Blackwell, 1966) p. 1, where Wittgenstein says that since Freud refused to commit changes in mental states to "chance," he was committed to the search for causal laws to explain them.

35. Sulloway, *Freud,* p. 117.

36. Ibid., p. 118.

37. Cf. ibid. Also Guntrip, *Personality Structure,* pp. 149-52, who points out the logical connection between Freud's "homeostasis" and his later theory of death instinct. Cf. Nigel Walker, "Freud and Homeostasis," *British Journal for the Philosophy of Science* 7 (1956) 61-72.

38. *Psychoanalysis,* p. 193. I need to guard against the possibility of equivocation here where I use the term "static." When "static" is applied to the classical substantival descriptions of the person, I mean primarily that the individual is conceptualized as a self-subsisting entity that is isolated from other persons. When Freud uses the term "homeostasis" it has a biochemical sense, referring to a constant equilibrium of forces. In neither case does "static" necessarily mean that there is simple inertia, a mere absence of motion. In both cases, however, the self is understood as a self-contained system; there is an analogous meaning to the term "static," because it remains quite different from the interpersonal models advocated by both Barth and object relations where the self is an open system, always acting and interacting with other individuals.

In similar fashion to Sigmund Exner (1846-1926),[39] Freud's early personality theory assumed that the central nervous system must be subject to certain quantitative laws of excitation. The inhibition or control of certain stimuli would later become the foundation for the "pleasure principle." In the Project, however, it served to explain the human mind in terms of a closed mechanism, subject to the constant exchange of energy. Again, all of this was undertaken not as a mere physiological explanation of neuronal events, but in order to explain such personal functions as cognition, remembering, observing, criticizing, and theorizing, the psychopathology of hysteria, sleeping, and dreaming.[40] The ambitious nature of the Project leaves little wonder why Freud's friend and chief biographer, Ernest Jones, would describe the Project as a "magnificent *tour de force*," which "unites and expresses the two opposite sides of Freud's nature, the conservative and the freely imaginative."[41] Nevertheless, both Freud and his later critics expressed reservations about the success of his physiological reductionism.

Freud's assessments of the Project were themselves far from constant. At first he seemed satisfied that he had found the key to the connections between physiology and psychology.[42] Yet within a few weeks Freud had given up on his ideas contained in the Project, concluding that it was pure "balderdash." He did not even attempt to publish it. The ambivalence perhaps stemmed from Freud's repeated attempts to find a physiological key to the human mind, while at the same time he was constantly uncovering clinical symptoms of his psychiatric patients that defied physiological explanation. Freud seemed wedged between his Helmholtzian physiological training and his constant collision with the clinical facts of mental illness that seemed to thwart any attempt to reduce psychology to brain physiology.[43]

39. Exner's major work, *Entwurf zu einer physiologischen Erklärung der psychischen Erscheinunggen* (1894) exerted a perceptible influence on Freud. See "Autobiographical Study," pp. 9-10. Cf. Jones, *Life and Work,* I, p. 417; and Sulloway, *Freud,* p. 116.

40. See "Project for a Scientific Psychology," *S.E.,* I, pp. 295-397.

41. *Life and Work,* I, pp. 420-21.

42. In a telling letter, describing his feelings about the original Project letter sent to Fleiss, Freud reveals: "I had a clear vision from the details of the neuroses to the conditions that make consciousness possible. Everything seemed to connect up, the whole worked well together, and one had the impression that the Thing [Jones: 'i.e. the mind'] was now really a machine and would soon go by itself. The three systems of neurones, the free and bound state of Quantity, the primary and secondary processes, the main tendency and the compromise tendency of the nervous system . . . all that was perfectly clear, and still is. Naturally I don't know how to contain myself for pleasure" (*Life and Work,* I, p. 419).

43. See Thomas Parisi, "Why Freud Failed," *American Psychologist* 42 (1987) 235-45. Parisi argues that Freud willingly gave up reductionist assumptions and is better interpreted as

Freud had run up against the "conceptual restraints" that confronted a pure physiological explanation of the human mind when he came into contact with two very accomplished neurologists who could not contain their studies of the person to the field of neurology. Unconscious processes were first made known to Freud through his senior colleague, Joseph Breuer. Breuer recounted to Freud his encounter with the unconscious processes in his treatment of Anna O.[44] Later, Freud went to Paris (in 1884-85) to study with the famed neurologist and hypnotist Jean-Martin Charcot (1825-93). From his studies with Charcot and his translation of Charcot's work into German, Freud says: "I received the profoundest impression of the possibility that there could be powerful mental processes which nevertheless remained hidden from the consciousness of men."[45] Charcot, Freud thought, had been one of the first to uncover the mechanism of hysterical phenomena. To explain hysterical symptoms Charcot appealed to "psychology," not physiology, as was the custom in Germany.[46] It was Charcot who influenced Freud to undertake research that would show the difference between hysterical paralysis and organic paralysis. From this research Freud concluded that hysterical paralysis *"behaves as though anatomy did not exist or as though it had no knowledge of it."*[47]

It was likely that Freud's scientific curiosity to find the connections between physiology and psychology led him to undertake the Project, and that his respect for the insurmountable differences between psychological and physiological symptoms led him to abandon that same Project.[48] When the realities of suffering patients resisted the imposition of a preconceived model, Freud had to adapt his theory to fit the facts. One has to admire his personal and scientific integrity in doing so.

The theoretical problems presented in his early undertaking have failed to be resolved up to the present, whether in the field of philosophy or psy-

---

an "emergentist" (p. 237). For a response to this interpretation of Freud see Slavin and Kriegman, "Freud, Biology, and Sociobiology," *American Psychologist* 43 (1988) pp. 658-61. Also Douglas M. Snyder, "Comment on Parisi," *American Psychologist* 43 (1988) 661-62. Freud's ambivalence over the reductionist paradigm perhaps explains the current disputes regarding whether Freud finally desired to reduce psychology to a natural science. This tension is well summed up by Guntrip, who states: "Freud the positivist by education was constantly being left behind unwittingly by Freud the realist face to face with suffering patients" (*Psychoanalytic Theory*, p. viii).

44. This was c. 1882.

45. "Autobiographical Study," p. 17. Cf. also *S.E.*, I, pp. 19-31.

46. See *S.E.*, I, p. 171.

47. *S.E.*, I, p. 169.

48. See Parisi, "Why Freud Failed," pp. 239-40.

chology. Nevertheless the Project is important for two reasons. First, because it reveals Freud's fundamental assumption that the physical world is a place where independent particles of matter in motion are seeking equilibrium. This theme will play itself out through the course of Freud's writings. Second, it points out the inherent difficulties in seeking to formulate any type of scientific psychology that does justice to both physical and mental realities. In such a quest, one crosses the threshold of consciousness time and again, first from the mental or psychological side, then from the biochemical or physical side, constantly seeking to figure out how the two relate. When this takes place, might not the theologian, who has been dealing with the same problem on a different level, benefit from a mutual exchange of ideas? Had Freud not gone beyond his thinking in the Project, there would be little room for dialogue. Thank goodness he did.

Freud's Biological Anthropology

The second and more extensive stage in Freud's psychoanalytical theory was based on a biological model of human behavior, largely derived from the evolutionary theories of Darwin and Lamarcke.[49] Freud's biological explanation began with the idea that human conduct is based on powerful "instincts" (*Triebe*) that evolved within the human species. In this stage, the neurones were replaced by "'instincts' and the physiology of the brain and nervous system by the biochemistry and the phasic development and maturation of the sexual component instincts."[50] It is important to pay close attention to the way in which Freud is employing the term "instinct." In Freud's studies, the instincts serve as more than purely biological phenomena. Instincts function on two levels, the biophysical and the psychical. Freud states: "by an 'instinct' is provisionally to be understood the psychical representative of an endosomatic, continuously flowing source of stimulation."[51] Freud began with the assumption that the primary instinctual needs are for self-preservation and for race preservation: hence the respective instincts of hunger and sex. Increasingly, Freud came to see the psychological significance of the unconscious manifestations of the sexual drive. Freud leaves little doubt about the powerful motivation that the sexual instinct supplies:

49. Guntrip, *Personality Structure,* p. 120, places this second stage of Freud's development at roughly 1898.

50. Ibid.

51. "Three Essays on the Theory of Sexuality," *S.E.,* VII ([1905; rev. 1910, 1915] 1953) p. 168.

It may be asserted . . . that the task of mastering such a powerful impulse as that of the sexual instinct by any other means than satisfying it is one which can call for the whole of a man's forces. Mastering it by sublimation, by deflecting the sexual instinctual forces away from their sexual aim to higher cultural aims, can be achieved by a minority and then only intermittently, and least easily during the period of ardent and vigorous youth. Most of the rest become neurotic or are harmed in one way or another.[52]

Freud's theory of instinct in many ways transcended the neurological reductionism in his Project. In this second stage, the biological has mostly supplanted the neurological; and yet the influence of thermodynamics is still very much in evidence. Once again Freud assumes a constant state of biological excitation as the starting point for human behavior. The laws of momentum and of conservation of energy still provide the scientific framework for his theory of personality. This time, however, Freud applied such laws to psychosexual energy, or "libido" *(Lust)*, rather than neuronal synapses.[53] The principle of homeostasis, or constant exchange of energy, still remains the terminus a quo for human motivation, with the terminus ad quem changed from neurological events to sexual gratification.[54] The extent to which Freud employed biological metaphors for explaining human psychology can be found in an essay where Freud used the example of a bird's egg as a model of a closed psychological system.[55]

52. "'Civilized' Sexual Morality and Modern Nervous Illness," *S.E.,* IX ([1908] 1959) p. 193. Who can deny that Freud has put his finger on a major social problem? But one must ask whether he has correctly diagnosed the source of the problem, much less prescribed the right cure. Cf. Guntrip, *Personality Structure,* p. 69.

53. Thus Snyder writes concerning Freud: "Instinctual functioning is similar to the functioning of physical objects according to Newton's first law of motion, which states that 'every body perseveres in its state of rest, or of uniform motion in right line, unless it is compelled to change that state by forces impressed thereon'" ("Comment," p. 662). See *Newton's Principia, the Mathematical Principles of Natural Philosophy,* tr. A. Motte (New York: Daniel Adee, 1846) p. 83.

54. In this regard, Jones observes that Freud's Project, although it was quickly abandoned by Freud himself, nevertheless contained many of the seminal ideas that were later applied to his psychology. Hence, "The language of physics and cerebral physiology in the Project was Freud's natural one, to which he in great part adhered later even when he was dealing with purely psychological problems. It is true that he then gave the terms he used psychological meanings which take them away from their original context, but all the same they are often terms that no pure psychologist would have employed to start with" (*Life and Work,* I, p. 420).

55. "Formulations on the Two Principles of Mental Functioning," *S.E.,* XII ([1911] 1958) pp. 218-27. "A neat example of a psychical system shut off from the stimuli of the external world, and able to satisfy even its own requirements autistically . . . , is afforded by a bird's egg with its food supply enclosed in its shell; for it, the care provided by its mother is limited to the provision of warmth" (p. 220n).

Why did Freud move beyond the neurophysiological to the biological model based on evolutionary theories of the instincts? The answer to this is found in Freud's apparent frustration with the physiological reductionism of the Project, coupled with his theory that the biological model seemed to strike a compromise between the physical and the psychical. Freud thus employs the biological phenomenon of instinct in order to explain the psychical. When he uses "instinct" to explain human "anxiety," it is plain that such terms refer to something beyond the biological realm. Freud theorized that an instinct served as a sort of bridge between the two realms of physical and psychical:

> If now we apply ourselves to considering mental life from a *biological* point of view, an "instinct" appears to us as a concept on the frontier between the mental and the somatic, as the psychical representative of the stimuli originating from within the organism and reaching the mind, as a measure of the demand made upon the mind for work in consequence of its connection with the body.[56]

In the same context, Freud makes an important distinction. While a "stimulus" is applied from the outside world to living things, an "instinct," according to Freud, is self-contained, arising from "within the organism itself." A stimulus registers a sudden impulse from the outside world. On the other hand, an instinct is not sudden but is constant like the laws of motion.[57] Freud refers to "instinct" as a constant flow of energy that is not sexual of itself, but becomes so when connected with certain erotogenic zones in the body. It apparently bridges the gap between somatic and psychical because it also "makes demands upon the mind for work." Instincts demand a somatic manifestation in order to be discernible one from another: "What distinguishes the instincts from one another and endows them with specific qualities is their relation to their somatic sources and to their aims. The source of an instinct is a process of excitation occurring in an organ and the immediate aim of the instinct lies in the removal of this organic stimulus."[58]

One can now see why Freud is sometimes accused of formulating a

---

56. "Instincts and Their Vicissitudes," *S.E.*, XIV ([1915] 1959) pp. 121-22.

57. *S.E.*, XIV, pp. 118-19.

58. "Three Essays on the Theory of Sexuality," p. 168. The above quotation is not in the original document of 1905, but was inserted in 1915, about the same time as the writing of "Instincts and Their Vicissitudes." In a later footnote (1924), Freud adds, "The theory of the instincts is the most important but at the same time the least complete portion of psychoanalytic theory" (ibid.).

static theory of the human being in which the ideal state is one of nonexcitation or inertia.[59] It is somewhat ironic that Freud's theory of instincts, which conjures up images of psychosexual energy surging throughout the human body in search of a somatic outlet, was ultimately based on the notion that humans tend to resist becoming overly excited. It is fascinating to conjecture how Freud's theories might have to be adjusted were he writing in the midst of a Hollywood-saturated twenty-first century rather than Victorian Europe. But even in Hollywood they understand that sex is not all. Violence also sells, and for this too Freud had an explanation.

Freud's emphasis on the instincts also led him to posit the aggressive instinct. The aggressive, or death, instinct represented the logical extension of the life-tensions theory based on classical physics. Since human aggression is undeniable, Freud theorized that the ego had an innate tendency to reduce life tensions by restoring the body to its original inanimate condition. Every organism therefore has a tendency to destroy itself and reduce tensions by returning to an inorganic state. This gave rise to the death instinct. Hence arose Freud's theory that there exists a psychological opposition between Eros and Thanatos.[60]

There is a crucial question that Freud must have asked himself at this stage of his theoretical journey: Whence comes this neurosis that consigns to "grief" the many who seem unable to deal successfully with their sexual tensions? The source of neurosis, Freud decided, comes from the social restraints that civilization places on the individual's sexual behavior. Freud theorized that "anxiety" was the ego's response to pent-up sexual tension with no outlet. Since individual sexual instinct always presses for an outlet, but the suppression of the sexual (and later, "aggressive") instinct is necessary in order for civilization to be able to form, it is the fault of civilization that anxiety develops within the individual. In other words, the energies available for the development of any civilization depend largely on the suppression of sexual excitation, and the suppression of sexual impulses causes various forms of psychological illness. From all of the above premises Freud drew the stark conclusion that society and the individuals who compose society are necessarily at odds:

59. This leads Guntrip to observe that Freud's constancy principle is actually a "stagnancy principle," and the pleasure principle is closer to a death principle than Freud would admit (*Personality Structure*, pp. 128ff.; cf. pp. 147ff.).

60. See "Beyond the Pleasure Principle," *S.E.*, XVIII ([1920] 1950) 7-64, esp. pp. 60-61n. Since Freud's translators capitalize "Eros" and "Thanatos," I have chosen to do the same in this chapter.

> Every individual is virtually an enemy of civilization, though civilization is supposed to be an object of universal human interest. It is remarkable that, little as men are able to exist in isolation, they should nevertheless feel as a heavy burden the sacrifices which civilization expects of them in order to make a communal life possible. Thus civilization has to be defended against the individual, and its regulations, institutions and commands are directed to that task.[61]

Therefore, Freud reasons that the demands placed on the individual by the civilization are so at odds with the needs of the individual to express his or her instinctual needs that the tension between the two cause most forms of psychoneurotic illness.[62]

Freud suggests three possibilities for dealing with individual neurotic anxiety. First, he recommends that a good deal of the sexual instinct can be "sublimated," that is, diverted into noninstinctual pursuits that are socially acceptable.[63] Second, suppression of libido is simply the cost of forming civilization and living together as human beings; hence a good deal of libido will simply have to be suppressed, with the unfortunate consequence that it inadvertently becomes lodged in the unconscious and "repressed," ultimately causing the individual to "take flight into neurotic illness."[64] Finally, of course, there remains the socially unacceptable option of untamed expression of instinctual urges. Hence: "The man who, in consequence of his unyielding constitution, cannot fall in with this suppression of instinct, becomes a 'criminal,' an 'outlaw,' in the face of society — unless his social position or his exceptional capacities enable him to impose himself upon it as a great man, a 'hero.'"[65] In order not to increase the number of neurotic individuals within society, Freud argued that society should not impose overly strict sanctions on the sexual instincts.[66]

In developing a comprehensive anthropology that places the primacy on the instincts, it becomes evident that Freud is pitting the needs of the indi-

---

61. "The Future of an Illusion," *S.E.*, XXI, p. 6. See also pp. 7ff.

62. "'Civilized' Sexual Morality," pp. 191ff.

63. *S.E.*, IX, p. 187. There nevertheless remain limits to sublimation. See ibid., p. 188.

64. *S.E.*, IX, p. 192. Freud affirmed the central importance of repression: "the doctrine of repression is the foundation-stone upon which the whole structure of psychoanalysis rests" (*Collected Papers* [1924], I, p. 297). On sexual repression as the cause of neurosis, see also "Three Essays on the Theory of Sexuality," pp. 164-65.

65. *S.E.*, IX, p. 187. One could mention several other forms of ego defense, such as "projection," "rationalization," "regression," and "isolation." But these are not quite as central as those listed in the text above, and are primarily explained by them.

66. *S.E.*, IX, p. 194.

vidual to gratify instincts against the needs of society to preserve itself through the consensus that instincts need to be suppressed. This paints a rather pessimistic picture of human nature. Freud's conclusions were often at odds with the concurrent notions of theological liberalism that the individual and culture would mutually complement each other's needs. But, more importantly, they created a puzzling contradiction regarding the human picture. Guntrip summarizes the dilemma Freud claimed to have uncovered:

> The denial of instinct is necessary for culture and civilization, whilst the gratification of instinct and the relaxation of culture is necessary for health. This pessimistic conclusion should arouse our suspicions. Social life, on this view, can never be any other than unending warfare between instinct and morality, the needs of the individual and the demands of the group, or, in another form, the flesh and the spirit.[67]

While Freud's view of instincts went through many modifications, it nevertheless remained at the core of his psychoanalytic theory throughout his career.[68] As late as 1930, Freud could write:

> It is impossible to overlook the extent to which civilization is built up upon a renunciation of instinct, how much it presupposes precisely the non-satisfaction (by suppression, repression or some other means?) of powerful instincts. This "cultural frustration" dominates the large field of social relationships between human beings. As we already know, it is the cause of the hostility against which all civilizations have to struggle.[69]

It is not surprising that the instinctual basis for his anthropology also led Freud to espouse a pessimistic picture of human nature:

> Men are not gentle creatures who want to be loved, and who at the most can defend themselves if they are attacked; they are, on the contrary, creatures among whose instinctual endowments is to be reckoned a powerful share of aggressiveness. As a result, their neighbor is for them not only a potential helper or sexual object, but also someone who tempts them to satisfy their aggressiveness on him, to exploit his capacity for work with-

---

67. *Personality Structure*, p. 69.

68. Freud's long-standing theme, described by Joan Riviere as the "irremediable antagonism between the demands of instinct and the restriction of civilization," is noted in her editorial comments preceding "Civilization and Its Discontents," *S.E.,* XXI, pp. 60-61.

69. "Civilization and Its Discontents," p. 97. This edition was first published in German in 1930 as "Das Unbehagen in der Kultur."

out compensation, to use him sexually without his consent, to seize his possessions to humiliate him, to cause him pain, to torture and to kill him. *Homo homini lupus.*[70]

Freud cites some historical examples of human bestiality and concludes: "anyone who calls these things to mind will have to bow humbly before the truth of this view."[71]

Freud, therefore, believes that his instinctual theory does a more than adequate job of explaining not only psychoneurosis but also human social problems. However, if this be true — that human beings are constituted primarily of instincts, both sexual and aggressive — what force, we might ask, draws individuals together into a society or civilization? This too would have to be explained on the level of instinctual functions. Freud attempts to explain the tendency to form groups and thus civilization as the diffusion of libido:

> I may now add that civilization is a process in the service of Eros, whose purpose is to combine single human individuals, and after that families, then races, peoples and nations, into one great unity, the unity of mankind. Why this has to happen, we do not know; the work of Eros is precisely this. These collections of men are to be libidinally bound to one another.[72]

The above represents Freud's attempt to explain civilization in terms of the various permutations of human instincts. But is this a sufficient explanation of civilization? Guntrip again comments on Freud's stark anthropology of human instincts: "it seems odd that our greatest achievements should arise out of the denial of our primary nature, and rest on our using for cultural purposes energies designed for different and anti-cultural uses."[73] Guntrip's point is well taken, for if every person stands against culture on the deepest psychic level, how can a composite sketch of so many innately antisocial individuals form a society? This question is a difficult one for Freud to answer in spite of his many and prolific attempts to do so. Unlike the medieval and Enlightenment thinkers who defined the human being in rationalist terms, Freud cannot appeal to the transcendent power of human reason to delimit the instincts and thus form society. Freud's anthropology is bound to the in-

---

70. "Civilization and Its Discontents," p. 111.
71. Ibid., p. 112.
72. Ibid., p. 122.
73. *Personality Structure*, p. 72.

stincts. He therefore appeals to his doctrine of repression, arguing that civilization is possible only because of the necessity to suppress the instinctual drives that would otherwise destroy any possibility of civilization. For Freud, the whole, represented by civilization, is inexplicably greater than the sum of the parts, which are composed of instincts.

Freud acknowledged that his theory of civilization was not novel. It bore marked similarities to ideas that were traceable back to Hobbes, Kant, and the Stoic philosophers.[74] Yet Freud's argument is original in its application, for it attempts to begin with instincts and end with an explanation of the origins of unconscious attitudes and actions that are representative of the psychological repression of the instincts. Freud's explanation for human society based on the repression of instincts, however, begs the question. So far he has not explained why the need to repress instincts and form social groups is stronger than the instinctual compulsion of every individual to destroy the group through unbridled sexual or aggressive actions.

Freud recognized that he had not yet explained why social groups form. He thus posited Eros as an explanation for the formation of civilization. As to why Eros exists, ultimately compelling persons to be drawn together in spite of their stronger instinctual inclinations to do just the opposite, Freud could provide no answer, until he developed his theory of the ego ideal and superego.

The Element of Object Relational Psychology in Freud's Thought

The third stage of Freud's theoretical development is the most significant for this study. Here we see the implicit beginnings of object relational psychology in his development of such terms as "sexual object," and also in his usage of the technical terms "ego" *(Ich)* and "superego." While these developments

---

74. Freud's theory of pitting the individual needs against the collective demand for a strong leader was largely borrowed from Thomas Hobbes, *Leviathan*, ed. Molesworth (London: J. Bohn, 1839-45) I, esp. chaps. 11 and 13; and Kant, "Anthropologie in pragmatischer Hinsicht," *Kants gesammelte Schriften*, 23 vols. (I-VIII, XIV-XVI, Berlin: Georg Reimer, 1902-14; IX-XIII, XVII-XXIII, Berlin: de Gruyter, 1922-55) VII, pp. 117-333, esp. §§82, 83. Though Freud does not mention that his theory of civilization came from either Hobbes or Kant, there can be no doubt that he read them carefully. See *S.E.*, V, p. 542, in which he refers to Hobbes's *Leviathan* regarding the origin of dreams. See also V, pp. 503-4; XVIII, p. 28, comparing psychology with Kant's concept of time. Freud also thought Kant's "categorical imperative" was the "direct heir of the Oedipus complex" (XIII, p. xiv, 22; and esp. XIX, p. 167).

come mostly in his later essays (1920 and later), they can be traced clear back to 1905 in his "Three Essays on the Theory of Sexuality." With this third stage of Freud's thought we see an interesting progression from the mechanical, to the biological, and finally, to a nascent object relations view.

The Development of the "Sexual Object"

From early on it was apparent to Freud that the sexual instinct implied a "sexual object," since the instinct of sexuality is incapable of being explained apart from the object toward which it is attracted. Freud thus attempted to take this into account in his psychoanalytic theory. In his "Three Essays on the Theory of Sexuality" (1905), Freud incorporated the idea that the sexual instinct could not be sufficiently explained merely as an impulse within an isolated individual; a sexual instinct implies relation to a sexual object. Freud thus defined the "person from whom sexual attraction proceeds" as the "sexual object."[75] The incorporation of the sexual object into Freud's theory indicates two basic truths about the nature of the human being. First, that a truly isolated individual is problematic even in a theory based on instincts. This is because, as Freud admitted, the normal course of sexual relation goes beyond autoeroticism to the higher plane of sexual relations with other individuals. Thus the interpersonal dimension is implied — if not found explicitly[76] — even in the instinctual definition of the human being. Second, the exclusively material and biological categories once again reveal themselves as insufficient models for human beings and their complicated afflictions.

The Development of the "Ego" and the "Ego Ideal"

Freud's "Three Essays on the Theory of Sexuality" illumines the seminal beginnings of object relations psychology. As we have seen, for Freud the psyche is revealed by the tension created between an individual's instincts and the ethical injunctions placed on him or her by society.[77] Freud had clearly perceived that the human being must contain something beyond raw instinct,

---

75. "Three Essays on the Theory of Sexuality," pp. 135-36.

76. In contrast to this view of Freud's, see Barth, *CD*, III/4, pp. 136ff. I discuss this passage at length in chapter six below.

77. Freud admitted that his insights better explain male than female development, hence the usage of the masculine pronoun. This raises one of the traditional criticisms of Freud's psychoanalytic theory: it is remarkably male-biased.

something to which social injunctions in the form of mores and taboos could appeal. For if human beings could be sufficiently described solely in terms of instincts, then, like the lower animals, those instincts would always be acted out automatically, or at every available opportunity. This is plainly not the case, for, as we have seen, the sublimation and repression of the instincts are peculiar to humans alone, and necessary for the maintenance of human civilization. If unlimited libidinal expression would be let loose, there would be much less neurotic anxiety for most individuals. Yet this cannot happen, for the fabric of society would then be torn to shreds. Freud therefore reached the conclusion that neurotic anxiety is the cost of living in a civilized world.

At this stage, however, Freud realized that the mechanism of repression is not sufficiently explained. In his search to account for the mechanism, it was plain that such could not be found in the instincts, since the instincts were precisely what were being repressed.[78] Hence some entity or structure within the individual had to be capable of transcending and thus censoring the instincts, and allowing them to be repressed, sublimated, or expressed. Freud thus developed the use of the term "ego" *(Ich)* in order to explain the psychological agent that comes into conflict with the unconscious instinctual drives. Collision between ego and instincts thus elucidates the source of psychical tension in the individual. Freud believed that with the discovery of the psychological ego he could explain the nature of group ties libidinally. Here Freud clearly steps beyond the bounds of biology and into the realm of psychology. By this I mean that while the id[79] could be identified with the biological realm through the instincts, the ego is not susceptible to biological explanation.[80]

At first the ego took a more or less adversarial role in relation to the instincts; he viewed it as quite separate from the instincts and playing a censorial role.[81] But the antipathy between ego and instinct proved to be unsatis-

---

78. It could be observed, of course, that the instincts vie one with another, as, e.g., the life and death instincts often do. However, there would still need to be an explanation as to why Eros and Thanatos do not either cancel each other out, or fuse, thus creating a widespread acceptance of sadomasochistic sex, etc. See below.

79. Initially the id was coextensive with the sexual-libidinal drive; but after 1920 Freud believed that the aggressive instincts were also contained within the id.

80. See "Group Psychology and the Analysis of the Ego," *S.E.,* XVIII ([1921] 1955) pp. 69-143. This is not to suggest that the ego is exclusively conscious. Many of its mechanisms for repression of the instincts are unconscious. This explains much of the difference between Freud and the rational psychologies of the philosophers and theologians who preceded him.

81. The antipathy between the ego and id again recapitulates the Platonic-Boethian theory of the higher intellectual and the lower appetitive soul that war with one another for the individual's allegiance. See Van Leeuwen, *Person in Psychology,* p. 34. Freud admitted that his tri-

factory. In "Beyond the Pleasure Principle" (1920) the ego takes on more than a mediating role between the unconscious libidinal self, or id *(Es)*, and society; it becomes rather the integrating structure for the whole person.[82] The integrative function of the ego becomes even more evident in Freud's ensuing essay, "Group Psychology and the Analysis of the Ego" (1921).

The genesis of Freud's "ego ideal" took place in several steps. Freud theorized that sexual overvaluation of one individual by another tended to create an idealization of certain love objects.[83] The idealization of the love object amounted almost to a divinization of the person so perceived. He then attempted to explain how groups are tied together by the part of the ego that identifies with the leader of any particular group. This Freud eventually named the "ego ideal." According to Freud's ego ideal theory, an individual within a group substitutes the leader of the group for the ego ideal. This explains why individuals place themselves under a leader's control. The acquiescence of individuals to a group leader is further explained by the fact that another part of the individual's ego allows that individual to identify him- or herself as a recipient of the leader's love (along with other group members). It is the leader's capacity to be identified with an ideal conception of the self, coupled with the perceived diffusion of that leader's approval to individuals within the group, that, in Freud's view, draws human individuals together into groups.[84] Here Freud, in my view, bumps his head against the glass ceiling of instinctual theory. The human being, at this stage of Freud's theory, is hardly reducible to a bundle of instincts seeking homeostasis. Guntrip observes that these distinctions are "not distinctions which are regarded as innate in the organism, but distinctions which arise in the ego after birth as a result of experiences in object-relationships."[85] Here we see that the "ego" and

---

partite psychology of id, ego, and superego reflects the classical anthropology that divides human beings into body, soul, and spirit. Nevertheless (see previous note), Freud's truly innovative contribution to modern thought was that the agency which mediates between morality and instincts is not often conscious of its own operations. In this sense he certainly did more than recapitulate classical anthropological dualism.

82. *S.E.*, XVIII (1950) 7-64. Guntrip refers approvingly to Freud's understanding of the ego here as the "basic unitary primary total psychic self" (*Personality Structure*, p. 90). See also p. 93. Nevertheless, the unitary ego is not something that Freud held to consistently; indeed, he seems to revert to describing the ego as part of the id modified by experience in *The Ego and the Id* (1923). It comes as little surprise then that the antipathy of the ego and id has not been completely abrogated, but remains a tenet of Freudian psychoanalytical theory even up to the present.

83. See "Group Psychology," pp. 112ff.

84. See "On Narcissism," *S.E.*, XIV ([1914] 1959) p. 95.

85. Guntrip, *Personality Structure*, p. 91.

the "ego ideal" derive at least in part from interpersonal dynamics. Yet even at this higher stage of psychoanalytical development, Freud still placed the primary emphasis on the instinctual impulses, with the object relations being the mere outgrowth of the impulses.[86]

The "Superego" and the Oedipus Complex

The necessity of explaining human society by positing the "ego ideal," along with Freud's later observation that the ego emanates "resistance" to psychoanalytic therapy, created problems for Freud's concept of the ego. He thus modified his theory about the ego, because it seemed that there must be a part of the person that was neither ego nor id. As we have seen above, the "ego ideal" was needed in order to explain the formation of societies or groups, which are based on the identification of the individual with the ideal conception of the leader. The question still remains why an individual would willingly project the idealized conceptions of a leader on any specific individual, who in reality was plainly inferior to the ideal. Why would any individual abide by the prohibitions such a leader would put forth? Freud was convinced there must be some developmental key somewhere along the pathway of childhood. This he found as he took a closer look at the prevailing ambivalence that so many of his patients felt toward their parents.

At first, Freud used the terms "ego ideal" and "superego" interchangeably.[87] Eventually, however, he saw the increasing need to designate a motivation by which the ego conforms to its ideal. The result was that the "superego" eventually replaced the "ego ideal" as the third leg of Freud's tripartite psychology. The chief difference seems to be that the ego ideal was primarily conscious, while the superego is primarily an unconscious structure.[88]

The superego came to represent the internalization of the social and cultural mores and taboos, particularly as they were reinforced by the same-sex parent during the stage of sexual attraction to the parent of the opposite sex at roughly four to five years of age. This process of attraction to the parent of the opposite sex received Freud's well-known label, derived from classical Greek mythology, "Oedipus complex." In order for the Oedipus complex to

86. Thus Sulloway emphasizes: "Freud envisaged the ego and the superego as jointly developing out of the *id* — or that part of the mind that contains the core of the unconscious, the source of all the passions, and the biologically innate in man" (*Freud*, p. 374). Cf. "The Ego and the Id," pp. 24-25, 34-38.

87. E.g., "The Ego and the Id," p. 28.

88. See Guntrip, *Personality Structure*, p. 97.

be resolved, during childhood the parental authority of the opposite-sex parent had to be accepted in the form of a prohibition against incest. Thus Freud described the superego as the "heir to the Oedipus complex," and said that it "introduced the most momentous objects into the ego."[89] By this Freud meant that the superego is the internalization of the moral law — not as an a priori moral imperative in the sense Kant thought of it, but as the internalization of parental prohibitions: "As the child was once under a compulsion to obey its parents, so the ego submits to the categorical imperative of its superego."[90] Freud believed all of this could be psychologically traced to the resolution of the Oedipus complex.

Once again, we see a crude type of object relations beginning to weave its way into Freud's psychoanalytic theory. For while the ego ideal was a mere projection of the individual's conception of the group leader, the superego results from rather complex relations with other persons, especially the parents. Therefore, the superego represents not a mere projection but an internalization of early relationships. This process is explained in the individual through the resolution of the Oedipal conflict, and collectively in the human race through the phylogenetic transmission of the father complex, or totem taboo.[91] In the case of the Oedipal conflict, the relation to the object is a relation to the parental authority. But, we might observe, it is not much of a relationship, for it is based on the repression of biological impulses due to the superior authority and power of the parent, often resulting in an enormous burden of irrational guilt.[92]

Along with the need to rename his third psychical entity, the "superego," Freud began to doubt whether anxiety could be described, as he had insisted earlier, as lack of libidinal discharge. Thus his theory of "ego anxiety" developed in which the anxiety stemmed not from purely instinctual origins, but rather from obviously psychological origins — from the psychological ego:[93]

> We have attributed the function of conscience to the super-ego and we have recognized the consciousness of guilt as an expression of a tension between the ego and the super-ego. The ego reacts with feelings of anxiety (*Gewissensangst*) to the perception that it has not come up to the de-

89. "The Ego and the Id," p. 48.

90. Ibid.

91. See ibid., p. 38. The phylogenetic component of the superego will be further explained below.

92. See ibid., esp. pp. 49ff.

93. Ibid., pp. 57-58. Cf. Guntrip, *Personality Structure*, p. 98.

mands made by its ideal, the super-ego. What we want to know is how the super-ego has come to play this demanding role and why the ego, in the case of a difference with its ideal, should have to be afraid. . . . The super-ego — the conscience at work in the ego — may then become harsh, cruel and inexorable against the ego which is in its charge. Kant's Categorical Imperative is thus the direct heir to the Oedipus complex.[94]

Statements like the above have led Guntrip to observe that in Freud's later personality theory the ego can nearly be equated with the whole psychological person. The result is that it is not merely the instincts, but also object relations that explain repression.[95] Freud's comparison of his Oedipus complex to Kant's categorical imperative is noteworthy. In drawing such a comparison he thinks to have found a scientific explanation for a philosophical concept; but has he? I think, rather, the superego signifies the logical conclusion of pitting the ego and id against one another. Once this fundamental dualism has been deciphered, it is difficult to see how the superego differs from the rational faculty in most forms of rationalist philosophy, where reason must suppress the desires of the lower appetites.

Discovering the fount of human guilt proved to be extremely difficult, stimulating a constant revision of psychoanalytical theories in the course of Freud's writings. In a final attempt to explain the origins of the superego in terms that might do justice to evolutionary theories about the instincts, Freud traced the "sense of guilt" back to the Oedipus complex, and finally back to the "killing of the father by the brothers banded together" — the totem taboo. In order to explain the phenomenon of human guilt, Freud theorized that the "brothers" who had banded together to kill the more powerful father afterward sensed remorse for having done the deed. Their guilt is really remorse since it was after the fact. Yet Freud acknowledged that this only begs the question when it comes to explaining the origins of guilt, for the "remorse" is explicable only if there had been some form of conscience that somehow communicated the moral nature of the deed in the first place. He therefore attempted to explain the conscience by proposing that it surfaced as a result of the conflicting forces of both love and hatred. The ambivalence toward the primal father is explained as a psychological counterbalancing act between love and hatred. While hatred compelled the deed to be done (the patriarchal murder), love compelled a pang of remorse over the deed and re-

94. "The Economic Problem of Masochism," *S.E.,* XIX, pp. 166-67.
95. "Repressed ego-object relationships which are needed to explain repression . . . " (Guntrip, *Personality Structure,* p. 101).

inforced the identification with the father and subsequent superego development.[96]

In both Freud's explanations of the Oedipus conflict and the origins of "guilt," we have come upon an irresolvable dualism within Freud's anthropology that is not altogether unlike the dualisms found within Kant, Schleiermacher, and the medieval theologians. I attempt below to show the difficulties this dualism caused Freud.

Conclusions Regarding Freud's Anthropology

Guntrip succinctly summarizes the three stages of development traced above in Freud's psychoanalytic theory:

> In his first period Freud struggled to transcend physiology and arrived at psychobiology. In his second period he began the struggle to transcend psychobiology and move on to consistent *psycho*dynamic theory of personal object-relations. With his concept of the super-ego, we begin to see, not an organism dominated by instincts, but an ego which has instinct among its various properties, shaped as a whole in the matrix of human interaction.[97]

We have surveyed the interesting attempt by Freud to reduce the human psychology to a complicated structuring of the instincts. In a sense, his attempt was largely based on materialist assumptions about the nature of human beings. The delineation of a materialistic psychology is not peculiar to modern anthropologies; such anthropologies can be traced all the way back to the time of Democritus (c. 460–c. 370 B.C.E.) and other pre-Socratic philosophers. However, the means by which such reductions were attempted by Freud and other psychologists in the twentieth century were without precedent, because they attempted to take into account the vast reservoir of unconscious processes that usually result from the repression of primitive instincts. Freud and some later Freudians attempted to reduce human actions, including religious actions, to their biological building blocks.[98]

Shall we throw out Freud's view of humanity at the outset and proceed to find a psychology that is more compatible with Christian belief? I hope

---

96. "Totem and Taboo," *S.E.,* XIII, p. 143; and "Civilization and Its Discontents," *S.E.,* XXI, pp. 131ff.

97. *Schizoid Phenomena, Object Relations, and the Self* (London: Hogarth, 1968) p. 381.

98. See "Future of an Illusion," *S.E.,* XXI, p. 35.

not. If we reject every aspect of instinctual anthropology we would likely overlook a fact of which Barth has begun to make modern theology aware: that there is very little which theological anthropology has to fear from material reality per se. The material and the psychical are not mutually exclusive. Barth's anthropology could be summarized by the statement that the psychical and physical are not to be confused, but neither should they be separated. Given the importance of special creation, theology has every reason to embrace the material realities of human life as an integral part of God's contingently created reality and a necessary component of human creatureliness. It is neither biology nor the biological facts of human existence that Christian anthropology needs to fear. It is, rather, the "biologians" who must be opposed: those who have dogmatically asserted that the biological is the *only* reality that explains human existence.[99] There is no need for biology and Christian theology to oppose one another when it comes to studying the human being. Quite to the contrary, I would argue that the theologian should wrestle with all of the theological implications of human biology (e.g., sexuality, appetite, aggressive impulses), rather than avoiding them as has so often been done in the past. Barth is especially keen to see the theologian take biology seriously by taking the Christian doctrine of the physical body seriously.

On the issue of biological reductionism, it seems that Freud stood somewhere in the middle. It would be unfair to classify him as a complete reductionist, for he never denied that there exists a real human consciousness, one seated on the mysterious throne of the ego, sandwiched between the equally mysterious (to a materialist) superego and id.[100] With the passing of time and careful observation of human emotional illnesses, Freud became convinced that there must be not only a conscious mind, but also an unconscious dimension to the human personality. The operation of unconscious processes was observed during psychoanalysis, hypnosis, and other means such as dream analysis. The powerful evidence for the existence of the unconscious mind sent modern psychology scurrying back and forth across the threshold of consciousness, across the barrier between body and soul, mental events and neurological entities. One of the strengths of modern scientific psychology after Freud is that it never let go of the real physical existence of human beings; it admits frankly the bodily and sexual exigencies of human life while at the same time attempting to understand the nature of the soul.

99. See *CD*, III/2, pp. 80-90, esp. 88.

100. See, e.g., "Psychical Qualities," *S.E.*, XXIII, p. 157: "The starting-point for this investigation is provided by a fact without parallel, which defies all explanation or description — the fact of consciousness. Nevertheless, if anyone speaks of consciousness we know immediately and from our most personal experience what is meant by it." See also the note on the same page.

We might prudently accept the emphasis on the instincts as an attempt to overcompensate for many years of exaggerated emphasis on the soul. In most Western Christian theology the rational faculty of the conscious mind was seen as the crowning glory of human personhood, with the body as little more than a miserable encumbrance, and subconscious processes mostly relegated to the netherworld of dreams and visions. One does not have to agree wholeheartedly with Freud in order to see that his sober study of human sexual and aggressive impulses has been given all too little consideration in most theological circles. If we grant that there is even a kernel of truth in his insights regarding the subtle but powerful influence of unconscious psychological processes, then there is little possibility of returning to Christian rationalism. Christian anthropology in the twenty-first century will have great difficulty viewing the soul as a *ratio superior* in quest of the *rationes aeternae*.

There are, of course, many points at which theologians are compelled to disagree with Freud. Freud held to some degree of biological reductionism right to the end, and it would be naive to overlook his almost complete commitment to materialism. But before I spell out a number of specific objections to Freud's instinctual theory of the person, I want to point out the dimensions of Freud's thought that I believe are instructive for modern theological anthropology. The following are some positive aspects of Freud's anthropology from a theological point of view.

First, Freud has focused our attention on the central importance of human sexuality. Coming on the heels of the Victorian era, the need for a frank discussion of the importance of sexuality is not to be questioned.[101] Western European culture was immensely repressed during that era and it would be foolish to think that every dimension of such repression was conducive to emotional health. How can we explain that up until the mid-twentieth century, most theologians would flinch at a frank assessment of the role that sexuality plays? The Bible certainly speaks to the topic loudly and clearly. Could it be that for the most part Christian theology has been overly influenced by the pervasive asceticism that stemmed from classical dualism and flowered during the medieval period, carrying its momentum right through the Enlightenment? Or perhaps the church's general avoidance of psychoanalysis is better explained by the possibility that theologians and clergy themselves have been more than a little bit sexually repressed. Or does the usual reticence of the church to acknowledge both the beauty and centrality of human sexu-

---

101. Although one could ponder whether, in light of the modern sexual revolution, a certain dose of Victorian prudery might not balance things out a bit and lead to a more civilized society.

ality stem from the traditional theological anthropologies with their intractable dualism of soul and body? Hans Küng captures the importance of Freud's insights poignantly: "Sexuality acquires a truly ubiquitous virulence if it is not processed and integrated into the personality structure."[102] A joyful and frank assessment of the central role of human sexuality is certainly not avoided in the Bible — it can be found in the biblical anthropologies from Genesis to the Song of Solomon. The importance of sexuality is less evident in the New Testament, but still finds a powerful endorsement from the life and teaching of Jesus, as well as its metaphorical expressions in the Pauline writings where the relations of male and female are likened to the relation of Christ to the church.[103]

I believe this is where Barth's interpretation of the *imago Dei* is especially instructive. For Barth, it is human sexuality, humankind as male and female, that describes our basic form of humanity. Our sexual differentiation as male and female defines the basic building block for all human relationships. Hence "we cannot say man without having to say male or female and also male and female. Man exists in this differentiation, in this duality."[104] It must be remembered, against the popularized interpretations of Freud, that he gave sexuality a broader interpretation than simple genital sexuality. Sexuality is rather a life force that assumes many psychological manifestations and is susceptible to many permutations. For Barth also, human sexuality receives a broader definition and application than simple excitation and usage of the sexual organs. Barth, however, gives human sexuality a much wider interpretation than does Freud. I say more about this in chapter six. For now it is sufficient to observe that both Barth and Freud see human sexuality as critically important to almost every aspect of our existence.

Second, Freud has not flinched from soberly assessing the capacity for human aggression. He suffers little from the lingering delusions regarding the goodness of the human heart that sprang up primarily out of nineteenth-century Romanticism. The world wars and countless other incidents of brutality such as "ethnic cleansing" in the late twentieth century offer little evidence to contradict Freud's observation: *Homo homini lupus.* The retrogression into bestiality remains an imminent and sometimes horrifying possibility that has all too often become an actuality. Freud is right to see that civilization's perch is usually a precarious one not only because nature threatens,[105] but because

102. *Freud and the Problem of God,* p. 104.

103. See Eph. 5:21–6:4.

104. *CD,* III/2, p. 286.

105. In "Future of an Illusion," Freud proposes: "the principal task of civilization, its actual *raison d'être,* is to defend us against nature" (*S.E.,* XXI, p. 15).

aggressive impulses from deep within the human heart threaten to break out at almost every opportunity.

At this point we might be tempted to wonder if Freud has cast some light on the theological doctrine of "original sin" — not its nature and origin of course, but has Freud perhaps illumined the means of original sin's transmission? Is there as much distance between Freud and the Puritans as he would like to think?[106] While the former exposed sexuality and the latter attempted to repress it, both inevitably drew attention to its central importance for human existence, as well as its pervasive role in revealing human infidelity and self-centeredness.

Might there not also be some common elements between Freud and the reformers, or more specifically, between Freud and Barth's insistence that God must remain transcendent and "Wholly Other," uttering a "No" to human attempts at self-justification, and judging human civilization as a whole? In Barth's earlier theology there was a dialectic between the individual and God, between time and eternity; for Freud there was a dialectic between ego and instincts, such that he was eventually forced to posit the judgmental character of the superego. In either case, the radical otherness of someone of great authority breaks through the isolation of the individual and forces on the conscience an external reality to be reckoned with. The similarities should not be stretched too far, and the differences must be acknowledged, even while making such comparisons. Yet there are some positive elements of comparison between the two that will be further amplified when we compare Barth and object relations.

Finally, we can admire Freud's boldness in stating eloquently the conditions of his unbelief. He thought to have explained the psychology of belief to such an extent that he dared to label religion as an "illusion." Furthermore, he questioned the notion that belief in God as an abstraction can be more plausible than the God of faith. Freud openly challenged the view that the philos-

---

106. See Paul Tillich, *Systematic Theology,* vol. II (Chicago: University of Chicago Press, 1957) p. 54: Freud "describes, from a special angle, exactly what concupiscence means. This is especially obvious in the way Freud describes the consequences of concupiscence and its never satisfied striving. . . . Up to this point, a theological interpreter of man's estrangement is well advised to follow Freud's analyses." Nevertheless, Freud ultimately failed to describe concupiscence because: "Concupiscence, or distorted libido, wants one's own pleasure through the other being, but it does not want the other being. This is the contrast between libido as love and libido as concupiscence. Freud did not make this distinction because of his puritanical attitude toward sex. . . . In Freud's thought there is no creative *eros* which includes sex. . . . Classical Protestantism denies these assumptions . . . for in man's essential nature the desire to be united with the object of one's love for its own sake is effective."

ophers are talking about God when they "give the name 'God' to some vague abstraction which they have created for themselves; having done so they can pose before all the world as deists, as believers in God, and they can even boast that they have recognized a higher, purer concept of God, notwithstanding that their God is now nothing more than an insubstantial shadow and no longer the mighty personality of religious doctrines."[107] Barth is in hearty agreement with Freud's assessment of the God of modern liberalism. Freud's criticism may very well aid us in understanding what Barth means when he affirms God as "Wholly Other," the God who reveals, rather than the God who is the sequel to religious thoughts or sentiments.

Nevertheless, some weaknesses in Freud's theories about the person create some incompatibilities with Christian anthropology. A contradiction remains at the heart of Freud's theory about the human being, a contradiction that centers on his insistence that instincts would be sufficient to explain the formation of human civilization.[108] It seems that one of the most important things that Freud uncovered, the possibility of modern psychology to assess psychologically unconscious processes, is the very thing that the presuppositions of his biological reductionism denied. The unconscious psychological processes, even if they might partly derive from repressed instincts, are nevertheless occasioned more by interpersonal encounters than by instincts themselves. The unconscious psychological processes proved to be increasingly difficult to locate in the region of the instincts; and that is why, as Freud's theory began to grow and develop, he had to create new terms such as "ego" and "super-ego" to describe certain nonbiological entities, which resembled the human faculties theorized by many earlier philosophers. Here we see something that Barth had predicted would be true of every anthropology that begins with a dogmatically oriented prejudice for evolutionary interpretations. Barth argued that the human being could not ultimately be leveled down to an animal; for even if we would overlook the growing amount of research that indicates our physical differences from the other animals, we "constantly see ourselves on other levels than those amenable to natural science."[109] The "other levels" are illumined by the practical reason of ethics. We are not only thinking beings, but also valuing, willing, and acting beings who function on the level of practical reason, as Kant observed.[110] Finally, of course, Barth insists that "real man," the human being considered theologi-

107. "Future of an Illusion," *S.E.*, XXI, p. 32.
108. A contradiction that applies to his concept of God as well. But this is not central to the topic at hand. See Meissner, *Psychoanalysis*, pp. 7, 44ff., 54-97.
109. *CD*, III/2, p. 91.
110. *CD*, III/2, pp. 91ff.

cally, can never be considered in isolation from God and fellow humans. Hence Barth concludes that there is something tragic about every nontheological anthropology because such anthropologies always throw humankind back on itself in an effort to explain both the distinction and the connection between the psychic and somatic realities. Barth believes that no secular anthropology can sufficiently explain this connection. Theological anthropology thus derives the benefit of being able to demonstrate the connection between psychical and somatic material because they are both revealed as real by the Word of God. This too I need to discuss in chapter six.

At the point where Freud employed Eros to explain the need to form civilization, his thought appeared to be "upwardly open." Yet in the sentence that follows, Freud asserts: "These collections of men are to be libidinally bound to one another." The equation of Eros with libido is difficult to swallow. The emphasis on libido shows the core of Freud's reductionist assumption applied to his view of humanity: all human interactions must reduce to lower biophysiological levels. He thus closed his anthropology off from any possibility of upward illumination. This is because the need to preserve society through the curbing of libidinal excitations is assumed, but never sufficiently accounted for. Eros can be accounted for only on the higher plane of practical reason: the ethical and ultimately some sort of philosophy or theology that can explain the meaning and purpose of human love. The existence of Eros is dependent on the spiritual dimension: Eros reflects the love of God in creation; this is why Barth could affirm Eros so heartily in his later anthropology. Perhaps this need for Eros to be explained from a higher source is hinted at by the fact that many of Freud's eminent colleagues parted from him because they sought ways to reincorporate the spiritual into their respective psychoanalytic theories.[111] In seeking to explain Eros, Freud retreated from the spiritual and sought his explanations from instinctual theories. Freud's anthropology therefore contains an element of cynicism because it lacks the capacity to explain the fine qualities of human love, sacrifice, and altruism. As David Cairns observes in his assessment of Freud: "He has no place in the instinctual nature of man for love, no place for even a rudimentary desire both to give and to receive."[112] Freud has frankly described the bestial side of human nature, but he has also omitted a large portion of that which is essential to the human being, for in his view every person's attraction is ultimately instinctual.

---

111. Viz., Carl Jung (1875-1961), Erich Fromm (1900-1980), and Viktor Frankl. See Küng, *Freud and the Problem of God*, pp. 109-22.

112. *The Image of God in Man* (London: SCM, 1953) p. 232.

Fairbairn begins where Freud left off, but rearranges his presuppositions about the nature of human beings. Fairbairn's object relations theory presupposes that human beings are essentially social in nature, and he attempts to explain deviant social behavior as a lapse in normal interpersonal development.

It is interesting, for the purpose of drawing together the various strands of thought contained in this study, to note the direction in which modern anthropologies have tended. Whereas the Enlightenment thinkers such as Kant and Hegel viewed the essential feature of the human being as the exercise of reason, the implicit anthropology in Freud's thought is precisely the opposite. For Freud, and much of modern social sciences, the function of reason has been supplanted by the function of instinct. Hence we have seen the arguments about the human essence come full circle. While Kant had thought the essence of human civilization to be based on enlightened self-interest, which was strictly rational, Freud saw the essence of civilization as explicable in terms of the pragmatic diffusion of instinctual attraction, which he claimed was purely instinctual. The former can be seen as an "angelic" anthropology. The latter is closer to an "apish" anthropology. It is precisely the inability of either model to give a sufficient explanation of the human being that compels us to seek a more suitable alternative.

With increasing clarity, then, we have begun to see the shortcomings of the types of anthropologies that picture the human being as composed of two competing forces. Both the rationalist and the instinctual theories reveal a radical dualism in their descriptions of the human being as an upper and lower faculty at odds with each another. The end result in Freud's biological anthropology is much the same as the Enlightenment thinkers for whom a sensible self vies with a rational self, a noumenal self is at odds with the phenomenal self, a self that is appetitive is suddenly confronted with the inexplicable pangs of guilt for indulging in things that come naturally or by way of instinctual endowment.

If the argument above has not sufficiently documented Freud's anthropological dualism, I would add to it by again drawing attention to his "Future of an Illusion." In this essay Freud pits the god of reason, *Logos,* against the god of religion, *Ananke.* The former, Freud thinks, represents the "reason" of the modern sciences, especially the growing data of the science of modern psychology; the latter represents the "necessity" of believing that which is absurd *(Credo quia absurdum),* because it is either above reason or necessary for the maintenance of civilization. This conclusion of Freud is somewhat ironic in view of the fact that he based all of his anthropology on a supposed rejection of traditional rationalist philosophies and proposed to base his view of the human being on biological impulses. But when it comes to explaining the origin of religion, he pulls a Promethean switch by maintaining that reason *(Logos)* is fully on the side of his biological psychology and against religion. This is a fitting illustration of the dualism that inadvertently pervades his thought. For Freud, Eros and Thanatos, love and hate, libido and aggression, are perpetual opposites, which are represented by competing instincts.[113] This is similar to the dualism that surfaced in the philosophies of Plato, the Stoics, and Kant — as well as the theology of Schleiermacher. In Freud's thought the dualism surfaces from the "lower" side. While the former philosophies viewed the human being as a rational being — a thinking self subsumed under the higher powers of the human intellect — Freud attempted to reduce the self to a highly complex manifold of instincts. The former ran up against the realities of the human inclinations toward sensuality, or propensity for radical evil, and found such realities difficult to explain. While seeming to provide an adequate explanation of human aggression and antisocial behavior, Freud could not adequately explain the ability of human beings to overcome the all-powerful instincts and form civilization.[114] The two types of dualism show the flip sides of the same coin. Christian anthropology will have few positive contributions to make if it cannot rid itself of a similar dualism.

What is needed, then, is an anthropology that can think of the whole person, body and soul, as a unity. An adequate anthropology would need to provide a satisfactory explanation for the drive of humans to form society, that is, to be in encounter with fellow humans. It would need to give adequate explication to the soul's need to form loving relations with other persons, while at the same time taking the body's biological realities into account. I believe that object relations represents a viable attempt to do this in the field of modern psychology, just as Barth attempts to achieve much the same balance in modern theology.

113. See, e.g., "Civilization and Its Discontents," *S.E.,* XXI, p. 122: "And now, I think the meaning of the evolution of civilization is no longer obscure to us. It must present the struggle between Eros and Death, between the instinct of life and the instinct of destruction, as it works itself out in the human species. This struggle is what all life essentially consists of, and the evolution of civilization may therefore be simply described as the struggle for life of the human species."

114. See Guntrip, *Schizoid Phenomena,* pp. 153ff.

The "Dynamic" Self in Object Relations Psychology

It was largely Freud's success in pointing out the importance of formative parent-child relations in the earliest stages in life that encouraged the development of object relations psychology. With this in mind, R. D. W. Fairbairn, while acknowledging the seminal importance of libido theory, proposes:

> It would appear as if the point had now been reached at which, in the interest of progress, the classic libido theory would have to be transformed into *a theory of development based essentially upon object-relationships.* The great limitation of the present libido theory as an explanatory system resides in the fact that it confers the status of libidinal attitudes upon various manifestations which turn out to be merely *techniques for regulating the object-relationships of the ego.*[115]

While the distinction Fairbairn makes sounds highly technical, it is an important one for psychoanalytic theory. Instead of libido, Fairbairn proposes to explain the human being on the basis of the interactions between human beings: "My point of view may, however, be stated in a word. In my opinion it is high time that psychopathological inquiry, which in the past has been successively focused, first upon impulse, and later upon the ego, should now be focused upon *the object* towards which impulse is directed."[116] Fairbairn believes that such a model explains both psychological health and illness more parsimoniously than does instinctual theory.[117] The important thing about object relations theory for this study is that it incorporates a truly dynamic understanding of the person into its anthropology. It does not attempt to explain the person merely in terms of an impulse that resides within, but incorporates the fact that the foundational structure of a personality is always shaped within a social matrix. Could it be that the interpersonal dynamic that object relations contains is analogous to Barth's insistence on the person as a "being in encounter"? We shall see in chapter six. First we need to outline the concept of the person in object relations psychoanalytical theory.

---

115. *Psychoanalytic Studies*, p. 31.

116. Ibid., p. 60.

117. Ibid., pp. 128-29, 160. This is not to say that *all* object relations theorists have cast out the instincts as the essential characteristic of human personality. See Buckley, *Essential Papers,* pp. xii-xiii.

The Essential Self: Instincts or Object Relations?

From observing his patients who exhibited schizoid personality disorders, Fairbairn began to reflect critically on the primary place of libido in the prevailing psychoanalytic system founded by Freud.[118] A fundamental feature of schizoid phenomena that the classical libido theory tended to overlook was the splitting of the ego due to bad object relationships.[119] As we have seen, libido theory was based on the idea that the impulses became localized as they flowed through successive erotogenic zones during respective stages of psychological and physical development. But Fairbairn questions the libidinal theory by observing that in such theory, the central importance of the object to which the impulses flow has been overlooked. He thus theorizes that Freud's erotogenic zones are better explained as the mere channels through which libido flows to its object, since *"the ultimate goal of libido is the object."*[120]

Fairbairn admits that in the infant the libidinal flow is automatically oral; but he contends that in the mature adult, it is not automatically genital. In the adult, libido flows through a number of paths of different options.

118. Fairbairn claims that his "schizoid" personality is much like what Jung defines as "introvert," although I fail to see the strength of the comparison, because Jung's "introvert" is mostly a personality type, while Fairbairn's "introvert" exhibits at least some degree of psychopathology. See *Psychoanalytic Studies*, p. 29. Fairbairn states: "What has convinced me of the paramount importance of the object-relationship is the analysis of patients displaying schizoid characteristics; for it is in such individuals that difficulties over relationships with objects present themselves most clearly" (p. 39). In more contemporary psychology, attention seems to have shifted from the "schizoid" to the "borderline" personality. Some theorists would almost equate the two, with the latter terminology being more prevalent (see Arnold H. Modell, "Primitive Object Relationships and the Predisposition to Schizophrenia," in Buckley, *Essential Papers*, p. 334). Nevertheless, many, including Fairbairn and the revised DSM III manual, would distinguish between the two, seeing the schizoid difficulty as stemming from an earlier developmental disorder than does the borderline personality.

119. Fairbairn is quick to acknowledge his indebtedness to Melanie Klein, who modified Freud's concept of ego splitting by developing an extensive (and sometimes graphic) theory of introjection and projection of both good and bad objects. See, e.g., "A Contribution to the Psychogenesis of Manic-Depressive States," *International Journal of Psycho-Analysis* 16 (1935) 145-74. This is not to say that Freud had completely overlooked the concept of ego splitting. But ego splitting for Freud was never more than he presented in Oedipus conflict. Cf. "Splitting of the Ego in the Process of Defense," *S.E.*, XXIII, pp. 271-78.

120. *Psychoanalytic Studies*, p. 31. See also p. 138. Fairbairn cites the latter page in his own definition of "libido": "The real libidinal aim is the establishment of satisfactory relationships with objects; and it is, accordingly, the object that constitutes the true libidinal goal" ("Observations in Defence of the Object-Relations Theory of the Personality," *British Journal of Medical Psychology* 28 [1955] 145). Cf. Guntrip, *Personality Structure*, p. 287.

Adult sexuality is therefore not strictly "genital," but rather "mature."[121] In staking out the claim of his disagreement with Freud — especially Freud's insistence on component instincts, that is, the successive libidinal discharge through certain sexual organs — Fairbairn attempts to explore new territory in psychoanalytic theory. Fairbairn's terminus a quo for human personality derives not from instinctual impulses or the derivative "pleasure principle." Rather, Fairbairn places the primary emphasis on the relationship. The impulses are therefore at the disposal of each person for the expression of love and satisfaction, or dissatisfaction, within the context of an interpersonal relation. Fairbairn agrees that repression holds the key to psychological investigation. But unlike Freud, Fairbairn proposes:

> Problems of the personality can only be adequately understood at a personal level and in terms of personal relationships. *Pari passu,* they involve explicit recognition of the inadequacy of any attempt to interpret problems of the personality in terms of post-Darwinian biology, and thus explicit abandonment of that part of Freud's theoretical system which aims at providing an explanation of problems of the personality in terms of instincts and erotogenic zones.[122]

In Fairbairn's view, none of the erotogenic levels is automatically or satisfactorily explained by itself, because even in Freud's theory raw libido could not explain itself; it made sense only as it bore the mark of an interpersonal relationship. Fairbairn's theory of sexuality, however, depends on successful object relations; it recognizes, but also transcends, the stages of erotogenic development defined by the instincts. Fairbairn infers, "Libidinal pleasure is not the end in itself, but the "sign-post to the object."[123] Fairbairn then offers a piercing critique of Freud: he proposes that instinctual theory was built on the false assumption of autoeroticism, not object-eroticism.[124]

---

121. *Psychoanalytic Studies,* p. 32. Elsewhere Fairbairn proposes, regarding libidinal zones: "the significance of the zones reduces itself to that of available channels by way of which libido may seek the object" (p. 73).

122. "Observations on the Nature of Hysterical States," *British Journal of Medical Psychology* 27 (1954) 106-7.

123. *Psychoanalytic Studies,* p. 33. Cf. Rom Harré, *Social Being: A Theory for Social Psychology* (Totowa, N.J.: Rowman and Littlefield, 1980) p. 2: "The deepest human motive is to seek the respect of others." Quoted in Van Leeuwen, *Person in Psychology,* p. 201.

124. *Psychoanalytic Studies,* p. 34. The primacy given to inherent autoeroticism applies primarily to Freud, of course. But it also applies to Freud's followers such as Karl Abraham, *Selected Papers of Karl Abraham* (London: Hogarth, 1927) p. 496.

The difference here between Fairbairn and Freud signifies something about the human being that is highly significant. I believe it represents a fundamental conceptual distinction in the nature of the human being. For Freud, the sine qua non of human existence was found in the instincts: component instincts that succeeded one another during the stages of psychological development. We are a self-contained bundle of instincts seeking the release of tension. Everything that is constitutive of human ontology derived from the pleasure principle. For Fairbairn the instincts are never an end in themselves, but always a means of expressing or repressing an object relationship. It is understandable, then, that Fairbairn would call into question the autoerotic premise of classical psychoanalysis. Freud's "ego" could be described as a sort of menagerie for libidinal energy, seeking the most readily available outlet; as such it precluded the possibility that those instinctual energies could be the vehicle of an interpersonal relationship. This would not necessarily have to be the case, because we can imagine a system that incorporates human instincts without eliminating the interpersonal dimension.[125]

Fairbairn supports his position by giving a simple example by which he illustrates the differences between himself and instinctual theory. In the case of an older child who sucks his thumb, classical instinctual theory would explain the libidinal manifestation as an instance of mere pleasure seeking. But this is not a sufficient explanation, argues Fairbairn, because not all children display such regressive behavior, nor to the same degree. Instinctual theory would explain thumb-sucking in terms of autoeroticism. But how would instinctual theory allow for the regression to an oral stage of libidinal satisfaction at a time when the child should have moved well beyond the oral stage? Fairbairn, arguing from an object relations standpoint, says that the thumb-sucking "represents a technique for dealing with an unsatisfactory object-relationship." Therefore, if there is deprivation in the relation to the external object — in this case, probably an unmet oral need in the early stages of infancy — the object becomes internalized. The child thus seeks satisfaction by regressive means (in this case sucking the thumb) because oral gratification was unavailable from the maternal object at the time when it was needed. But, according to Fairbairn, it is more than a simple need for pleasure that stimulates the autoerotic behavior. The need to internalize the bad-object relationship is based on the difficulty such a bad relationship causes the child. Since the early disappointment had been external and outside the child's control, the child needed to exert some kind of control by internalizing the disappointment of not being orally gratified.

125. See "Instincts and Their Vicissitudes," pp. 122-23.

Fairbairn continues: "It is no exaggeration to say that *the whole course of libidinal development depends upon the extent to which objects are incorporated and the nature of the techniques which are employed to deal with incorporated objects.* . . . It must always be borne in mind, however, that it is not the libidinal attitude which determines the object-relationship, but the object-relationship which determines the libidinal attitude."[126] In other words, real object relations in early childhood form the basis of the libidinal attitudes for the rest of life. According to Fairbairn, where those object relations break down and become technically "bad," the child internalizes such bad relations and is likely to develop some kind of symptoms, possibly including a deviant form of sexual behavior, schizoid withdrawal, or aggression. In object relations the term "bad" does not designate a moral category. It means primarily relationships that are unsatisfying. An unsatisfying object relationship in early childhood does seem to trace the blame to the parents or parental figures; but moral guilt or blame is not necessarily implied by such a theory. Introversion can be precipitated by a number of factors, including the strength (or lack) of the infant's sucking reflex, an illness in the mother during the postnatal period, the innate disposition of the infant, or any number of social factors that could adversely affect the child's attachment to the mother (or primary object). Hence a "bad" object relation does not necessarily mean that the mother can be accused of moral dereliction or child neglect. Such may or may not be the case. Fairbairn has sometimes been criticized for not spelling out clearly whether a bad object relation is due to bad parenting. In this context, at least, it is merely a technical designation.[127] What Fairbairn does clearly point out, however, is that a bad object relation can usually be traced to a breakdown of a normal and healthy relationship pattern during the crucial formative years of early childhood.

One of the major insights of object relations, which has been confirmed by a good deal of empirical observation of young children,[128] is that Freud fixed the pivotal psychological events too late in the child's life. While Freud tended to focus on the father and the Oedipus complex at roughly four or five years of age, object relations shifts the primary emphasis in psychological development to the

126. *Psychoanalytic Studies*, p. 34.

127. *Psychoanalytic Studies*, pp. 33, 56. Cf. Fairbairn, "Observations on the Nature of Hysterical States," p. 107.

128. E.g., Edward Z. Tronick, "Emotions and Emotional Communication in Infants," *American Psychologist* 44 (1989) 112-19. The author points out that research indicates that other-directed affective communication of infants is far more organized, reciprocal, and significant than had been previously believed.

infantile dependence on the mother.[129] Building on the observations of Melanie Klein's work with very young children, Fairbairn explains the schizoid personality in terms of an extreme reluctance to abandon *infantile* dependence.[130] At the same time, the schizoid personality is filled with ambivalence because schizoid persons, although desperately dependent, usually desire to renounce their infantile dependence and grow beyond it. But the only way to wean a child from infantile dependence is to establish a stable relationship in which the child is unconditionally accepted in spite of the dependency. Fairbairn therefore emphasizes the need for interpersonal reciprocity in establishing a normal and healthy "ego."[131] Fairbairn expresses the need for interpersonal relations within the family: (a) each infant and child has a psychological need to be genuinely loved by parents, and (b) the parents must genuinely accept the child's love toward them.[132] Parental assurance enables the transition from infantile dependence to "mature dependence." Again, Fairbairn places the emphasis on the relationship of the child with the parents or parental figure:

> Frustration of his desire to be loved as a person and to have his love accepted is the greatest trauma that a child can experience; and it is this trauma above all that creates fixations in the various forms of infantile sexuality to which a child is driven to resort in an attempt to compensate by substitutive satisfactions for the failure of his emotional relationships with his outer objects. Fundamentally these substitutive satisfactions (e.g. masturbation and anal eroticism) all represent *relationships with internalized objects, to which the individual is compelled to turn in default of a satisfactory relationship with objects in the outer world.*[133]

With the above statement Fairbairn's theory becomes more complicated, for he theorizes that objects to which the child relates can be either ex-

---

129. Thus Guntrip states in *Schizoid Phenomena*, p. 119: "*We have no choice now but to focus our thinking more on the problems of ego-development in the first year than on the oedipal problems of the later infancy though they are real problems.*" The importance of infancy in constituting one's psychological makeup is also developed in the writings of Donald W. Winnicott, e.g., "The Theory of the Parent-Infant Relationship," in Buckley, ed., *Essential Papers*, pp. 231-53.

130. See Melanie Klein, "Notes on Some Schizoid Mechanisms," in *Developments in Psycho-Analysis* (London: Hogarth, 1952) pp. 292-320, esp. p. 297. Fairbairn attempts to describe the etiology of disorders such as paranoid, obsessional, hysterical, and phobic according to his own dynamic theory. However, I largely omit the clinical names and manifestations herein, since they seldom pertain to the main point of this thesis.

131. Fairbairn's concept of "ego" is discussed below.

132. *Psychoanalytic Studies*, p. 39.

133. Ibid., pp. 39-40.

ternal and "real" or internal and psychological, in much the same fashion Freud believed that the superego could be internalized at the stage of the Oedipus complex.[134] Fairbairn believes that external object relations are internalized and become an integral part of the individual's psychological structure. Internalized objects, in Fairbairn's view, are usually the result of unsatisfactory relationships to objects in the external world, and sometimes become pathological.[135] It is the internalization of external objects that elicits Fairbairn's reinterpretation of the Freudian concept of repression. Fairbairn does not deny that repression is the key tenet of psychoanalytic theory; he does, however, deny that it is explained primarily by the Oedipus complex, that is, the energetic "reaction formation" against incestuous impulses.[136]

The conclusion one may draw from our study of Fairbairn thus far is that his theory allows for a development of the human being that is more "real" in a human sense. Psychological development is not dictated by a succession of biologically defined erotogenic zones, but includes a category for personal, moral development. In Fairbairn's theory the normal individual develops beyond an incorporating, predominantly "taking" infancy, to an increasingly nonincorporating and predominantly "giving" adulthood that is compatible with mature human sexuality.[137]

The Dynamics of Form and Structure in Object Relations

Both Freud and Fairbairn would agree that in order for a parent to have a psychological impact on an infant, there must be bodily contact of various types.[138] The body, with all its biological functions, cannot be overlooked as a

---

134. See "The Ego and the Id," p. 75.

135. *Psychoanalytic Studies,* pp. 110-11. See also pp. 40-41, 53ff. Fairbairn's insistence that the internalized object is usually a "bad" (unsatisfying) object differs from Melanie Klein, who believed that both good and bad objects would become internalized. For the most part, contemporary object relations has followed Klein in allowing that the internalized object usually consists in a "good object" and a "bad object," represented by the good and bad parent, which are in need of being integrated for normal psychological development to occur. Fairbairn's theories went through a number of changes, which perhaps explains Buckley's comment: "The nature of this process of internalization, however, remains murky in Fairbairn's writing (as it does in psychoanalytic theory in general)" (*Essential Papers,* p. xviii). See Guntrip, *Personality Structure,* pp. 341ff. Cf. Kernberg, *Internal World,* p. 70.

136. See *Psychoanalytic Studies,* pp. 61-62.

137. Cf. Kernberg, *Internal World,* p. 64.

138. See *Psychoanalytic Studies,* p. 40.

necessary instrument of psychological development. But are the body and its instinctual impulses *sufficient* to explain psychological development? Freud's theory emphasized the functioning of the instinctual energy that directed the individual toward the object, while Fairbairn emphasizes the object-directed nature of the ego. For Freud, libidinal energy is impersonal and isolated in the id, with manifestations that flow through various erotogenic zones as if they were mere conduits. For Fairbairn, the libidinal energy is integrated with the actual psychological structure. Libido serves the ego, and always seeks a real person with whom to attach, rather than merely seeking self-gratification. Fairbairn describes his chief difference with Freud: "although Freud's whole system of thought was concerned with object-relationships, he adhered theoretically to the principle that libido is primarily pleasure-seeking, i.e. that it is directionless. By contrast, I adhere to the principle that libido is primarily object-seeking, i.e. that it has direction."[139] Fairbairn continues to explain his disagreement with the theoretical foundations of Freud's interpretation of the scientific method:

> No man, even the greatest and most original, can remain wholly independent of the scientific background of his day; and it cannot be claimed that Freud provides any exception to this rule. Here we must remind ourselves of the scientific atmosphere of the nineteenth century in which Freud was nurtured. This atmosphere was dominated by the Helmholtzian conception that the physical universe consisted in a conglomeration of inert, immutable and indivisible particles to which motion was imparted by a fixed quantity of energy separate from the particles themselves. The energy in question was conceived as having been, for some unknown reason, unevenly distributed at the beginning and as subsequently undergoing a gradual process of redistribution calculated to lead eventually to an equilibrium of forces and an immobilization of the solid particles. Such being the prevailing conception of the contemporary physicist, it is not difficult to understand how it came about that, when Freud, in advance of his time, set himself the arduous task of introducing order into the hitherto confused realm of psychopathology, he would have remained sufficiently under the influence of the scientific atmosphere of his day to conceive impulse (psychical energy) as separate from structure and to cast his libido theory in an equilibrium-seeking mould.[140]

139. Ibid., p. 126.
140. Ibid., pp. 126-27. Cf. Fairbairn, "Observations on the Nature of Hysterical States," p. 109.

Some have argued that Fairbairn raises a moot point, since object relations and instincts (especially in the form of the pleasure principle) are not necessarily exclusive.[141] However, the chief difference between Freud and Fairbairn is not one of "either instinct or object relations." Fairbairn does not deny the existence of the instincts or the pleasure principle, per se.[142] It is rather a question of how, and in what order, the instinct and object relations are related to one another as they form the foundation of the individual's psychology. One of their principal disagreements is seen in their assumptions about the person's relation to the external object. Freud assumed that all object relations would be governed by instinctual impulses in the form of the pleasure principle. Fairbairn, on the other hand, argues that the libido is better explained as a unity of structure and energy in the form of an intrinsically object-related drive.[143] In this way, Fairbairn attempts to unify the libidinal energy with the structure of the ego and thus describe the ego as the place in which the structure and the energy are not separated, but complementary and dynamically related. From this premise, Fairbairn concludes that an individual who is governed in sexual relations purely by pleasure has experienced unsatisfying object relations. This illustrates an important distinction between Fairbairn and instinct theory. Instinctual theory proposes that the natural inclination of the individual is egocentric, with various developmental permutations of the egocentricity being called upon to explain later genital sexuality, which is allocentric. On the other hand, Fairbairn proposes that the original condition of the individual is allocentric. Egocentricity or "fixations" are explained by bad object relations.

Where Freud thought to implement basically Newtonian concepts in order to explain the human personality structure, Fairbairn attempts to update Freud's theory by employing concepts largely under the influence of Einstein and the so-called new physics.[144] Fairbairn describes his theory as providing an alternative, couched in terms of personal relationships and

141. See, e.g., Karl M. Abenheimer, "Critical Observations on Fairbairn's Theory of Object Relations," *British Journal of Medical Psychology* 28 (1955) 29-41. The author's chief complaint seems to be that Fairbairn has constructed a psychoanalytic theory that bears strong resemblance to Jung's "complex" theory, but has given too little credit to Jung, or at least failed to note their similarities.

142. See "A Critical Evaluation of Certain Psycho-Analytical Conceptions," *British Journal for the Philosophy of Science* 7 (1956-57) 52.

143. Fairbairn states: "relationship with the object, and not gratification of impulse, is the ultimate aim of libidinal striving. These conclusions involve a complete recasting of the classic libido theory" (*Psychoanalytic Studies*, p. 60).

144. Thus Fairbairn asserts that his integration of energy and structure in psychoanalytic theory is more in keeping with a postmodern worldview under the influence of the new physics. See *Psychoanalytic Studies*, pp. 127-28.

dynamic ego-structure, to Freud's description of the psyche in terms of id, ego, and super-ego, based as this is upon a Helmholtzian divorce of energy from structure no longer accepted in physics, and combined as it is, albeit at the expense of no little inconsistency, with a non-personal psychology conceived in terms of biological instincts and erotogenic zones.[145]

The extent to which Fairbairn has broken new ground is evidenced by the criticisms some subsequent object relations theorists have directed toward him. For example, Winnicott and Khan agree with Fairbairn that the root of the schizoid personality is the infant's failure to feel the mother loves him in his own right. However, they reveal their Newtonian bias by stating: "What Fairbairn is referring to then is an infant with needs, but with no 'mechanism' by which to implement them, an infant with needs not 'seeking' an object, but seeking detension, libido seeking satisfaction, instinct tension seeking a return to a state of rest or un-excitement; which brings us back to Freud."[146] It is precisely the strength of Fairbairn's theory that he refuses to allow the person to be conceived as an "ego" driven by a disparate "mechanism" to seek detensioning, and so on. Fairbairn's critics, in this case, seem to have either overlooked or rejected Fairbairn's insistence that energy and structure should coinhere. However, the significance of the paradigm shift that Fairbairn advocated for psychology was appreciated early on by his friend and colleague, John Sutherland.

Sutherland observes that Fairbairn's ego suggests "a superordinate structure of great flexibility and perhaps in the nature of a 'field force,' its primary function [being] the container of motives from all the subsystems which have differentiated from it. Subsystems such as the behavioral systems of the ethologist, or the higher level organizations we call the subegos and internal objects all fall within its influence." Sutherland suggests that the self be conceptualized as the overall dynamic structural matrix, such that "we can give underpinning to the personal level of action as 'I' and yet allow for the self to be dominated at different times and in different situations by any of its sub-systems such as the superego, the antilibidinal ego, the exciting object, etc. etc."[147]

Sutherland's biography on the life and work of Fairbairn sheds a good

---

145. "Observations on the Nature of Hysterical States," pp. 109, 114-15n.

146. Book review of *Psychoanalytic Studies of the Personality,* by W. R. D. Fairbairn, *International Journal of Psycho-Analysis* 34 (1953) 332.

147. "The British Object Relations Theorists: Balint, Winnicott, Fairbairn, and Guntrip," unpublished paper presented at a scientific meeting of the Association for Psychoanalytic Medicine, May, 1979. Quoted in Kernberg, *Internal World,* p. 79. Brackets Kernberg's. More will be said about the "field" concept and its bearing on the discussion at hand in chapter six.

deal of light on Fairbairn's continuous revision of Freud, and the extent to which he respectfully departed from both Freud and Klein:

> Fairbairn distinguished four features of the early oral attitude that shape the adult personality. The first marks his departure from the classical libido theory, because the libidinal object, that is, the *primary object that is sought by the primal instincts, is in his view the mother as a whole person.* This is the crucial statement that separates Freud's theory, founded on instinctive energies internal to the infant, from one that views development as a creative emergent from innate factors that occurs only through the psychological factors in the mother-infant relationship. What is referred to is a clearly felt need in the infant to be recognized, accepted and responded to as a unique autonomous being, yet a being that can only exist through being in relationships.[148]

Kernberg also agrees with Fairbairn's "consistent stress on the link between particular self and object components as dynamic units," a stress that

> represents the earliest effort to link with metapsychology the clinical observation that we never see pure drives but always object relations under the effect of drive derivatives. Fairbairn's stress on considering endopsychic structure both as structure and an energy system seems to me, in the light of contemporary biological thinking as well as clinical evidence, a more sophisticated basis for updating psychoanalytic metapsychology.[149]

Whereas Freud had sought to place primary emphasis on the instincts, Fairbairn conceives the person as a psychosomatic whole.[150] The unity of body and soul signifies emotional health; conversely, fragmentation indicates illness.[151] However, the complementarity of body and soul cannot be described as unordered parity. They are not equal halves but an ordered whole. There is order even in the unitary and complementary relation; hence, in

---

148. *Fairbairn's Journey into the Interior* (London: Free Association, 1989) p. 99.

149. *Internal World*, p. 84. However, Kernberg has reservations about the extent to which Fairbairn overthrew the instinctual theory, particularly the dual instinct theory; cf. p. 83.

150. See Guntrip, *Schizoid Phenomena*, p. 10.

151. Fairbairn rarely spells out specifically what forms this unity of body and soul usually take. However, implied in his and other object relations theories are such things as: a psychosomatic harmony that is indicated by normal social adaptation, absence of psychosomatic illnesses, and ability to control oneself in normal social settings. The fragmentation of the ego caused by a bad object relation often results in either schizoid withdrawal or violent and belligerent antisocial behaviors, often accompanied by psychosomatic diseases and sexual dysfunction, etc.

Fairbairn's thought, the instinctual impulses are relegated to a secondary place (whether they be libidinal or aggressive), while the object relation is primary.[152] Object relations is primarily interpersonal. The logic of the interpersonal relations is therefore "dynamic." [153]

Guntrip summarizes the essential feature of Fairbairn's object relational view as "a fundamental ego-theory which makes psychodynamics a genuine science of a real self or person, a unique center of meaningful experience growing in the medium of personal relationships."[154] This shows that the dynamic understanding of the self that is contained in object relations is not simply a more "up-to-date" theory, but an altogether different type of theory from one based on instincts. The interpersonal structure of object relations is again described by Guntrip: "The business of psychodynamic research is with that aspect of the whole man which we call the motivated and meaningful life of the growing 'person,' and his difficulties and developments in object-relationships with other persons. A dynamic psychology of the 'person' is not an instinct-theory but an ego-theory, in which instincts are not entities *per se* but functions of the ego."[155] How, then, does object relations define the essential psychological self, or "ego"?

The Unitary Ego of Object Relations

According to Fairbairn, "the pristine personality of the child consists of a unitary dynamic ego."[156] Ideally, one's psychological health would be denoted by the unity and integrity of the ego; this seldom seems to be the case in the real world, however. Nearly every individual experiences some degree of ego fragmentation, for no one's childhood object relations are solely "good."[157] The ego therefore becomes split, and this split explains the root of repression and psychological illness. Fairbairn states:

152. *Psychoanalytic Studies*, p. 39.
153. Sutherland states regarding Fairbairn's psychodynamic theory: "The development of a self is, in short, inconceivable without relationships" (*Fairbairn's Journey*, p. 104). Although all the things to which the term "dynamic" refers are not necessarily limited to interpersonal relations, the sense in which Fairbairn uses the term usually fits closely with the definition that I give in this study: applying it to the interpersonal relations that comprise one's being.
154. *Schizoid Phenomena*, p. 127.
155. Ibid., p. 124. Fairbairn's theory is, of course, an ego theory that emphasizes the interpersonal dynamics more than the development of the ego itself.
156. "Observations on the Nature of Hysterical States," p. 107.
157. See *Psychoanalytic Studies*, p. 64.

According to my point of view, however, repression and splitting of the ego represent simply two aspects of the same fundamental process. Such a view was rendered possible for me by the fact that, after finding it necessary to replace a psychology conceived in terms of impulses by one conceived in terms of object-relations, I also found it necessary to resolve Freud's divorce of impulse (viz. id) from ego by adopting the unitary conception that ego-structure is itself inherently dynamic.[158]

Fairbairn therefore describes emotional pathology as an "internalisation or introjection of the unsatisfying object."[159] In general agreement with Klein, Fairbairn believes psychopathology results from the "splitting" of the originally unitary ego. But, as we have seen above, unlike Klein, Fairbairn sees the internalization of external objects as the determining factor of psychopathology. In Fairbairn's theory, the object that is internalized is usually the "'bad' object," resulting from an unsatisfactory object relation.[160] Internalization, then, is the mechanism by which the ego is split, and it rarely if ever describes healthy emotional development.[161] Repression is thus directed not against impulses per se, but against bad objects. As an example of this kind of repression, Fairbairn cites the clinical evidence of delinquent children who have experienced unsatisfactory relationships in their early infancy and childhood with parents, but who are reticent to identify the parents as the bad objects. How could this be explained, asks Fairbairn, unless the children have actually "identified" with the parents, and subsequently internalized the parents as bad objects? It is explicable in terms of the internalization whereby the children direct their unconscious anger not at their parents but toward themselves. The children internalize the bad objects because in most instances there is simply no choice. The children are so completely dependent on the parents that the rejection of them is psychologically impossible; internalization offers the only way for the children to defend the ego from the powerless

---

158. "Observations on the Nature of Hysterical States," p. 106.

159. Ibid.

160. Fairbairn's departure from Klein finds some support in the theory of Winnicott, who states: "It will be seen, therefore, that the work of Klein on the splitting defence mechanisms and on projections and introjections and so on, is an attempt to state the effects of failure of environmental provision in terms of the individual" ("The Theory of Parent-Infant Relationship," in Buckley, ed., *Essential Papers*, p. 246).

161. See *Psychoanalytic Studies*, pp. 110ff. Fairbairn seems to contradict himself by asserting the unity of the pristine ego, while earlier he had posited that the "basic position in the psyche is invariably a schizoid position" (ibid., p. 8). It seems that the ego as an unfragmented whole is postulated only in the case of a "theoretically perfect person whose development had been optimum; but then there is really nobody who enjoys such a happy lot" (ibid.). Cf. p. 56.

situation foisted on them by bad external objects.[162] Therefore, it is the internalization of bad object relationships that explains the origin of anger, and of schizoid behavior.[163]

When the "bad objects" are internalized, the ego splits. The "splitting of the ego" leads us to observe that Fairbairn's "unitary ego" is not unitary because it is monolithic. It is a means by which Fairbairn can explain what a healthy individual might look like — what a person might become if raised in a perfectly loving environment. The unitary ego is also a means by which Fairbairn can describe the drive for the person to form relations apart from mere instincts. Fairbairn's "ego" is unitary not in the sense that it is singular, or lacking in component parts, but in the sense that it is the fundamental stratum of the person. In addition to being the psychological core of the self, the ego is highly motivated. The ego does not depend on the libido to seek relations to other persons; it is intrinsically motivated to form relations to others. The ego's aim (in its "pristine" condition at least) is to seek objects, whether internal or external.[164] In this context Fairbairn states:

> I feel it desirable to draw attention to a fundamental feature of my general theory, viz. that it is essentially a theory of *dynamic structure*. I do not, however, regard the *developed* psyche as a *single* dynamic structure. I regard it as composed of a multiplicity of dynamic structures falling into two classes: viz. (1) ego-structures, and (2) internal objects. . . . It may be added that the terms "ego-structure" and "internal object" are employed in an antithetical sense, and that *"an internal object" may be defined as "an endopsychic structure other than an ego-structure, with which an ego-structure has a relation comparable to a relationship with a person in external reality."*[165]

In other words, the psyche is not composed of a simple ego in static repose, but an ego that is constantly being shaped by real relations to mother (and later the father and others), and quasi relations to its own introjections.

For Fairbairn the ego is not inherently torn between the instincts and the superego, as with Freudian theory; it is, rather, an ego that is libidinally motivated to seek the object. In this sense, the "ego" according to Fairbairn is much more comprehensive than Freud's "ego." But in the case where the ob-

---

162. Ibid., p. 67.

163. The aim of the therapist should therefore be to "de-cathect" bad objects that have been internalized. The clinical applications are, however, not directly pertinent to this study.

164. "Object-Relations Theory," p. 145.

165. Ibid.

ject is unavailable, or unwilling to form personal relations at a crucial time, it becomes an unsatisfying object. The "bad object" thus internalized, the ego splits. Fairbairn continues: "My general position is that, from a psychological standpoint, all aims must be regarded as personal, and all forms of object relationship as libidinal. Viewed from this standpoint, libido is more comprehensive than sex; and I should define 'libido' as *'the object-seeking principle.'*"[166] In other words, the ego is not split between instincts (libido) and superego (ethical injunctions), nor between a libidinal urge (Eros) and an aggressive urge (Thanatos). The splits in the ego occur, rather, when unsatisfying object relations necessitate the defensive posture of the ego, and bad relationships become internalized, taking on a life of their own in the individual's inner psychology.[167] In one of his latest psychoanalytic essays Fairbairn affirms that the ego "is present from birth." His integration of the libido and the ego is evidenced by his conclusion: "Libido is a function of the ego."[168] Fairbairn again affirms that the ego is fundamentally object-seeking, and in this sense "pristine." To say the ego is primarily object-seeking means that the child immediately seeks attachment to the mother's breast ("part-object"), and later to the mother as a whole person ("whole-object").[169] As we watch Fairbairn's personality theory develop, we get a picture that the goal of attachment is ultimately to form a satisfying relationship with the mother. Thus Sutherland observes: "The oral fixations did not represent the failures of satisfactions at the breast as such, but were the result of a deprivation in the overall constellation of 'mothering.'"[170] This represents a clear departure from the pleasure principle.[171]

Contrary to Kernberg, who proposes that Fairbairn's "object-seeking ego" represents an arbitrary elevation of libidinal instinct over the aggressive instinct, I believe that Fairbairn's rejection of the instinct of "aggression" constitutes a fundamental shift in psychoanalytical paradigms.[172] Fairbairn's theory is an attempt to shift modern psychology from an organic to a dynamic

166. Ibid.

167. Cf. Guntrip, *Schizoid Phenomena*, p. 388: "The 'ego' for Fairbairn was not an 'apparatus' nor merely a structural part of a psychic system. It is the personal self, so that when the primary ego is split in experience of other real persons, each aspect of it retains 'ego' quality as a functioning aspect of the basic self."

168. "Synopsis of an Object Relations Theory of the Personality," *International Journal of Psycho-Analysis* 44 (1963) 224.

169. Ibid., pp. 224ff.

170. *Fairbairn's Journey*, p. 108.

171. Ibid., p. 111.

172. *Internal World*, p. 67.

interpersonal model: from picturing the person as an organism seeking satisfaction to seeing the person as a human being in search of meaningful relationships who uses various organs as means of seeking pleasure and also establishing such relationships. In normal human development the instincts are thus subservient to the forming of meaningful relationships. Whereas with Freud genuine relationships are nearly always suspect, because beneath every relation is some form of libidinal pleasure, with Fairbairn the opposite is the case. On this note Sutherland observes, "As regards 'libido,' the real libidinal aim is the establishment of satisfactory relationships with objects; the object thus constitutes the true libidinal aim. Sexual aims are essentially personal, but all personal aims are not necessarily sexual."[173]

To describe the ego as essentially "object-seeking" is a technical way of accounting for human sociability. It is important to note that, in spite of taking issue with Freud's instinctual theory, Fairbairn does not attempt to throw out the instincts altogether. In fact, Fairbairn highlights some recent evidence from ethological studies that indicates that the young among the higher animals are born with a strong tendency to "imprint" and attach to the parent.[174] Even the studies of instincts among the lower animals point to the fact of object attachment. Hence the pleasure principle, which focuses almost exclusively on libidinal attraction, does not suffice to explain human behavior nearly as cogently as does the object relation or reality principle, which shows that instinctual attraction itself takes many different forms and covers a much broader category than sexual gratification.[175] From the ethological studies, among other things, Fairbairn concludes that object seeking is the primary motivation in human interactions, with aggression representing the frustration of object relations. Drawing on this evidence, Fairbairn proposes: "There is no death instinct; and aggression is a reaction to frustration or deprivation."[176]

It is important to draw out the implications of Fairbairn's insistence that aggression cannot be explained by an aggressive instinct; rather, acts of aggression are responses to bad object relations and can have several different manifestations. Whether aggression is turned inward, resulting in schizoid personality disorders, or outward, resulting in hysterical states or violent aggression, depends on the types of ego splitting that occurred, according to Fairbairn. The schizoid personality generally experienced an object loss in the

173. *Fairbairn's Journey*, p. 148.
174. Cf. John Bowlby, *Attachment* (New York: Basic Books, 1969).
175. "Psycho-Analytical Conceptions," p. 52.
176. "Synopsis," p. 224.

early oral stages of life, while the depressive had usually experienced loss in the later oral stage of development.[177] In either case the loss of an object relation in the early stages of life threatens the ego and precipitates a withdrawal of libidinal energy from external objects. Such a loss of libido can have disastrous consequences: "The fact is that in renouncing libido the ego renounces the very form of energy which holds it together; and the ego thus becomes lost. *Loss of the ego* is the ultimate psychopathological disaster which the schizoid individual is constantly struggling, with more or with less success, to avert by exploiting all available techniques."[178] According to Fairbairn, then, the schizoid and the depressive states represent a regression due to unsatisfactory object relationships in early childhood: "The traumatic situation in either case is one in which the child feels that he is not really loved as a person, and that his own love is not accepted."[179]

When Fairbairn uses the term "object relation," is it safe for the theologian to equate an object relation with human love? Probably not. Nevertheless, there could be a significant relation between them. While the parallel in behaviors (e.g., imprinting) between the higher animals and humans does not warrant the conclusion that the higher animals experience "love" in the fullest sense, it may be that the human propensity to form relations to objects could have some theological significance if we reflect on it in light of Barth's insistence that the image of God can be traced to the human need to "be in encounter" with God and others. Object relations illumines the psychological propensity, the possibility, or the openness of human beings to love and be loved. Barth's interpretation of the image of God as "being in encounter" points out the relational dimension of human personhood. At this point, I wish to point out that a relation between a "satisfying object relation" and Barth's theological understanding of human love is an exciting possibility. It is especially intriguing to note that, like Fairbairn, Barth defines human evil relationally; there are interesting parallels between Barth's description of evil as "non-being" and Fairbairn's insistence that aggression stems not from an aggressive instinct, but from bad object relations.

I now turn to the primacy of love, and the secondary status of the phenomenon of fear and aggression, as explained by object relations theory.

---

177. *Psychoanalytic Studies,* pp. 48-49, 53-54.
178. Ibid., p. 52.
179. Ibid., p. 55.

The Origin of Aggression and Antisocial Behavior
according to Object Relations Psychology

Fairbairn's insistence that a "dualistic instinct theory" (or any other instinct theory for that matter) is unacceptable forces us to pose a "practical" question to the object relations theorists. Instinctual psychology seems to have little difficulty in explaining aggressive human behavior, because Freud eventually adopted the view that aggression is an instinct: a "death instinct," Thanatos, which balanced out Eros, the "life instinct." I have pointed out how Freud stumbled, however, when it came to explaining human socialization. In contrast, this seems to be the singular strength of object relations psychology. Object relations provides a sounder explanation for the human propensity to form social groups. In nontechnical terms, it designates mutual attraction as the essence of human existence. But, according to object relations theory, how might one explain *aggressive* human behavior? A prima facie look at object relations theory could lead one to doubt whether antisocial behavior is explicable in such a model, since the natural condition of the ego in object relations theory is to be "object-related." Furthermore, there is some merit to the argument that Fairbairn's choice of Eros over Thanatos represents an arbitrary choice. Object relations would fall into a dualism that would be much the same as Freud's if it were forced to posit two equal but opposite forms of object relations: one based on object attraction, another based on object repulsion.[180] If we wish to formulate a unitary ego at the root of object relations theory, a simple reversal of Freud's dichotomous anthropology will not suffice. Displacing Thanatos with Eros would only shift the problem from an incapacity to explain society to an equal incapacity to explain human aggression. The way in which Fairbairn deals with the dualistic problem therefore warrants our close attention.

Fairbairn attempts to explain the so-called death instinct by appealing to the libido's ability to attach not only to good objects, but also to bad objects:

> We have seen, furthermore, that libido may be attached to bad objects which have been internalized and repressed. Now a relationship with a bad object can hardly escape the alternative of being either of a sadistic or

---

180. This seems to be the position of Klein, whose theories generally portray a rift between love object and the persecutory or sadistic object, and likely explains the major theoretical differences between Klein and Fairbairn. See Klein, "A Contribution to the Psychogenesis of Manic-Depressive States," in Buckley, ed., *Essential Papers,* pp. 40-70. Cf. Klein, *The Psycho-Analysis of Children* (London: Hogarth; New York: Grove, 1960), esp. chaps. VIII and IX.

of a masochistic nature. What Freud describes under the category of "death instincts" would thus appear to represent for the most part masochistic relationships with internalized bad objects.

Fairbairn continues: "A sadistic relationship with a bad object which is internalized would also present the appearance of a death instinct."[181]

A similar explanation for human aggression is developed by Guntrip, who builds on Fairbairn's theory. Guntrip points out the great psychological need that the infant has for object relations:

> However caused, the danger of separation, whether by desertion or withdrawal, is that *the infant, starting life with a primitive and quite undeveloped psyche, just cannot stand the loss of his object. He cannot retain his primitive wholeness for more than a short period in the absence of mother, and cannot go on to develop a strong sense of identity and selfhood without an object-relation. Separation-anxiety then is a pointer to the last and worst fear, fear of the loss of the ego itself, of depersonalization, and sense of unreality.*[182]

Since depersonalization, that is, separation from the parental object, engenders certain aggressive defenses by the ego, "the chronic aggression which has always seemed to be the hallmark of 'man' is but a defence against and a veneer over basic ego-weakness."[183] This basic ego weakness is dynamically defined, and thus lends itself to the unitary concept of the ego. In other words, aggression, according to Fairbairn and Guntrip, represents the secondary reactions of fear and anxiety that are defensive reactions to bad object relations. Aggression then is a type of cover-up for the schizoid position, which reveals that we are weak and fearful.[184] Again, Guntrip points out that in an intractable environment, fight or flight, aggression or schizoid withdrawal, are the only options. Hence: "Human beings hate because they are afraid. If the weak and dependent infant finds his environment unsupporting and even hostile while he is as yet quite unable to defend himself, fear dictates withdrawal and the breaking off of relationships. It is fear that makes it impossible to love, and the conflict between love and fear is the fundamental problem. . . . It takes a strong and stable person to love; hate is a defence of weakness and fear."[185] Guntrip's observations bring to mind the compelling statement in

---

181. *Psychoanalytic Studies*, p. 79.
182. *Schizoid Phenomena*, p. 128.
183. Ibid., p. 129.
184. Ibid., p. 137.
185. Ibid., p. 386. Cf. pp. 153, 155-56, 164.

the epistle of John that there is no fear in love, "but perfect love casts out fear."[186]

I find Fairbairn's position to be a highly plausible interpretation of human psychological development because it explains both love and fear, attraction and aggression, more cogently than do the positions that assume that love and hatred are equal but opposite components of one's psychological structure. I concede, however, that not everything can be answered from the assumption that love is primary. For it still remains to be explained why aggressive and antisocial behavior would issue from an ego that is inherently object-seeking. Mustn't there be an aggressive instinct — albeit a latent instinct in many cases — in order to explain aggressive reactions to unloving situations? Or could it be that "aggression," as Freud defined it, represents not so much a positive endowment as a distortion of the normal drive to attach to objects? In the remainder of this chapter I attempt to show why the latter is more likely to be the case.

While Fairbairn's departure from Freudian orthodoxy was precipitated largely by his clinical work with schizoid patients, his theoretical deviation from Freud was likely to have been influenced by Ian Suttie's major work, *The Origins of Love and Hate* (1935).[187] Suttie was one of the first to question Freud's exclusive emphasis on the instincts. The bulk of his work was ignored, however, because of his vitriolic attacks on Freud, coupled with the aura that had begun to surround Freud at the time when Suttie's works were being published.[188] Nevertheless, I believe Suttie provided an important service to modern psychology in pointing out the way in which psychological "hatred" (Suttie uses the term "hate" instead of "aggression") can be explained as the negation of love. At the same time, Suttie argued that the converse is not

186. *hē teleia agapē exō ballei ton phobon*, 1 John 4:18. Cf. Barth, *CD*, II/1, pp. 32-43. Barth affirms that humans *may* love and *must* fear God. Does this place love and fear on an equal plane? No. By this he affirms the primacy of love and the necessity of being fearful of love's negation: "Fear has to follow love, and not conversely. Love has to be named and understood as the basis of fear" (p. 35). Cf. *CD*, III/2, p. 480.

187. (London: Kegan Paul, Trench, Trubner, 1935). See Guntrip, *Psychoanalytic Theory*, p. 24: "Ian Suttie, in his 'Origins of Love and Hate,' an early Tavistock man, was in a sense a forerunner of Fairbairn, who once said to me, 'Suttie really had something important to say.'" See also Sutherland, *Fairbairn's Journey*, p. 118.

188. Cf. Bowlby, *Attachment*, p. 376: "Suttie and others of the prewar Tavistock group postulated that 'the child is born with a mind and instincts *adapted to infancy*,' of which 'a simple attachment-to-mother' is predominant. . . . Had Suttie linked his ideas to those that Freud was advancing from 1926 onwards they might have been given attention in psychoanalytical circles and have led to a valuable development in theory. As it was, he coupled them with an attack on Freud which led to resentment of his book and neglect of his ideas."

plausible: love cannot be explained as a mere negation of instinctual aggression. Love is more than the absence of hate. Love fails of explanation if one assumes that only "hatred," or lower instinctual capacities, can explain human behavior. Suttie had rejected the Freudian argument that hatred is a primary instinct (in the form of Thanatos). He argued rather that the infant is in primary need of love. Far beyond libidinal satisfaction, the child needs moral encouragement, attention, protectiveness, and company. He therefore rejected the biological and sexual reductionism of Freud, along with Freud's explanation of culture. Suttie argued: "Freud, as I have shown, adheres to the older *kind* of view in regarding love and hate as wholly independent of each other in their origin, as conflicting in 'ambivalence,' and as *uniting* in sadism and masochism. I do not take this view, but regard hate as the *frustration aspect of love, as 'tails' is the obverse of 'heads' in the same penny.*"[189]

Suttie explained negative emotions and human aggression as the dread of loneliness, the absence of love that is "the conscious expression of the human form of the instinct of self-preservation which originally attached the infant to its mother."[190] The prolonged dependence of the human infant provides the seminal beginning of social development. The lack of instinctual endowment is precisely what Suttie thinks provoked the need for human society. Love threatened becomes anxiety, and love denied becomes hatred; therefore, hatred "is just a standing reproach to the hated person and owes all its being to a demand for love."[191] Human actions are purposive, because, in Suttie's perspective, even the sexual act aims to elicit a response; hence sociability is the extension of the need for love.[192] And when love is spurned or ignored, it becomes aggressive; hence aggression is a negative mode of love seeking.[193]

Suttie also disagreed with Freud's overemphasis on the role of the father, and was one of the earliest theorists to place a major weight on the role of the mother, and the infant's attachment to the mother, for psychological

---

189. *Origins*, p. 60.

190. Ibid., p. 19.

191. Ibid., p. 23. In a pithy paraphrase of Shakespeare, Suttie proposes: "Hell hath no fury like a baby neglected."

192. Ibid., p. 38. Suttie sees both the Calvinist and the Freudian as espousing a view of original sin: the infant is born with immoral tendencies. I say more on this later.

193. *Origins*, p. 63. Cf. Guntrip, *Schizoid Phenomena*, p. 386: "Human beings hate because they are afraid. If the weak and dependent infant finds his environment unsupporting and even hostile while he is as yet quite unable to defend himself, fear dictates withdrawal and the breaking off of relationships. It is fear that makes it impossible to love, and the conflict between love and fear is the fundamental problem."

development.[194] Repression, Suttie suggests, stems more from the mother than the father.[195] All of this results in, or perhaps issues from, a much more amicable interpretation of religion than the one given to it by Freud: "Broadly speaking religion springs from dis-satisfactions of development, and is concerned in its higher forms to better our affective relationships with each other (i.e. is ethical)."[196]

Suttie's thoughts were sometimes extreme, and often undocumented by sufficient clinical research. He nevertheless illumined one of the fundamental tenets of the object relations theory of aggression: it is unsatisfying or "bad" object relations that engenders fear and hatred. If we accept Suttie's position, then human hate cannot be categorized as an unrestrained aggressive impulse. Aggressive behavior is more than an unrestrained impulse. It represents a deviation from the normal, even if some degree of aggression is found in nearly every human being. The natural inclination of the ego is therefore to be attached to an object. And it is the failure of the environment to nurture the ego in normal interpersonal relations that results in ego splitting and ego defenses that can tend to be either secondarily aggressive or primarily schizoid. I believe that the implications of this view for human ontology are both profound and parallel to Barth's insights in more than a superficial way. I work out some of these implications in chapter six.

I have mentioned Suttie's contributions to object relations psychology partly to shed light on the historical development of object relations theory by way of showing his influence on Fairbairn. But I have also mentioned Suttie because I believe his insights on the nature of love and hate serve to indicate that the implicit anthropology of object relations warrants a broader interpretation and comparison with certain theological studies of the person. This leads to one of the theoretical links between object relations and the dynamic theological anthropology of Barth. In addition to influencing Fairbairn, Suttie exerted a profound influence on the philosopher John

194. In *Origins*, in contradistinction from Freud's totemic explanation for civilization, Suttie affirms: "we need not hesitate to proceed with our own hypothesis, that in all his social activities — Art, Science and Religion included — man is seeking a restoration of or substitute for that *love for mother* which was lost in infancy" (p. 71). Cf. ibid., pp. 125-26. Freud did, however, begin to place some emphasis on the child's relation to the mother in his latest writings. See "An Outline of Psychoanalysis," *S.E.*, XXIII, p. 188. But even so, Freud's nascent object relations theory is truncated, for it is always subsumed under the larger category of instinctual drives, especially the resolution of the Oedipus complex and fear of castration.

195. *Origins*, pp. 101-2.

196. Ibid., p. 127. Unfortunately, Suttie's interpretation of religion warrants a closer inspection than we have time to give it.

Macmurray. I encourage the reader to spend time with Macmurray's philosophical thought, especially as contained in his Gifford Lectures of 1953-54. Nevertheless, while Suttie and Macmurray took a more philosophical approach to their critiques of Freud and organic anthropologies that explained the human mind by instincts, Fairbairn took a more clinical path to the same destination.

Summary of the Importance of Object Relations
for Modern Theological Anthropologies

Having studied some of the findings of object relations psychology, we find that it presents several possible parallels to Barth's anthropology. For one thing, both Barth and object relations have attempted to point out the shortcomings of the mechanical and biological (organic) anthropologies, especially those reductionist anthropologies that have surfaced in the wake of the evolutionary theories of Darwin and the Romantic philosophers.[197] For another, both Barth and Fairbairn have tried to forge a unitary anthropology. They attempt to view the person not as a composite of segregated parts, but as a dynamic whole in which the energy and structure coinhere. For Barth it is the Spirit that unites the human being as an ensouled body and embodied soul; this describes the unitary structure of the "whole man." The person acts, and never acts in isolation, but always toward God and others. For Fairbairn it is the wholeness of the "ego," as integrated energy and structure, that underlies his description of the psychological life of each individual. The anthropological holism that Barth advocates thus finds a parallel in object relations. We have seen that Barth begins with the premise that no isolated dimension of human beings would be adequate to describe the "real man." Neither the human will, nor intellect, nor soul apart from body, nor body apart from soul could provide a firm ground for theological anthropology. Rather, Barth considers the human being as a dynamic and integrated whole, in ordered relation to God, self, and others. In similar fashion, object relations developed to the point where it could not accept the Freudian compartmentalization of the human being. Fairbairn sees the whole person as emotionally healthy; the fragmentation of the ego, caused by bad object relations in early life, describes a significant factor in the development of

---

197. By this I do not mean to imply that Fairbairn rejected evolutionary theories altogether. Rather, he rejected the reification of the instincts by psychology. See Sutherland, *Fairbairn's Journey*, p. 162.

psychopathology. The splitting of the ego sometimes results in a schizoid or withdrawn condition; at other times it results in aggressive antisocial behavior. It is interesting to note, however, that even though aggression may be endemic to human nature, it is not the normal course for human conduct to take, according to Fairbairn. Aggression is a symptom of a more fundamental human brokenness, a brokenness that occurs at a deep interpersonal level. Barth similarly did not view human sin as "normal." Sin is the symptom of a highly abnormal condition precipitated by a broken relation between human beings and God. Sin is nonbeing.[198]

Earlier in this chapter we saw that Freud himself attempted to give a psychological explanation for belief in God. This has served to make theologians understandably suspicious of psychological explanations for many things. However, I hope that the study of object relations has indicated that modern psychologists should be among the last to predicate realities about the world based on the strength of purely subjective states of consciousness. It is rather the interplay between the objective bodily realities and inner states that has occupied most psychoanalytic theories ever since Freud. Freud got things off on the right track to suggest that there must be interplay between the psyche and the soma. It was not his willingness to approach the problem but his particular solution, in which he nearly reduced the psyche to a complex epiphenomenon of the soma, that I find unsatisfactory. It remained for the object relations theorists, Fairbairn, Guntrip, and others, to note that endopsychic structure can be explained only by looking at the complicated patterns of interpersonal relationships during the early months and years of life. When this is done, we arrive at the conclusion that the human psyche strives not merely for libidinal pleasure, but for object relations. In common parlance, the human soul contains an irreducible hunger for human love.

It is precisely the object relations theorist's insistence on the need of the infant to form object relations that represents a material parallel to Barth's position that we derive our being not from some prior "stuff" or being (entis), but rather from a dynamic relationship (relationis) to God. In the case of psychology, the "other" is of course the mother or parental figure. But the analogy is striking, because the "mother's" relationship itself constitutes the psychology of the individual in no uncertain terms, and Barth is certain that

---

198. The relationship has, of course, been broken by humans, not by God himself. It is only by God's grace that the animosity that the human race holds toward God can be overcome. The theological truth that Barth emphasizes so strongly would be interesting to compare and contrast with Freud's attempts to abolish God's objective existence by trying to explain psychologically the need for God's paternal protection. This, however, would entail another study altogether.

the need for relation to God will be reflected in the creature and his or her relations to others. The analogical relationship between Barth and object relations is reinforced by Barth's insistence that in the human being we see a reflection of the love expressed within the triune God and poured out in the divine-human covenant. Hence human beings are by nature beings who encounter one another: I with Thou, mutually conditioning one another's being and shaping one another's destiny.[199] Barth has argued that we *are* as we *act* toward one another, and object relations has provided a tool to glimpse the material reality of this truth. There are many other ways to state it, but this statement will do for now. I make a closer comparison in chapter six.

Could it be that in the final few years of Freud's life we have an admission from his own writings that true love must be governed by a higher calling than that of the instincts? Certainly, a good deal of his own discoveries tend to lean in the direction that part of the human being transcends the instincts altogether. Having fled to England before the outbreak of World War II, Freud wrote a response to a letter from Albert Einstein. Einstein had asked if Freud could shed any insight on how war might be prevented. In the letter Freud mentioned two kinds of emotional ties that could be encouraged among human beings to mitigate the chance of war. The first is by means of "identification." This is thoroughly understandable in light of the discussion on Freud's "ego-ideal" theory above. The other, said Freud, "may be relations resembling those towards a love object, though without having a sexual aim. There is no need for psycho-analysis to be ashamed to speak of love in this connection, for religion itself uses the same words: 'Thou shalt love thy neighbour as thyself.' This, however, is more easily said than done."[200]

199. See esp. *CD*, III/2, pp. 322-24.
200. "Why War?" *S.E.*, XXII ([1932] 1964) p. 212.

CHAPTER 6

A Comparison of the Anthropologies Contained in Barth and Object Relations Psychology

The religious and the sexual are close akin.

KARL BARTH

In chapter five I argued that object relations psychology has dealt with some of the problems that it inherited from Freudian psychoanalytic theory. Although it was built on certain seminal ideas within Freud's thought, object relations represents a significant step forward in our attempt to understand the psychology of the human being. Object relations is a new wine that bursts the old wineskins of both the mechanistic and organic anthropologies based on instinctual drives. The human being, defined object-relationally, is not merely a biochemical bundle of impulses seeking equilibrium but an acting agent who is seeking meaningful relations with other persons. The logic that undergirds object relations is based on interpersonal dynamics: the dynamic of interpersonal relationships that can be reduced neither to the mechanical categories of classical Newtonian physics nor to the language of biological organisms.[1] In the chapters prior to chapter five, I argued that Barth also devel-

---

1. Barth rarely mentions the new physics. Yet in the *Dogmatics* he hints that the most recent developments in physics may hold some new possibilities for pushing beyond the old dualisms of the Greek and traditional Christian conception of the human being: "And there may well be the added reason to-day that a quite unexpected ally can be found for this view in physics, which has undergone so revolutionary a renewal in the last decade" (*CD*, III/2, pp. 390-91). (By "this view" Barth means the position that organic materialism is inherently pessimistic

ops a theological concept of the person that is dynamic. His theological anthropology is dynamic because it attempts to break free from the classical dualisms that extended into the period of the Enlightenment and modern Protestant theology as well. Rather than accepting that the person is an autonomous thinker enclosed in a physical body, Barth emphasizes the person as a unitary acting agent, constituted by dynamic interpersonal relations to God, self, and others.

We have now come to the place where it is appropriate to explore the similarities between the dynamic concept of the person in both Barth and object relations psychology. In this chapter I explore specific parallels between Barth's description of "real man" as a "being in encounter" and the dynamic self in object relations. I have three reasons for pointing out these specific similarities. First, I wish to show that there are certain structural similarities between Barth and object relations in their dynamic concept of the person. By structural similarities I mean that both the methods which they employ and the categories in which they choose to discuss the person contain some significant parallels. These structural similarities are highly important because they point out that Barth's anthropology compares favorably with some of the discoveries that modern psychology has made regarding the nature of the person. This shows how Barth's anthropology can interact with the human sciences on a level that has seldom been acknowledged. Second, I wish to demonstrate how both Barth and object relations have constructed models that overcome the traditional anthropological dualism that has exerted a predominant influence over Western thought for most of the past two thousand years. Third, I wish to show how the dynamic-relational concept of the person in both theology and psychology can engender a fruitful dialogue between these two disciplines and pave the way for the healing of persons in a modern world. I will also follow Barth's interactions with several psychologists, including Freud, in order to show the extent to which it is legitimate, even by Barth's own self-prescribed theological method, to compare his theological anthropology with some of the findings of the human sciences.

---

and theoretically weak.) Even here theologians must be careful to exercise caution in employing the dynamic categories of postmodern physics, because the interpersonal world will necessarily demand a higher level of explication.

Some Structural Similarities between Barth and Object Relations in Their Concept of the Human Person

The Interpersonal Element in Barth's "Real Man" and Fairbairn's "Ego"

The first and most important parallel between Barth and object relations is the emphasis each places on interpersonal relations in constituting the person. Both Barth and object relations show how the person is shaped by a social context: by relation to an "other." In each case the person is defined not only by what mental faculties or instinctual energies an individual might *have,* but also by what the individual *does* — especially in relation to an other or others. Both show, on their respective levels of inquiry, how interpersonal relations are the fundamental building block of an individual's personhood; each person is shaped by his or her peculiar history of interpersonal relations. This can be called the "dynamic" of interpersonal relations. In the case of one person relating to another there is an "outer dynamic." But the outer dynamic has immediate implications for an "inner dynamic." Object relations has shown how certain important relations to others can become internalized ("introjected") and assume a life of their own within the individual's psyche. The correlation between external objects and internal psychological representations of the external object relations could have some interesting implications not only for psychoanalytic theory, but also for the development of cognition, will, and emotions — and the relation of mind and body. (It is significant to note Barth's insistence that each person must have a relation to the "self" as well as to God and others.) In Barth's anthropology, relation to God is the primary relation. We might say that God is the primary external object. Nevertheless, this relation has some important implications for the development of individual consciousness. It is only in the relation to God as an "object" that consciousness begins to develop, that cognition, volition, and affection take on a valid existence. This I explain in the following pages.

In object relations, self-identity develops only within the history of complex social interaction. The self is born within a social matrix. For Barth, of course, the social coefficient of knowing and being has a theological foundation. From Barth's theological perspective the social matrix of human personhood reflects the relational character of the triune God. God is a being who is in relation to himself, not just within the economic Trinity, but also within the immanent Trinity. Therefore, the human being who reflects God's nature cannot be actualized as fully human apart from a right relation to the Creator, other creatures, and self.

The social development of human consciousness highlights another similarity between Barth and object relations: both insist on the unity and integrity of the person as a whole, rejecting any dichotomies between body and soul, mind and matter, or psychological self (ego) and instinctual self (libido). The explicit holism of both Barth and object relations shows the extent to which both attempt to discover the unity of the theoretical and the practical person, the biological and the psychological. There is little that smacks of idealism in either anthropology. Their respective anthropologies are not merely derived a priori but give a good deal of respect to the empirical observation of the person's physical existence. On the other hand, neither falls into materialism in their reflections on the nature of the person. Rather than idealism or materialism, a deep-seated realism runs through the thought of both Barth and Fairbairn. Barth's realism leads him to respect both the revealed nature of the person as it is interpreted in the person of Christ, and the physical existence of the person — which the Scriptures clearly indicate has an almost equal importance with the spiritual and psychological realities. Once again, the Trinity plays a major role in Barth's understanding of the person. This means that the incarnation of the Son must shatter the traditional categories that separated soul and body, instincts and reason, replacing them with a hearty affirmation of the dynamic interdependence of each with the other.

Fairbairn's realism leads him to integrate his clinical observations with his theory, his understanding of early childhood relations in forming the adult psyche with his respect for the biochemical conditions that create the possibility for object attraction in the first place. Such a realism tends to push them along a similar conceptual path, skirting idealism on the one hand and the reductionist tendencies of positivism or naturalism on the other.

In the process of comparing Barth and object relations, one needs to ask some crucial questions: What is the relationship between Barth's understanding of "real man" as a being who encounters God, others, and self, and the human being who the psychologist says is shaped by early childhood object relations? At what points do they compare favorably? At what points do they differ? If, as I have proposed, the "real man" described by Barth's theology is analogous to the insights about the human being that have been discovered by object relations, then what kind of similarities and differences shall we see if we compare them closely? And what importance might these similarities signify for the study of Barth — for his doctrine of humanity and its relation to the human sciences?

It is important to acknowledge at the outset that, in spite of the similarities, the anthropologies of Barth and object relations do differ. The respective differences are almost as important to discover as the similarities because they help to define the respective boundaries of each discipline. For example, there is a primary difference of perspective. Theologians look at the person from the perspective of the Word of God. In theological anthropology the relation to God is the primary relation upon which all others are founded. The spiritual dynamic is fundamental — and this is the first sphere of relationship to which theologians must give attention. Psychologists, on the other hand, are not given the task of understanding the spiritual dynamic: psychologists are not concerned to study the relations between human beings and God. Psychologists are given the task of combing through the research and the clinical evidence in order to conform their theoretical formulations to the reality of the human subject being studied. Psychologists oriented toward object relations theory can observe the other-directedness of an infant from the earliest stage of infancy through adulthood. In this process, psychologists can develop and use a set of technical terms to better understand the development of the human psyche. These terms may have little or no meaning to theologians. Yet psychologists do not see the other-directedness of their patients as a reflection of the image of God. Only theologians can see the person's other-directedness as a reflection of the triune God. Therefore, when theologians describe God as "love," there is a shift in meaning from the psychologists' description of human "love." Human love reflects divine love, it corresponds to it and stands only in relation to it; yet human love cannot be *equated with* divine love. This is a point that Barth emphasizes repeatedly, and it has some important ramifications for the relation between theological anthropology and the human sciences.

The relationship between Barth and object relations could also be revealed by pointing to Barth's employment of certain dynamic terms, such as *analogia relationis*. The *analogia relationis*, in addition to serving a theological function, may also provide us with a heuristic device for probing parallels between theology and other sciences, parallels that are appropriate to the personal object being studied. Since this cross-disciplinary study is one in which the *relations* between living subjects is being compared, the term *analogia relationis*, I propose, is an especially appropriate tool for the task at hand.

In this chapter, therefore, I attempt to weave together many of the strands of thought from the previous chapters in support of my contention that Barth's anthropology reveals a significant conceptual similarity to the findings of object relations psychology.[2] As far as I am aware, such a compari-

---

2. I have already given the criteria by which such a comparison is made in chapter one, and thus reiterate that it is not a natural theology, but a working out of the logic of Barth's *analogia relationis*, that facilitates this discussion.

son has not been brought out by anyone else who has studied either Barth or object relations.

The Dynamic Concept of the Person in Both
Barth and Object Relations Psychology

The adjective "dynamic" is a term that Fairbairn and other object relations theorists use frequently.[3] Barth too is fond of the term in the context of his theological anthropology.[4] The respective meanings are, of course, not univocal. We have to respect the different frameworks in which both of them use the term. But are they genuinely analogous? Or could I be accused of stretching an analogy in order to construct a convenient comparison between the two?

The anthropologies of both Barth and object relations are "dynamic" not only because they contain an implicit reference to motion as opposed to an inert state, but also because these anthropologies predicate this motion on the basis of interpersonal relations. The person in both respective disciplines is always acting, choosing, and moving in relation to other persons. It is not mere physical motion, determined by prior causes related to drive discharges, and so on, but interpersonal motion, understandable only in terms of interpersonal relationships, that is indicated by the term "dynamic."

Barth's and Fairbairn's concepts of the person are also dynamic in the sense that they do not construe the person as a closed system determined by antecedent causes and tending toward a state of equilibrium. They are dynamic in the sense that neither allows the reductionist criteria to stand. They are dynamic because the person in each case is open to an almost infinite variety of creative options in respect to possible interactions with other persons. While certain patterns of human behavior can be observed within the field of interpersonal relations, there is nevertheless an overriding openness to the almost infinite variety of possibilities that obtain between human beings who engage in relations one to another. Below I say more about the ways in which a dynamic anthropology creates the possibility for human freedom.

A dynamic anthropology attempts to balance both the physical and psychical realities of the person. While neither Barth nor object relations assumes that the human being is reducible to biology, chemistry, or physics,

---

3. See, e.g., Fairbairn, *Psychoanalytic Studies,* pp. 148-50.
4. See *CD,* III/2, p. 248. Cf. III/2, pp. 158-59.

neither overlooks the importance of the biophysical realities. Both the psychical and the somatic components are taken into account, but neither is seen as sufficient to explain the whole person apart from the other. The human being is not reducible to a mechanism or an organism; a person can be adequately described only when the added dimension of his or her interpersonal history is taken into account. In object relations, the self is formed biologically within the womb, and psychologically and spiritually within a social matrix, of which the most fundamental building blocks are the earliest relations between parents and children. The dynamic person in object relations provides a material illustration of the capacity for interpersonal communion, which Barth sees as the best interpretation of the *imago Dei*.

Dynamic Anthropology Is Open-Ended

An important aspect of what both Barth and Fairbairn mean when they use the term "dynamic" is that they do not think the individual person can be defined as a self-contained system. The person who is described in terms of interpersonal dynamics is not a closed system. In the closed mechanistic or organic anthropologies, the person's behavior is supposedly accounted for in terms of instincts (as with Freud's libido). On the other hand, the rationalist anthropologies attempted to account for a certain degree of openness by positing the intellect and will as faculties that enable the person to act according to either law or reason, or both. Nevertheless, rationality itself does not contain any reference to the interpersonal dimension; it merely unfolds as an inherent human faculty (e.g., Kant's categories of understanding, or Descartes's *ratio*). But a dynamic anthropology also includes the dimension of interpersonal relations, and relations are open-ended. For Barth, the person is "dynamic" in the sense that we live within a relational and thus "historical" context — faith is dynamically understood as a covenant relation with God that entails an encounter with other human beings. Object relations generally sees the earliest relations to parents as the beginning for the basic building blocks of human psychology.

Fairbairn believes that his dynamic anthropology bears a certain similarity to the new physics in that it integrates the psychical energy with the psychological structure. We can see why Fairbairn thought this was a significant theoretical improvement of Freud's concept of id, ego, and superego, for it is difficult to see how mental structure and mental energy could possibly interact with one another (e.g., id and superego) unless both are structures endowed with energy. In other words, how could the superego restrain the id if they are completely unlike entities? It is a problem similar to the relation between soul and body in philosophy and theology (viz. how do soul and body interact if they are by definition completely unlike entities?). Fairbairn tries to solve the problem by arguing that both energy and structure are "dynamic," proposing that they coinhere in the psychological ego. The constant interpenetration of energy and structure illustrates the extent to which Fairbairn constructed his theory of the person more along the lines of a field theory than the classical concept of motion contained in the Newtonian framework.

A similar observation could be made with regard to Barth's anthropology. His person is dynamic in the sense that interpersonal actions cannot be explained merely in terms of linear causation. Interpersonal actions are usually characterized by an element of spontaneity and freedom that arises as a result of the capacity for reciprocal interpersonal actions.[5] If Barth's anthropology is analogous to a "field theory," as has been suggested of Fairbairn's object relational anthropology, it is primarily in the sense that it is relational, not simply mechanical.

Dynamic Anthropology Is Relational

The employment of field theory in describing the relational nature of the person is advocated by T. F. Torrance; he comments on Clerk Maxwell's field theory:

> We must now take up Clerk Maxwell's concept of the *field* . . . and not least the concept of *relational thinking* which he found, for example in the teaching of Sir William Hamilton. Evidence for this is apparent in Clerk Maxwell's 1856 essay on analogy where he showed that analogical resemblances and differences are embedded in the structural patterns of nature throughout the universe. Analogies are sets of relations which bear upon each other and point beyond themselves and thus supply us with fundamental clues for heuristic inquiry beyond the limits of empirical and observational knowledge. Hence, he claimed, "in a scientific point of view the *relation* is the most important thing to know." Clerk Maxwell insisted, however, that the relations he referred to were not just imaginary or putative but *real* relations, relations that belong to reality as much as things do, for the inter-relations of things are, in part at least, constitutive of

5. See esp. III/2, p. 126.

what they are. Being-constituting relations of this kind we may well speak of as "onto-relations."[6]

By inference, then, a relation is not peripheral or incidental to human ontology but is constitutive of the human essence. This is what Barth has said on a theological level, and what object relations confirms by its empirical studies of human psychological development. Again, Torrance comments on the historical stream of thought that explains the person in dynamic-relational terms:

> Here we have a distinctive element in Scottish and Reformed theology which dates back to Duns Scotus' development of the concept of the person as it emerged from the Trinitarian teaching of Richard of St Victor, and was passed on through Duns Scotus' *Commentaries on the Sentences of Peter Lombard* to John Major in Paris and then to John Calvin and back, not least through the *Syntagma Theologiae Christianae* of Amandus Polanus, to Scotland. This was a theological mode of thinking which rejected the analytical, individualist notion of the person that was put forward by Boethius and Thomas Aquinas and was later reinforced and built into western social philosophy through the positivist individualism of John Locke and August Comte who thought of persons as separated individuals connected through their external relations, rather like Newtonian particles.

Barth clearly stands within the stream of theological reflection that views the individual in terms of relations rather than isolated particles. Torrance continues:

> In the Reformed theological tradition the notion of the person is held to be controlled by the person-constituting and person-intensifying activity of God in the Incarnation, such that union with Christ becomes the ground for interpersonal relations in the Church. Relations between persons have ontological force and are part of what persons are as persons — they are real, person-constituting relations.[7]

The relational structure of both Barth's and object relations' anthropology allows them to understand the person as a reality that is analogous to the modern field concept developed by Faraday and Maxwell.[8] The "field" is, accord-

---

6. *Transformation and Convergence*, pp. 229-30.
7. Ibid., p. 230.
8. In addition to Torrance, see also W. J. Neidhardt, "Thomas F. Torrance's Integration of Judeo-Christian Theology and Natural Science: Some Key Themes," *Journal of the American Scientific Affiliation* 41 (1989) 87-98, esp. 93-94.

ing to Torrance, a better model for a dynamic anthropology than the more mechanistic terms that, for example, describe human beings as if they could be explained in terms of antecedent biophysical causes. Humans are of course connected to other things in the world, because no person has autonomous existence. However, they are connected by interpersonal relations, not just impersonal causes. Neither matter in motion nor biochemical reactions can provide a sufficient explanation for human behavior. Relations are essential, not accidental, in the development of the person. We must go beyond Torrance's observation to mention that *personal* relations contain an element of spontaneity and rational response-ability that cannot be fully subsumed under the more general category of simple mechanical "relations." In other words, there is something unique about personal relations. While noting Torrance's suggestion that a field theory might provide a more adequate paradigm for human existence than that provided by the notions of classical physics, we would do well to apply the field theory to the realm of interpersonal relations somewhat cautiously because the field of personal relations will contain certain elements that cannot be fully explained by any types of relations that are strictly nonpersonal.

Dynamic Anthropology Is "Historical"

Another important aspect of Barth's anthropology is his description of the interpersonal encounter as a "history." There is ample evidence to suggest that Barth and object relations understand the term "history" in an analogous sense.[9] Both respect the importance of each individual's history, and see it as more than a chronological arrangement of past events. A history is composed of an encounter or series of encounters between one person and another.[10] Thus defined, a history shatters the limitations of any mechanistic model that suggests that the person is something like an isolated particle

9. One must admit, of course, that Fairbairn uses the term "history" sparingly, and differently from its rich and varied meaning in German philosophical and theological circles. Nevertheless, Macmurray seems to attach a good deal of importance to the term in the context of his understanding of object relations. See above, pp. 224-25, and Macmurray, *Persons in Relation*, p. 46: "Human behaviour cannot be understood, but only caricatured, if it is represented as an adaptation to environment; and there is no such process as social evolution but, instead, a *history* which reveals a precarious development and possibilities both of progress and of retrogression" (italics mine).

10. Misiak defines "encounter" in phenomenological and gestalt psychology: "Basically, encounter refers to a meeting or a meaningful communication between people" (*History of Psychology*, p. 423).

moving through space and time and acted upon by external forces. An interpersonal history is more than a mechanical motion or even a self-impelled organic process. But how can a personal history take place if it is not connected to past physical and biochemical events?

Again, there is an integration going on here between the form and content, between energy and structure: this time it is an integration that expresses the unitary relation between the personal field and the historical. Rather than personal identity being separated from history, as if it could stand in the timeless reaches of some ideal world, the person is a predicate of history, and history is a predicate of human interactions. For Barth, "history" *(Geschichte)* is not the stage upon which an endless procession of dramatis personae act out their separate roles. It is rather the real interaction between human beings that creates the stage of history. For Barth, of course, this historical process is Christologically interpreted. That is, the stage of history is established by revelation and the incarnation. In Barth's theology, all human history is established by God's own history — by his self-revelation that unfolds in the person and work of Christ. What Barth seems to be saying is that God reveals himself *as* history: the triune God is the center of all time and the very ontological ground for the sequence of all events on earth and in heaven. This does not necessarily set into motion a deterministic framework for historical events. While some events are fixed, those events that involve interpersonal histories contain elements of spontaneity, creativity, and openness to innovation that break out of the deterministic framework.

Barth's distinction between a "history" and simple motion of inanimate things or the "state" of organisms is helpful. The term "dynamic," used in this context, can apply only to an interpersonal history. It is dynamic because it is interpersonal. It is a "history" that is signified by its interpersonal character. A history is dynamic not because it entails mere motion nor even because it unfolds toward a particular end (entelechy); it is dynamic because it necessarily entails interpersonal reciprocity. History is an encounter between two or more persons. It is an I interacting with a Thou in such a manner that there is a mutual shaping of one another's being. As human creatures we are historical beings in the sense that we really shape one another at the deepest level. A history is dynamic not merely because of the motion that it entails, but because it is motion that contains a personal intention. In this sense, both Barth and object relations mean the same thing when they describe human interaction as "action." With John Macmurray, they both agree that a "history" is a motion that includes a personal intention.[11] Apart from motion with

11. See Macmurray, *Persons in Relation*, p. 46.

intentionality there could be no human action, only motion. Only an interpersonal intent initiates an encounter that can break through the closed circle of mechanical determinism and allow for human freedom. There is, of course, a sense in which the past influences each human encounter. But the very nature of human encounter is such that each encounter is open-ended: there is always opportunity for the spontaneous irruption of new and creative actions within the relationship. Certain patterns of relating one to another can determine to a large degree the type of relation that will take place, but the patterns that tend to influence the nature of a present encounter can never fully predict future encounters.

For Barth, the basis of each human encounter begins with God. The divine-human relationship revealed in Christ is the basic building block for all human relationships. For object relations, interpersonal encounter must begin with the human parent, usually the mother. In either case, there is a strong similarity between the meaning and usage of the term "dynamic." It denotes an interpersonal history in which the being of one person can actually affect the being of another at the deepest ontological level. There is a mutual shaping of one another in the moment of encounter such that there is a mutual exchange of personal form and content, of energy and structure.

As we begin to understand the logic of interpersonal relations, we see why a history *(Geschichte)* is "dynamic," and why raw physical motion is not — in the technical sense in which I am using the term. Even the motion of an organism is not strictly "dynamic" in the sense in which both Barth and object relations use the term. A history differs from organic motion in that organisms have no conscious and volitional interactions one with another. Human beings, on the other hand, possess the ability to respond; we can speak and listen; we hear and interact; we perceive the needs of another person and make decisions about whether to render our assistance. We can become conscious of the other person and choose, or choose not, to enter into relationship with him or her. In the course of normal human interactions, we can choose to allow our histories to intersect and coinhere. The human possibility to shape one another by interpenetrating each other's being at the deepest level is another way of explaining how both "object relations" on the one hand, and Barth's "being in encounter" on the other, are "dynamic" in the historical sense.[12]

12. See *CD*, III/2, pp. 157-60.

*Dynamic Anthropology Encompasses
Both Relation and Differentiation*

It is important to keep in mind that in a healthy interpersonal encounter there should be no loss or confusion of identity. The identity of each human being becomes increasingly distinct in relation to the other. In object relations theory the child is looked upon as the subject of study. There can be little doubt, however, that the being of the mother is also affected by the relations with the child.[13] In the dynamic of the relation there is a real encounter in which the persons intersect with one another; therein are both integration and differentiation of personalities. The child's ego develops only in relation to the parent, and the parent can be a parent only in relation to the child: there is reciprocity of relationship, but of course in a different sense. Object relations deals primarily with the formative aspects of the parent's relation to the child; but we can easily conceive how a much wider circle of relations could be mapped out and studied. One can see that for purposes of narrowing the field of study the focus of object relations must be primarily on the ways in which the parent or parents influence the child's psychological development. Nevertheless, it can hardly escape our notice that there are intriguing parallels between the narrowed attention of the object relations theorist and the broader picture that Barth paints of humanity when he insists that the basic formula for interpersonal encounter is "I am as Thou art."[14]

In Barth's theology the encounter between God and humanity, as well as between one human being and another, is unified in the person of Jesus

13. Some day perhaps there shall be a more unitary means for psychology to study the relationship from both perspectives rather than simply the perspective of the child. It seems that Winnicott has made some progress in this direction: "The infant and the maternal care together form a unit. Certainly if one is to study the theory of the parent-infant relationship one must come to a decision about these matters, which concern the real meaning of the word dependence. It is not enough that it is acknowledged that the environment is important. If there is to be a discussion of the theory of the parent-infant relationship, then we are divided into two if there are some who do not allow that at the earliest stages the infant and the maternal care belong to each other and cannot be disentangled" ("The Theory of Parent-Infant Relationship," in Buckley, ed., *Essential Papers*, p. 235). Much more needs to be said, of course, about other object relations that enter into the child's world than simply the relation to the mother. Relations to father, siblings, and others need to be accounted for. Nevertheless, in choosing to focus primarily on the mother-child relation, object relations is seeking to explain the most fundamental relation from which all others follow. The integration of object relations with family systems theory is probably an area of psychology that will see further theoretical developments. See N. Gregory Hamilton, "A Critical Review of Object Relations Theory," *American Journal of Psychiatry* 146, 12 (1989) 1557-58.

14. See esp. *CD*, III/2, p. 248.

Christ. As both God and man, Christ represents the encounter that moves downward from God to humanity. At the same time, Christ embodies the upward movement of humankind toward God. Christ is God in relation to humankind, and humankind in relation to God. In addition to this, he is the person who is a man for others. Finally, he is related perfectly to himself. Christ therefore initiates every form of relation in which we can participate. The point I wish to emphasize here is that Christ both differentiates God from humanity and at the same time forms the basis of relation between God and human beings. In becoming a particular man, he chooses to subject himself to a communion of reciprocity with all humanity.[15] Yet there is no confusion between God and humanity. God remains God and human beings remain themselves. Once again, in interpersonal relations there is not only union of the traits and personalities of two distinct persons, but also differentiation: one from another as distinct individuals.

Again, it is important to clarify how the encounter between one person and another does not confuse their respective individual identities. Encounter does not entail a mystical fusion of identities, any more than object relations insists on a symbiotic relation between parent and child as the only stage of development. Quite the contrary, the dynamic of encounter always differentiates one individual from another at the same moment in which it brings them both into communion. It is therefore not separation alone that differentiates one individual from another, but an encounter with another person that initiates the process of one individual differentiating from another.[16] Healthy interpersonal relations therefore enable a person to develop mature relationships characterized by creativity, spontaneity, autonomy, and freedom. But separation by itself cannot enable an authentic differentiation of persons one from another. In the case of the child's attachment to the parent, the relationship normally progresses from a condition of symbiosis or

15. Does humanity actually encounter God in such a way that God is changed? Yes. According to Barth, in the incarnation, God brings humanity into himself. There is, therefore, no lack of humanity in God: "we are not God. . . . But God is man" (*CD*, II/1, p. 151); "God's deity does not exclude, but includes his humanity. . . . His deity encloses humanity in itself" (*Humanity of God*, pp. 46-47).

16. Cf., e.g., Teilhard de Chardin, *The Phenomenon of Man*, tr. Bernard Wall (London: Collins, 1959) p. 294, who affirms the personal nature of God, but for whom the "Omega Point" seems very close to an energy that absorbs rather than defines individual identity. Yet at other places he suggests that the "Omega Point" is the highly transcendent "other" who calls us into being from a supernatural vantage point, "by the differentiating and communicating action of love (God all *in everyone*)" (p. 308). The latter statement, although it is framed in terms unfamiliar to the trinitarian theology of Barth, is closer to a dynamic anthropology than it might first appear.

extreme identification, to dependence, to so-called independence, and finally to interdependence or "mature dependence." In each stage of relationship the bonding of the parent with the child and child with parent helps the child differentiate and become his or her own person.

Object relations psychology has discovered through empirical and clinical studies that there is a reciprocity of relationship in which persons mutually shape and transform each other. This discovery has come from studying the parent-child relations in the earliest stages of development. This is not a discovery that should surprise the theologian; for the dynamic relation between parent and child provides a reflection of the dynamic nature of God himself in which the Father and Son mutually condition one another in the Spirit.[17] As Barth states: "I and Thou" is an "inviolable constant of human existence"[18] because it mirrors the original "I and Thou" of God himself. For Barth, that human beings cannot fulfill their destiny as solitary beings provides an inevitable reminder that God himself is not alone. God "exists in relationship and fellowship. As the Father of the Son and the Son of the Father He is Himself I and Thou, confronting Himself and yet always one and the same in the Holy Ghost."[19] Human beings are designed to be in communion because they reflect the very nature of God — and God himself is in communion *ad intra*. From revelation, Barth adduces the human capacity to love and therefore to reflect the divine love. From watching human subjects carefully, object relations concludes that a child's capacity to love is shaped by the presence or absence of parental love. Each reflects on the human being from a different starting point, but each arrives at the similar conclusion that there is a social coefficient to human personal development.

There are, of course, some differences between the theological and the psychological anthropologies, differences that must be respected and that deserve further exploration. Nevertheless, the similarities between the two are intriguing, so much so that they serve to illumine the analogical relation between revealed humanity and human beings studied by the human science of object relations psychology. There is likeness even amid the unlikeness between God's relations and human relations. It is a likeness rooted in God himself. He is the archetypal Being who exists in dynamic relation within himself. As such he is self-sufficient and could remain aloof. But he does not remain aloof. He chooses to become human. Even at the highest level of rela-

---

17. See *CD*, I/1, pp. 480-84. "Because God is antecedently love in Himself, love is and holds good as the reality of God in the work of reconciliation and in the work of creation. But He is love antecedently in Himself as He posits Himself as the Father of the Son" (p. 484).

18. *CD*, III/2, p. 289.

19. *CD*, III/2, p. 324.

tions (between God and humanity) there is reciprocity of relation because, given the incarnation, we cannot deny that God is affected by his relation to humanity. He extends himself to us and calls us to extend ourselves to him and to others. Our capacity to be in relation to one another is therefore a reflection of God's relation within himself; we become ourselves as we encounter the One who is a perfect relation within himself. And as we become ourselves, we are compelled to encounter others.

Some Important Differences between Barth's Anthropology and That of Object Relations

Thus far I have argued that the dynamic anthropologies contained in Barth and object relations psychology bear an analogical relationship to each other. But even in their similarities there are obvious differences. This is what an analogical relation entails: both similarity and dissimilarity — a correspondence in some respects between things that are otherwise different. As an example of one of the differences, Barth draws attention to the dimension of human sexuality that is mature adult sexuality: he follows Genesis 1:27 (and Genesis 2, esp. vv. 18-25) in emphasizing the importance of the God-given relationship between male and female. For Barth the human "I and Thou" is interpreted primarily within the context of the biblical statements about male and female. For modern psychology, on the other hand, the relation between one person and another is believed to have its profoundest influence in the earliest stages of life in which an infant is parented. Barth discusses human sexuality from the perspective of the revealed Word of God; his source is the scriptural teachings about the creation of humankind as male and female, who in the relational aspect of their sexuality represent the very image and likeness of God. In the New Testament, Christ himself incarnates this image, bringing human beings into relation with God the Father.[20] Christ is the image of God, and Barth is quick to point out that the male-female relation of Genesis is interpreted by Paul to be a reflection of Christ's relation to the church.[21] Fairbairn, on the other hand, stresses the importance of human sexuality (in its most comprehensive sense) primarily from the perspective of the relation between parent and child.[22] In fact, object relations sees the latter

20. Col. 1:15-20; 3:10; 2 Cor. 4:4.

21. See Eph. 5:21–6:4; and *CD*, III/2, pp. 312ff.

22. As we have seen, Fairbairn does not interpret the parent-child relation as purely libidinal, but primarily interpersonal. His concept of sexuality is therefore much more broadly interpreted than Freud's — as is Barth's. See below.

as affecting every dimension of the former: earliest object relations affects the sexual-relational disposition of the person for the whole course of life.

I have pointed out that an important similarity between Barth and object relations is that they both emphasize the central importance of human sexuality in the growth and development of the human being. The difference is that Barth recognizes the importance of the male and female differentiation as the basis for intimate interpersonal communion. Object relations pays closer attention to the relation between a child and parent. While the differences should not be minimized, it is intriguing to note that from the time of Freud's psychoanalytic theory onward, modern psychology has seen the continuity of sexual attraction throughout the whole life cycle. In other words, parent-child relations will exert a tremendous influence on that child's later relations to persons of the opposite sex. And, if we carry the cycle of human sexual relations out still further, the nature of the relations of the male and female who become parents will have a profound impact on their relation to their child.

One of the important differences, therefore, between Barth and object relations is the stage at which each decides to stress the central importance of human sexual relations. In spite of their different emphases on the respective stages of development, it should be noted that modern psychoanalytic theory acknowledges the connection between one type of sexual-interpersonal relation and the others. In this regard, it could hardly be perceived as a coincidence that Paul mentions the theological significance of the husband-wife relationship and of the relation of parents to children as if the latter followed naturally with the next breath.[23]

The Whole Person as a Dynamic Unity:
Pushing beyond Anthropological Dualism

Both Barth and Fairbairn attempt to describe the human being as an indissoluble unity. They aim to describe the integrity and unity of the *whole person*. This holism avoids spiritualism or psychologism on the one side and reductionist materialism on the other. This holism is seen in Barth's emphasis on both body and soul, which constitute the whole person in mutual reciprocity and interaction. In object relations, the holism is seen in the unitary psychological ego which is the sine qua non of emotional health. Object relations also assumes the interrelation between soul and body in the very fact

23. Col. 3:18-21; Eph. 5:21–6:4.

that the external material object can be internalized and brought into the psychical structure. Object relations theory is predicated on the assumption that there is a constant dynamic interaction between the psychical and somatic. The psychosomatic unity of the human being informs and shapes the whole scope of psychoanalytic discussion. Such an assumption is so obvious that it can almost be overlooked.

The Unitary Ego in Fairbairn's Object Relations Psychology

The psychological self in object relations is also a whole person. Fairbairn proposes an "ego psychology" in which the ego is the "primary psychic self in its original wholeness, a whole which differentiates into organized structural patterns under the impact of experience of object-relationships after birth."[24] At the core of the human being is a unitary dynamic ego.[25] It is unitary because it is not inherently at war with itself, as if it were equally torn between conflicting drives such as attraction and aggression. There is no separation in Fairbairn's thought between structure and libidinal energy. His concept of the person is dynamic because it is actively "other seeking." As such the ego is constantly shaped by its encounters with external objects; over a period of time and a number of encounters with the external (usually parental) object, the ego begins to differentiate self from other, and self-awareness begins to develop. As the ego encounters the external objects it can be threatened by a bad relation over which it has no control. The need to protect the ego from bad object relations stimulates the internalization of the external objects with the result that relations develop between one part of the split ego and another.[26] The splitting of the ego due to bad object relations is the cause of many psychological problems, and the reunification of the ego is the only means to renewed psychological health. This is accomplished, according to Fairbairn, by the reintroduction of a good object to the patient. The inner psychological world therefore reflects the relationships with external objects in the physical world.

24. Guntrip, describing Fairbairn's psychoanalytic theory, *Personality Structure*, p. 279.

25. See Fairbairn, "Observations on the Nature of Hysterical States," *British Journal of Medical Psychology* 27 (1954) 107.

26. One must concede that Fairbairn's "ego" is not monolithic. It is usually split into representations that seem to be at odds with one another, such as the "libidinal ego" and "antilibidinal ego," or "exciting object" and "rejecting object." Nevertheless, the point is that these split-off structures are dynamically defined; i.e., they are subject to the vicissitudes not of instinct, but of interpersonal relations. See "Observations," pp. 107-9.

The highly complex interplay between the internal and external objects is something that Fairbairn describes in details that are not pertinent to the discussion at hand.[27] What pertains here is the discovery by object relations theory that the constant interaction between the psychical representations of somatic realities and the physical realities themselves explains an enormous amount about human psychology. It is precisely the need to integrate the psyche with the soma, rather than allow them to remain separated by the older dualisms and parallelisms, that provides the implicit starting point for modern object relations theory. With this in mind, it is difficult to overlook that one of Freud's chief contributions to modern thought was his tireless pursuit of the necessary unity between mental events and physical events in human life. His quest was ultimately unsuccessful because of his unexamined positivistic presuppositions. Nevertheless, he set modern psychology off in the right direction. With a few exceptions, modern psychology has presupposed the unity between the psychical and somatic ever since, constantly seeking to explain such a unity.

We have seen Fairbairn's attempt to integrate energy with structure in his endopsychic structural theory. In Fairbairn's framework an ego abstracted from the libido is meaningless, because an energyless structure makes no sense and lacks the practical capacity to function as a regulative agency over the libido. Might we find a similar sort of integration in Barth's description of the relation between body and soul?

Barth's "Whole Man"

Barth does not, of course, deal in his anthropology with endopsychic structures. Yet he does deal extensively with the problem of the relation between soul and body. If we consider that in Barth's thought the soul is person as subject, and the body the person as object, then it could be said that energy and form are integrated such that neither makes sense apart from a functional relation to the other. It should be conceded that Barth's conception of the soul and body is not strictly identical with the "ego" and "libido" of modern psychoanalytic theory. Yet there are certain parallels in each anthropology such

27. For Fairbairn's description of his more dynamic (and very complex) interpretation of structural theory, see *Psychoanalytic Studies,* chap. 7, "A Synopsis of the Development of the Author's Views Regarding the Structure of the Personality," esp. pp. 170-79. One does not have to agree with all the particulars of Fairbairn's structural theory to accept his point that the separation of energy and structure in Freud's theory is no longer the best way to conceptualize psychical structure. See p. 171.

that I do not think it out of order to suggest a strong analogical relationship between them.

Barth proposes that through the Spirit of God, "real man" is: "the subject, form and life of a substantial organism, the soul of his body, wholly and simultaneously both, in ineffaceable difference, inseparable unity, and indestructible order."[28] Drawing on the theological truth that in Jesus we see and witness "real man" *(vere homo)*, Barth looks to the New Testament and finds that Jesus is a whole man: "embodied soul and besouled body." In the New Testament the pneumatic and the somatic form an active whole.[29] The oneness and wholeness of Jesus is Barth's starting point for theological anthropology.[30]

For Barth, the soul is not some eternal substance that is encumbered by a body. Such a dualistic view stems from Hellenic philosophy, and it has been the prevailing anthropology of Western theology for nearly fifteen hundred years. Barth is struggling to push beyond this dualistic view. He has denied the possibility that either the soul or the body could be a self-sufficient substance, or the person a juxtaposition of soulish and bodily substances.[31] Rather, soul and body are dynamically related. The soul is neither to be confused with nor separated from the body. Any severance of soul and body creates chaos and death. Soul and body are in "inseparable unity" *(in untrennbarer Einheit)*. The soul and body are integrally related, and it is not a coincidental relation.

Barth views the soul as the life of the body — here we have "being": the soul provides a rational and volitional structure for the animating force of the human body. Human life is more than a mere organism. The human being is therefore a soul inasmuch as the soul indicates the subject as the life of the body.[32] Here Barth is in agreement with most theological anthropologies:

28. *CD*, III/2, p. 325, the heading for §46.

29. E.g., in giving up of himself *(heauton;* Gal. 1:4), Jesus gives up both his soul *(psychēn autou;* Matt. 20:28) and his body *(ta sōma mou;* Luke 22:19).

30. *CD*, III/2, pp. 328-31. It is not the oneness and wholeness of the two natures, divine and human, that Barth is concerned with here, but the oneness and wholeness of his *human nature* as ensouled body and embodied soul. Nevertheless, there is an analogy between the human being and the divine. The Christological councils were right to deny that the mere bodily existence of Jesus could comprise his humanity, while the supplanting of his soul with the eternal Logos could comprise his deity (as with Apollinarianism and Nestorianism).

31. Such a position is argued for in recent times by, e.g., Robert Gundry, *Soma in Biblical Theology: With an Emphasis on Pauline Anthropology* (Cambridge: Cambridge University Press, 1976). He proposes that the body and soul comprise "two substances which belong together though they possess the capability of separation" (pp. 83-84).

32. *CD*, III/2, 373-74, quoting H. Cremer: "Soul is 'life as it stirs in the individual and quickens the material organism which serves as a means for its activity.'"

"man is soul." But there is a difference between Barth and traditional anthropologies. Barth describes the human being not as mere soul, but as a "soul of his body." As "soul of his body" human beings belong to the material world of space and time.[33] Each human exists as an organic, physical, material body: a person is a soul of a particular body. Barth makes clear, contrary to many theological anthropologies, that the soul does not dwell in a body incidentally:

> He is neither before nor beside nor after his material body. He is the life of his physical body, not a life in itself, and not a life hovering freely over his body or dwelling in it only incidentally. . . . The statement that "man is soul" would be without meaning if we did not immediately enlarge and expound it: Soul of one body, i.e., his body. He is soul as he is a body and this is his body. Hence he is not only soul that "has" a body which perhaps it might not have, but he is bodily soul, as he is also besouled body.[34]

Is there a sense in which energy and structure, soul and body, coinhere for Barth? Yes. While the soul is the animating subject of the body, "Soul would not be soul, if it were not bodily."[35] And, while the body is the objective form of human existence, it would "not be body, if it were not besouled."[36] There is no strict separation then between the soul as subject and the body as object. While there is an ineffaceable difference (*unaufhebbare Verschiedenheit*) between body and soul, they are not separable. They relate to one another dynamically, and form an undivided whole human being. Soul and body are "two moments" of one undivided human nature.[37] We cannot speak of the soul without speaking of the body. Because each person is a unity, the soul and the body are necessarily connected. If we interpret the soul as the animating force in some sense, then we also may interpret the body as the objective form of human existence. The soul and body are not merely connected by some extraneous third thing, but actually coinhere. That is, soul and body exist only as they interpenetrate within a living human being.

The coinherence of a human soul and human body means that they are not connected in some way that is incidental to a human being's existence; but each exists only as it is integrated into the existence of the other. The soul is, according to Barth, "not without a body. . . . Hence every trivialization of

33. *CD*, III/2, p. 349.
34. *CD*, III/2, p. 350.
35. Ibid.
36. Ibid.
37. *CD*, III/2, p. 393.

the body, every removal of the body from the soul, and every abstraction between the two immediately jeopardizes the soul. Every denial of the body necessarily implies a denial of the soul."[38] On the other hand, there is no human being unless the body is besouled: "We obviously do not see man if we will not see that, as he is wholly his body, he is also wholly his soul, which is the subject, the life of this body of his."[39]

The inseparable unity of body and soul prohibits Barth from thinking of them as if they were separate substances. For if we conceive of soul and body as separate substances, then either we must depend on some third entity (tertium quid) to link them,[40] or we must allow them to coexist side by side in the manner of psychophysical parallelism:

> We are, in fact, caught in an endless spiral, so long as the idea of the two substances is not wholly abandoned, and the concrete reality of the one man set up definitively at the start, in the middle and at the end of all consideration, soul and body being understood, not as two parts, but as two moments of the indivisibly one human nature, the soul as that which quickens and the body as that which is quickened and lives. . . . The abstract dualism of the Greek and traditional Christian doctrine, and the equally abstract materialist and spiritualist monism, are from this standpoint a thoroughgoing and interconnected deviation.[41]

Barth clearly rejects both traditional dualism and materialist monism as viable options for Christian anthropology. Fairbairn and most object relations theorists adopt a similar perspective. When Wundt and others first began to study human behavior, they adopted a form of philosophical parallelism that was essentially dualistic. Freud, on the other hand, exchanged a dualist perspective for a more or less materialistic monism. Yet the materialist assumptions began to show their theoretical weakness as soon as Freud was forced to posit the ego and superego and the like. Object relations theory generally rejects both the dualist and the materialist assumptions, and implicitly assumes a more or less interactionist type of anthropology. In some ways Barth's anthropology reveals a certain similarity with interactionism. I say more about this below.

38. *CD*, III/2, p. 373.
39. *CD*, III/2, p. 383.
40. Barth does in fact see the Spirit as the means of uniting body and soul, but he denies that the Spirit constitutes a third entity that would create a trichotomous anthropology. See *CD*, III/2, p. 354.
41. *CD*, III/2, p. 393.

According to Barth, the soul is inner — it represents the self as subject. Yet the soul could not be a soul if it had no outer. As we have seen, any denial of the body denies the soul.[42] For Barth this is not merely a theoretical observation, but also a historical and practical one. The devaluation of the body has nearly become the "gospel" of many Christian anthropologies. Yet a dynamic anthropology would have to conclude that those who deny the body will eventually impugn the soul. This is precisely what Barth proposes: the neglect of the importance of the human body has often resulted in a compensating materialism that makes the opposite mistake of denying the soul. For example, Marxism, among other things, illustrates the vengeance that history exacts from the church when it overlooks the material conditions that rob the worker of his or her soul.[43]

Comparing the Two: Soul and Body, Ego and Libido

Neither Barth nor object relations is satisfied with the traditional anthropologies that have accepted either dualism (parallelism) or monism. Both Barth and Fairbairn endeavor to think them together — to perceive the inherent unity and reciprocity between body and soul, ego and libido. With due consideration for all the differences between the two fields, we can nevertheless perceive some significant parallels between them. Both attempt to understand the human being in a more unitary fashion than traditional dualism.[44] Among other things, a unitary anthropology denies the separability of body and soul. Body and soul differ, but they cannot be separated. They are differentiated, yet they form a unity. The body has been traditionally seen in Western anthropologies as the seat of one's physical appetites, and therefore something to be tolerated at best, and sometimes discarded. The soul, on the other hand, received the stronger emphasis. The bifurcation of the person into the body and soul, and the lopsided importance attached to the soul, can no lon-

---

42. *CD*, III/2, p. 373.

43. More will be said about this below.

44. I use the term "unitary" in much the same manner as T. F. Torrance. Even though it is a term that Barth never uses, according to Torrance it is an apt description of Barth's theological form and content. A "unitary" anthropology seeks to conceive of the unity of the empirical and theoretical dimension of human existence. In this case we are referring to Barth's insistence on the unity between "soul" and "body" as theoretical constructs, and the empirical reality of living persons, who for the most part can be categorized neither as a soul nor as a body, but a living person in whom these two coinhere. See Barth, *Dogmatics in Outline*, tr. G. T. Thomson (New York: Harper & Row, 1959) p. 9; also Neidhardt, "T. F. Torrance's Integration," pp. 87-98, esp. 89-90.

ger attain credibility among most modern studies of the human being. What is needed is a means of conceptualizing their integration.

The problem of how the soul and body are related, and whether soul or body plays the primary role in constituting the person, has posed an insurmountable theoretical obstacle to theology and philosophy through the centuries. The problem of dualism tends to surface where it is sometimes least expected. For example, Freud attempted to explain human psychology, first in terms of biochemistry, and later in terms of instinctual drives. In positing the instincts as the human essence, Freud sought to do away with the soul altogether, or at least explain it as an epiphenomenon of the body. Yet the body and its instincts could not support so great a weight; for the nonbodily entities like the "ego-ideal" or "superego" kept appearing almost like phantoms. As we have seen, the model for explaining the ways in which these various psychological entities played themselves out was borrowed from various theories in classical physics and thermodynamics. But by the time Freud formulated his most mature psychology he had nearly recapitulated the ancient trichotomous anthropology that conceptualized the person as body, soul, and spirit. On the other hand, in the dynamic anthropologies proposed by Fairbairn and Barth, there is a sense in which the energy is inherently connected with structure. In a dynamic anthropology there can be no dichotomies or trichotomies between separate component parts of the self. Rather, there is an integration and constant interaction. For example, Fairbairn asks how any conceptual framework for human psychology can talk about a structure that is not "energized." Any such thing as an existing structure without any energy is inconceivable when it is applied to the psychology of human beings. Analogously, in Barth's anthropology, a body without a soul is not a "dead person," it is simply a "body." The disturbing thing about a corpse is that it is no person at all, which nevertheless bears the outer appearance of that person. The disintegration of the unitary structure of human beings is therefore — literally — death. A disembodied soul is a false analogy taken from the crude application of physical metaphors to personal realities, as if the body could be an empty container into which a soul can be poured.[45]

So a body that is not besouled and a soul that is not embodied are unhelpful abstractions. Time and again Barth makes clear that he intends to avoid these abstractions. Barth attempts to push beyond anthropological dualism in espousing a unitary anthropology; his position is one that deserves our close attention, for it has become increasingly evident that the anthropol-

---

45. Barth denies that the soul resides in a material body as if it were "an oyster in its shell" (*CD*, III/2, p. 376).

ogy of the Bible is not as dualistic as most of the theologians of the church had supposed. At the heart of biblical anthropology the Scripture is always concerned about the *whole* person in relation to God. Also, at the foundation of the modern human sciences and medicine a similar view is beginning to prevail. The endless and mostly fruitless speculations as to whether the biological or the psychological components are primary have begun to give way to newer paradigms that accept biological priority and psychological supremacy. These paradigms are usually constructed on models that reject both dualism and reductionism, arguing instead that reality is structured as a bidirectional hierarchy in which things are ordered according to their complexity — beginning with the physical, and graduating upward to the chemical, biological, social, and psychological components. At the highest level, all the lower levels are not excluded but included.[46] What makes the hierarchy bidirectional is that the components at the lower level have priority, while the higher-level components exert a certain amount of control over functions at the lower levels.

These hierarchical paradigms have gained increasing acceptance in the human sciences. Yet they are mostly belated theoretical attempts to explain the practical death of anthropological dualism, a death that has been a self-evident fact of modern medicine for many years. For example, do we not live in a world today in which increasing numbers of psychological illnesses are susceptible to treatment with chemical drugs? Do we not also live in a time when the psychosomatic origins of many physical illnesses have been revealed? Can we ignore the fact that highly sensitive instruments can register amazingly slight electrical impulses in the human central nervous system that correlate to certain emotions? There is, therefore, no going back to the naive but attractive notion that the psychical and somatic run down parallel tracks — as if they were simultaneously at a similar milestone but never intersecting one another and exerting a mutual influence. If Christian anthropology continues to endorse anthropological dualism it will find itself defending a position that is both scientifically untenable and biblically indefensible. Such a position will continue to push many of the thoughtful people of our age headlong into either materialist or spiritualist monism, both of which have enormous shortcomings.

Let us see how Barth attempts to transcend the dualist categories.

---

46. See, e.g., Hector C. Sabelli and Linnea Carlson-Sabelli, "Biological Priority and Psychological Supremacy: A New Integrative Paradigm Derived from Process Theory," *American Journal of Psychiatry* 146, 12 (1989). In order to push beyond the old stalemate of "either biology or psychology," the authors look back to the philosophy of Heraclitus for more dynamic and integrative paradigms. I see no reason not to include the "spiritual" at the highest level of the hierarchy.

The Interaction of Soul and Body

If Barth rejects both parallelism and substantival dualism, what does he propose? The option of either materialist or spiritualist monism is obviously ruled out at the start. It might seem that the only choice would therefore be some type of interactionism in which body and soul engage in constant mutual interplay.[47] Modern studies in neurophysiology have shown a tremendous correlation between conscious processes and brain events. If we deny the possibility of attempting to reduce all consciousness into brain events, then interactionism looks increasingly attractive.

John Eccles has proposed an interactionist anthropology. Like Barth, Eccles rejects materialist monism. Unlike Barth, Eccles comes from a scientific background where most of his colleagues adhere to a materialist monism as their theoretical framework.[48] Eccles argues for dualism rather than materialist monism in attempting to explain the human mystery. But he proposes a type of "dualism" that is not like that of Descartes. It is rather an interactionist dualism in which a "frontier" is crossed between mind (soul) and body in both directions: from sensations to mental events and from mental events to actions in the material world. Nevertheless, even within such a dynamic interplay, mental events are given order by a thinking self: "A key component of the hypothesis in the unity of conscious experience is provided by the self-conscious mind and not by the neuronal machinery of the liaison areas of the cerebral hemisphere."[49] Without the presence of a self-conscious unity (soul), Eccles asks, how can the brain events come to be synthesized into any kind of conscious experience? He continues: "The experienced unity comes, not from a neurophysiological synthesis, but from the proposed integrating character of the self-conscious mind."[50] He concludes: "the selectional and integrational functions are conjectured to be attributes of the self-conscious mind, which is thus given an active and dominant role."[51] In other words, while there is an undeniable reciprocity between body and mind, there is also an order between the body and mind such that it is impossible to equate the identity of the individual merely with the physiological events of the brain. Rather, there is a human subject who is capable of exerting self-conscious control over certain physiological events,

47. Interactionism excludes both parallelism and epiphenomenalism, but not necessarily dualism of all types.
48. *The Human Mystery* (Berlin and Heidelberg: Springer, 1979) p. 9.
49. Ibid., p. 227.
50. Ibid., p. 228.
51. Ibid., p. 229.

including brain events. How else can we talk meaningfully about human consciousness? The only alternative would be to argue that the physiological events of the brain somehow coalesce in order to form human consciousness, in which case human beings turn out to be nothing more than very complicated machines whose actions are dictated by the neuronal events of the brain.

In Eccles's interactionist anthropology we see once again a bidirectional hierarchy that accounts for the priority of lower levels such as physics and chemistry, but the supremacy of higher levels, which exert a rational influence on the lower-level components. In other words, a body, with all its physical and biochemical realities, is the necessary condition for human existence, but it is not sufficient. A person can exert control over his or her own body by acting spontaneously, freely, and rationally.

Although Barth rejects interactionism per se, it is interesting to note the similarities between Barth and the position put forth by Eccles. Both insist on the differentiation of the soul and body. Both also insist on the unity of the soul and body. There is unity in the differentiation, and there is differentiation in the unity. In both theories there is a constant bilateral connection between the body and soul. For example, Eccles points out that kinesthetic experience correlates with the development of language, with the capacity for sense perception. Bodily experiences therefore influence the identity of the self.[52] This illustrates the constant interaction between body and soul as the necessary condition for normal human consciousness. Barth likewise will not allow any split between the soul and body. They are not identical or interchangeable, but neither are they separable. The soul needs the body in order for a person to exist.[53] But the body needs a soul; both Barth and Eccles posit the soul (or mind) as the organizing center of mental events. The soul can therefore exert a willful effect on the body and bodily movements. It is the whole person that acts, and the soul that orders actions even as it is inextricably bound to the body. The human being cannot therefore be reduced to a body; but neither can the person exist without the body.[54]

52. Ibid., pp. 131ff. Eccles notes his agreement with Macmurray's emphasis on the importance of tactual stimulation in the development of conscious awareness and self-conscious identity. Cf. *Persons in Relation*, p. 75.

53. See *CD*, III/2, pp. 372-73.

54. See *CD*, III/2, p. 375.

The Spirit as the Basis of Unity between Body and Soul

There is, however, an important point of difference between Barth and Eccles. Eccles describes the self-conscious mind as a "self-subsistent entity."[55] Barth describes the self-conscious mind as sustained by the Spirit of God.[56]

Whereas Descartes got himself into trouble by locating the convergence of the mind and body in the pineal gland, Eccles, as a neurologist, seems to locate the point of convergence in the more complex neurological functioning of the brain. But has Eccles put forth a fundamentally different position from that of Descartes? Eccles avoids the crudity of placing the body-soul connection in the pineal gland; but is this really a fundamental step forward? Are body and soul really connected in the complex neurophysiological events of the brain?

One of the problems with interactionism is finding the human essence. Barth asks the interactionist where the "real man" ultimately resides: "We have to ask: Who or what operates from one side or the other? Where is real man in this play of thrust and counterthrust? Is he on the one side or the other? Is there a decision on this? Or is he on both sides? And if so, how is he the subject of such a criss-cross and competitive activity?"[57] Barth has warned that any parallelism or interactionism would ultimately reduce to dualism. This seems to be the case even in more modern attempts to articulate the interactionist position. Yet we should not dismiss dualism simply because a position allows for the dual realities of body and soul. Barth is himself a dualist and not a monist in the sense that he believes in the existence of both body and soul because these are the most obvious components in biblical anthropology. The unacceptable aspect of dualism comes when it fails to allow for any interaction between body and soul and fails to provide an adequate conceptual framework for their unity. In a sense, then, interactionism is a step in the right direction. Interactionism seems to stumble, however, when it attempts to describe the point at which the body and soul interact. Barth on the other hand is not particularly interested in locating the *point* at which body and soul interact. He wishes merely to describe the fact that they do interact and coinhere.

Will Barth attempt to resolve the theoretical problem of the relation between soul and body? To a large degree, finding the right answer depends on asking the right question in the first place; Barth therefore refuses to frame the question of the body-soul relation in the traditional categories:

---

55. *Human Mystery,* p. 226.
56. See *CD,* III/2, §46.2, "The Spirit as Basis of Soul and Body," pp. 344-66.
57. *CD,* III/2, p. 429.

We cannot participate in the solving of the riddle which seems to burden and engage the participants in this discussion. In face of the whole discussion we can only declare our fundamental objection that the soul and the body of the man of whom they speak are the soul and body of a ghost and not of real man. . . . We do not have the body here and the soul there, but man himself as soul of his body is subject and object, active and passive — man in the life-act of ruling and serving, as the rational being as which he stands before God and is real as he receives and has the Spirit and is thus grounded, constituted and maintained by God.[58]

Rather than attempt a theoretical rejoinder to the mind-body problem, Barth points to the presupposition that enables theological anthropology to avoid the problem at the start. It is by the Spirit that the soul and body are sustained in their interconnection; and it is the Spirit that orders soul and body such that the human being is a rational subject whose soul rules over the body. Since Barth sees the inevitable wholeness and rational unity of the human being as a necessary starting point, he wonders how it can be scientific to split off either the soul from the body or the body from the soul and expect to make any progress in understanding the real person.

When Barth proposes that the Spirit of God is the basis of the unity of the body and soul, it sounds nearly as if he is calling on a "God of the gaps" to solve the mind-body problem. However, he is not attempting to solve the problem of how the body and soul are united. It is simply a means of confessing that the unity of the human being as besouled body and embodied soul rests in the revealed mystery of God's being. Here Christian anthropology must walk on the stepping stones of faith, and psychological anthropology would be stepping beyond its boundaries. Nevertheless, this God who makes body and soul come together in the forming of a human being is not some unknown God, such as we have seen in Schleiermacher. He is rather a God who has given himself to be known as an object of real knowledge.

The Whole Person in Order and Disorder

In this section I suggest some more parallels between Barth's anthropology and Fairbairn's object relations. These parallels are mostly discovered in the relational dynamic between body and soul, or instincts and ego. They do not constitute a one-for-one correspondence between theology and psychology,

58. Ibid.

but are analogies that are mostly heuristic in nature. I hope they may suggest some possibilities for the articulation of future dynamic anthropologies in both psychology and theology, and will open the way for further dialogue between these respective disciplines.

If we accept the premise of Barth's dynamic and unitary anthropology, we must concede that the body and soul cannot be separated, for their separation means death: death not merely of the body but of the whole person. The body and soul together comprise a unitary self. But neither is the confusion of body and soul acceptable, according to Barth. The soul is not the body, and the body is not the soul. For Barth, the soul and body are connected in order: soul first, then body. The human being is a duality of soul and body such that the "elements of his being are not identical, and that neither of them can be reduced to the other. . . . Soul is not organic body; for life is not corporeal body, time is not space, and existence is not nature. Similarly, body cannot be soul."[59] Soul and body are differentiated and ordered. Barth observes that their order is reminiscent of the relation between Creator and creature in which "there is a higher and a lower, a quickening and a quickened, a factor that controls space and one that is limited by it, an element which is invisible and one which is visible."[60] While the unity of soul and body is undeniable, there is not a perfect symmetry between them: "That he is wholly and simultaneously both soul and body does not exclude the fact that he is always both in different ways; first soul and then body."[61] That Barth insists on the soul as the "first" indicates that the soul is the integrating agency for the person. The soul transcends the body even as it is inseparable from it. The soul is the seat of freedom; it is the center of the subject, and thus capable of exerting control over the body, which is the periphery.[62]

This position put forth by Barth is developed in an analogous way by object relations. Fairbairn rejects instinctual theories of the person because they separate energy and structure. Fairbairn's usage of the terms "energy" and "structure" is almost the opposite of what one might expect. Energy might seem to be the counterpoint to the "soul" in theology, with structure being the outer form, or body. In Fairbairn's usage, however, "energy" is more closely related to the body, because it is connected to bodily instincts: instinctual drives are the source of psychical energy, according to Freud. And "structure" is analogous to the soul, because the ego is the "structure" that exercises

59. *CD*, III/2, p. 367.
60. *CD*, III/2, p. 368.
61. *CD*, III/2, p. 372.
62. *CD*, III/2, p. 397.

rational restraint over the instincts.[63] Fairbairn insists on the importance of a "libidinal ego" and other integrated psychical components. He therefore sees the integral relation between ego and impulse. It is apparent that each influences the other, but they do not influence each other similarly. Apart from the impulses there would be no somatic energy; apart from the ego there would be no subject to order the impulses. In Fairbairn's object relations there is also order. The instincts are integrated with the ego, forming a dynamic whole. Instincts are therefore object-seeking; they are a means of expressing an object relation. Libido is an "object-seeking principle."[64] In normal human development, the instincts ultimately seek expression through object relationships with other human beings. The human being is therefore rational in the sense of being endowed with an inherent need to engage in communication with the other; this fact is especially observable during the unconscious and preverbal earliest stages of life. In Fairbairn's theory there is order in the natural condition of the human being. The ego is normally object-directed; it is not wedged between the superego and libido. Humans are not normally characterized by some feeble "ego" struggling to mediate between social expectations and powerful impulses. The original condition of the ego is that it seeks objects to which it can meaningfully attach. In other words, human beings are innately motivated to seek human relationships. Aggression surfaces only when there is a failure to attach successfully to external objects — where relationships have become unsatisfactory.[65]

But perhaps Barth and Fairbairn have painted too optimistic a picture of human nature. In what sense do we see the instincts as inherently "object seeking"? There are many circumstances in which one could say that raw instinct seems to hold sway over the desire for interpersonal relations. This is certainly the case when one human being murders another; it is apparently the case where sex has become depersonalized, or "demonised," as Barth labels it. There are numerous circumstances in which the soul does not govern the body,[66] in

63. By unitary I mean that, even if they are distinguishable, there is no separation between the body and the soul; Barth points out that in the Bible the person is always both a *res* and an *idea* or *nomen*: "The Bible does not think in terms of this opposition. The real man who would have to be a *res* on this view is not a *res* but the human person self-animating and self-animated in the act of existing under the determination of the Spirit." The arguments for anthropological dualism, Barth concludes, are mostly Greek in origin. See *CD*, III/2, pp. 433ff. But as we have seen above in chapters two and three, similar dualisms were perpetuated in Descartes, Kant, and modern theology and philosophy, almost up to the present.

64. See chapter five above.

65. See chapter five above; also Hamilton, "Critical Review," p. 1554.

66. I refer here to Barth's insistence that the human being is "the unity of a ruling soul and serving body" (*CD*, III/2, p. 427).

which human actions are irrational and damaging to an extreme, inflicting pain and useless suffering on self and others. In what sense then can we insist along with Barth that the soul should, and must, govern the body? In what sense can we allow, along with object relations, that the instincts are always directed toward the personal object? The more unpleasant aspects of human behavior confront us with a difficulty: the facts often reveal the extent to which the aggressive instincts seem to overrule any rational consideration for the personhood of the other. In many cases the human exercise of raw libidinal or aggressive instinct seems to be the rule rather than the exception to human behavior.

If we go back to the theories of civilization put forward by both Kant and Freud, we must admit they were not naive concerning human nature. They rightly observed that many seek for power, glory, and accumulation of possessions with little consideration for the needs of others — let alone a desire to allow personal relationships to enter their self-seeking ventures. Humans are, at times, remarkably obsessed with gratifying themselves. How can we explain such egotism?

Those who hold the former dualistic categories have a straightforward explanation for the occurrence of impersonal behavior among humans. In a dualistic framework we simply explain erratic, lustful, and irrational actions as actions that stem from the flesh rather than the soul (or spirit).[67] The dualistic psychologist would say that antisocial behavior arises from aggressive instincts that have somehow gained the upper hand over the libidinal instincts. It stems from a human willingness to choose death over life, aggression rather than libidinal attraction, or, to put the same choice in more theological language, to live by the lower rather than the higher faculties. This

---

67. At times Paul sets the flesh against the Spirit in what seems to be an almost Hellenic dualism. See Gal. 5:13-25; Rom. 8:4-14. But these passages do not depict a thoroughgoing anthropological dualism. For in the New Testament, *sarx* is never set against *pneuma* in such a manner that the Spirit is the higher nature and the flesh the lower nature of an individual. Rather, the flesh expresses an orientation away from God while the Spirit indicates one's orientation toward God. Barth is not the only theologian to reject the Kantian dualism between theoretical and practical; e.g., Pannenberg affirms: "A dualism between an ethical and religious sphere, on the one hand, and a 'natural and biological sphere,' on the other, cannot appeal to Pauline thinking; it likewise finds little support elsewhere in the New Testament writings" (*Anthropology*, p. 129). Cf. *CD*, IV/3 (2), pp. 670-71: "Surely the victory of the Spirit over the flesh as described by Paul cannot be equated with the supposed or actual prevailing of human morality over human immorality." These are somewhat different types of dualisms: Kant's was primarily a dualism between the theoretical and ethical spheres of reason, while the main forms of anthropological dualism have been those which pitted the higher rational sphere against the lower biological sphere. Nevertheless, in chapter two we have seen that Kant tended to perpetuate the older dualisms, albeit in an altogether different way.

is where instinctual anthropologies fall into a track that runs parallel to classical and modern dualism.

But a dynamic anthropology must seek a different explanation for human bestiality. A dynamic view does not allow us to say that human dereliction arises from the victory of the instincts over the capacity for self-restraint. If there is an aggressive impulse vying with an attracting impulse, the dynamic anthropology must account for both in terms of a higher principle that explains both attraction and aggression. The individual who lapses into irrational and gratuitous violence may very well have chosen to succumb to his or her aggressive impulses. Yet a dynamic anthropology insists that there should be an ordered integration between them. Hence the disorder must be explained by an external referent: by a lapse in a relation to an external object, by a disruption in the relations that normally constitute its order.

Barth has argued that there is a basic human form from which we can fall. The form of our humanity is always related to God. Hence to fall away from God is to fall away from our real humanity; this is what Barth means when he describes evil as "non-being." It is an attempt to describe that which seems impossible but which nevertheless occurs. It describes (without explaining fully) how our essential goodness has been ontologically breached. This is analogous to what object relations attempts to explain when it shows how the drive to form relations to real objects can be thwarted and thus result in internalized bad objects. In each of these respective fields any breach in the interpersonal relations that normally sustain the individual threatens the integrity of the order between the body and mind. When the normal sphere of relations is threatened it precipitates a defensive reaction that leads on the psychological level to aggression, antisocial behavior, or on the theological level to what Barth describes as "non-being," the "ontological impossibility," and the like. Both are precipitated by brokenness of vital relations between the individual and the other.

But how can aggression surface if it is not at least a latent potential deeply embedded within human nature itself? Could it not be that the bad object relations merely precipitate the latent tendency toward aggression? In other words, how can human beings act in accordance with something that is not in their nature to do? According to object relations theory, we are naturally attracted to objects; why do we find ourselves so often "object-repulsed"? Why would aggression sometimes be the result of a bad object relation? Where does aggression come from if it is not a latent human possibility to begin with? A similar question can be asked of Barth: How can sin become a possibility when it is impossible? How can it come to be unless it is fully a possibility?

Macmurray has been helpful at this point. We have seen how he described aggression or anger as the negative pole of love. That is, anger is the defensive response employed when a relation is thwarted and the self is in need of protection until the positive pole of engaging in relation becomes possible once again. The dissolution of the relation is therefore something that the individual struggles to overcome — even to the extent that an individual might allow anger to lead to aggression in order to defend against the loss of the relationship. Relation to an other, therefore, is the primary thing, and aggression serves to defend against the loss of a relation. When there is a loss of relation or a damaging relation, the person activates certain defensive reactions in order to defend against the threat to the self that those broken relations pose. The defensive reactions such as aggression indicate a need to restore right relations. However, aggression serves to defend the self only against some of the possible consequences of the loss of relation. Aggression itself cannot restore the lost relation. This is where forgiveness is an essential part of the field of personal relations, where grace is the sine qua non of all interpersonal relationships. As we have seen, Barth criticized Kant's practical anthropology for not giving adequate attention to the need for grace or forgiveness. Here again the logic of trinitarian anthropology and object relations psychology shows the enormous need for forgiveness for the healing of broken interpersonal relations. We can begin to understand, then, why Paul sees the forgiveness that comes from God as the indispensable condition of any Christian community.[68]

Macmurray has denied that instincts play a significant role in human behavior. But I do not believe we need to eliminate the aggressive drive or instincts simply because we have adopted an object relations approach. The presence of instincts need not threaten the reality of interpersonal relations. The important thing to consider here is whether the human being is torn between two competing drives: one loving, the other aggressive; or whether there is some design and order that mandates a relation to the loved object. In the dynamic and unitary anthropology that emerges from Barth, there is little doubt that he sees the latter as the case: our personal character is not decided by choosing to side with either the higher or lower faculty of human nature, but rather by our decision to respond or not respond to God. We are rational, therefore, only when we respond to the divine categorical imperative. It is not, however, an imperative that we impose on ourselves, as Kant proposed, but an imperative that God imposes on us. It is an imperative that establishes right relation to the One who commands us.[69] To act rationally is to act in re-

---

68. See esp. Eph. 2:11-22; 4:3; Col. 3:12.
69. *CD*, III/2, p. 423.

sponse to God: "to be open to the will and action of God and to give God a place within."[70] When we act irrationally, we fall into nonbeing, out of relation to God, and into an inability to rightly order our soul and body. Rationality for Barth is therefore "object-related." We can act only rationally as we are related to God; and relation to God enables us to act as *soul* of our body. Outside of relation to God the soul and body fall into chaotic disorder.

The important thing to note here is that Barth's emphasis on the necessity for relation to God is much the same as Fairbairn's interpretation of the child's relation to an ideal parent. In both cases a fundamental "object relation" provides the basis for normal human personhood.

When it comes to the breakdown of positive relationships, the analogy between Barth and object relations begins to weaken. In some ways Barth's concept of "non-being," and so on, simply cannot be compared to the human frustration that results from a broken interpersonal relation. The differences become especially clear if we compare Barth and Macmurray. For Macmurray, the negative pole of human behavior occurs when one is cut off from relation to an other and thrown back upon oneself. The response is likely to be a form of aggression or anger; and this is necessary, according to Macmurray, in the natural rhythm of "withdrawal and return." The negative always constitutes its positive by standing in opposition to it. Aggression and anger are thus necessary for human development. In Barth, however, there can be no ontological status whatsoever to nonbeing. Evil cannot have any positive existence; evil is explicable only as an inexplicable surd. It is nothingness: the privation of the good *(privatio boni),* and as such it cannot be constitutive of positive relations. The power of nonbeing is wholly negative.[71] Nonbeing assumes a far more sinister status than human anger or aggression.

So while there is a similarity here in the way in which Barth and the anthropology of object relations both eschew the dualist framework that pits soul over against the body, mind against matter, and ego against the instincts, there are also some differences that must be taken into account. Some of the differences can be seen in the questions that each brings to their respective level of inquiry. Barth is dealing primarily with questions presented by Christian anthropology and long-standing philosophical debates about soul and body. Fairbairn is asking about the relation of the instincts to the object relations in the development of human psychology. When psychologists deal

70. *CD*, III/2, p. 402.
71. See *CD*, III/3, §50, "God and Nothingness," esp. pp. 349ff. Cf. *CD*, IV/3, pp. 174ff. By labeling evil "non-being" Barth does not in any way wish to ignore its real destructive power and opposition to God.

with the problems of why human beings withdraw from one another, they do not normally say that a human lapses into "nonbeing" in the absence of any meaningful relationships. They make no statements about reality or truth as such, but simply attempt to describe the patterns of behavior that usually occur. A psychologist can observe that when thwarted, humans tend to get angry, sometimes acting aggressively, other times psychologically internalizing the anger and manifesting depression, schizoid behavior, and so on. On the other hand, when Barth describes the "nothingness" that opposes God and is opposed by God, he is making a claim to truth based on revelation. In Barth's theology the opposition to God that is described as "nothingness" is not in any way constitutive of God's being. Neither does "nonbeing" contribute in any positive way to the being of the human being.

In spite of these differences, however, it is fascinating to notice the immense importance that both Barth and Fairbairn attach to primary object relations in defining personhood. The order between soul and body, or ego and instincts, depends largely on the relations that form the basis for their unity. Conversely, it is not surprising that the ordered unity of the self can be greatly damaged from broken relations, especially to God or parents.

The Dynamic Self and the Development of Consciousness

For Barth, consciousness begins not with the abstract Cartesian "I think," but with the soul's consciousness of itself, which immediately entails the psychosomatic awareness of all that is other. Self-consciousness is psychosomatic because, while it is primarily a function of the soul, it cannot be independent of the body. Consciousness is dynamic in origin because it is both particular and active. It entails the actions of a particular person. The awareness of one's self necessarily encompasses both the body and the soul:

> I come to myself, discover myself and become assured of myself. It belongs to my capacity for action that I continuously do this, that I am continuously engaged in the act of becoming self-conscious and therefore in this return movement. It all takes place in me and therefore in my soul. Yet it cannot be denied that this act in which my soul is at once subject and object is also wholly a corporeal act. . . . I am not this material body of mine. . . . But I do not exist without also being this material body. I do not live otherwise than as I live in my body.[72]

72. *CD*, III/2, p. 375.

Barth warns against neglecting the bodily realities in the process of coming to self-consciousness. It is only when the soul is both subject and object that it can recognize other objects. The recognition of other objects is necessary in order to know one's self, even the self as knowing subject. Self-consciousness therefore develops within a social matrix.

Once again I propose that Barth and object relations are similar in their views on the development of consciousness. For example, what does Fairbairn mean when he describes an "internalized object"? An internalized object is a psychical representation of something that was originally outside the infant's body. The external object, in the form of the mother, the mother's breast, and so on, presents itself to the infant. At the earliest stages of life it is not perceived as an object, for its availability lends itself to the illusion that it is part of the infant itself. The infant's sense of self at this early stage is not at all developed; it is not differentiated from real external objects.[73] External, physical objects, namely the mother and the mother's breast, very soon become internalized and represented within the endopsychic structure.[74] Indeed, the internalization of the mother's breast is probably a psychological consequence of the physical incorporating of the mother's milk: a very literal physical internalizing. But, subjectively, much more than the milk is being taken in. The effect of the disappearance of the milk will develop psychical representations that may well affect the child for the rest of his or her life. Literal physical incorporation of milk at the earliest stages of life results in a "taking" attitude that is psychological and characterizes the earliest stages of life.[75] The important thing to notice is how object relations assumes the possibility of reciprocal action between the body and the mind: the infant's relations to external physical objects, mostly in the person of the mother and the mother's breasts, exert a direct influence on internalized psychical structures.

According to Fairbairn, if the feeding of the infant is accompanied by a number of unsatisfactory conditions, both physical and emotional, it is likely to introduce persecutory objects into the endopsychic structure of the child. If modern psychology teaches us anything about the emotional development of a child, it is that physical interactions with significant persons from the

73. See *Psychoanalytic Studies*, p. 145. esp. footnote.

74. "The first social relationship established by the individual is that between himself and his mother; and the focus of this relationship is the suckling situation, in which his mother's breast provides the focal point of his libidinal object, and his mouth the focal point of his own libidinal attitude. Accordingly, the nature of the relationship so established exercises a profound influence upon the subsequent relationships of the individual, and upon his subsequent social attitude in general" (*Psychoanalytic Studies*, pp. 10-11).

75. Ibid., p. 146.

earliest preverbal stages of life are readily transformed into internal psychical representations that shape one's psychology for every subsequent stage of life. There is, therefore, a dynamic interaction between the physical and the psychological in the development of consciousness. Object relations makes no specific mention of the "soul"; there is the ego, however, which may very well be regarded as the soul's sequel.[76] At any rate, as with Barth, also in object relations psychology the bodies of both the self and the other are explicitly assumed to play an important role in the shaping of a person's psychology and the development of consciousness.

The interplay between the somatic and psychical in object relations is analogous to Barth when he insists that the soul's awareness of itself must necessarily incorporate the body: "It would be very hazardous even to affirm that from this return movement I do not need my corporeal senses. Without having some command and making some use of them, I cannot be aware of objects different from myself. And without being aware of objects different from myself, I cannot distinguish myself from others as the object identical with myself, and cannot therefore recognise myself as a subject."[77] The point that can be drawn from both Barth and object relations is this: Consciousness surfaces with the capacity to differentiate the self from the other while both exist in the temporal and spatial setting of the physical world. The possibility of self-consciousness existing quite apart from any contact with spatio-temporal realities had been assumed from earliest Hellenic philosophers and reinforced by Descartes and others in modern thought. From the perspective of the more dynamic view, the assertion that self-consciousness reveals a self-subsistent thinker is no longer plausible. It has been challenged by a reexamination of biblical anthropology, and further challenged by the findings of modern psychology from Freud onward.[78]

Among those psychologists who have done extensive study on the social components of human knowing is G. H. Mead. Mead's major work, *Mind, Self and Society*, deftly avoids the pitfalls of parallelism on the one side and radical behaviorism (which denies the reality of human consciousness altogether) on the other, in proposing the social genesis of the self. Disputing the parallelism of Wundt, Mead proposes:

---

76. For Fairbairn, "An ego is present from birth" ("Synopsis of an Object-Relations Theory of the Personality," *International Journal of Psycho-Analysis* 44 [1958] 224).

77. *CD*, III/2, p. 375.

78. The insights of existential philosophy should also be mentioned as a source of thought that has served to challenge the dualistic epistemology; the existential school has undoubtedly exerted an influence on certain strains of both theology and psychology.

The difficulty is that Wundt presupposes selves as antecedent to the social process in order to explain communication within that process, whereas, on the contrary, selves must be accounted for in terms of the social process, and in terms of communication; and individuals must be brought into essential relation within that process before communication, or that contact between the minds of different individuals, becomes possible. The body is not a self, as such; it becomes a self only when it has developed a mind within the context of social experience.[79]

As we have seen, Macmurray also draws attention to the social context of cognitive development: "The distinction of Self and other is the awareness of both; and the *existence* of both is the fact that their opposition is a practical, and not a theoretical opposition."[80] The dynamic relation between inner world and outer world is a common factor for the development of consciousness in both Barth and object relations, just as the dynamic relation between "Self" and "Other" is a necessary condition for the development of human beinghood according to Macmurray. There is here a practical unity of object and subject.[81] With both Barth and object relations the theoretical distinction between self and other is not important, nor is the theoretical identity of the self. The origin of consciousness is, rather, described practically: not in the Kantian sense of the individual's relation to the legal demands of the categorical imperative, but in terms of a personal relation to an other.

When it comes to the derivation and description of consciousness, neither Barth nor object relations allows us to retreat to the purely organic nor the purely psychical explanations offered by the dualistic philosophers. The insight common to both is that the dynamic interaction between the "soul and body" (to use the terms of theological anthropology) gives rise to consciousness. In this context we can better understand Macmurray's rejection of the Cartesian "cogito." This is because to know existence we must participate in existence in the form of action. And to act is to meet resistance in the form

---

79. (Chicago: University of Chicago Press, 1934) pp. 49-50. See also pp. 135-226, esp. p. 140. Cf. Pannenberg, *Anthropology,* pp. 185-90. One does not have to agree with Mead's emphasis on the importance of "gestures" as a carryover from biological evolution in order to appreciate his elucidation of the social dimension of consciousness.

80. *Self as Agent,* p. 109.

81. The neo-Kantians, in their attempt to prescribe the proper field of psychology, perceived the need for such a unity; e.g., Paul Natorp argues that objectification and subjectification are flip sides of the same epistemological coin: "Only from the standpoint of the objective is there a subjective, but, furthermore, objectivity signifies a proper character of being *(Seincharakter)* only in opposition to the former" (*Philosophie: Ihr Problem und Ihre Probleme* [Göttingen: Vandenhoeck & Ruprecht, 1911] p. 151).

of the other. The isolated cogito is thus a reductio ad absurdum, because in order to think we must think truly or falsely, and an isolated mind cannot verify the truth or falsity of its thoughts by checking them against the thoughts of others. A pure thinking substance therefore vanishes as if it were an illusion.

Macmurray has pointed out the philosophical weakness of Descartes's position,[82] and Barth points out the unbiblical nature of such a position. The point to be emphasized here is the epistemological similarity between the understanding of consciousness in Barth and that which is implicitly put forth by object relations. Both see consciousness arising in the dynamic interplay between mind and body within a social context. Both formulate the development of human consciousness in dynamic and interpersonal terms, rather than either idealist or positivist modes of thought. Let us look at the similarities more closely.

Macmurray proposed that one of the epistemic implications of object relations could be distilled into the affirmation that "all cognition stems from recognition."[83] It is recognition of the mother, or maternal object, that creates the possibility for each stage of cognitive development thereafter. In Barth's thought, the seat of cognition is the knowledge of God. We need to follow Barth's argument carefully at this point, because the parallels to object relations theory are intriguing. Both indicate the extent to which all knowledge is personal — and therefore interpersonal — at its foundation. Human consciousness develops not within a closed circle of individual experience as Descartes, Kant, and most Western theologians had assumed, but from a shared experience.[84] Let us see how Barth explains this.

How is it possible for the human being to perceive? asks Barth. Humans are percipient as they are able to perceive God and others, distinguishing them from themselves. To perceive thus means to be able to perceive *another:*

> To perceive *(vernehmen)* means to receive another as such into one's self-consciousness *(Selbstbewusstsein)*. To be percipient thus means to be capable of receiving another as such into one's self-consciousness. A being

---

82. While modern philosophy has largely failed to solve the mind-body problem, it is nearly in agreement regarding the inability of the older Greek and Cartesian dualisms to solve it. See, e.g., Gilbert Ryle, *The Concept of Mind* (London: Hutchinson, 1949) esp. chap. 1, "Descartes' Myth."

83. A remarkably similar line of reasoning is presented by L. W. Grensted's Bampton Lectures, *Psychology and God* (London: Longmans, Green, 1931), esp. pp. 81ff. The degree to which Grensted may have influenced Macmurray is difficult to tell.

84. See ibid., p. 81, n. 1.

capable only of a purely self-contained self-consciousness would not be a percipient being. Man is not such a self-contained being. He is capable of self-consciousness, but he is also capable of receiving another as such into this self-consciousness of his. Man can not only posit himself. In so doing he can also posit another, and therefore himself in relation to this other and this other in relation to himself.[85]

Perception is thus a unity of "awareness and thought" *(Wahrnehmung und Denken)* in the context of a relation.

Here Barth once again harks back to the epistemological problems that Kant introduced, in which Kant decided that scientific knowledge was a combination of concepts and percepts. Barth, however, attempts to reinterpret the problem in a more dynamic context. He does not wish merely to analyze pure human reason into its component parts, but also to integrate it into the practical dimension. Like Macmurray, Barth sees the need to integrate the practical and theoretical so as not to end up with a "pure act of thought" that cannot "surmount the limits of self-consciousness."[86] Knowledge, according to Barth, is constituted neither by a pure act of thought nor by a pure act of awareness (for until awareness interacts with one's own thoughts it remains external and is not admitted into one's self-consciousness). Rather, Barth insists, in a similar fashion to Kant: "the perception proper to man is itself an undivided act, in which awareness makes thinking possible and thinking awareness."[87] But similar to Macmurray, and unlike Kant, Barth does not isolate scientific thinking from practical or ethical thinking: both types of thought are integrated into a unitary epistemology by the encounter between *persons.*

At first glance, Barth seems to argue that the body contains perception, and the soul thought. Thought is primarily a function of the soul, while awareness is ordered primarily through the body. According to Barth: "Man thinks, therefore, in so far as he is the *soul* of his body."[88] But since the soul is the soul of the body, and the body is besouled, it is more complicated than that. Awareness is not only bodily and thought is not only of the soul. The body also thinks:

> Thinking is not only with the soul. How could his soul think, if it were not the soul of his brain, his nerves and his whole organism? Even when he thinks, man lives the life of his body. Even his thought is necessarily

85. *CD*, III/2, p. 399.
86. *CD*, III/2, p. 400.
87. Ibid.
88. *CD*, III/2, p. 402.

disturbed by the disturbance of the life of his body; and it necessarily ceases if he is deprived of his body. Even his thinking is executed as it is accompanied and assisted on one way or another by the action of his whole body.[89]

This is where Barth differs from Descartes and most traditional Christian anthropologies. Descartes was right to see the soul as the seat of consciousness; but he was wrong to believe that the soul could not only be distinguished but also detached from the body.[90]

From what source did Barth derive his ideas about the oneness of soul and body? Barth's thoughts stem mostly from his capacity to reflect on the anthropological problems — especially presented by Kant and the German idealists — in light of the biblical anthropology. Barth points out that in both the Old and New Testaments there are no instances of rationality abstractively interpreted. The rationality of each person is the capacity of a rational response to God; thought, will, and act are described in terms of openness to God. Knowledge, or rationality, in the Bible, is therefore object-related; it entails relation to God as the object of human knowledge. Barth affirms that to know the man Jesus is to know not only God, but also ourselves. The point is that in all human cognition there is a constant object of knowledge; to know one's self is to know, and be known by, an other. There is no such thing as knowledge that is pure self-knowledge; there is no consciousness in a vacuum.[91]

---

89. *CD*, III/2, p. 401.

90. See *Meditations, and Selections from the Principles of Philosophy;* repr. in W. T. Blackstone, ed., *Meaning and Existence* (New York: Holt, Rinehart, 1971) p. 517: "I exist, and because, in the meantime, I do not observe that aught necessarily belongs to my nature or essence beyond my being a thinking thing, I rightly conclude that my essence consists only in my being a thinking thing [or a substance whose whole essence or nature is merely thinking]. And although I may, or rather, as I will shortly say, although I certainly do possess a body with which I am very closely conjoined; nevertheless, because, on the one hand, I have a clear and distinct idea of myself, in as far as I am only a thinking and unextended thing, and as, on the other hand, I possess a distinct idea of body, in as far as it is only an extended and unthinking thing, it is certain that I [that is my mind, by which I am what I am] am entirely and truly distinct from my body, and may exist without it." Cf. also: "And even if we supposed that God had conjoined some corporeal substance to such a conscious substance so closely that they could not be more closely joined, and had thus compounded a unity out of the two, yet even so they remain really distinct. For however closely he had united them, he could not deprive himself of his original power to separate them, or to keep one in being without the other; and things that can be separated, or kept in being separately, by God are really distinct" (*Principles of Philosophy,* section LX).

91. *CD,* III/2, p. 54.

Barth can describe the noetic effects of sin as the self "depriving itself of its first and last object and being abstractly directed to other objects. Such a perception can only be deranged and perverted. Neither in the Old Testament nor the New does the Bible recognise such human perception which is estranged from its first and last object and therefore improper and abnormal, but proper and normal in respect of other objects."[92] In biblical anthropology, consciousness depends on God as the primary object of knowledge: the one who is the beginning and end of all knowledge.[93] Let us be clear what Barth is saying. He is not saying that God is the only object of human knowledge. Other objects are obviously known, and for many people their reality seems much more certain than the knowledge of God himself. The capacity to know seems quite possible apart from God. Nevertheless, Barth follows biblical anthropology closely at this point, and insists that God is the overarching purpose behind all the events of nature and history. For those who are open to God in faith, all the knowledge of other objects mediates the knowledge of God himself. This is analogous to the affirmation of Macmurray, in view of object relations, that all cognition stems from recognition. Rarely would an adult become aware of the fact that earliest object relations had facilitated later cognitive processes. However, this does not mitigate the fact that most adults could not perform their abstractive reasoning processes effectively had not their mothers, or some parent or parent figure, bonded to them by talking, cooing, holding, and generally being available for them in order that they might become psychologically attached. Personal relations are the source of cognition. This is analogous to what Barth means when he describes God as the seat of human rationality. This does not mean that God is always the object of our conscious processes; but rather that he is perceived by the eyes of faith to be the original source of all cognition — and the ultimate goal of all our knowledge. The knowledge of God is often mediated to the faithful through common things.[94] In both cases the bedrock of

92. *CD*, III/2, p. 403.

93. *CD*, III/2, p. 403. Cf. Prov. 1:7. "The fear of the Lord is the beginning of knowledge *(da'at)*."

94. In *CD*, III/2, p. 402, Barth states: "Man may sense and think many things, but fundamentally the perceiving man is the God-perceiving man. It is true, of course, that the other which he perceives is not identical with God, and that he continuously perceives other things as well as God. But when the Bible speaks of perceiving man, there is nothing else which it is important or necessary for man to perceive. Man perceives and receives into self-consciousness particular things — the action and inaction of his fellow-men, the relations and events of nature and history, the outward and the inward sides of the created world around him. But these are important and necessary for man only because God does not usually meet him immediately but mediately in His works, deeds and ordinances, and because the history of God's traffic with him takes place in the sphere of the created world and of the world of objects distinct from God."

human knowledge is not found in the merely conscious mind, but grounded in more primary relation to an other, which may be found either by exploring unconscious processes or assuming a stance of faith.

On the basis of object relations, Macmurray has drawn attention to the fact that the first knowledge we have in life is knowledge of the personal other. And the primary sense for coming to the knowledge of the other in the earliest stages of life is the tactile.[95] From this, Macmurray concludes:

> The primary perception of the other must arise from the discrimination between being tactually cared for and the absence of this; and this discrimination cannot serve to distinguish different others. Since the infant's motivation contains an implicit reference to the other, the recognition of the other as "What responds to my cry" must become explicit so soon as any power of discrimination is acquired. And since this is the first cognition, we can understand why "all cognition is recognition."[96]

It is in the ongoing process of the tactile, and to a lesser degree, audiovisual, recognition of the other that we discover "the dawn of knowledge." The findings of some more recent object relations theorists provide interesting confirmation of Macmurray's emphasis on the tactile in the cognitive development of children.[97] The importance of the tactile sense in early development is further evidence for the interplay of the somatic and the psychic in the development of consciousness. Of course the visual sense also depends on the somatic apparatus of the eye, and so on; but nothing characterizes the somatic boundary quite as vividly as the tactile sense. For example, Donald Winnicott has recently emphasized the tactile component in the psychosomatic development of the child:

> Associated with this attainment [becoming an individual person as distinct from the mother] is the infant's psychosomatic existence, which begins to take on a personal pattern; I have referred to this as the psyche indwelling in the soma. The basis for this indwelling is a linkage of motor and sensory and functional experiences with the infant's new state of being a person. As a further development there comes into existence what might be called a limiting membrane, which to some extent (in health) is

---

95. One of Macmurray's most original insights was his critique of Western philosophy's overemphasis on the visual and neglect of the tactile in its reflections on the process of cognition. See *Self as Agent,* pp. 107-13.

96. *Persons in Relation,* pp. 75-76.

97. E.g., D. W. Winnicott, "The Theory of Parent-Infant Relationship," in Buckley, ed., *Essential Papers,* pp. 241, 245.

equated with the surface of the skin, and has a position between the infant's "me" and his "not-me." So the infant comes to have an inside and an outside, and a body-scheme. In this way meaning comes to the function of intake and output; moreover, it gradually becomes meaningful to postulate a personal or inner psychic reality for the infant.[98]

This quotation demonstrates how Winnicott and other object relations theorists describe the infant's development in terms of the dynamic psychosomatic interaction with the mother. According to Winnicott, the infant advances from the earliest stage of "Absolute Dependence," to "Relative Dependence," to the third stage of "Toward Independence," wherein intellectual functioning begins. Time and again he emphasizes the continuous interaction between a child's psychic reality and various organs of the body. The interplay of the psychic and somatic is one of the salient features of modern object relations psychology; and the holistic approach of modern psychology is not accidental. Where the older philosophical psychology approached the psyche by abstractive reflection alone, modern scientific psychology approaches the psyche by allowing its reflections to be shaped by the observable psychosomatic realities of whole persons. The development of this unitary anthropology has presented modern psychology with the theoretical framework to make some major steps forward. Apart from the assumption that the psychical and bodily phenomena constantly interact, modern psychology would have little means for pushing beyond a Cartesian type of reflection on the nature of the soul and engaging in empirical studies of human behavior. In this context, it is easy to see why neither dualism (which includes parallelism and interactionism) nor materialism could provide the framework for understanding the human being in all his or her complexity. As long as a dualism of the Cartesian type prevailed there was little motivation for modern psychology to develop because the processes of the mind were believed to be inaccessible to empirical research. But on the other hand, how could materialism provide a sufficient paradigm for modern psychology? How could the materialist develop a psychological theory that is truly *psycho*logical when the materialist disbelieves in the soul's existence?[99] The only consistent option for

---

98. Ibid., p. 241. Winnicott refers to the importance of the tactile, and other three-dimensional stimuli, such as "holding" (p. 245).

99. See Brand Blanshard and B. F. Skinner, "The Problem of Consciousness — A Debate," in *Philosophy and Phenomenological Research* 27 (1966-67). Blanshard states: "If there are in fact conscious events distinct from bodily events, a method that disregards them and confines itself to the body cannot be adequate to the study of mind. If behaviorism is to be adequate as a method, it must also be sound as a philosophy; it will give us an adequate science of mind only

the materialistic psychologist would be a reductionist type of human science that would study human behavior as if it were a very specialized branch of classical physics.

Likewise, Barth's interpretation of biblical anthropology attempts to do justice to both the psychical and the physical realities of human existence. He resists a monist spiritualism just as much as a monist materialism.[100] Barth is guided rather by the "concrete monism" *(konkrete Monismus)* that he believes is found in the biblical concept of the soul. Even with the many differences taken into consideration, it would be difficult to overlook the extent to which the framework of investigation for object relations is parallel to that of Barth. Both believe that the identity of an individual arises only as a psychosomatic event that is engendered by an ongoing history or relationship with an other. For object relations the foundation for mental health, or "continuity of being," is laid down by the relationship to the mother or parents. For Barth the continuity of our being is founded in God.[101] Barth proposes: "Only thought and awareness of God are comprehensive, proper, normal and therefore sound thinking and awareness. This is the first and most important lesson to be learned from biblical anthropology."[102] In Barth's thought, the human ability to be percipient is endowed by God. In the case of object relations, the percipient ability is endowed by the mother: in both cases the capacity for perception and cognition is teased out by a primary relation to an other.

Object relations' psychosomatic explanation for the genesis of consciousness reveals a parallel insight to Barth's insistence on action as the unification of knowing and being. Apart from action, we have neither knowing nor being. But action is always relative and dynamic; it takes place in relation to an other.[103] As we act in relation to an other our consciousness is shaped by the psychosomatic interactions between ourself and the psychosomatic other. As we interact with the other, both as psychosomatic whole persons,

---

if mental behavior *is* bodily behavior. And this bold conclusion is one that both Watson and Professor Skinner have had the courage to draw."

100. *CD*, III/2, p. 393.

101. Perhaps these similarities are what led Freud to speculate that God is nothing more than the projected idealizations of the human desire for the protection from the forces of nature by a larger-than-life Father. On the other hand, Barth explains this readily within his theological framework as just the reverse. God's triune reality, which is in itself interpersonal and dynamic, enters into human history. He embodies himself in the psychosomatic realities of human existence and calls us to conform our actions to a way of being that reflects his own.

102. *CD*, III/2, p. 403.

103. Barth says in *CD*, III/2, p. 406: "To act generally is to set oneself freely in motion in relation to another. A doer is always one who is capable of such free movement in relation to another." See below.

we differentiate ourselves from the other and our consciousness comes alive. Consciousness comes into being with our self-consciousness, and self-consciousness comes into being with other-consciousness. All of these are simultaneous and unified events that can only be separated out as if they were different moments of the same event.

The epistemological implications of such a unitary perspective on the origin of consciousness should not be overlooked. While Kant and the neo-Kantians had divided philosophy into three separate forms of knowing: logical-theoretical, practical, and aesthetic, Macmurray has attempted to unify them by tracing cognition to a single origin. According to Macmurray's schema, the practical[104] is the primary mode of knowing; both theoretical and aesthetic reason are delimitations of the original knowledge gained at infancy. There is therefore one primary type of consciousness that is interpersonal in origin and unites all types of consciousness. According to Macmurray, all consciousness stems from, and represents various permutations of, the primary I-Thou encounters of earliest childhood. In this sense, then, it is unitary in that it unites the theoretical structures for knowing and the object known; it unites the subject and object by allowing for one only as it allows a simultaneous recognition of the other.

This object-related development of consciousness was anticipated by neo-Kantian philosophers such as Hermann Cohen, who stated:

> All pure consciousness is consciousness of the object. The *Gegenstand* is the content which pure generation effects. The problem cast before consciousness is accordingly that which the object presents. The rational quest for the object is the rational quest of or the possibility of the object. Thus one again sees how consciousness and possibility belong together. Moreover one thereby sees that the possibility of consciousness signifies the possibility of the object.[105]

The problem with the pursuit of the object, as Cohen and other neo-Kantians allowed it, was that their idealist philosophy reached an impasse in their threefold Kantian division of knowledge; they therefore sought the unification of scientific, ethical, and aesthetic knowing in the unfolding of culture itself. For Cohen, three modes of consciousness exist: the logical, ethical, and aesthetic, and the integration of these modes of knowing could be found only

---

104. In the expanded sense that Macmurray gives it, building on Kant, but going well beyond him.

105. *Logik der reinen Erkenntnis,* in *Werke,* VI (Olms, 1981) p. 426. Cited in Fisher, *Revelatory Positivism?* Translation Fisher's.

in the surrounding culture.[106] For Cohen, the I is precipitated by the correlation with the Thou; but this is not a theoretical correlation, it is practical. In other words, the moral demand of the Thou calls the subject into being. This bears a certain similarity to the practical integration of cognition that can be found in the thought of both Macmurray and Barth. Yet the realist epistemology of Barth and Macmurray goes further because they will not allow the person to be split up into three categories of knowing. The idealists such as Cohen must allow for a theoretical self[107] that stands in some nebulous relation to the practical, while the realism of Barth and Macmurray allows the subject understood practically, the I in relation to the Thou, to be ontologically primary. In other words, in the dynamic anthropology advocated by Barth and Macmurray, the I in relation to the Thou shapes the intellectual, the ethical, and the aesthetic modes of existence.

The parallels between Barth and object relations with regard to the origin of consciousness shed light on Barth's "actualism." We have established above that the action of a personal agent is one of the primary characteristics of a dynamic anthropology. It is only as we act, Barth says, that we have knowledge of ourselves both as subject and object. How could it be otherwise? Since only a besouled body can act, then only the soul that experiences bodily action can know itself as the subject of bodily action.[108] And only the soul that acts in and with the body can experience the body as object. Since knowledge of one's own body as object is necessary for the development of self-consciousness, then action is required for the development of one's own sense of self — an action that takes place primarily in relation to an other.

Barth, as a theologian, once again employs his understanding of God as triune in order to explain his anthropology. Having rejected the possibility that human existence could be "absolute" or self-subsisting, Barth proposes that the primary "other" must be the Spirit, who "grounds, constitutes and maintains man as soul of his body."[109] Apart from the Spirit, there is nothing

---

106. See Fisher, *Revelatory Positivism?* p. 51.

107. For Cohen, "Only thinking itself can generate *(erzeugen)* what validly counts as being" (*Logik der reinen Erkenntnis*, p. 81; ET, *Religion of Reason*, tr. S. Kaplar [New York: F. Ungar, 1972]).

108. Barth presents a biblical argument against the Greek concept of the immortality of the soul — to my mind, a very convincing one. See *CD*, III/2, pp. 378ff. The soul is usually equated with the whole "life" of the human, and it is anything but immortal; for it can be killed (Num. 31:19), "devoured" (Ezek. 22:25); it can die (Judg. 16:30; Ezek. 13:19), etc. *Nephesh* is the life of the body as well as the soul. Similarly with much in the New Testament. Whether this view we are surveying necessarily entails a denial of the immortality of the soul, as Barth infers, is beyond the scope of this study. It does seem to be implied by the necessary coinherence of body and soul as whole person. This does not deny the resurrection, of course, but reinforces it as an act of God's grace.

109. *CD*, III/2, p. 393.

but a constant and puzzling duality of immortal soul on the one side and mortal body on the other. Barth is not optimistic that philosophy will ever solve the mind-body problem as long as it frames the question only in terms of "man for himself," that is, humans persons apart from the Spirit. Barth concludes:

> Our only relief will then be found in the see-saw movement between ideas and appearance, thinking and speculation and so on, which pervades the history of philosophy in every age. If there is no knowledge of the Spirit, even the practical recollection of the one man can only lead to the materialistic or spiritualist reaction, and therefore to the realm of spectres.[110]

It is quite interesting, in view of the developments of linguistic analysis, that Barth closes this section by mentioning the ways in which common speech confirms a unitary anthropology. For example, we do not say "my brain thinks" or "my body has a toothache." Rather, we say simply, "I think" or "I have a toothache." Barth points out that our speech contains more wisdom than our theoretical reflections. There is no division of body and soul in our speech about ourselves. In such cases as those mentioned above, we should not neglect the fact that when we use the first person singular pronoun, "I," we are speaking meaningfully about ourselves as a unified human subject.[111]

I have attempted to show, by comparing Barth, object relations, and the epistemic interpretation of object relations in Macmurray, that there is a significant analogy between the origins of human knowledge and the ways in which God gives himself to be known in revelation. If we are justified in the observation that there is an analogy between the way God gives himself to be known and the way humans know themselves and others, and that this knowing is based on dynamic relations more than on static concepts of being, should we not concur with Barth that it is more helpful to describe it as an *analogia relationis* than an *analogia entis?*

Dynamic Anthropology and Human Dignity

Neither Barth nor object relations paints a pessimistic picture of human nature, a pessimism that often resulted from the dualistic picture. Neither of

---

110. *CD,* III/2, p. 394.
111. Ibid.

them impugns human dignity and freedom. This optimism regarding human nature may surprise those who are familiar only with Barth's dialectical anthropology in which he emphasized the *diastasis* between God and humanity. With his earlier emphasis on the Wholly Otherness of God and his "No" to the sinful condition of humanity, Barth seemed almost to reiterate the Calvinist in crying out "total depravity!" Yet we have seen in chapter four that Barth's mature anthropology did not render humanity vile, godless, and depraved from the effects of sin (as Calvin had suggested and many Calvinists propounded).[112] Rather, we have seen that for Barth "real man" is essentially and ontologically good. Sin may cast a veil over human goodness, but this does not alter the fact of this goodness at the real core. How did Barth arrive at such a positive conclusion?

Barth refused to discuss the human being only in terms of secular or scientific phenomena; he discussed the person in terms of Christology. The image of God describes human destiny, because the basic goodness and dignity of the human being is restored to the image of God in Christ. The image of God represents human freedom because each person is able to respond to God through relation to Christ. And the image of God elevates human dignity beyond any other possibility, theoretical or practical, because each person's humanity is yoked to the humanity of Christ, and therefore to the divinity of God. There can be no higher elevation of humanity than to be the covenant partner of God. Barth affirms this in many of his later writings:

> It is when we look at Jesus Christ that we know decisively that God's deity does not exclude, but includes His *humanity*. . . . How could we see and say it otherwise when we look at Jesus Christ in whom we find man taken up into communion with God? No, God requires no exclusion of humanity, no non-humanity, not to speak of inhumanity, in order to be truly God. But we may and must, however, look further and recognize the fact that actually His deity *encloses humanity in itself.*[113]

Likewise, for object relations the human being is not reducible to mere instincts, nor cloven between loving and aggressive instincts, libidinal and aggressive, as Freud suggested. There is a noticeable absence of Freud's pessi-

---

112. Calvin's view of total depravity (or "perversity") has been somewhat misconstrued by many subsequent theologians; for him it was simply the corollary to the Reformation cry *sola gratia*. See T. F. Torrance, *Calvin's Doctrine of Man* (London: Lutterworth, 1949) pp. 83ff. Cf. Barth, *CD*, IV/1, p. 367, who disagrees with this, mostly because Calvin does not work out his doctrine of sin Christologically.

113. *Humanity of God,* pp. 49-50.

mistic assessment of human nature in object relations. Fairbairn and Guntrip argue that antisocial behavior can be explained through the disruption of good object relations at the earlier stages of human development; the earlier the disruption, the more severely damaged the individual is likely to be in one's later capacity to form stable relationships. Therefore, hope always remains for human healing and restoration as long as the possibility for good object relations exists.[114]

If our lives lack order, wholeness, and dignity — and who can doubt that much of the time they do — a dynamic anthropology must conclude that it is because we have become alienated from our true selves: we have fallen from the sphere of relationships that define and sustain our personhood. It may be that such a "fall" can be blamed on one's own choices; but it may also be that the individual who is estranged from God and others had little or nothing to do with the breach in such relationships. Other people around us may have cut off such life-shaping relationships without our knowledge or consent. At any rate, the broken condition of the divine image in humans does not occur because we are inherently torn between two radically different and ever-present selves: one noble and intelligent, and another fleshly and base. It is rather because we have excluded, or been excluded from, the sphere of relations that positively shape our human personhood.[115] Whether it be the lapse from the pristine state of a unitary ego due to bad object relations, or the fall from a sinless state of perfection in which body and soul are perfectly united in a harmonious union with God, either case implies that human brokenness is a negation of the human reality. Although human beings are sinful and beset with all manner of psychological illnesses in many instances of the present life, they are essentially good. Sin and emotional brokenness are endemic to the human race, but they are not ontologically normative. The sinful person is an impostor. For those who receive the grace of God in Christ the blemish of sin is removed and true humanity is restored because a right relation between the creature and its Creator has been re-

---

114. The optimism contained in object relations is not only theoretical, but practical; it manifests itself in the possibility for later therapeutic intervention to aid a person who has endured many bad object relations during childhood.

115. Pannenberg (*Anthropology,* pp. 119-28) does a fine job of pointing out the social context of human sinfulness and the need to push beyond the simple explanation of Augustine that sin is transmitted biologically. Kant, Schleiermacher, Ritschl, and P. Schoonberg have all preferred to talk about a "kingdom of sin" as a designation for the corporate and social dimension that it possesses. Pannenberg reminds us that while Augustine was wrong to explain original sin in terms of sexual desire, we should not react against him so strongly that we allow a division between the biological and psychosocial dimensions of sin.

stored. Fragmentation and chaos are unnatural to humans. Wholeness and order are our "natural" condition: having been lost through sin, they are restored in Christ.[116] Human wholeness is not the condition of the Christian only, but a condition that only the Christian knows — and is therefore compelled to proclaim to others.[117]

From a dynamic anthropology, hope emerges. This is because the damaged condition of our interpersonal relations can be restored. The grace of God extended in Christ contains the good news that the damaged relation between God and humanity is in the process of being healed. This grace also mends the damaged relations between human beings.[118] However tarnished the human condition may appear to be, hope always remains for the healing of persons. For psychology it may mean restoring the soul and body to their proper order, and for theology it must include the higher order of restoring relation to God. Theologically, the prospect for the healing of relations is always hopeful, because the restoration of all relationships rests ultimately on the fact that our relation to God has already been restored in Christ.

Theology and Psychology in Dialogue

Theology and Psychology at the Boundaries

We have seen that both Barth and Fairbairn's object relations psychology advocate a type of realism that allows their anthropologies to be open-ended. That is, they are constantly seeking to describe better the nature of the object to which they refer. Neither expects their concepts to be finalized, because they attempt to describe objects that are real living subjects. A realist anthropology will thus constantly revise its thoughts about human beings in light of the further study, observation, and reflection on the human subject. Why? Is this due to indecisiveness? an unwillingness to be committed to a specific program? No. Rather, realists are engaged in constant dialogue with the nature of the object to which they desire to conform their language.

---

116. See 2 Cor. 3:18–4:6; Col. 3:1-10.
117. See *CD*, IV/3, §71.6, "The Liberation of the Christian," esp. pp. 673ff.
118. See 2 Cor. 5:16-21.

Open-Ended Anthropology

In Christian theology, Barth has argued that the language appropriate to our understanding of the human being is the language of revelation: it is the Word from the triune God to humanity. The Word that becomes human language and human flesh is the starting point for theological anthropology. Christian anthropology begins with the humanity of Christ. For object relations, the language seeks to conform to the person in the context of his or her psychological development from the earliest stages of childhood. But unlike the psychology of Freud and certain forms of modern behaviorism, object relations entails a kind of realism that does not close itself off from dialogue with other higher systems of thought such as philosophy or theology. As we have seen, object relations, especially of the type Fairbairn advocates, is not positivistic. It respects empirical research, but it is not rigidly empiricist. It attempts to take the biological realities of human existence into account, without being slavish to biological reductionism. Object relations does not operate from the premise that only the empirical method can do justice to the study of human beings; it does not claim to have an exhaustive description of human beings even if it might attain a degree of accuracy in describing the dynamics of primary object relations and their implications for psychological development and clinical treatment. Object relations does not try to reduce all explanations for human behavior to the lower levels of biology, chemistry, and physics, nor does it attempt to reduce theology to psychology. In this sense it is open: open to new truth, open to new levels of discovery, open to the possibility of describing its object with an increasing degree of accuracy. But what of Barth's "dogmatic" anthropology?

The common understanding of the term "dogmatic" makes dogmatic anthropology sound remarkably closed. It would be a mistake, however, to believe that dogmatic anthropology is "dogmatic" in the pejorative sense of the term. Dogmatic anthropology is dogmatic because it seeks to explain its understanding of human beings as creatures made in God's image, as creatures who are the brothers and sisters of Christ. This does not mean that dogmatics assumes an air of infallibility. We have shown that Barth's dogmatic method is continually open to receive new truth.[119] It is "dogmatic," therefore, in the sense that it seeks to explain the ground of its belief. At the same time it is open-ended because it cannot assume that it has explained its belief exhaustively or with perfect accuracy. It is bound to the revealed truths about God and humankind, but it can never assume that it has described accurately

---

119. See above, chapter four.

or spoken every word that is needful about the human being as God's creature. Because of the openness to new truth, dogmatic anthropology can seek to dialogue with scientific and philosophical anthropologies of every age.[120] If dogmatics is faithful to its own foundation in the Word of God, it is not bound to agree with other views of the human being; at times it is compelled to disagree strongly. But even in its faithfulness to its own foundation in revealed truth, it may find itself in agreement with certain aspects of nontheological anthropologies. Dogmatic anthropology must not, however, allow itself to be tossed to and fro by the current winds of secular belief. It may employ secular language at times, and even secular philosophy, but it must never stray from its real objective of describing the human being as the creature made in the image and likeness of God. In this, Barth has held firm, and he has done theological anthropology — and every other form of anthropology — a great service.

Psychology at Its Limits

Object relations attempts to view the ego as both unitary and whole in its pristine state. Yet object relations is also realistic about the fact that no such "whole" egos are phenomenally observable. In chapter five we saw that this is an area where Fairbairn seems to equivocate, sometimes insisting on the unitary nature of the "pristine ego," and other times regarding the ego structures and the internalized objects as two separate and disparate entities. One of the major criticisms aimed at Fairbairn has been that he did not clearly explain whether the bad object relations were the fault of the parent only, or were caused by a projection of hatred from the infant toward the mother.[121] I would suggest that here we see an element of psychoanalytic theory that is pressing against the boundaries of its own discoveries. When the psycholo-

---

120. It is appropriate here to cite Barth's affirmation: "In dogmatics we cannot presume to know and declare in advance, as a more than hypothetical certainty, what is and what is not fundamental. An hypothesis as such is not to be repudiated but exploited. But it cannot be given the rank and function of a principle. A serviceable heuristic canon cannot be treated as if it were a classic text. . . . When this happens . . . dogmatics condemns both itself and the Church in which it ought to have kept watch to death from suffocation" (*CD,* I/2, p. 865). See also pp. 866ff.

121. Kernberg observes that Fairbairn's critics agreed: "with Fairbairn's stress that at the root of the schizoid personality is the infant's failure to feel that the mother loves him in his own right, but pointed to the difficulty of finding out whether Fairbairn considers this the mother's failure or the result of the child's projection onto her of his own hate" (*Internal World,* pp. 76-77).

gist looks at symptoms that might be described as "bad object relations," are these bad object relations stemming from the parent's less than adequate emotional and physical nurture of the child? Or is there something within the child right from the moment of birth (conception?) that could spontaneously project hatred upon the parent? Who but the theologian could appropriately reflect on such matters? It seems here that psychoanalytic theory must halt, and if there is need for further discussion must appeal to the theologian or moral philosopher for meaningful discussion, or perhaps illumination.

When pressed up against certain theoretical impasses, such as: Where do bad object relations originate from — neglectful mothers or angry children? psychoanalytical theory has already begun an implicit dialogue with the theologian. Would not the psychologist here benefit from an explicit cross-disciplinary dialogue with those whose task it is to talk about the nature of the Fall, guilt, sin, atonement, and forgiveness? My hope is that this will increasingly be the case, and that the dialogue in this study will be but one contribution to an ongoing series of such dialogues.

Yet I would be remiss to propose that the dialogue would be a one-way conversation, as if the theologian could gain nothing from the psychologist. The psychologist who aims to understand the mechanisms of various neurotic or psychotic disorders poses no greater threat to theology than Galileo did by looking through his telescope. Some of the scientific studies of human beings will hold little interest for the theologian; others will appear to threaten certain cherished dogmas of the faith *(fundamentum dogmaticum).* Still others will seem to confirm or provide a material parallel for a dogmatic understanding of the person. At times the psychologist may be able to provide the dogmatician with certain heuristic tools with which to further explain his or her dogma. For example, when the psychologist points out the social dimensions of psychoneurotic illnesses, could it be that the theologian is here provided with a description that might illumine some aspects of the doctrine of original sin? For while the psychologist has nothing to say about the doctrine of original sin per se, neither have theologians found a thoroughly acceptable alternative to the crude insistence by Augustine and others that original sin is transmitted through the physical human seed. It would seem that the model used by the object relations theorist could provide a good deal of insight into the means by which human brokenness is transmitted from one generation to the next. The medium through which sin passes is one of broken interpersonal relations. While I would hesitate to equate sin with "bad object relations" univocally, who could deny that there must be some relation between them? The fracturing of the originally "pristine ego" is not to be equated with the Fall, but it nevertheless bears some analogical relation to the theological concept of the Fall, although in quite different language from that given in Romans 2, 3, and 5.[122] Both signify a brokenness of relations between persons, a fracture of the shared experience of human life.

The "Real Man" in Space and Time

A crucial question surfaces in light of the relation between dogmatics and psychology. Does this "dialogue" between Barth and modern scientific psychology indicate that the Kantian distinction between the noumenal and phenomenal has been overcome?

In matters that pertain to the relation between Christian theology and natural theology, we have seen that Barth cautiously accepts the Kantian critiques of natural theology — with the notable exception that he rejects Kant's moral proof for the existence of God. But what of the fundamental distinction between practical reason and the sensible forms of space and time that constrain the phenomena of scientific inquiry to mere appearances; has this fundamental epistemological split been denied in Barth's anthropology? I believe that the answer is yes. Barth's anthropology, when seen in the light of the wider scope of the *Dogmatics*,[123] indicates that Barth had no intention of abiding by Kant's distinction between noumenal and phenomenal, speculative and practical reason. Barth even goes so far as to claim that both the body and the soul are found within the space-time world of material and physical reality. Soul is the determination of an earthly being in space and time. The soul is indissolubly bound to the world of material and temporal reality, but at the same time it is not victimized or imprisoned by them. Here we find that

---

122. "Therefore as sin came into the world through one man and death through sin, and so death spread to all men because all men sinned."

123. See chapters two and four above; also *CD*, II/1, p. 464, where Barth states, regarding God's omnipresence: "In the older theology God's omnipresence was usually coupled with His eternity. The reason is not far to seek. His omnipresence seems to have reference to His relation to space, His eternity to His relation to time. The two, it was thought, could be comprehended under the more general conception of infinity (*infinitas*) and expounded according to the common pattern thus provided. . . . The parallel between omnipresence and eternity appears obvious. It gives a logical and metaphysical clarity which has perhaps seemed even more satisfactory since the conceptions of space and time began to play their prominent role in Kant's theory of knowledge. For space and time can be understood as the limits within which we ourselves exist and within which the world also exists for us. These are the conditions under which the activity of our human existence, our knowing and willing, take place as such (in time), and in relation to objects (in space)."

the long journey through Barth's anthropology after his critique of Kant comes to one of its crucial conclusions: a unitary and dynamic anthropology is one in which the theoretical and practical selves must be together. They are two moments of the same creaturely reality; and like the unity of soul and body, they cannot be thought of as separate.

We could wish that Barth had been more explicit about his rejection of Kant's severance of the space and time sphere of the sensible forms from the ethical and religious spheres. Nevertheless, that Barth is willing to place the soul, as well as the body, within the spatiotemporal world speaks for itself. Kant's "real" (noumenal) self, his ethical self, could be approached only outside the sensible forms of space and time. On the other hand Barth's self stands within space and time. Barth's dialogue with Freud and other psychologists (see below) gives evidence that Barth has chosen to supersede Kant's dualisms; Barth does not wish to allow the behavioral sciences to study the body, while theology is relegated to the study of disembodied souls.[124] We therefore have every reason to expect to find parallels between the biblical witness to our revealed humanity in Christ, and the theories of modern psychology that are ultimately accountable to the empirically observable realities of human existence.[125]

The "Feeling of Absolute Dependence" Revisited

Does Schleiermacher's "feeling of absolute dependence" take on a different hue in light of our study of Freud and object relations? Is there a sense in

124. For an account of the post-Kantian dualism, see C. P. Snow, *The Two Cultures: And a Second Look,* 2d ed. (Cambridge: Cambridge University Press, 1964) (originally published in 1959 as *The Two Cultures and the Scientific Revolution*).

125. In the *Dogmatics* Barth spells out clearly his rejection of Kant's distinction between the theoretical and ethical; e.g., III/4, p. 25: "Wherever and whenever the command of God encounters a man, it is always determined by the fact that He is this God. The presuppositions, plans, intentions and methods of this God will always be normative. This event will always take place at a point on the ways of this God — and to this extent not in empty space. Looking back upon past and forward to future encounters with His command, we can have absolute assurance. The One who commands is the one who as Father is the sovereign Lord of His creature, who in His Son has given Himself for it, and who as Spirit will lead it into all truth and thus perfect it." Again: "When man in faith in God's word and promise realizes how God from eternity has maintained and loved him in his little life, and what He has done for him in time, in this knowledge of human life he is faced by a majestic, dignified and holy fact. . . . We may confidently say that the birth of Jesus Christ as such is the revelation of the command as that of respect for life. This reveals the eternal election and love of God" (p. 339).

which the feeling of absolute dependence can be accounted for in terms that would cause us to question its validity as a foundation for Christian theology? Perhaps so. It is not coincidental that the theme of dependence has rung loud and clear from the bell tower of developmental psychology. Time and again, the psychologists have mentioned the absolute dependence of the infant on the mother or primary caretaker, and its implications for all stages of emotional life. Infant dependency is not only a physical dependence, but a psychological dependence as well. It would not be an exaggeration to say that all of the building blocks of the human psyche are founded on the cornerstone of complete emotional and physical dependence of the child during the first three to four years after conception.

Does modern psychology adversely affect Schleiermacher's insistence that the "feeling of absolute dependence" is anterior to the functions of knowing and doing?[126] In appealing to the "feeling of absolute dependence" was Schleiermacher referring to the preverbal unconscious stage of life that is so fundamental for all other stages? Has the feeling of absolute dependence been weakened, or strengthened, by the insight of psychoanalysis that the state of complete psychological dependence is the primary state of human development?

The parallels between Schleiermacher and psychoanalytic theory are intriguing, and potentially damaging to the theological significance of the "feeling of absolute dependence." But before we go too far with such a comparison, we should remember that Schleiermacher did not intend his "feeling of *absolute* dependence" to be a description of any kind of purely psychological phenomena. It was intended to be anterior to any other kind of dependence that is susceptible to natural explanation. He had intended "the feeling of absolute dependence" to provide a transcendental foundation for Christian piety: having thus explained the origin of religious piety, Schleiermacher thought to explain the object of our knowledge — God. In the feeling of absolute dependence Schleiermacher thought he had found an epistemological *prius* that would fall outside the range of Kant's critiques. He intended to erect a foundation for Christian theology that might maintain some intellectual credibility. As a matter of method, it would of course go against the grain of this study to assert that a psychological finding could invalidate a theological truth. Barth, of all theologians, would be skeptical of such a method of criticizing Schleiermacher or any other theologian.

However, some critical questions about the feeling of absolute dependence cannot be avoided. Barth's question was this: Does the feeling of abso-

---

126. *Christian Faith,* §3.

lute dependence provide an adequate foundation for Christian theology? He decided it could not. My question is this: If the feeling of absolute dependence can be accounted for by the psychologist, does this in any sense confirm Barth's suspicion that its usage by the theologian was illegitimate? The latter question deserves some careful attention.

There is a sense in which modern psychoanalysis draws our attention to Schleiermacher's genius. Schleiermacher was a keen observer, and in his search to find a way around the critical philosophy of Kant, he expanded on certain aspects of human experience that would later be discovered by scientific psychology. If our study of modern psychoanalytic theory has gained us some insight into the truth about the development of human consciousness, then we must agree that there is something in the individual soul that does precede both knowing and doing. There is something that is the unconscious foundation on which all later conscious experiences are built, and that powerfully influences the capacity both to know and do throughout life. Schleiermacher was a keen observer of the self; we can almost marvel at his insight into the precognitive dimension of human consciousness.

The possibility remains, however, that the feeling of absolute dependence fails as a foundation for theology because it describes human psychology and nothing more. This was, *in nuce,* Barth's criticism of Schleiermacher. Barth argued that if we begin with psychology (in the general sense) then we can end only with psychology, and never attain a true theology. Curiously, when faced with a similar form of religious expression, this was also Freud's position (following Feuerbach): the psychology of religious experience cannot verify the objective truth of the experience. I mentioned in chapter three that the feeling of absolute dependence was particularly susceptible to psychological explication. Let us see if this might be the case.

After Freud published his opinions on the psychological explanation of religion in *The Future of an Illusion,* he received a letter from a friend, Romain Rolland. In the letter Rolland agreed with Freud's assessment that religion itself was an illusion, and agreed that religious beliefs as such were nothing beyond an illusion. Nevertheless, Rolland insisted that within the realm of subjective feelings one could appreciate the true source of religious sentiments. It may not promise immortality, or the reality of religion, but it provides the impetus for religious energy, Rolland argued. The source of religious sentiment is the feeling that allows for the sensation of "eternity." Such a feeling Rolland referred to as an "oceanic" sense of oneness with the external world as a whole.

Freud admitted that the occurrence of such a feeling is not possible to deny. He questioned, however, if such a feeling had been correctly interpreted:

"From my own experience I could not convince myself of the primary nature of such a feeling. But this gives me no right to deny that it does in fact occur in other people. The only question is whether it is being correctly interpreted and whether it ought to be regarded as the *fons et origo* of the whole need for religion."[127]

Naturally Freud sought a psychological explanation for this "oceanic" feeling. He explained it like this. There is nothing we are more aware of than our own ego. Such self-awareness is somewhat deceptive, however, for as we have seen, Freud believed that the ego develops on the surface of the id. The ego is less real than it appears and thus fades into the unconscious recesses of the id. In passionate love, however, the ego boundaries begin to diffuse. Therefore, the ego boundaries are not constant. Freud reminds his reader that in a great number of pathological conditions the ego boundaries begin to break down. The ego states are anything but constant, and go through a number of developmental stages from infancy to adulthood. (In object relations we have seen this confirmed in more detail, in the theory that in the complex world of interaction between infant and mother, the ego begins to differentiate from non-ego, the objective world, through a number of experiences and sensations, some of them pleasurable, some of them painful. The first distinguishable object is the mother or the mother's breast.) Freud continues his argument by drawing attention to the earliest psychological state of life.

According to Freud, the importance of the original undifferentiated state of the ego is this:

> Our present ego-feeling is, therefore, only a shrunken residue of a much more inclusive — indeed, an all-embracing — feeling which corresponded to a more intimate bond between the ego and the world about it. If we may assume that there are many people in whose mental life this primary ego-feeling has persisted to a greater or less degree, it would exist in them side by side with the narrower and more sharply demarcated ego-feeling of maturity, like a kind of counterpart to it. In that case, the ideational contents appropriate to it would be precisely those of limitlessness and of a bond with the universe — the same ideas with which my friend elucidated the "oceanic" feeling."[128]

Hence the religious feeling that one is reaching eternity, or feeling absolutely at one with the universe, is readily explained by the residue of the original infantile state of undifferentiated ego. The feeling of oneness with the universe

---

127. "Civilization and Its Discontents," *S.E.*, XXI, p. 65.
128. Ibid., p. 68.

could be leftover feelings from infancy; that such a residue of feeling would be felt later in life fits in with Freud's theory, for the primary states are never completely removed; they are simply buried beneath the remains of the more recent states.[129] Freud concludes: "Thus we are perfectly willing to acknowledge that the 'oceanic' feeling exists in many people, and we are inclined to trace it back to an early phase of ego-feeling. The further question then arises, what claim this feeling has to be regarded as the source of religious needs."[130] Freud admits that the psychological explanation for the origin of apparently religious feelings does not invalidate the possible objective reality of such feelings. He does, however, think that his theory casts sufficient doubt on the validity of religious feelings to practically disregard them — which is precisely what Freud chose to do.

Freud has provided an interesting, and if true, damaging, account of the religious experience from a psychological perspective. Later object relations theorists have substantiated Freud's reference to the undifferentiated sense of oneness between mother and child at infancy. But what does all this mean for religious experiences? Has psychoanalytical theory really provided an explanation for the "oceanic feeling of oneness with the world" that Freud's friend, Romain Rolland, refused to let go? More importantly for this study: does this same criticism apply to Schleiermacher's "feeling of absolute dependence"? We must proceed with caution at this point. For later in the same volume of the *Standard Edition,* Freud attempts to explain the occasion of a colleague's conversion to Christianity in terms of an unresolved Oedipus complex.[131] If Freud accounts for the former situation, then what is to prevent his psychological explanations from accounting for the latter and, indeed, all forms of religion?

With regard to the feeling of absolute dependence, it should be admitted that it corresponds well to an undifferentiated primitive ego state of which the modern psychologist has made us aware. The similarities are not difficult to find. In *The Christian Faith,* Schleiermacher refers to all true feeling as a self-consciousness that is determined by something other. It is not dependence per se, but the *absolute (schlechthiniger)* feeling of dependence that gives Schleiermacher his starting point for human religious consciousness. He distinguished the *absolute* dependence, which is religious, from the *relative* dependence, which is earthly. Has he overlooked the "absolute" nature of infantile dependence? It seems so. Schleiermacher would probably object that

---

129. Freud gives the *Roma Quadrata,* the four levels of Rome, as a metaphorical example of the psyche with its simultaneous layering of experiences from earlier stages of development (ibid., pp. 69ff.).

130. Ibid., p. 72.

131. "A Religious Experience," *S.E.,* XXI, pp. 169-72.

we are equivocating in referring to infantile dependence as "absolute," that we are failing to understand the technical way in which he is describing the term. He is clearly attempting to find a philosophically primary form of dependence, anterior to any form of earthly dependence. He is intending to surmount human psychology (in the general sense) and reach, by way of a religious epistemology, to God himself. The problem is this: in his quest to find a foundation for theology, did Schleiermacher inadvertently refer to a primitive psychological state? If he did, or even if he envisaged something behind the psychological state as the foundation for theology, then we would do well to look elsewhere for a dogmatic starting point for Christian theology. For since Schleiermacher has located both the feeling of absolute dependence and God as its counterdeterminant in the subjective realm of human consciousness, the difficulty in disentangling the truly religious intuition from the psychological processes of the earliest stages of life would seem to be formidable, if not impossible. If, on the other hand, we begin with revelation, with the Word of God, then there should be little doubt that we are intending to signify something besides a state of human consciousness.

The latter route was clearly the one taken by Barth. It was possibly due to the criticisms such as the one that Freud could make of a more or less Schleiermacherian form of Christian faith that Barth intended to take theology in an altogether different direction: grounding it in revelation rather than the feeling of absolute dependence. It is important to note that I am not dismissing the feeling of absolute dependence because modern psychology will not allow it; rather, I am pointing out that when theology embarks on certain tasks that are more closely aligned with psychology than theology proper, theology has begun to compromise its own credibility.

One must admit that Freud saw the possibility that he had not invalidated the objective truth of religion simply by giving the psychological account of religious feelings. Yet on the practical level he disregarded the possibility that religious feelings could be based on a more objective form of truth: a given, such as revelation. Could it be that he was mistaken to believe that a psychological account of religious experience could invalidate the objective truth of that religious experience? After all, many have pointed out that he applied his psychological explications of religious feelings rather selectively and narrowly. He steadfastly maintained that religion was nothing more than a vehicle for the expression and maintenance of infantile needs and dependencies. But one of his major insights into human psychology was to uncover the ambivalence that we often feel toward our parents, especially the father. He could just as well have applied his psychological razor to the need for *unbelief* as belief; for the Oedipus conflict, which falls at the center of his psychoanalytic theory, contains a very powerful wish for the annihilation of the father. If religion is a mere projection of human psychology, could not *irreligion* also be a purely psychological projection? For in light of the Oedipus conflict, the desire for the individual to be rid of "God the Father" seems every bit as plausible as the need to invoke a deity as a fatherly figure in order to protect from the forces of nature and compensate for the harshness of life. The desire to have a father and the desire to be rid of one's father could be equally well explained according to Freud's theories. They seem to cancel one another out.

How then do we explain the origin of religious beliefs? Either we can explain religious beliefs as a projection of human needs for love, or we can explain human love as a reflection of divine love. In Schleiermacher's theology we arrive at God by analyzing religious consciousness. Barth had decided that any attempt to make predications about God based on religious consciousness could only lead theology into a cul-de-sac of subjectivism. The plausible psychological explanation that a modern psychoanalyst such as Freud can offer for the feeling of absolute dependence tends to support Barth's skepticism toward any theology predicated on religious consciousness.

Freud and Barth Closely Compared on Human Sexuality

Barth's comments on psychotherapy and psychological theory are not extensive. They are nonetheless incisive. In his final volume on the doctrine of creation,[132] Barth engages in dialogue with Freud on a level that shows that he understood the importance and the implications of some of Freud's basic premises.

As we have seen, both Barth and modern scientific psychology put sexuality at the very center of their respective anthropologies. Colin Gunton has criticized Barth for his interpretation of the *imago Dei* as human sexual polarity, male and female. Gunton admires Barth's dynamic ontology, and thinks that Barth's view of God compares favorably with that of Charles Hartshorne's process theology. Gunton thinks that Barth's anthropology, however, is given a somewhat less dynamic interpretation because of Barth's emphasis on the *imago Dei* as male and female.[133] I propose, to the contrary,

132. *CD,* III/4, §§52-56.

133. *Becoming and Being: The Doctrine of God in Charles Hartshorne and Karl Barth* (Oxford: Oxford University Press, 1978) p. 188: Barth's "rather strained use of the male-female relationship at the heart of his conception of human nature appears to have called attention away from the fact that his position is as radically destructive as any empiricist, existentialist, or neoclassical attack on conceptions of the person as a timeless substance problematically linked to a changing body."

that Barth's emphasis on humanity as male and female contains one of his more helpful insights. Furthermore, I believe that Barth's interpretation of the *imago Dei* as male and female shows the extent to which he has transcended the classical and neoclassical substantival categories. Interpreting the *imago Dei* as the structural differentiation into male and female, Barth spells out in very specific terms *(in concreto)* what it means for human beings to reflect the likeness of God. "Male and female" is the basic form of of the *imago Dei*. It is not a theoretical or abstract definition of the *imago*, but a concrete and specific definition that is observed in the historical moment of encounter itself. Barth's interpretation of the *imago Dei* encompasses human sexual love, but human sexuality is much more broadly interpreted by Barth than, for example, by Freud.[134] Let us see what Barth means when he argues that male and female is the form of our fellow humanity.

In chapter five we have seen how modern psychology has illumined the central role that human sexuality plays in the psychological development of the human being. In light of this, would not the theologian do well to reexamine the biblical data, especially the creation sagas in Genesis 1 and 2? And who has done this with more originality, and perhaps audacity, than Barth? In his interpretation of the *imago Dei* as male and female, Barth strikes a common chord with modern psychoanalytic theory. They have this theme in common: both emphasize the central role of sexuality for human beinghood. Sexuality is therefore central to human beinghood. For Barth, male and female is the pivotal differentiation of human personhood. For modern psychology, sexuality provides the basic motivation to form relations. In both cases, human sexuality is determinative in providing both the structure and motivation for interpersonal encounter. The similar themes in both Barth and modern psychology are important because they indicate the extent to which Barth's theological anthropology is analogous to certain aspects of the human sciences. The nature of human sexuality, however, needs to be further defined.

As we have seen, Freud conceptualized sexual instinct as the fount of psychical energy and the core of human psychology. Object relations found human sexuality almost equally important, but interpreted the libidinal impulses in terms of the drive to form primary relations to other persons. Barth's anthropology also gave sexuality a place of primary importance. We have seen that Barth's portrait of human sexuality was not one of a self-contained system of energy that stimulates human actions. It was rather a description of a relationship that mirrors the interpersonal dynamism within

---

134. See *CD*, III/2, p. 288.

God himself. Sexuality, the human encounter as male and female, is thus central to the image of God.

In a section where he discusses the ethics of freedom and responsibility for human sexual expression, Barth comments on 1 Corinthians 6:13ff.: "In the relation between man and woman more is at issue than the χοιλια.[135] It is a question of the σωμα. Thus for the Christian, the ethical prohibition against adulterous relations with a harlot is a question of man himself in his psychophysical totality. Not a part or a special function of his being, but the man himself as a whole belongs to the Lord."[136] In exegeting the above passage, Barth draws attention to the psychosomatic unity that is assumed in Scripture. The ethical implications of Christian sanctification (v. 11) are based on the prior assumption of this psychosomatic unity by the apostle Paul. This unity of body and soul, coupled with the union of the believer with Christ, entails the responsibility to avoid gluttony and extends to Paul's prohibition against intercourse with a harlot:

> This [command] would not preclude intercourse with a harlot if the σωμα of which also this is said were one thing and sex and its needs something different; if the Christian life described could be lived out in one sphere and sexual life, following its own law, in another. But this is not the case. . . . This is just what he who is one Spirit with the Lord cannot do. His sexual needs and their satisfaction (even within marriage, as the context shows us) cannot be sundered from the other aspects of his being and from the total responsibility of his relationship with woman. He cannot regard the sexual sphere either as being specially unclean or as being specially clean. In this sphere, too, he must and will be wholly himself, and allow the woman to be wholly herself. He will realise that he can enter into such a relationship with her only if each is concerned for the whole being of the other, so that for both of them it is not a question of something partial or furtive, as in whoredom, but, as the terms indicate, as something total: μία σάρξ, ἐν σῶμα.[137]

It almost sounds as if Barth is here denying the importance of sexuality for biblical anthropology. It is important to realize, however, that he is merely giving sexuality an expanded definition. Sexuality is interpreted in terms of the "total responsibility" that a personal relationship entails. Barth thus uses

---

135. *Sic;* Barth is undoubtedly referring to *koilia* (v. 13); this seems to be a printer's error, since *koilia* is in the German edition.

136. *CD,* III/4, p. 135.

137. Ibid.

the Pauline text above and similar texts to argue for the psychosomatic wholeness and against a strictly biological interpretation of human sexuality. He then contrasts his theological anthropology with some important aspects of Freudian psychology:

> We are to-day in the pleasant situation of being able to point to the fact that even from the standpoint of medical psychology thinkers are increasingly inclined to accept and emphasize this view[138] of the matter. Only thirty or forty years ago, in the age of Sigmund Freud, it would have been otherwise. . . . Among these, as the research of the period saw it, the sexual libido played a decisive if not an exclusive role. Not only was it to be recognised as more powerful than had previously been supposed, but practically all the impulses and tendencies of the life of the soul were to be understood in terms of its manifestation. In certain forms of the teaching, at any rate, it seemed that the human element as such was to be brought under the denominator of the specifically sexual. We withhold all the comments and criticisms to which we are not entitled as those unable to co-operate in this sphere of enquiry. We simply take note that this phase in the interpretation of the matter now seems to have been left behind even in medical psychology, so that we should be tilting against windmills if we were to make our relevant theological affirmations in opposition to the received standpoint in the medical sphere. The opposition to Victorianism in the widest sense had its season and its justification. But even in the medical sphere it has been clarified, in the development characterised especially by the names of Alfred Adler and C. G. Jung, into the general opinion that while the specifically sexual is to be estimated very differently from previous views, *it must now be understood in relation to the psycho-physical existence of the whole man and not vice-versa.*[139]

It is too bad the Barth did not proceed to cite Jung and Adler, since their writings are widely available and they are more akin to the object relations theorists we have been studying. He does, however, cite from several psychologists who also emphasize that human sexuality includes both psyche and soma.

---

138. Barth is referring to the "psycho-physical" wholeness of human sexuality.

139. *CD*, III/4, pp. 135-36; italics mine. Barth of course overlooks the dynamic component within Freud's thought; and it could be mentioned in balancing his evaluation of Freud that Freud did not interpret sexuality only in terms of genital sex, but within a much wider context. Nevertheless, Barth put his finger on the essence of Freud's anthropology, and rejected Freud's biological reductionism as the basis for an adequate concept of human sexuality.

Sexuality and Self-Transcendence

As a specific example of the trend away from the Freudian interpretation of sexuality, Barth cites Oswald Schwarz, whose psychology of human personality includes an understanding of sexuality that takes account of sexual impulses in the developmental stages, but then opens upward at the highest level of emotional development and indicates the spiritual dimensions of the sexual drive.[140] Barth notes that recent developments[141] in psychology have encouraged it to grow beyond a theory of personality based on uncontrollable impulses and toward the realization that sexuality possesses an "indissoluble unity with love and with the spiritual element of moral purposes. In this union the force of sexuality as a mere biological urge becomes truly human. Bodily sexuality is no more and no less than the stamp set upon the apprehension and finding of the Thou and even of the I, from which the path leads into the world of the objective and the realm of spirit."[142] Barth emphasizes the trend in psychology to include in its theory a component of self-transcendence that allows for *eros,* but "does not make sexual indulgence inevitable." Rather, such sexual expressions are "free to bring the biological impulses as such into conjunction with the other aspect of life, i.e., to control them instead of being controlled by them."[143]

As we have seen, Freud sometimes advocated that the sexual instincts should be given more freedom so as to reduce the amount of neurotic anxiety within individuals who are frustrated by pent-up sexual desires. Nevertheless, Freud had not altogether denied that one must control sexual impulses: his concept of sublimation described the capacity to redirect sexual energy toward cultural activities. When it came to accounting for the structure that controls such impulses, however, Freud would not allow any talk about the Spirit — not even the human spirit. He attempted, rather, to explain human sexual attraction in terms of a complex structuring of instincts themselves; so much so that the "ego" was described as growing on the surface of the id. Barth is right, therefore, to point out that it was not the mere fact of human sexuality that Freud had attempted to explain. It was rather the place of biological sexuality as the *fons et origo* of human personhood. Freud describes sexuality as an impersonal energy force, which is not only detached from psychical structures, but is also the reductionist principle by which he attempts

---

140. *Sexualität und Persönlichkeit* (1943).
141. Barth is writing in the late 1940s–early 50s; *KD,* III/4 was published in 1951.
142. *CD,* III/4, p. 136.
143. Ibid.

to explain all human interactions. Barth, on the other hand, is appealing to a unity of transcendence and immanence, heavenly and earthly, visible and invisible, when he insists on human sexuality as a "psychosomatic" totality.[144] He advocates a unitary anthropology, but not a monist anthropology. He denies both material and psychical monism as a sufficient grounds for theological anthropology.

The idealist and rationalist anthropologies fixed their attention on the psychical and mental, respectively, and usually relegated the somatic realities of human life to a place of secondary importance. By contrast, Freud and others had fixed their attention on the somatic, and sought to describe the psyche as an epiphenomenon of the instinctual impulses.[145] This, we have seen, had its shortcomings; for in order to speak about the psychological, Freud was forced to adopt terms that described psychological structures closely resembling the functions of the older rational psychology. The superego closely resembled the conscience, or categorical imperative, and the ego itself closely resembled the soul of the rationalist anthropologies. The similarities between Freud and rational psychology do not ipso facto invalidate Freud's insights. But they do point out the extent to which a dualism of body and soul has often been employed to explain the basic human capacity to either transcend or succumb to the bodily impulses. There is a sense in which the dualist paradigm contains an element of truth, of course; for freedom of choice, which entails the capacity to deny instincts, must be explained if we are to do justice to the common experience of a society existing under some form of moral law. But is the dualist framework intelligible in the materialistic context in which Freud operated?

Barth reinforces his insistence on the human freedom to self-transcend, and thus use the sexual urge for personal purposes by noting that human sexuality can be sublimated into artistic or other activities and can be lived out in the intellectual rather than the physical plane. Again, Barth seems to overlook that Freud would have agreed with him that sexual impulses must generally be controlled (sublimated) by a majority of citizens within any given civilization. But this raises an important question for Freud's doctrine of sublimation. How might one arrive at the capacity to sublimate sexual impulses apart from some capacity for rational self-transcendence? Is not the superego's capacity to control the impulses similar to the concept of the person that was advocated by the rationalist psychologies of the classical and traditional Christian think-

144. *CD*, III/2, pp. 350-51.

145. What else could be meant by Freud's description that the ego develops on the surface of the id? ("The Ego and the Id," *S.E.*, XIX, pp. 24ff.).

ers? Fairbairn astutely points out that Freud began with an empirical method, but in order to explain unconscious processes had been forced to introduce certain psychical entities that are strangely familiar to those found within many rationalist psychologies.[146] For example, in the superego we see an instance of a higher faculty exercising control over a lower impulse. Freud differed from the former rational psychologies mostly inasmuch as he sought to find a psychohistorical explanation for the capacity to deny instincts; he sought to ground such a capacity in the Oedipal conflict. But he ultimately skirted the issue of how the mind actually transcends the instincts in order to redirect them. Any anthropology based on instinctual impulses seems eventually to reach this impasse. Here we see the force of Barth's critique. It is precisely, Barth argues, the self-transcendent element that allows for human sexuality to fulfill its highest and most human purposes.

It is time now to ask what are the parallels between Fairbairn's emphasis on the object relatedness of the impulses and Barth's insistence that we are created to be in encounter as male and female.[147] Both Barth and Fairbairn espouse the view that the libidinal impulses alone cannot do justice to human sexuality. Both adhere to the psychosomatic reality of the person without trying to reduce the person either upward into a thinking substance or downward into a mechanism governed by biological impulses. In this sense, there is a phenomenological element in both Barth and Fairbairn. Both make an effort to bracket the specific presuppositions or biases that their respective fields tended to bring with them in their study of human beings and look carefully at the human phenomena to see what can be seen. What, then, do they see? There is an undeniable dimension of consciousness, and there is an equally undeniable sense in which consciousness is intentional and always seeking rapport with an object. All acts of consciousness are naturally related to or directed toward something or, more universally, toward *someone.* H. Misiak describes Edmund Husserl's phenomenological influence on modern psychology in terms that illuminate the discussion at hand: "There is no love without someone or something loved, no desire without something desired, no perception without something perceived, and the like. Knowing the contents of consciousness is knowing the object itself."[148] This attempt to conceptualize the unity of consciousness and its object applies to both Barth and Fairbairn.

---

146. See Fairbairn, "A Critical Evaluation of Certain Psycho-Analytical Conceptions," *British Journal for the Philosophy of Science* 7 (1956-57) 55.

147. See *CD,* III/2, pp. 319-20.

148. Cf. Misiak, *History of Psychology,* pp. 410-11.

Human sexuality, therefore, encompasses both the physical and the psychical dimensions in a total union of interpersonal reciprocity. A truncated sexuality will therefore have potentially devastating consequences on the person who is treated impersonally, in other words, as a mere object for one's own gratification.

"Demonized" Sexuality and the "Healing of Persons"

That the human being is a psychosomatic unity leads Barth to explain:

> The truly erotic man is whole and free even in the sexual act; he thus seeks and discovers in it the free and total person of the other. He attains *eo ipso* to an atmosphere common to both and to its continuance, to the most varied and enduring fellowship with the beloved, to the fullest possible inward penetration of their personalities to a common erotic world. This world is called marriage, which represents for man the only perfect form of *eros* and the sexual impulse.[149]

While marriage is the telos of interpersonal encounter, Barth concedes that the institution of marriage does not itself guarantee the personal character of sexuality. Nevertheless, the point once again is that human sexuality includes the psychical as well as the somatic: it seeks the total personhood of the other. Barth argues that sexuality crosses over into its higher spiritual threshold when it reflects the covenant character of God's own covenant love.[150] Perhaps it will not always be the case that human sexual love reflects the character of God's love. Male and female remain, however, as the ineradicable basic form of humanity. This is the case because the mystery of human encounter is a reality that is revealed and enacted through Christ's relationship to the church; as such, human love reflects divine love, unveiling the dynamic reality of God's triune character.

Citing a work by the Roman Catholic Ernst Michel,[151] Barth argues that any sexual expression that disregards the psychosomatic wholeness of an interpersonal relationship

> is not the product of a strong biological impulse but of a strong self-centredness and bondage to self which merely exploits that natural im-

---

149. *CD*, III/4, pp. 136-37.
150. See *CD*, III/2, pp. 291-94.
151. *Ehe: Eine Anthropologie der Geschlechtsgemeinschaft* (1948).

pulse, detaching it from the psycho-physical unity of natural love and using it in the service of self-preoccupation or a flight from the self. Used in this way, it is not bestial but demonic, i.e., human in a negative determination and in conflict with man's ineradicable relationship to the Thou, as a relapse into self-exaltation or an evasion of the self. Without self-giving to a Thou the sexual act becomes the magical practice of a demonised sex; the attempt by a sort of conjuration, by fusion with the sexual polar opposite (masculine or feminine), to secure that which is to be had only in mutual individual and personal self-surrender. Not what is called fleshly lust, or animal impulses, but this attempt, this violation of the human, is what is really evil in this sphere, i.e., apostasy from the authentic human conception of sexuality. Deliverance from such non-human sexuality can be effected only by a reintegration from the heart's core by love and fellowship.[152]

By "demonic" Barth refers to that which thoroughly depersonalizes the other. He could not affirm more strongly his belief in the interpersonal character of human sexuality. He is saying much the same in the field of theology as the object relations psychologist who proposes that the integration of energy and structure in the psychology of the self shows that raw libidinal energy apart from any meaningful object relations creates a susceptibility to human pathology. In both fields the conclusion is that libido is certainly not, *eo ipso*, the fundamental building block of human psychology. The energy that motivates human attraction must also encompass an interpersonal relationship. If it does not, it becomes egocentric: not biological, but actually personal in the negative sense, and takes the form of emotional and spiritual illness.[153] For Barth, such pathology receives a theological interpretation of the strongest order: depersonalized sex is "demonic." It is demonic because it violates human personhood at the deepest ontological level, engaging in the biological at the expense of the psychical. In these days of supposed sexual liberation his summons to repair damaged and depersonalized sexuality by the reintegration of the "heart's core by love and fellowship" is especially timely. In the face of the enormous depersonalization and commercialized exploitation of sexuality in modern life, the answer is surely not to retreat to a new form of Victorian prudery, but to re-emphasize the need for sexuality to contain a personal dimension.

152. *CD*, III/4, p. 137.
153. I have noted above that for Fairbairn: "Frustration of his desire to be loved as a person and to have his love accepted is the greatest trauma that a child can experience" (*Psychoanalytic Studies*, pp. 39-40). The result of the trauma is to resort to substitutive satisfactions and thus internalize bad objects.

To the object relations theorist the libidinal ego seeks a satisfactory object relation and develops a susceptibility toward pathology where the object relations are unsatisfactory. Fairbairn, for example, has pointed out that bad external object relations can become psychologically internalized, and thus buried in the unconscious mind in the form of "bad objects." It is then the task of the therapist to engage in a therapeutic relationship in such a way that he or she might come to be trusted as a "good object." The bad object relations are therefore capable of being rectified in light of a good object relation.[154] Fairbairn notes Freud's willingness to dig through the archives of the church in order to discover case studies of demonization, which he thought to explain by his psychoanalytical insights. Freud dusted off the fascinating case of the painter-demoniac Christoph Haizmann. In analyzing Haizmann's case, Freud attempted to explain the origin of "demons" as neuroses that stem from evil and base wishes deriving from the impulses.[155]

In Haizmann's case, the death of his father left him in a state of depression, and drove him to resort to the desperate measure of signing a pact with the devil. Who would dispute the fact that psychobiological factors came into play, including Haizmann's very troubled relation to his own father? Yet, Fairbairn insists, Freud overlooked the key to Haizmann's illness. Freud failed to see that it was more than repressed libido that produced Haizmann's demonic possession, just as it was more than the liberation of libido that seemed to have effected his cure. It was, Fairbairn argues, an internalized "bad object" in the form of a bad relation to his father that accounted for Haizmann's "demonization" — and only the restoration of a good object relation (in this case to the Virgin Mary) that initially cured him. In tracing the etiology of an emotional illness to an internalized bad object, Fairbairn is saying much the same thing as Barth. For the internalized bad object represents a fundamental wound to the human soul that stems from "depersonalized sex" — albeit primary sex, sex when the libido functions at the earliest stages of childhood (whereas Barth discusses only the more mature level: sexuality between "male and female"). In object relations, depersonalized sexuality in the form of an unsatisfying object relation violates the emotional wholeness of the person, because sex always seeks for a sexual object. This shows how, for object relations theory, the sexual and the interpersonal coinhere. For Barth, depersonalized sex violates the fundamental "I-Thou" of human encounter: again the sexual and interpersonal dimensions coinhere. The similarities are

154. *Psychoanalytic Studies*, p. 74.
155. See Freud's case study, "A Seventeenth-Century Demonological Neurosis," *S.E*, XIX, pp. 67-105.

more than coincidental. They indicate that there exists an analogy between human brokenness as a revealed broken relation to God and others, and on the psychological level as internalized bad object relations.

Barth's description of depersonalized sexuality as "demonization" gives us some insight into his own description of evil as "nothingness" *(das Nichtige)*, or "non-being."[156] "Non-being" is a way of designating that a relationship has been breached. What else could it represent, since for Barth being itself is a relationship? The riddle of sin is the riddle of a broken relationship. Sin is enigmatic because it indicates a lapse of being caused by a lapse of a vital relationship. In light of the Christian doctrine of redemption, human sin is even more paradoxical because God has done everything necessary to repair the brokenness of the relationship between himself and the human race.[157] "Nothingness," "non-being," and other such terms designate Barth's attempt to give the paradox of sin a dynamic definition. Since our being is contingent on our relations, the absence of relation would have to result in our nonbeing. It is not wholly surprising then that Barth would allow the term "casting out demons" to denote a means of restoring human wholeness.[158] For Barth, the term "demonization" is used somewhat metaphorically; yet he does not discount the possibility that the demons are "real," even though their reality is ontologically negative. For Fairbairn, the demons are psychological. Yet they might not be exhaustively described in terms of endopsychic human states, for they represent an unhappy interpersonal history, and a history of bad object relations can readily become repressed and stored in the unconscious with the result that they may become a sinister psychological force in the life of the individual. Who knows if such a sinister psychological force might not begin to assume a life of its own — acting independently of the person whose soma-psyche it occupies? In the theology of Barth and the psychology of Fairbairn, this seems to be an open possibility.

At the very least, it is safe to say that both Barth and Fairbairn disagree

---

156. See e.g., *CD*, III/3, §50, "God and Nothingness"; and IV/3, p. 174.

157. For Barth, sin is always seen as a repudiation of grace, a rejection of relation to Christ. See *CD*, III/3, pp. 307ff. Cf. Berkouwer, *Man: The Image of God*, pp. 343-44: "When Barth speaks of the 'ontological' impossibility of sin, he means that it is impossible for man to fall out of the grace of God. No matter how much sin as an actual power has loaded man with guilt and shame, his essence — his relation to God — could not be affected, since God's grace triumphed over this choice and excluded it ontologically."

158. See Fairbairn, *Psychoanalytic Studies*, pp. 70-74; and cf. *CD*, IV/3, pp. 172ff., where Barth recalls the exorcism of a demonized woman by J. C. Blumhardt. The cry of the demon (on the lips of one of those observing) at the point of exorcism, "Jesus is Victor!" provides the title for §69.3 of the *Dogmatics*.

with Freud's opinion that "demons" are nothing more than a projection of repressed reprehensible wishes and impulses toward one's father. Since Fairbairn's object relations is "upwardly open," there might be a good deal of room for dialogue among object relations psychologists, pastors, and theologians regarding the relation between emotional illness and demonization.[159] Of course, many psychologists would likely steer clear of investigating such unusual phenomena for fear of appearing "unscientific." It might prove, however, that psychologists would be more willing to look at demonization than would many theologians. This seems to be the case if we compare Freud's and Fairbairn's willingness to give the Haizmann case their thorough scrutiny with Bultmann's dismay that Barth would even mention the exorcism performed by Johann C. Blumhardt (1805-1880) in his *Dogmatics*.[160]

From the above discussion we can conclude that both Barth and Fairbairn believe that "demonization" usually goes with a broken interpersonal history; furthermore, there is little chance of cure apart from the intervention of a trustworthy "good object." Regarding Haizmann, Fairbairn finally observes: "it was only after his pact with the Devil was replaced by a pact with God that his freedom from symptoms was finally established. The moral would seem to be that the appeal of a good object is an indispensable factor in promoting a dissolution of the cathexis of internalized bad objects."[161] In other words, people expend an enormous amount of emotional energy in order to preserve the status quo of their emotional illnesses; it is only when an apparently trustworthy and accepting "good object" allows them to release the emotional vise grip on their illness that any progress can be made. This psychological insight has some important ramifications for the "cure of souls."[162]

Barth's recollection of an exorcism performed by J. C. Blumhardt turns

---

159. In his essay "Notes on the Religious Phantasies of a Female Patient," *Psychoanalytic Studies*, pp. 183-96, Fairbairn notes the connection between "the original attitude towards parents prevailing during early childhood, and displacement of this attitude towards supernatural beings" due to disillusionment of the child with parental powers. Nevertheless, Fairbairn is highly skeptical that "higher values" can be accounted for purely in terms of their psychological origins (pp. 188-89).

160. See Bultmann, *Kerygma und Mythos*, ed. H. W. Bartsch (Hamburg, 1948) I, p. 150, where Bultmann mentions that the stories about the Blumhardts were an abomination to him ET, *Kerygma and Myth*, ed. H. W. Bartsch, tr. R. H. Fuller (London: SPCK, 1953).

161. *Psychoanalytic Studies*, p. 74.

162. In light of one of the major themes of this study, a better term for "cure of souls" would be a term used by Paul Tournier, "healing of human persons" (*The Healing of Persons*, tr. E. Hudson [New York: Harper and Row, 1965]).

out to be especially pertinent at this point. Regarding the exorcised spirit's shrieking "Jesus is Victor!" Barth observes:

> Like similar events in the New Testament, the occurrence during which Blumhardt heard this cry: "Jesus is Victor," has three aspects. On the first, it is realistically explained in the sense of ancient and modern mythology. On the second, it is explained in terms of modern psychopathology, or depth psychology. On the third, it is not explained at all but can only be estimated spiritually on the assumption that the two former explanations are also possible and even justifiable in their own way.[163]

A preliminary observation of the above statement yields the important point that Barth does not allow the third, spiritual, explanation to exclude the second, psychopathological, explanation. Nevertheless, he insists that the spiritual is the level on which he seeks to understand this striking account documented by the elder Blumhardt. But even more pertinent is that it is none other than Christ himself who is credited with the exorcism performed by Blumhardt. The internalized "bad object," or demon, is thus displaced by the ultimate "good object," Jesus. For Barth, of course, the Jesus who is credited with the exorcism is not a mere psychological figure, nor even a mere human figure, but the living and risen Lord. The latter understanding can be apprehended only on the level of faith. This nevertheless is strongly reminiscent of Fairbairn's insistence that the "bad objects" can be released only in the context of a patient's acceptance of a "good object." The point is worth noting, because it is likely to have a wider application than either of these extreme cases indicates. Even in less dramatic instances of human emotional and spiritual illness, the curative power of a good relationship cannot be underestimated. Establishing a relationship with a good object, it would seem, is the sine qua non of human wholeness, and the only path to healing the "sin-sick soul."[164] How might this happen? This is a question that I believe the minister and psychologist should have every reason to discuss together. Let us now return to the discussion of marriage and human sexuality.

163. *CD*, IV/3, p. 170.

164. There is an echo to this insistence on the "good object" as the means for psychological and spiritual healing in the psychology of Carl Rogers. Accurate empathy, warmth and congruence, and unconditional positive regard are all essential characteristics of the therapist in the therapeutic process, said Rogers. Rogers's therapeutic triad has been given a good amount of attention by pastoral theologians such as Oden, *Kerygma and Counseling*.

Parallels between Barth and Post-Freudian Psychology

Barth cites the psychological theory of Charlot Strasser,[165] declaring that in Strasser we find an "apparent agreement or material parallelism *(Parallele)*[166] between what we have presented on a theological basis with the findings of modern clinical psychology."[167] He paraphrases Strasser, whose ideas stand in marked contrast to Freud: "We do violence to nature, writes Strasser, if we measure the nature of man by that of the animal. Human nature has a physical but also a psychical structure. Hence it is erroneous to suppose that human nature is frustrated if in the time of physical sexual maturity it cannot be sexually active, but it must await a suitable opportunity for this activity. Nobody has yet been made ill or destroyed through sexual discipline."[168] Strasser, like the object relations theorists, represents a departure from Freud's explanation of the origin of neuroses. Both Strasser and Fairbairn interpret the object relationship as that which determines the libidinal attitude, not vice versa. Barth then quotes from Strasser directly:

> Sexuality is no affair of the inferior bodily impulses alone. Only the mistaken, specialised treatment of sexuality could make fashionable the expression "sex appeal." The only kind of sex appeal which is salutary is that which does not satisfy the needs of the body at the expense of those of the mind. Sexual impulses and love are indissolubly united; love without mental control is impossible. . . . The sexual impulse is through and through spiritualised in man. Beyond the biological need there stands spiritual decision. Love means much more than bodily satiety in sexual intercourse. Love is something beyond an organically conditioned disturbance of our ego below the navel.[169]

Barth concludes: "As a theologian, one could and would have to say these things very differently, and much else besides. But there is every reason to rejoice that a modern doctor can say what he has to say in such parallelism

---

165. "Seelische Gleichgewichtsstörungen im geschlechtlichen Eheleben," *Die lebendige Ehe* (1948).

166. Barth is fond of the term "material parallelism" to describe certain findings in the human sciences that tend to agree with his dogmatic anthropology. These parallels are specific similarities between dogmatic anthropology and human sciences, which bridge the so-called gap between theology and the other sciences. They are specific instances that indicate the analogical relation between dogmatics and human sciences.

167. *CD*, III/4, p. 138.

168. Ibid.

169. Strasser, pp. 216-17. Quoted in Barth, *CD*, III/4, p. 139.

(Parallele) to Christian truth, almost as though he had taken his bearings from Eph. 5 and I Cor. 6, as may well be the case with Charlot Strasser by way of Jeremias Gotthelf and Dostoievski."[170]

Several important implications can be drawn from Barth's interesting notes on human sexuality above. First, we see that both Barth and the post-Freudian psychologists whom he cites (in general agreement with object relations psychology) acknowledge the fundamental importance of sexuality for human personhood. Sexuality cannot be ignored. It is necessary to human personhood. But neither can sexual instincts per se serve as a sufficient explanation for human behavior, let alone human personhood. Both Barth and the post-Freudian psychologists[171] agree that human sexuality deserves to be interpreted in a broader context than that which is provided by instinctual theories. It is the *need* to form relationships that is primary, and the instinctual *drives* should be governed by this spiritual reality. Any reversal of the order, or severance of the personal from the biological, can only lead to a truncated and false conception of human sexuality. It is not sexuality per se, but sex divorced from all the other dimensions of our personhood that indicates the brokenness of human beings. It is not pleasure per se, but the dehumanizing component in the midst of the pleasure that Barth opposes: not the lust, or impulses per se, but the absence of authentic interpersonal intercourse accompanying the sexual intercourse that empties sexuality of its significance.[172]

Second, in the above passages we see an example of Barth's willingness to bring Christian anthropology into dialogue with the findings of scientific psychology and state the grounds of agreement or disagreement with respective psychological theories. He mentions the "apparent agreement or material parallelism between what we have presented on a theological basis with the findings of modern clinical psychology." This signifies that Barth's trinitarian theology, which operates on the principle of *analogia relationis,* does not seek to burrow itself into a self-enclosed circle of revelation detached from the space-time realities of natural human phenomena. Barth has discovered what he believes to be certain "parallelisms" between theological anthropology and the findings of medical psychology. Such parallels indicate that the *analogia relationis* allows for a real and meaningful analogical rela-

---

170. *CD,* III/4, p. 139.

171. The psychologists whom Barth cites — Jung, Adler, and the lesser-known Schwarz, Michel, and Strasser — are not strictly speaking "object relations" theorists. They nevertheless represent a Continental movement away from Freud's extreme emphasis on the sexual impulses similar to that of British object relations.

172. See *CD,* III/4, pp. 135-37.

tionship between eternity and time, between reality and appearance, between the noumenal world of value and the phenomenal world of fact. With this concrete example before us, we see that the *diastasis* between revelation and human science has grown considerably smaller than it had been in Barth's earlier dialectical theology. This is a point that many of Barth's critics have tended to overlook.[173]

Barth's dialogue with Freud and the other post-Freudian psychologists cited above helps us to see that we are on the right track to seek to expand such a dialogue. In other words, it shows Barth's willingness to dialogue with the modern human scientist and search out points of agreement. Barth does not see Christian anthropology as an isolated field, exclusive of any dialogue with the human sciences. Rather, he is willing to dialogue, to interact, and to compare what the Scripture says about the human being with the findings of modern scientific research, including modern psychoanalytic theories.

Conclusion

In the course of this study I have shown how Barth's approach to Christian anthropology has been influenced by his broad respect for the historical problems that he inherited from modern philosophy, along with the subsequent theological problems that came in the wake of Kant and Schleiermacher. Alongside Barth's commitment to deal with the historical problems that Continental philosophy and theology handed on to him, Barth was also committed to a biblical anthropology that he believed centered on a dynamic understanding of the triune God. As Barth's theology matured, he placed an increasing amount of weight on the divine self-disclosure of the triune God. It has become an almost unquestioned conclusion among Barth's critics that his theological method and content would serve to alienate theology from the

---

173. Cf., e.g., Ronald Gregor Smith, *The Doctrine of God* (Philadelphia: Westminster, 1970) p. 91; and R. H. Roberts, "Karl Barth's Doctrine of Time: Its Nature and Implications," in S. Sykes, ed., *Karl Barth: Studies of His Theological Method* (Oxford: Clarendon, 1979) pp. 88-146, esp. 114, 123, 124-25. Roberts goes so far as to say: "Through a profound ontological exclusiveness Barth has attempted to preserve Christian theology from the indifference and hostility of a secular world. The triumphalist aggrandizement of his theology was made at the risk of a total disjunction and alienation of his theology from natural reality. The disturbing irony of his efforts is that Barth achieved this alienation by skilled and energetic use of traditional Christian theological categories. His creation stands before us as a warning as to what may happen if the God of the orthodox Christian Gospel is prized apart from the structures of contemporary human life. . . . In almost Proustian manner Barth has re-created a lost world" (p. 145).

natural sciences (including the human sciences). In this study, I have shown that a theology which is based primarily on the Trinity does not necessarily deserve the label "positivity of revelation," as though it inevitably places itself beyond the reach of the other sciences. I have argued that Barth believed that a dialogue between dogmatics and other sciences is possible, provided that each respects the other discipline's boundaries.

I have attempted to refute the "positivity of revelation" accusations by pointing to the ways in which most of Barth's critics neglected to take into account some important changes in Barth's doctrine of humanity in his later writings. I have presented certain evidence from Barth's own writings, along with the intriguing analogies between Barth's dynamic anthropology and that of object relations psychology, to show that Barth's trinitarian anthropology was far less hostile to the human sciences than many have supposed. From an extended comparison between Barth's anthropology and that of Fairbairn, I have concluded that they have a number of inherent similarities. The chief similarity is in the dynamic-interpersonal ontology of the human being that both advocate. In both cases the person is composed of the relations that are constitutive of their personal being. Some of the parallels between modern psychology and dogmatic anthropology were suggested by Barth himself in the section of the *Dogmatics* where he discussed the ethics of human sexuality and marriage. The discovery of a number of parallels between Barth and object relations psychology should modify the common perception that Barth's theology excludes the possibility of dialogue with other sciences. Furthermore, the implications of the similar themes found in the dynamic anthropologies of both Barth and modern object relations psychology could serve to facilitate dialogue between the human sciences and Christian anthropology, with the hopeful prospect of exploring new paths for the healing of persons. The dynamic nature of the person that both Barth and object relations espouse confirms that the analogy of relations *(analogia relationis)* serves as a more adequate model for Christian anthropology than do the more traditional dualistic categories. It shows that the consideration of the whole person is more than a theoretical consideration. The healing of whole persons must be psychosomatic in origin — ministering to the physical, psychical, and spiritual components of human existence.

Finally, the dynamic trinitarian anthropology that Barth develops in his *Dogmatics* should encourage the church to shift its perspectives regarding what it means to be fully human. Since we are creatures created in the image and likeness of God, our pathway to God-likeness is achieved only through a shared journey with God and others. This should encourage us to see that there is no authentic humanity apart from fellow humanity — to understand that the basis for Christian community is found right within the very nature of God himself. This study has illumined a good deal about the scriptural admonition to love as God loves: "Beloved, let us love one another; for love is of God, and he who loves is born of God and knows God. He who does not love does not know God for God is love. . . . So we know and believe the love God has for us. God is love, and he who abides in love abides in God, and God abides in him."[174] We are called to become for others what God has become for us: a cleansing, healing, life-giving presence.

I began this study by asking, What is man? I have concluded by showing that this question is best answered by asking, Who is God? I have attempted to show, by a careful consideration of Barth's doctrine of the human being, how the Christian doctrine of the Trinity can provide a means for discussing the nature of the human being that is relevant to modern thought. A trinitarian anthropology not only informs us who we are, but also informs us who we are called to become. The God who is antecedently love within himself calls us to love outside ourselves, to reach beyond our selfish inwardness and reflect the love of the Father and Son and thus be made fully alive — fully human. "We love because he first loved us."[175]

174. 1 John 4:7, 8, 16.
175. 1 John 4:19.

Bibliography of Works Cited

Abenheimer, Karl M. "Critical Observations on Fairbairn's Theory of Object Relations." *British Journal of Medical Psychology* 28 (1955): 29-41.

Abraham, Karl. *Selected Papers of Karl Abraham.* London: Hogarth, 1927.

Allan, Walter. "Sociology and Theology: A Study of Their Relationship with Reference to Berger, Luckmann and Barth." Ph.D. dissertation, Drew University, 1969.

Anderson, Ray. *On Being Human.* Grand Rapids: Eerdmans, 1982.

Ashley, Benedict. *Theologies of the Body: Humanist and Christian.* Braintree, Mass.: Pope John Center, 1985.

Athanasius. *De Incarnatione.* London: David Nutt, 1901.

———. *Contra Gentes.* Ed. P. Schaff, H. Wace, and A. Robertson. In *Nicene and Post-Nicene Fathers* IV. Repr. Grand Rapids: Eerdmans, 1980.

Augustine. *De Trinitate. On the Trinity.* Ed. P. Schaff. Tr. A. W. Haddan. In *Nicene and Post-Nicene Fathers* III. Repr. Grand Rapids: Eerdmans, 1956.

———. *De Civitate Dei. The City of God.* Tr. and ed. Marcus Dods. 2 vols. New York: Hafner, 1948.

Baille, John. *Our Knowledge of God.* New York: Scribner, 1959.

Barth, Karl. *The Word of God and the Word of Man.* Tr. Douglas Horton. London: Hodder and Stoughton, 1928.

———. *Die kirchliche Dogmatik.* 4 vols. in 14. Zollikon-Zurich: Evanglischer Verlag, 1939-57.

———. *Church Dogmatics.* Ed. G. W. Bromiley and T. F. Torrance. Tr. G. W. Bromiley, et al. 4 vols. in 14. Edinburgh: T & T Clark, 1956-75.

———. *Dogmatics in Outline.* Tr. G. T. Thomson. New York: Harper & Row, 1959.

———. *From Rousseau to Ritschl.* Tr. Brian Cozens. London: SCM, 1959.

———. *Anselm: Fides Quaerens Intellectum.* Tr. I. W. Robertson. London: SCM, 1960.

———. *Theology and Church.* Tr. L. P. Smith. New York: Harper & Row, 1962.

———. *Christ and Adam: Man and Humanity in Romans 5.* Tr. T. A. Smail. Edinburgh. London: Oliver and Boyd, 1963.

———. *The Epistle to the Romans.* Tr. E. C. Hoskyns. 6th ed. New York: Oxford University Press, 1968.

———. *Fragments Grave and Gay.* Tr. E. Mosbacher. London and Glasgow: Collins, 1971.

———. *Protestant Theology in the Nineteenth Century.* Tr. B. Cozens, et al. London: SCM, 1972.

———. *The Humanity of God.* Tr. J. N. Thomas and T. Weiser. Repr. Atlanta: John Knox, 1978.

———. *Karl Barth: Letters 1961-1968.* Ed. J. Fangmeier and H. Stoevesandt. Tr. and ed. G. W. Bromiley. Grand Rapids: Eerdmans, 1981.

———. *The Theology of Schleiermacher: Lectures at Göttingen, Winter Semester of 1923-24.* Ed. D. Ritschl. Tr. G. W. Bromiley. Grand Rapids: Eerdmans, 1982.

Baxter, Christina Ann. "The Movement from Exegesis to Dogmatics in the Theology of Karl Barth, with Special Reference to Romans, Philippians and the *Church Dogmatics.*" Ph.D. thesis, University of Durham, 1981.

Beck, L. W. "What Have We Learned from Kant?" In Allen W. Wood, ed. *Self and Nature in Kant's Philosophy.* Ithaca, N.Y., and London: Cornell University Press, 1984.

Berkouwer, G. C. *Man: The Image of God.* Tr. D. W. Jellema. Grand Rapids: Eerdmans, 1962.

Blanshard, Brand, and B. F. Skinner. "The Problem of Consciousness — A Debate." *Philosophy and Phenomenological Research* 27 (1966-67).

Bloom, Allan. *The Closing of the American Mind.* New York: Simon & Schuster, 1987.

Bonhoeffer, Dietrich. *Life Together.* Tr. John W. Doberstein. New York: Harper & Row, 1954.

Bowlby, John. *Attachment.* New York: Basic Books, 1969.

Bradshaw, Timothy. "Karl Barth on the Trinity: A Family Resemblance." *Scottish Journal of Theology* 39 (1986): 145-64.

Brandt, Richard B. *The Philosophy of Schleiermacher.* New York: Harper and Bros., 1941.

Bromiley, Geoffrey. *An Introduction to the Theology of Karl Barth.* Grand Rapids: Eerdmans, 1979.

Brunner, Emil. *Die Mystik und das Wort.* Tübingen: Mohr, 1924.

———. *Natural Theology: Comprising "Nature and Grace" by Professor Dr. Emil Brunner and the Reply "No!" by Dr. Karl Barth.* Tr. P. Fraenkel. London: Geoffrey Bles, Centenary, 1946.

———. *Man in Revolt.* Tr. Olive Wyon. 3d ed. London: Lutterworth, 1947.

———. "The New Barth." *Scottish Journal of Theology* 4 (1951): 125-35.

———. *Revelation and Reason.* Tr. O. Wyon. Philadelphia: Westminster, 1956.

Buber, Martin. *I and Thou.* Tr. R. Gregor Smith. Edinburgh: T & T Clark, 1937.

Buckley, Peter, ed. *Essential Papers on Object Relations.* New York and London: New York University Press, 1986.

Bultmann, Rudolf. *Kerygma and Myth.* Ed. H. W. Bartsch. Tr. R. H. Fuller. London: SPCK, 1953

Busch, Eberhard. *Karl Barth.* Tr. John Bowden. London: SCM, 1976.

Cairns, David. *The Image of God in Man.* London: SCM, 1953.

Calvin, John. *Institutes of the Christian Religion.* Tr. F. L. Battles. Ed. J. T. McNeill. 2 vols. Philadelphia: Westminster, 1960.

Cantore, Enrico. *Scientific Man: The Humanistic Significance of Science.* New York: ISH Publications, 1977.

Cassirer, Ernst. *Rousseau-Kant-Goethe.* Tr. J. Gutmann, P. O. Kristeller, and J. H. Randall Jr. Princeton: Princeton University Press, 1945.

Chapman, J. Arundel. *An Introduction to Schleiermacher.* London: Epworth, 1932.

Clark, Stephen R. L. *Aristotle's Man.* Oxford: Clarendon, 1975.

Cohen, Hermann. *Religion of Reason.* Tr. S. Kaplan. New York: F. Ungar, 1972.

Colby, Kenneth M. *Energy and Structure in Psychoanalysis.* New York: Ronald, 1955.

Come, Arnold. *An Introduction to Barth's Dogmatics for Preachers.* Philadelphia: Westminster, 1963.

Condorcet, Antoine-Nicolas de. *Sketch for a Historical Picture of the Progress of the Human Mind.* Tr. J. Barraclough. London: Weidenfeld and Nicholson, 1955.

Copleston, Frederick. *A History of Philosophy.* 6 vols. Westminster, Maryland: Newman Press, 1946-60.

Cupitt, Don. *The Nature of Man.* London: Sheldon, 1979.

Deegan, D. L. "The Ritschlian School, the Essence of Christianity and Karl Barth." *Scottish Journal of Theology* 16 (1963) 390-414.

Descartes, René. *Meditations on First Philosophy.* Tr. Elizabeth S. Haldane and G. R. T. Ross. In vol. I of *The Philosophical Works of Descartes.* 2 vols. Cambridge: Cambridge University Press, 1931.

————. *Meditations, and Selections from the Principles of Philosopy.* Tr. John Veitch. La Salle, Ill.: Open Court, 1952.

Eccles, John, Sir. *The Human Mystery.* Berlin and Heidelberg: Springer, 1979.

Eichrodt, Walter. *Man in the Old Testament.* Tr. K. and R. Gregor Smith. London: SCM, 1951.

Einstein, Albert. *Ideas and Opinions.* Tr. S. Bargmann. Ed. C. Seelig. New York: Crown, 1954.

Fairbairn, W. Ronald D. *Psychoanalytic Studies of the Personality.* London: Tavistock, 1952.

————. "Observations on the Nature of Hysterical States." *British Journal of Medical Psychology* 27 (1954): 105-25.

————. "Observations in Defence of the Object-Relations Theory of the Personality." *British Journal of Medical Psychology* 28 (1955): 144-56.

————. "A Critical Evaluation of Certain Psycho-Analytical Conceptions." *British Journal for the Philosophy of Science* 7 (1956-57).

———. "Synopsis of an Object Relations Theory of the Personality." *International Journal of Psycho-Analysis* 44 (1963): 224.

Feuerbach, Ludwig. *The Essence of Christianity*. Tr. M. Evans. London: Trubner, 1843.

Fisher, Simon. *Revelatory Positivism? Barth's Earliest Theology and the Marburg School*. Oxford: Oxford University Press, 1988.

Freud, Sigmund. *The Standard Edition of the Complete Psychological Works of Sigmund Freud*. Ed. J. Strachey. Tr. J. Strachey, et al. 24 vols. London: Hogarth, 1953-74.

Gay, Peter. *The Enlightenment: An Interpretation*. 2 vols. New York: Knopf, 1966.

Gerrish, B. A. *A Prince of the Church: Schleiermacher and the Beginnings of Modern Theology*. Philadelphia: Fortress, 1984.

Graham, W. Fred. *The Constructive Revolutionary*. Richmond, Va.: John Knox, 1971.

Grensted, L. W. *Psychology and God*. London: Longmans, Green, 1931.

Gundry, Robert H. *Soma in Biblical Theology: With an Emphasis on Pauline Anthropology*. Cambridge: Cambridge University Press, 1976.

Gunton, Colin. *Becoming and Being: The Doctrine of God in Charles Hartshorne and Karl Barth*. Oxford: Oxford University Press, 1978.

Guntrip, Harry. *Personality Structure and Human Interaction*. London: Hogarth, 1961.

———. *Schizoid Phenomena, Object Relations, and the Self*. London: Hogarth, 1968.

———. *Psychoanalytic Theory, Therapy, and the Self*. New York: Basic Books, 1971.

Haezrahi, Pepita. "The concept of man as an end-in-himself." In *Critical Essays on Kant's Foundations of the Metaphysics of Morals*. Tr. L. B. Beck. Indianapolis: Bobbs-Merrill, 1969.

Hamilton, Kenneth. "Schleiermacher and Relational Theology." *Journal of Religion* 44 (1964): 29-39.

Hamilton, N. Gregory. "A Critical Review of Object Relations Theory." *American Journal of Psychiatry* 146, 12 (1989).

Harré, Rom. *Social Being: A Theory for Social Psychology*. Totowa, N.J.: Rowman and Littlefield, 1980.

Harré, Rom, and Paul Secord. *The Explanation of Social Behaviour*. Oxford: Blackwell, 1972.

Hartwell, H. *The Theology of Karl Barth*. London: Duckworth, 1964.

Hedges, Larry. "How Hard Is Science, How Soft Is Science?" *American Psychologist* 42 (1987): 443-45.

Hegel, G. W. F. *The Phenomenology of Mind*. Tr. J. B. Baillie. London: Allen and Unwin, 1949.

Henry, Carl F. H. "Chaos in European Theology: The Deterioration of Barth's Defences." *Christianity Today* 9 (1964): 15-19.

————. "Image of God." In *Evangelical Dictionary of Theology.* Ed. Walter A. Elwell. Grand Rapids: Baker, 1984. Pp. 545-48.

Hobbes, Thomas. *Leviathan.* Ed. C. B. Macpherson. Baltimore: Penguin, 1968.

Hume, David. *A Treatise of Human Nature.* Ed. L. A. Selby-Bigge. Oxford: Clarendon, 1896.

Hunsinger, George, ed. and tr. *Karl Barth and Radical Politics.* Philadelphia: Westminster, 1963.

Jaki, Stanley. *Cosmos and Creator.* Edinburgh: Scottish Academic Press, 1980.

————. *Angels, Apes and Men.* LaSalle, Ill.: Sherwood Sugden, 1983.

Jenson, R. W. *Alpha and Omega: A Study in the Theology of Karl Barth.* New York: Nelson, 1963.

Jones, Ernst. *Sigmund Freud: Life and Work.* 3 vols. London: Hogarth, 1954.

Jones, W. T. *A History of Western Philosophy.* 4 vols. Vol. 1, *The Classical Mind.* New York: Harcourt and Brace, 1965.

Jüngel, Eberhard. *The Doctrine of the Trinity: God's Being Is in Becoming.* Grand Rapids: Eerdmans 1976.

————. *Karl Barth: A Theological Legacy.* Tr. Garrett E. Paul. Philadelphia: Westminster, 1986.

Kant, Immanuel. *Kant's Introduction to Logic.* Tr. T. K. Abbott. London: Longmans, Green, 1885.

————. *Kritik of Judgment.* Tr. J. H. Bernard. London and New York: Macmillan, 1892.

————. *Kants gesammelte Schriften.* Königlich Preussische Akademie der Wissenschaften. 23 vols. I-VIII, XIV-XVI, Berlin: Georg Reimer, 1902-14; IX-XIII, XVII-XXIII, Berlin: de Gruyter, 1922-55.

————. *Kant's "Opus postumum."* Ed. A. Buchenau. Vol. I. Berlin: de Gruyter, 1938.

————. *Critique of Pure Reason.* Tr. N. Kemp Smith. London: Macmillan, 1950.

————. *Critique of Practical Reason and Other Writings in Moral Philosophy.* Tr. L. W. Beck. 1949; repr. New York: Garland, 1976.

————. *Religion Within the Limits of Reason Alone.* Tr. T. M. Greene and H. H. Hudson. Chicago: Open Court, 1934. Later edition. Tr. T. M. Greene and J. R. Silber. New York: Harper & Row, 1960.

————. *Foundations of the Metaphysics of Morals.* Tr. L. B. Beck. Indianapolis: Bobbs-Merrill, 1969.

Kehm, George. "The Christological Foundation of Anthropology in the Thought of Karl Barth." Ph.D. dissertation, Harvard University, 1967.

Kemp Smith, Norman. *A Commentary to Kant's 'Critique of Pure Reason.'* Repr. London: Macmillan, 1979.

Kernberg, Otto. *Internal World and External Reality.* New York and London: Aronson, 1980.

Kierkegaard, Søren. *Kierkegaard's Philosophical Fragments.* Tr. David F. Swenson. London: Oxford University Press; New York: American-Scandinavian Foundation, 1936.

————. *Kierkegaard's Concluding Unscientific Postscript.* Tr. David F. Swenson and Walter Lowrie. London: Oxford University Press, 1941.

————. *Fear and Trembling and the Sickness unto Death.* Tr. Walter Lowrie. Princeton: Princeton University Press, 1954.

————. *On Authority and Revelation.* Tr. Walter Lowrie. Princeton: Princeton University Press, 1955.

————. *The Concept of Dread.* Tr. Walter Lowrie. Princeton: Princeton University Press, 1973.

Klein, Melanie. "A Contribution to the Psychogenesis of Manic-Depressive States." *International Journal of Psycho-Analysis* 16 (1935) 145-74.

————. "Notes on Some Schizoid Mechanisms." In *Developments in Psycho-Analysis.* London: Hogarth, 1952.

————. *The Psycho-Analysis of Children.* London: Hogarth; New York: Grove, 1960.

Klooster, Frederick. *The Significance of Barth's Theology.* Grand Rapids: Baker, 1961.

Kuitert, H. M. *The Reality of Faith.* Tr. L. B. Smedes. Grand Rapids: Eerdmans, 1968.

Küng, Hans. *Freud and the Problem of God.* New Haven: Yale University Press, 1979.

Lake, Frank. *Clinical Theology.* London: Darton, Longman & Todd, 1966.

Lasch, Christopher. *The Culture of Narcissism: American Life in an Age of Diminishing Expectations.* New York: Norton, 1979.

Leibnitz, Gottfried Wilhelm. *Leibnitz: Selections.* Tr. P. P. Wiener. New York: Scribner, 1951.

Lott, Stanley G. "The Significance of Man in the Theology of Karl Barth." Ph.D. dissertation, New Orleans Baptist Theological Seminary, 1968.

Lovin, Robin. *Christian Faith and Public Choices: The Social Ethics of Barth, Brunner and Bonhoeffer.* Philadelphia: Fortress, 1984.

Lowe, W. "Barth as a Critic of Dualism: Re-Reading the *Römerbrief*," *Scottish Journal of Theology* 41 (1988) 377-95.

Mackintosh, H. R. *Types of Modern Theology.* 1937. Repr. London: Nisbet, 1962.

Macmurray, John. *The Self as Agent.* London: Faber and Faber, 1957.

————. *Persons in Relation.* London: Faber and Faber, 1961.

————. *Religion, Art and Science.* Liverpool: Liverpool University Press, 1961.

Marquardt, F. W. *Theologie und Sozialismus: Das Beispiel Karl Barths.* Munich: Kaiser, 1972.

McKinnon, Alastair. "Barth's Relation to Kierkegaard: Some Further Light." *Canadian Journal of Theology* 13 (1967): 31-41.

McLean, Stuart. *Humanity in the Thought of Karl Barth.* Edinburgh: T & T Clark, 1981.

McNeil, J. T. *A History of the Cure of Souls.* New York: Harper & Bros., 1951.

Mead, George H. *Mind, Self and Society.* Chicago: University of Chicago Press, 1934.

Meissner, W. W. *Psychoanalysis and Religious Experience.* New Haven and London: Yale University Press, 1984.

Meng, H., and E. L. Freud, eds. *Psychoanalysis and Faith: The Letters of Sigmund Freud and Oskar Pfister.* New York: Basic Books, 1963.

Miegge, Giovanni. "A Roman Catholic Interpretation of Karl Barth." *Scottish Journal of Theology* 7 (1954): 59-72.

Misiak, Henryk. *The Philosophical Roots of Scientific Psychology.* New York: Fordham University Press, 1961.

Misiak, Henryk, and Virginia Staudt Sexton. *History of Psychology.* New York and London: Grune & Stratton, 1966.

Moltmann, Jürgen. *Man: Christian Anthropology in the Conflicts of the Present.* Tr. John Sturdy. Philadelphia: Fortress, 1974.

Mondin, Battista. *The Principle of Analogy in Protestant and Catholic Theology.* The Hague: Martinus Nijhoff, 1963.

Mueller, David Livingstone. "Karl Barth's Critique of the Anthropological Starting Point in Theology." Ph.D. dissertation, Duke University, 1958.

Neidhardt, W. J. "Thomas F. Torrance's Integration of Judeo-Christian Theology and Natural Science: Some Key Themes." *Journal of the American Scientific Affiliation* 41 (1989): 87-98.

Newell, Roger. "Participatory Knowledge: Theology as Art and Science in C. S. Lewis and T. F. Torrance." Ph.D. thesis, University of Aberdeen, 1983.

Newton, Sir Isaac. *Newton's Principia, the Mathematical Principles of Natural Philosophy.* Tr. A. Motte. New York: Daniel Adee, 1846.

Niebuhr, Reinhold. *Essays in Applied Christianity.* Ed. D. B. Robertson. New York: Meridian, 1959.

———. *The Nature and Destiny of Man.* 2 vols. London: Nisbet, 1941.

Oden, Thomas. *Kerygma and Counseling.* Philadelphia: Westminster, 1966.

———. *Agenda for Theology: Recovering Christian Roots.* San Francisco: Harper & Row, 1979.

O'Donovan, Joan E. "Man in the Image of God: The Disagreement Between Barth and Brunner Reconsidered." *Scottish Journal of Theology* 39 (1986): 433-59.

Pais, Abraham. *Subtle Is the Lord: The Science and the Life of Albert Einstein.* Oxford and New York: Oxford University Press, 1982.

Pannenberg, Wolfhart. *Theology and Philosophy of Science.* Tr. Francis McDonagh. Philadelphia: Westminster, 1976.

———. *Anthropology in Theological Perspective.* Tr. Matthew O'Connell. Philadelphia: Westminster, 1985.

Parisi, Thomas. "Why Freud Failed." *American Psychologist* 42 (1987): 237-45.

Paulsen, Friedrich. *Immanuel Kant: His Life and Doctrine.* Tr. J. E. Creighton and A. Lefevre. London: John C. Nommo, 1902.

Peacocke, Arthur. *Intimations of Reality.* Notre Dame, Ind.: University of Notre Dame Press, 1984.

Plato. *Laws.* Tr. A. E. Taylor. London: 1934.

———. *Republic.* Tr. F. M. Cornford. New York: Oxford, 1945.

———. *Plato's Meno.* Ed. R. S. Bluck. Cambridge: Cambridge University Press, 1964.

Polanyi, Michael. *Personal Knowledge: Towards a Post-Critical Philosophy.* Corrected ed. Chicago: University of Chicago Press, 1962.

———. *The Study of Man.* Chicago: University of Chicago Press, 1959.

Ramm, Bernard. *After Fundamentalism: The Future of Evangelical Theology.* San Francisco: Harper & Row, 1983.

Ricoeur, Paul. *Freud and Philosophy: An Essay on Interpretation.* Tr. D. Savage. New Haven and London: Yale University Press, 1970.

Ritschl, Albrecht. *A Critical History of the Christian Doctrine of Justification and Reconciliation.* Tr. J. S. Black. Edinburgh: Edmonston and Douglas, 1872.

Rousseau, Jean-Jacques. *Of the Social Contract, or Principles of Political Right & Discourse on Political Economy.* Tr. C. M. Sherover. New York: Harper & Row, 1984.

Ryle, Gilbert. *The Concept of Mind.* London: Hutchinson, 1949.

Sabelli, Hector C., and Linnea Carlson-Sabelli. "Biological Priority and Psychological Supremacy: A New Integrative Paradigm Derived from Process Theory." *American Journal of Psychiatry* 146, 12 (1989).

Schleiermacher, Friedrich. *Über die Religion, Reden an die Gebildeten unter ihren Verächtern.* 1799, 1806, 1821, and 1831. Translations: *Schleiermacher on Religion.* Tr. J. Oman. London: Kegan Paul, Trench, Trübner, 1893, from the 1st edition. *On Religion.* Tr. T. N. Tice. Richmond, Va.: John Knox, 1969, from the 3d edition.

———. *The Christian Faith.* Ed. H. R. Mackintosh and J. S. Stewart. Edinburgh: T & T Clark, 1928.

Snyder, Dale N. *Karl Barth's Struggle with Anthropocentric Theology.* The Hague: Wattez, 1966.

Sperry, R. W. "Psychology's Mentalist Paradigm and the Religion/Science Tension." *American Psychologist* 43 (1988): 607-13.

Stamm, Johann Jakob. "Die Imago-Lehre von Karl Barth und die alttestamentliche Wissenschaft." In *Der Mensch als Bild Gott.* Ed. Leo Sheffczyck. Darmstadt: Wissenschaftliche Buchgesellschaft, 1969.

Sulloway, Frank J. *Freud: Biologist of the Mind.* London: Burnett, 1979.

Sutherland, John D. *Fairbairn's Journey into the Interior.* London: Free Association Books, 1989.

Suttie, Ian L. *The Origins of Love and Hate.* London: Kegan Paul, Trench, Trubner, 1935.

Sykes, Stephen, ed. *Karl Barth: Studies of His Theological Method.* Oxford: Clarendon, 1979.

Teilhard de Chardin, Pierre. *The Phenomenon of Man.* Tr. Bernard Wall. London: Collins, 1959.

Tillich, Paul. *Systematic Theology.* Vol. II. Chicago: University of Chicago Press, 1957.

Torrance, Alan. "Self-Relation, Narcissism and the Gospel of Grace." *Scottish Journal of Theology* 40 (1987): 481-510.

Torrance, James B. "Interpretation and Understanding in Schleiermacher's Theology: Some Critical Questions." *Scottish Journal of Theology* 21 (1968): 268-82.

―――. "The Vicarious Humanity and Priesthood of Christ in the Theology of Calvin." In *Calvinus Ecclesiae Doctor.* Ed. W. H. Neuser. Kampen: Kok, 1978.

Torrance, Thomas F. *Calvin's Doctrine of Man.* London: Lutterworth, 1949.

―――. *Karl Barth: An Introduction to His Early Theology.* London: SCM, 1962.

―――. *Theology in Reconstruction.* Grand Rapids: Eerdmans, 1966.

―――. *Space, Time and Incarnation.* Oxford and London: Oxford University Press, 1969.

―――. *Theological Science.* London: Oxford University Press, 1969.

―――. *God and Rationality.* London: Oxford University Press, 1971.

―――. *Space, Time and Resurrection.* Grand Rapids: Eerdmans, 1976.

―――. *Reality and Evangelical Theology.* Philadelphia: Westminster, 1982.

―――. *The Mediation of Christ.* Grand Rapids: Eerdmans, 1983.

―――. *Transformation and Convergence in the Frame of Knowledge.* Grand Rapids: Eerdmans, 1984.

―――. *Reality and Scientific Theology.* Edinburgh: Scottish Academic Press, 1985.

―――. *The Trinitarian Faith.* Edinburgh: T & T Clark, 1988.

―――, ed. *Belief in Science and in Christian Life.* Edinburgh: Handsel, 1980.

Tronick, Edward Z. "Emotions and Emotional Communication in Infants." *American Psychologist* 44 (1989): 112-19.

Ulanov, Anna. *The Feminine in Jungian Psychology and in Christian Theology.* Evanston, Ill.: Northwestern University Press, 1971.

Van De Pitte, Frederick P. *Kant as Philosophical Anthropologist.* The Hague: Martinus Nijhoff, 1971.

Van Leeuwen, Mary Stewart. *The Person in Psychology.* Leicester: Intervarsity Press; Grand Rapids: Eerdmans, 1985.

Vitz, Paul. *Psychology as Religion.* Grand Rapids: Eerdmans, 1977.

Von Balthasar, Hans Urs. *Man in History: A Theological Study.* London and Sydney: Sheed and Ward, 1968.

―――. *The Theology of Karl Barth.* Tr. John Drury. New York: Holt, Rinehart, and Winston, 1971.

Walker, Nigel. "Freud and Homeostasis." *British Journal for the Philosophy of Science* 7 (1956): 61-72.

Walrond-Skinner, Sue. *A Dictionary of Psychotherapy.* London and New York: Routledge & Kegan Paul, 1986.

Webb, Clement J. *God and Personality.* London: Allen and Unwin; New York: Macmillan, 1918.

Weber, Otto. *Karl Barth's Church Dogmatics.* Tr. Arthur C. Cochrane. Philadelphia: Westminster, 1953.

―――. *Foundations of Dogmatics.* Tr. D. Guder. Vol. I. Grand Rapids: Eerdmans, 1981.

Wells, W. W. "The Influence of Kierkegaard on the Theology of Karl Barth." Ph.D. dissertation, Syracuse University, 1970.

Whitehead, Alfred North. *Process and Reality*. Cambridge: Cambridge University Press, 1929.

Williams, Robert R. *Schleiermacher the Theologian*. Philadelphia: Fortress, 1978.

Willis, R. E. *The Ethics of Karl Barth*. Leiden: Brill, 1971.

Wilson, Edward O. *Sociobiology: The New Synthesis*. Cambridge: Harvard University Press, 1975.

————. *On Human Nature*. Cambridge: Harvard University Press, 1978.

Winnicott, Donald W. *Mother and Child: A Primer of First Relationships*. New York: Basic Books, 1957.

Winnicott, Donald W., and M. Khan. Book review of *Psychoanalytic Studies of the Personality*, by W. R. D. Fairbairn. *International Journal of Psycho-Analysis* 34 (1953): 329-33.

Zizioulas, John. *Being as Communion*. London: Darton, Longman & Todd, 1985.

Index

Abraham, Karl, 205n.124

Anderson, Ray, 4n.8, 19n.25, 146n.172, 159n. 223

Anselm, Saint, 110n.51

Anthropocentrism. *See* Cosmology, anthropocentric

Aristotle, 7n.17, 55

Ashley, Benedict, 36n.19, 50n.80

Augustine, Saint, 279n.115, 283

Barmen Declaration, 68-69

Barth, Karl
Analogy of Relations *(analogia relationis),* 11-18, 132-35, 137-38, 305-7
Calvin's influence upon, 9-10, 99, 129, 132n.129, 148n.182, 157, 237
Christocentric, 16
church as place for dogmatics, 27
dialectical theology, 5, 56-60, 86, 117, 198, 278
dialogue with E. Brunner, 5, 6n.12, 14n.28, 49n.77, 117, 123n.89
"history" (Geschichte), 60n.115, 141-45, 163, 227
individualism, 13, 97
male and female, 158, 197, 244, 292
and modern thought, 19-21, 61-96
postmodern thought and, 20, 170
'real man', 18-19, 97, 104, 106-8, 116-17,

123-30, 143, 153, 231-34, 248, 255-57, 278, 284-85
revelatory positivism, 10-12, 307
science and, 11-12, 101-7, 109, 116
social sciences, 14
Trinitarian anthropology, 7, 10, 57-58, 109-11, 116, 133, 144, 231-32

Being as
act, 94, 120-24, 136-37, 144, 152, 266-67
communion, 14, 139
dynamic (in Barth), 9-10, 13, 15, 19-24, 94-99, 118-22, 133-46, 149, 163, 166, 194, 229-30, 233, 235-44, 261
dynamic (in object relations), 13, 20, 24-25, 166, 174, 203, 212-17, 224-27, 229-30, 235-44
relation to other, 126, 142-48, 153
static substance, 13, 237

Berkouwer, G. C., 136n.145, 160n.224, 301n.157, 160n.224

Boethius, 13n.26, 237

Bonhoeffer, Dietrich, 10n.20, 151

Bowlby, John, 126n.104, 222n.188

Brunner, Emil, 6n.12, 14n.28, 49n.77, 117, 123n.89

Buber, Martin, 120, 139, 143

Buckley, Peter, 167n.6, 169n.8, 241n.13

Bultmann, Rudolf, 101, 106

319